FREE PIZZA FOR LIFE

ALSO RELEASED BY SECRET SAILOR BOOKS

BIG OLDIE
A Collection of Comic Zines by Rick V.
Years of Rick V's personal, funny, and entertaining comic zines come together in one superlative book.

TOUR SUCKS
A compilation of tour stories from various punks. Writers include: Chris Clavin, Spoonboy, Dave Dondero, Todd Congelliere, Rymodee, John No, Megan Mink March, Ginger Alford, Rick V, and Dani Kordani.

WE SHALL BRING A DARKNESS
A comic book by Emily Timm and Chris Clavin
A tale of a shadow world that posseses sinister power over our own and the one band that could cross over into those dark lands to fight back. This comic is a couterpart to the Los Gatos Negros LP.

VOCES LIBERTARIAS
Los orígenes históricos del anarquismo en Puerto Rico
By Jorell A. Meléndez Badillo
In order to analyze the origins and influence of anarchism on the island of Puerto Rico, Voces Libertarias traverses through the history of the emergent labor movement during the first two decades of the twentieth century. A product of rigid research, the book hopes to open a breach inside Puerto Rican historiography for the study of the past from a critical perspective. 225 pages. *Spanish language.*

Plan-It-X Records • Secret Sailor Books
P.O. Box 2312
Bloomington, IN 47404
www.plan-it-x.com

Or contact your local punk

FREE PIZZA FOR LIFE

The Early
Days of
Plan-It-X
Records

CHRIS CLAVIN

Secret Sailor Books
Bloomington, Indiana

A SECRET SAILOR BOOK
Published by
Secret Sailor Books
a division of
Plan-It-X Records
P.O. Box 2312
Bloomington, IN 47402

Edited by John Cahill
with special thanks to Ryan Fletcher, Abbey Friedman and Emily Timm

Cover art by Chris Clavin
Cover layout by Emily Timm
Text design and layout by Emily Timm

This book was published with the help of:
Sean Gilmore, Brian, Domenica Pileggi, Aaron Cabe, and Matt Flanagan

ISBN 978-0-9848829-1-5

Photo of Chris and Sam on the back cover by Amy Giambelluca
Other Photos by Chris Clavin & ?

Contact:
planitxrecords@gmail.com
www.plan-it-x.com

CONTENTS

INTRODUCTION   *viii*

A LETTER FROM SAM   *ix*

1.   ORIGINS   *2*

2.   INTERMISSION   *33*

3.   BLOOMINGTON   *35*

4.   SAM   *43*

5.   COTTAGE GROVE   *47*

6.   RETREAT   *77*

7.   DAYS OF CHAOS   *89*

8.   8 LONG MONTHS   *110*

9.   HOW I SPENT MY SUMMER VACATION   *119*

10. VAN LIFE   *130*

11. SAM'S IN JAIL   *156*

12. WAITING FOR JUDGEMENT   *196*

13. ON THE ROAD (AGAIN)   *209*

14. PLAN-IT-X RECORDS (THE STORE)   *221*

15. MR. DUPLEX   *226*

16. THE DOCTOR   *236*

17.	STARTS & ENDS	241
18.	THE MADISON	245
19.	GET A JOB	250
20.	ROCKIT'S	253
21.	THE ENDING	292

EPILOGUE: THE GULF OF MEXICO	297
STRAP YERSELF IN #1, #2, & #4	300
LIST OF PLAN-IT-X RELEASES	374

This book is for Samantha, but it is also dedicated to anyone who's ever written me a letter or ordered music from Plan-It-X records, including the first person to send in an order: James "Moz" Brand, rest in peace, and the most crucially fun person that I've ever known: Anthony Poynter, I miss you already.

INTRODUCTION

I'm sorry if you think this book is only about pizza scams and dumpster diving. There will be a lot of pizza parts, but there will be a lot of other stuff too. Most of all, this book is about my best friend Samantha and how both of us found the DIY punk scene.

You might get confused, because I'm gonna tell a lot of stories about my friend Sam. You might wonder who this Sam guy is and when Samantha comes into the picture, but they are one person. Samantha starts out as boy named Sam and ends up as a girl named Samantha. I refer to her as Sam, because that was who she was in these stories. Samantha and I talked about it one day in Olympia, because I was writing some songs about my life in Bloomington and she was the subject of a few of them. I asked her what I should do about her gender change in the songs. I didn't know if I should call her a "she," retrospectively, or a "he." She said that I should use "he," since it was history, and that she was a "he" back then, so Sam is Samantha. They are the same amazing person.

I'm not that good with dates, and, in the spirit of chaos, I decided not to do too much research into my own life, so some things might be out of order, but I think I got it right for the most part, and I doubt anyone will know if I didn't.

I tell stories about a lot of people in this book and I use their real names. I'm sorry if you're one of those people and you don't like my version of the story. I tried to be honest, but I know I'm only telling the story the way it felt to me and the way I remember it years later.

There are also some stories that I can't tell, or can't tell in full because I promised to keep them secret.

A LETTER FROM SAM

Dear Chris,

Holy fucking vagina! Hopefully I will have figured out a way to talk to you before you get this but if not, here I am. Don't let this shit get you down man. You've gotta keep going out there, get that record put out and shit. I feel like I'm in 12 monkeys or something, "Just let me make one phone call, it's a voice mail system, I need to call my friend." It's nuts in here. The fucking Christians run everything. I can make phone calls all day long, but only collect, and I can't think of who to call that I'd feel like going through all that stuff with. My bond is $10,000 so I'm gonna be in here for a few days. I had to trade some milk for this paper and pencil. I haven't gotten too much shit for being a green-haired fuck up yet, except from the guards. What is it that prisoners are supposed to say, "man it's been 9 hours since I saw a girl, what's it like having them around?" Oh yeah, I wrote/am writing, Miranda a letter too, speaking of beautiful girls, tell her I love her.

Okay, here's the whole story of what happened, I'm sure you are dying to hear it. Oh yeah, I'm not heterosexual or anything, I just love her. Heh. Anyway, here's what happened, as soon as I made the call I got a weird fucking feeling about it. That's why I forgot the cokes. The lady didn't say anything wrong, it was just the way she was talking. My feeling was just to fuck it and leave, but I figured that one last time would be okay. When I went down to get the pizza, the pizza guy was already there, looking nervous. He handed me the pizza. I handed him the check. I saw the detective and BAM, I take off running, but I'm really unhealthy and he said afterwards that he runs 10 miles a day. So, eventually, I figure out that I'm not going to think of anything cool + I'm running out of fuel, so I try kicking/tripping him up + elbowing him. But he rips off my magic necklace and grabs me around the neck. I saved the necklace, but I can't believe it came off!

What the hell, I look nuts in this funny little shirt. This place is crazy, like, uh, a prison or something. They just locked everyone in. I don't have a cell of my own yet, just a little cot.

Anyway, back to the story, they take me to IUPD and read me my rights and charge me with forgery, a class C felony. I say I won't talk + I won't do handwriting samples. Cops chow down on our pizza. They take me to the Monroe county jail. Cops cut off my chains with bolt cutters and ask me a million questions: Am I prejudiced against any group of people? Yes, white people. Have you ever been attracted to members of the same sex? Yeah! Wrong answer, huh? Oh yeah and no one ever lets me make my one phone call. I just figured out that I never be able to make any calls, except collect. But, anyways, they throw me in with this mean redheaded white man that has me strip down and looks up my asshole and stuff. He says mean shit the whole time, the funniest being "Get your rabbit ass in there" and I take a really cold shower w/ nasty chemicals. Then they lock me in de-tox for 2 hours and finally give me some blankets and a pillow and show me a cot. No real interesting prison stories yet. I'm not too scared of other jail fuckers, the guards are scarier. They gave me small clothes that don't fit and there were no shoes in my size. The asshole guard is around a lot. They woke me up a 6 a.m. although I didn't sleep much anyway. I wasn't gonna get breakfast, but this guy wanted my cookie + offered me cigarettes, so I just got it and ate my banana + cereal + gave him my cookies and milk.

I got this fucked up little book called the "Inmate Handbook." It seems like something Adolf Hitler's men would write, pretty much says that all I can do is read the bible, write letters + get baptized. Fuck that! I need some books through bars. I'm supposed to keep that book, or I get charged for it, but I'll probably lose it anyway, so I'll send you some of the funny parts. It says to never borrow cookies or cigs... if you do, then the guards can't protect you if you are sexually abused. Funny huh? But, anyway, I think I'll catch some sleep. Aww fuck, I need some soda! I love you and if anyone tries to make you feel guilty about this tell them to fuck off. You're the best friend that I've ever had. It's just a little run of bad luck I'm having.

-Sam

P.S. It's not too bad, still kind of interesting.
P.P.S. Don't let any Chinos steal my stuff.

This is how I found out that Sam was in jail, but let's take it back a few years...

CHAPTER 1
ORIGINS

I'm an only child. I was born in Louisville, Kentucky, the same place that my mom is from. She grew up poor and she never really had a job. Her father was a deadbeat who was run over by a train. My dad was born across the river, in Indiana. He grew up surrounded by cornfields and farm country, and was raised by his grandparents because his mom didn't want him. She came back for him when he was 14, but he refused to go with her. He worked at a cemetery in Louisville for around 40 years. They gave him a watch to celebrate his 30th year on the job. They also gave him a good deal on a grave for my mom and himself. During the last few years he worked there, he could see his own grave with his name and birthday carved into the stone.

For most of my childhood, we lived in Indiana, on a dead-end street named Car Circle. It was shaped like a big "P," with four houses in the middle and houses all around it. There were cornfields on one side and a thicket of vines and trees on the other. Across the nearby train tracks was a mini-mart called Convenient, where I would buy candy. Behind Convenient was a trailer park where local kids killed cats and had teenage sex in tool sheds. Down the highway was a drive-in porn theater. Further down the highway were the seeds of a still-young suburbia, with a mall and some fast food places.

The first part of my life was boring. I didn't have a teenage rebellion and I wasn't full of angst and anger. I was just a geek. I didn't know anything about anything. I spent my time building really awesome clubhouses in the woods. I organized the few friends I had into a secret society of well-trained warriors, and we learned to move silently through the underbrush. We learned to track animals and local hunters. I never hunted. I never killed an animal. We learned how to build traps for our invisible enemies. We were ready for a war that never came. We wore camouflage. Eventually, my comrades turned 16 and got their driver's licenses and went AWOL. My family moved 12 miles up the hill, and I left my backyard empire behind.

I'm the one with the knife.

My new high school was full of redneck yuppies. I spent those last two years like a ghost. I took art classes and started playing Dungeons and Dragons to make up for my lack of real world adventure. That's all I have to say about high school, really.

Somehow, I managed to graduate. My intricate system of balancing F's with C's to earn a D average worked out well. All I needed was a D to pass, and that's all I tried for. It got me to that day with the cap and gown. The girls wore gold and the boys wore green. My grandma came with her huge VHS camera. I wasn't happy about being filmed or posing for pictures with my pizza face and nerdy haircut, but I was happy that my time in that place with those people was coming to an end.

After graduation, I went back to work at the cemetery. I had worked there every summer since I was 14-years-old, trimming the weeds between the stones. Next time you're in a cemetery, just think about how much work that is. I was a weed-eater. Sometime in early July, I realized that there would be no end to that summer. There was no more school. "What the fuck was I going do in August?" I wondered.

Troy—my neighbor from the old neighborhood—and I stayed in touch. We played D&D on a weekly basis. He was one year ahead of me in school, and he was my only friend who went to college, even though it wasn't really college. It was a two-year college—Vincennes University —in Vincennes, Indiana, a small town on the border of Indiana and Illinois. You probably haven't been there. Some supposedly heroic white people killed some people there once. Anyway, my lack of direction led me to succumb to Troy's pressure, and I joined him at Vincennes. He said that we could be roommates, and he assured me that it would be fun. He made some gross sexual jokes that I pretended to understand.

When I told my parents that I wanted to go to college, the first word out of my mother's mouth was, "Why?" I thought she would be happy about the idea, but she was just surprised. My dad didn't have much to say about it. It was easy enough to get accepted into Vincennes. I received a student loan and all of that dumb stuff people say that you're supposed to do. That August, I packed up my things for the first time and went off to college, two whole hours away.

My first year of college was rough. I didn't adjust well. My acne reached a critical mass and I tried to hide it with a Guns N' Roses hat. Troy and I stopped getting along, you see, because Troy was a wannabe redneck. He acted like a country radio stereotype, if you know what I mean (if you don't, just listen to country radio for a few hours—that was Troy). Growing up together, I thought it was funny. His nickname, or codename, was Redneck. We thought of him like the cowboy character in any good action movie. He was our cowboy, our comic relief, but living with him every day was too much. He made racist jokes. He made homophobic jokes. It was too much to take, even though I knew he wasn't serious. He was complicated. For example, he once dated a black bisexual woman who'd take him to gay bars, where guys would hit on him and call him Cowboy. He told me these stories and he loved it. He's a really hard character to explain. He wore a cowboy hat everywhere he went, and I grew to hate the sound of his size-16 steel-tipped pointed boots coming down the hall. I could hear them the second he walked through the door from the stairway to our floor. Clump, clump, clump. I lay low, very low.

I somehow managed to almost get straight A's. I think it was the lecture format. In high school, homework was a big problem for me, but in college, I didn't have to read anything or do any homework to get good grades. I have a really good memory, so all I had to do was go to class and listen. It was easy.

Troy and I drove home every weekend—like everyone else—in his big old car. He'd drop me off at my parents' house, then come back that evening to play D&D. Vincennes is a suitcase college, and almost everyone would leave on Fridays. Thursday was the big party night, not that I know much about those parties—I didn't party.

The year was almost over, and I still hadn't grown as person.

Sometime that April, I went back to my dermatologist, expecting the same useless advice and ineffective cream that he usually gave me.

You need to wash your face at least two times a day," he'd remind me without looking up from his clipboard. I washed my face way more than that. This time, however, he recommended Accutane—a medicine that came in pill form that was very effective at getting rid of acne. I asked him if it was new and he said, "No, it's been around for years." I asked him why he hadn't mentioned it before, and he said that he preferred not to prescribe it, because of its side effects. He made me read over the list of side effects before deciding whether or not I wanted to try it. The list:

- Red, cracked, and sore lips
- Dry skin, eyes, mouth, or nose
- Nosebleeds
- Changes in skin color
- Peeling skin, especially on the palms and soles
- Changes in the nails
- Slowed healing of cuts or sores
- Bleeding or swollen gums
- Hair loss or unwanted hair growth
- Sweating
- Flushing
- Voice changes
- Tiredness
- Cold symptoms
- Headache
- Blurred vision
- Dizziness
- Nausea
- Vomiting
- Seizures
- Slow or difficult speech
- Weakness or numbness of one part of the body
- Stomach pain
- Chest pain
- Difficulty swallowing or pain when swallowing
- New or worsening heartburn
- Diarrhea
- Rectal bleeding
- Yellowing of the skin or eyes
- Dark colored urine
- Back, bone, joint or muscle pain

- Muscle weakness
- Difficulty hearing
- Ringing in the ears
- Vision problems
- Painful or constant dryness of the eyes
- Unusual thirst
- Frequent urination
- Trouble breathing
- Fainting
- Fast or pounding heartbeat
- Fever
- Rash
- Red patches or bruises on the legs
- Swelling of the eyes, face, lips, tongue, throat, arms, hands, feet, ankles, or lower legs
- You should know that Accutane may cause changes in your thoughts, behavior, or mental health. Some patients who took Accutane have developed depression or psychosis (loss of contact with reality), have become violent, have thought about killing or hurting themselves, and have tried or succeeded in doing so. You or your family should call your doctor right away if you experience any of the following symptoms: anxiety, sadness, crying spells, loss of interest in activities you used to enjoy, poor performance at school or work, sleeping more than usual, difficulty falling asleep or staying asleep, irritability, anger, aggression, changes in appetite or weight, difficulty concentrating, withdrawing from friends or family, lack of energy, feelings of worthlessness or guilt, thinking about killing or hurting yourself, acting on dangerous thoughts, or hallucinations (seeing or hearing things that do not exist). Be sure that your family members know which symptoms are serious so that they can call the doctor if you are unable to seek treatment on your own.

...

I read the list and asked the doctor if Accutane would really clear up my face.

"In most cases, yes," he said. I asked how long it would take to work. He told me that I would see great improvements within a week.

"I'd really like to try it," I said.

My skin started drying up immediately, and two weeks later, I still had dry, flaky skin, but I didn't have any zits. In my mind, it was a miracle. I'd been living with acne since middle school, and it had really ruined my life. It transformed me from the fun-loving class clown who was always getting in trouble in elementary school to the shy ghost who sulked through the halls in middle school and high school. I drew demons and dismembered bodies in my notebooks and stayed quiet while the other kids stumbled through the awkward stages of growth. I wasn't passing notes. I wasn't making out under the bleachers. I wasn't going to the mall on the weekends. As far as anyone knew, I wasn't even there. I wasn't growing. I was invisible.

All of a sudden, I could look in the mirror again, because of this pill that I hadn't even known existed. I was so angry with that doctor for keeping this secret from me for so long. I would've gladly suffered all of the possible side effects to avoid seven years of solitude and sorrow. I was ready to be seen again.

The school year was almost over, and I was anxious to put my new face to use. The only problem was that I didn't have a clue as to how to go about it. I had a crush on this heavy metal girl in one of my classes, and I spent the whole semester staring at her and looking away when she caught my gaze. That was my only tactic. I knew it was ineffective. I told myself that I would talk to her. I kept telling myself that I could do it, and the days kept passing. I failed to make my move, again and again. Finally, on the last day of class, my last chance came.

She walked out of the classroom and I walked behind her like a chain was pulling me. I knew that what I was doing was wrong. I knew that she would think I was a stalker and a creep and that, in some ways, she would be right. I knew that I should have stopped following her. I knew that I had my chance and blew it. I knew I needed to turn around and admit my defeat, but I kept walking.

After a few minutes, she stopped, turned around, and said, "Hello." I froze and muttered something. I'm not sure what I said, but she took pity on me. She asked me if I wanted to sit and talk for a while. I mumbled something. We found a bench to sit on. It was sunny, but cold outside that day, and the bench was freezing. My black leather jacket kept me warm, but I was still shaking from the nervousness. I hoped that she thought it was because of the chilly wind. I hoped that she just didn't notice. I'm sure that she did. She wasn't nervous at all and she didn't seem cold, despite her thin denim jacket. She talked, and I watched her lips. We sat close enough together that I could smell her breath, and it made me light headed. I thought about what it would be like to kiss her, and instantly started worrying about my lack of skill. I had only kissed a few girls in my life, and most of those kisses went really badly. When the acne came, the kissing ceased fire. The heavy metal girl's name was Jenny. She came from somewhere in Indiana, but I can't remember where. I knew I would never kiss her.

We talked for an hour or so. She did most of the talking, because I didn't have much to say. My life wasn't very interesting. I got a few words in every now and then, and tried my best to not seem like a total dork. She was so nice to me. I'm glad I chose her to be the first girl I talked to, because a colossal failure or a total rejection at such a crucial stage in my life would have done a lot of damage to my sprouting self-confidence. Jenny wasn't interested in me in the way I was interested in her, or in the way I thought I was interested in her. She didn't give me my first real kiss, but she gave me something much better. The next day, she introduced me to some of her friends.

There was a guy named Matt. Matt had long, black hair and thick-rimmed glasses. He introduced me to death metal. His roommate, Jim, was from Louisville, Kentucky, and was surprised that I didn't know about the music scene there. I tried to explain that I didn't know about anything or anyone. He tried to explain what straight edge meant. He was straight edge, and, according to him, it meant that you don't do drugs or drink, and that you hate the people who do. He had a green and white letterman jacket but, instead of a school name, it said "straight edge" on the back. He showed me his Louisville Slugger baseball bat. It said "straight edge" on it too, engraved with a wood burner.

"Cigarettes are okay though," he said, as he lit one up by the fan.

He offered me one, and I told him that I didn't smoke or do drugs. "Good," he said. Then he told me that death metal sucked. He argued with Matt about it for a while, then played Danzig for me, because he wanted me to hear some good metal. It's so weird trying to remember how it made me feel. I listened to Guns N' Roses and Metallica and I owned Paranoid by Black Sabbath, so I thought that I was pretty aware of what metal was, but then I heard Napalm Death, or whatever it was that Matt played for me. Then I heard Danzig. I remember the song very well. Jim grabbed his guitar and played along. He sang, and Matt mocked him...

Ooh
I can feel it move me
Feel it shove me
As I break the law
Said yea
I can feel its jabbing
Cuts the numbness then I
I come alive

Twist of Cain
Yea drives my brain
Yea twist of Cain
Make me come alive...
          - Danzig

I'd never heard anything so raw. I thought the vocals sounded like Elvis, but I really liked it. It was like heavy metal Elvis. It sounded so much more evil than anything I'd heard before. I picked up the CD case, and looked at the weird half-man/half-bull skull on the front. I opened the insert to the black-and-white band photo. They looked so tough. They looked like they would beat the shit out of you. Jim poked the picture and said, "That's Danzig right there." I stared into the dark eyes in the picture and started falling in love.

I was so bummed that the school year was ending just as I started making friends, but they were freshmen too, so we would all be back next year. Matt and Jim were getting a house together off campus and were gonna start a band. They assured me that next year was gonna be great, and, for the most part, I believed them. I just had to endure another summer at my parents' house in southern Indiana.

It was the first summer with my new acne-free face. I spent most of it with my friend Joe. Joe was the most social of my high school friends, which isn't saying much. After graduation, we would go to the mall on weekend nights with the hopes of meeting girls. We were so hopeless. We'd walk around, play some video games, go up and down the escalators, and end up in the parking lot of a fast food place eating burgers—together, but alone.

Fortunately, my pizza face, one of our biggest disadvantages, was gone. I was still a dork, but now I knew about death metal and Danzig, and my face looked okay. I also convinced Joe to shave his head, so the hair helmet that he used to have was gone. We were fairly okay to look at. The alternative era of the early '90s was in full swing and we were both dabbling in grunge. We wore flannels and ripped jeans, and Converse, of course. That summer would be ours, I thought. We were ready.

I met Joe during my senior year at Floyd Central High School. I hated almost everyone at that school. I transferred there during my junior year, which I spent adjusting to the huge differences between this new school and my old one. I wasn't doing well before, but at least I knew the names of the kids whom I didn't talk to. At least I remembered when we were friends in elementary school. At this new school, I was more invisible than ever. I was an outsider and completely uninteresting.

Joe sat next to me in English. He wore skinny, acid-washed jeans and polo shirts.

During the first week of class, Joe leaned forward to tap the shoulder of the kid sitting in front of me. This kid was on the track team, and had a sports jacket with his name and number on it. I think it was for track, but I'm not really sure. I wasn't a sports fan. I was curious about what the nerd with the hair helmet had to say to this kid who was clearly of a higher social class. The jock turned around, and Joe said, "Hey, your last name is Davis, right?" The guy looked confused and nodded. "Why do your socks say McGregor then?" Joe asked. Looking more confused, the jock explained that McGregor was the name of a sporting goods company. I thought for sure that Joe was gonna get his ass kicked for this ridiculous and totally random antagonism, but the guy turned out to be really nice and just laughed it off. Joe didn't drop it. "That's dumb," he continued. "Why would you want to wear socks with someone else's name on them?" I couldn't believe his nerve and I couldn't understand what he was trying to prove. The jock laughed again and refused to take the bait. He turned around and went back to his work. I looked over at Joe, and he gave me this sinister smile. I knew we were gonna be good friends.

We spent the rest of that year pulling pranks on the other nerds and jocks in class. We had some great moments. We also somehow managed to get the best grades in the class, which focused heavily on paper writing. We were both fairly creative, and, despite the fact that the teacher hated us, she liked our work. She used a grading curve, and it was usually either one of us or this other girl, Tonya Husson, who set the bar for the rest of the class. This made us pretty unpopular, but, like the teacher, everyone went easy on us because they liked our work. Not our papers, but our pranks. The rest of our classes without each other were dismal and depressing. We weren't strong enough to stand on our own. Divided, we were just shy and quiet nerds, but together, in our tiny kingdom, we were kings.

So there we were, our second summer since high school had ended. I had gone off to college while Joe stayed home and worked. We saw each other every weekend and, though I'm pretty sure he hated it, he played D&D with us on Friday nights. Now I was a new boy, ready to attack the world and make up for my lost teenage years, and, with Joe at my side, I knew that I could do it!

We were still losers. It didn't matter that my zits and his hair helmet were gone—we were still nerds with no social skills. "If only there were a way to show the girls at the mall how cool we had been in English class," I'd think. I started worrying that we would look back on our senior year as the good old days. I worried that we had already reached the peak of our social lives. We walked around the mall, played video games, went up and down the escalators, and ended up eating fast food in the car.

A few weeks into that summer, my grandmother died. I convinced Joe to come to the funeral home in Louisville with me. After the funeral, we decided to check out this record store that we had heard about called Ear-X-Tacy. They had these bumper stickers that we saw all over the place. It became a trend to cut up the stickers and make them say something else, like "rEar-X-Tacy" or "caT-X-ray." The sticker rearrangements added to the allure of this mysterious place. We decided to check it out. I found a pay phone in the hallway of the funeral home. I was happy to be out of that room full of distant relatives pretending to be nice to each other. I looked up the address of the store, and we left.

The store was much smaller than I'd imagined it would be, but I was quickly impressed by their selection and organizational skills. I was also really impressed by the referrals written on the dividers. I was mostly interested in buying some Danzig, and when I found the Danzig section, the divider said, "See: the Misfits & Samhain." I didn't take their advice that day. I bought my Danzig album and I found a cool Nirvana CD titled Hormoaning. It had a sticker on the front that said "Imported" and most of the text was written in Japanese. We had discovered a new world.

Not long after that day, at the beginning of our musical enlightenment, I found a cassette in Joe's car. It had a florescent green cover with weird, planet-looking artwork, in black. The spine said "DESCENDENTS: SOMERY." I asked Joe what it was. He acted embarrassed and didn't want to talk about it. I pressed him and eventually he explained that he'd heard the band on the Pump Up The Volume sound track. Pump Up The Volume is a great movie about a kid who uses his pirate radio station to battle the corrupt authority at his school. The soundtrack was a mix of alternative and punk music. The Descendents song that inspired Joe to buy their album was "I Like Food."

I like food, food tastes good!
I like food, food tastes good!
Juicy burgers, greasy fries,
Turkey legs and raw fish eyes
Teenage girls, with ketchup too!
Get out of my way, or I'll eat you
I like food, food tastes good!
I like food, food tastes good!
I'm going to turn dining back into eating
I like food, food tastes good!
I like food, food tastes good!
            - The Descendents

I'd seen the movie, but I didn't remember the song. I asked him what they sounded like. He was still being weird about it and didn't want to talk about the tape. I wouldn't drop it, because we were best friends. We spent most of our free time together. I was perplexed by this mystery band and by the fact that Joe bought it without telling me. I wore him down and finally he said, "I don't know, they sound like an amateur metal band or a garage band." Back then, to us, "garage band" meant a band that practiced in a garage. The title had nothing to do with the band's sound. Joe was basically saying that they sucked. He didn't know that they were a punk band. As far as we knew, punk bands were really fast and screamed a lot.

After several more minutes of coaxing, I convinced him to let me put the tape in. The first thing that struck me was how poorly the album was recorded, which is funny, because it's actually recorded very well, but until that time, I'd never heard anything that wasn't layered with overdubbed guitars and backup vocals. This was simple, stripped-down pop punk and it was new to my heavy metal ears. We listened to the whole tape, and, song after song, I became more intrigued. I thought they were a joke, but I was starting to like the joke. They seemed like real people. I started thinking, "I could do this."

"It's kinda good sometimes," Joe said, and I agreed. All of the songs were different, and the lyrical content was fairly diverse, which was something else I wasn't accustomed to. When the tape was over, I asked Joe if we could listen to it again. He smiled and said okay.

A few days later, we were at the mall. It was the usual routine, but we were feeling pretty confident, and we knew that we were way cooler than we used to be. We were pretty sure that this time would be different.

It wasn't. We ended up in the record store and I stumbled upon a Misfits album. It was self-titled and had a creepy, skeletal face on the cover. I remembered the suggestion in the Danzig section of Ear-X-Tacy, and I decided to take a chance and buy it. Joe was an amateur tech nerd and had rigged up an ⅛-inch input jack into his car stereo, meaning he could plug his Discman in and play CDs in the car. It was 1992, and we didn't know anyone with a CD player in their car. We were cutting edge cyberpunks. In the mall parking lot, we put the CD in and pressed play. The first song was "She." I could barely make out the lyrics, but I knew that voice. It was Danzig for sure, but he sounded so much younger and more intense. There were no guitar solos. The song was over quickly. I liked it a lot. "Hollywood Babylon" came on and continued to confuse us. We just sat there and listened. "Bullet" took it to another level and made us both feel a little uncomfortable:

President's bullet-ridden body in the street
Ride, Johnny ride
Kennedy's shattered head hits concrete
Ride, Johnny ride...
Texas is an outrage when your husband is dead
Texas is an outrage when they pick up his head
Texas is the reason that the president's dead
You gotta suck, suck, Jackie suck

Arise Jackie O, Jonathon of Kennedy
Well, arise and be shot down
The dirt's gonna be your dessert
My cum be your life source
And the only way to get it
Is to suck or fuck
Or be poor and devoid
And masturbate me, masturbate me
Then slurp it from your palm
Like a dry desert soaking up rain
Soaking up sun
Like a dry desert soaking up rain
Soaking up sun
- The Misfits

After that, we drove home with the windows down and the summer wind blowing in. I cranked up the volume as we drove through the suburbs and into the cornfields, feeling tough and punk, singing "I ain't no goddamn son of a bitch, you better think about it baby." I could feel my world changing.

…

Summer was speeding by, and I tried to convince Joe, just like Troy had convinced me, to join me at Vincennes. I wasn't going to miss living with Troy, but I wasn't very excited about living with whatever random redneck they stuck me with either, and I thought it would be great if Joe and I lived together, because we were cool, and we could be cool together in college. He didn't have any other plans, so I was making good progress, and I was pretty sure that he was gonna give in.

Our efforts to meet girls at the mall remained unsuccessful. We started to wonder if the girls at the mall were even cool enough to hang out with us anyway. We went to Louisville sometimes and hung out at Ear-X-Tacy, but we were pretty sure that the girls there were too cool to hang out with us. We were in limbo between two stages of cool.

Sometime in late July, Joe gave in and enrolled for classes. We had given up on going to the mall. We could sing along to every song on the Descendents and the Misfits albums, and we both got really into Tori Amos. I wish I had some video footage of that era—Joe and I riding around in his red Pontiac Firebird, singing Tori Amos at the top of our lungs.

I decided to try to find Valerie, my only ex-girlfriend, whom I met at the skating rink right before my acne started getting really bad. I didn't so much meet her as get attacked by her.

You see, there was a brief period of time in my teenage life when I was kind of cool. I wasn't cool at school, but I was cool at the skating rink. I'd go skating two times a week, from open 'til close, and, back then, my parachute pants and mullet were a boon, not a burden. A few times a night, the D.J. would announce that the next song was "couples only" and that all non-couples had to clear the floor. I used to have to wait sadly for the song to end, but for a few weeks before my exile, I was out there on the floor holding hands with girls. Some nights I would skate with a different girl each time. I even kissed some of them on the plastic seats surrounding the rink.

The first time a girl put her tongue in my mouth, I really didn't like it. The second time was okay, but by the third time, I was starting to pretend that I liked it. I knew I was supposed to like it anyway. There were nights when the girls would get jealous of each other over me. I know it's hard to believe, but you should have seen my mullet and my moves. I was pretty cool.

Valerie was one of those girls. We met when she tripped the girl I was skating with and took my hand.

"Hi, I'm Valerie," she said. "You don't want to skate with that girl, she's a slut." I looked back at my skate date, lying on the floor, and kept going, hand in hand with this strange new girl. I liked her style. No one had ever knocked anyone down to be with me. I had no clue how to handle it. We hung out all night and kissed a few times. I was still pretty horrible at kissing, but she went easy on me. We exchanged phone numbers, and made plans to meet at the rink again.

The next few weeks involved a lot of long phone conversations, periodically interrupted by one of our moms picking up the phone and telling us to hurry it up. We'd go skating twice a week, but we only went on one real date. We went to the movies. My mom drove me to Valerie's house and we picked her up. We saw Pink Cadillac starring Clint Eastwood. We made out a bit, and I think I felt one of her boobs. It was really awkward. I had no idea that it would be years before I'd make out with anyone again, and I never would have guessed that it would be with her. We broke up over the phone a few days later. I'm not sure why. It was my idea. I got it into my head that she was a liar. I think I was scared of her experience and my extreme lack thereof. She cried. I felt horrible. I didn't see her again for a long time.

At the skating rink a few weeks later, a girl asked me why I was wearing foundation. I told her I wasn't. I was wearing an acne medication with cover up in it. I didn't even know what foundation was. A few other girls were standing around listening. One of them took a closer look and said, "He really is wearing makeup." They all laughed. I sank. I didn't skate with anyone that night. I called my mom and got picked up early. I never recovered. I stopped going skating. I stopped being cool.

Five years later, in the heat of July, during the twilight of my rebirth, I decided to try to find the only girl I really knew. I opened the phone book and found three listings with her last name. Only two were in New Albany, where I assumed she still lived. I didn't know her mom's name, so I had to call both numbers. I dialed the first number on my rotary phone. A girl's voice answered.

"Is Valerie there?" I asked.

"This is Valerie," she said.

"Who is this?"

"It's Chris Johnston," I said. There was a pause, and then she asked if it was really me, how I found her number, and why I was calling. I tried to seem as normal as I possibly could, but it was pretty difficult. I can't remember what I said exactly, and I can't remember what reason I gave for calling her after five years, but somehow we kept talking, and it went pretty well. My self-confidence was off the charts, and I had nothing to lose. I asked her if she had a boyfriend. She said no. She asked me if I had a girlfriend. I said no. I didn't mention that my date with her was the last date that I'd went on, and, eventually, I asked her if she wanted to hang out with me and my friend Joe. She said yeah, and we made plans to meet at the Hardee's near her house the next day.

When I told Joe about my phone call and my plan, he was not impressed. He accused me of being pathetic and I couldn't really argue with him, but our attempts to meet girls at the mall and the record store were all tremendous failures, so I asked him if he had any better ideas. He didn't say anything. He didn't want to go with me to meet her. I spent most of the night convincing him to.

I should take a minute to tell you more about Joe. You may have formed a mental picture in your head of what he looks like, with and without the hair helmet, but I doubt you've got him pegged. He was thin and lanky with sharp eyes and a narrow nose. His face rarely revealed his feelings. He was like a memorial statue of a World War soldier, stern and bold with a frozen gaze. That's what made him so great. He was such a funny guy, but he almost never cracked a smile. It made everything he said seem that much funnier. It also made it hard to take him seriously when he was angry or complaining about something. We were a horrible team. Me looking mean and tired all the time, and Joe looking grim and bored. It's no wonder that the girls at the mall didn't want to talk to us.

Joe could be cruel sometimes, too. He was too honest. Honesty can be cruel. He suggested that when we go to meet her, we park across the street so we could get a look at her before she saw us. That way "in case she's ugly, we can just drive away." I told Joe that he was awful, but in the end, I agreed with him.

We waited.

I saw her walking, and I recognized her right away. She looked almost the same as she looked five years before. She was still taller than me. She was still thin and pale. She still had shoulder-length, curly, dishwater-blond hair. We drove across the street and honked the horn. Our first few minutes together were really uncomfortable, but once we got over the strangeness of the situation, we relaxed. We started laughing and having fun. I think she was relieved to see that Joe and I were kind of alternative. I was pretty relieved to make the same observation about her. Neither of us could have had any idea what we'd be like now, based on what we knew about each other from five years before. We were so young then. We hadn't picked sides yet.

We hung out all day and well into the night. We talked about music, Joe and I eager to impress her with our newly found expertise in the underground, but she already knew all about Danzig, the Misfits, and Tori Amos. She told us about other bands and asked us about other bands. We had no clue what she was talking about. She told us about punk shows in Louisville, and I told her that I really wanted to be a singer in a band, but I didn't know if I could sing well enough. She told me that you don't have to sing to be in a band. She said that no one sang at shows, they screamed. This was the first time I'd heard the word "show" used to describe a concert. I remember how strange it sounded. I wanted to ask her what she meant, but I just pretended to know instead.

The night went on, and we got hungry. I asked her where she wanted to eat, and she told us that she was a vegetarian. I had never met a vegetarian before and it really blew my mind. Joe was pissed off. We both started interrogating her. We wanted her to explain why she thought it was wrong to eat meat. We were vicious and ignorant. I used all of the arguments I now hate. I said things like, "If you don't eat the cow, someone else will," and "Where would all the cows go if people quit eating them?" I said that we needed meat to survive and that there was no way to get enough protein or vitamins from vegetables. I really had no clue what I was talking about and I have no idea why I was so opposed to her being a vegetarian. I guess I was afraid. It was the first time my ethics had been challenged, and I fought back with blind fury. It was something new.

We wore her down, eventually winning the argument when we found out that she owned leather shoes and a leather jacket. She admitted it was hypocritical, and decided to give up her foolish diet. That night, we went to Rally's and we all ate hamburgers in the car. It was just like the other summer nights for me and Joe, except this time we weren't alone. Nine months later, I'd become a vegetarian myself, and I'd grow to hate people that say the stupid things that Joe and I said. I still feel horrible about that night.

Later that night, when we dropped her off, she told us to wait a minute. She ran into the house and came back out a few minutes later with a handful of cassette tapes. She gave them to me and said, "Here's some local music for you guys to borrow and some other stuff—Dinosaur Jr. and the Violent Femmes." We said goodbye and we drove off.

"She seems pretty cool," Joe said. I agreed with him. I was pretty excited.

We studied the tapes. The local bands tape included Dybbuck, Enkindel, Bush League, End Point, and Crain. I didn't really know what to think about these bands on my first listen. They were like nothing I had ever heard before. I couldn't tell if they were metal or punk or alternative—I didn't know what they were. Little did I know, I was listening to some of the most original music from the greatest era of the Louisville hardcore scene. Louisville had a great music scene back then, and I missed out on most of it. I found the underground a little too late.

The Violent Femmes are one of the greatest bands to ever exist. When I heard them, my first thoughts were, "This is horrible, what is wrong with this band?" A few songs in, I thought, "This is great, I love this. This music makes me feel dangerous and dirty and misunderstood. These guys are outcasts and weirdoes just like me." I raced though the hills of southern Indiana in my Ford Mustang singing along to every song. I loved it. It changed me. I really believe that music can do that. Music can permanently change a person—I would never be the same. Years later, when the folk punk movement started, I realized that the Femmes were the first folk punk band. They got their start by playing on the street, totally acoustic, outside of big concerts. They'd play for the people standing in line. That's how they got their record deal. Some big-shot record label guy saw them and loved them. I would love to have seen them back then, young and rowdy, playing on the street.

Day after day, I will walk and I will play
But the day after today, I will stop and I will start

Why can't I get just one kiss?
Why can't I get just one kiss?
There may be some things that I wouldn't miss
But I look at your pants and I need a kiss

Why can't I get just one screw?
Why can't I get just one screw?
Believe me, I know what to do
But something won't let me make love to you

Why can't I get just one fuck?
Why can't I get just one fuck?
I guess it's got something to do with luck
But I waited my whole life for just one...
— The Violent Femmes

Dinosaur Jr.'s Green Mind was also on one of the tapes. It didn't impress me that much at first, but it crept into my head, and slowly became one of my favorite records. J Mascis' slacker vocals and guitar solos seemed like such a weird combination at first, but now they seem like peanut butter and jelly to me. I searched Louisville that summer until I found their purple shirt with the cartoon cow on the front and the monkey on the back. A few years later, I'd drive to Amherst, Massachusetts to find his house, to find him. Twenty years later, I still wear that shirt and I still love the music. It's like an old friend to me. It's like how a peanut butter and jelly sandwich always makes you feel better.

That summer was revolutionary for me. My monster face was gone. I was a real boy now. Valerie and I started dating; I had a girlfriend! I discovered so much new music and my best friend was going to be my college roommate. I was excited—I was finally starting to live! I was ready to be visible. I was ready to be loud.

The rest of that summer flew by. Valerie, Joe and I drove to Vincennes in my Mustang. My parents followed us with all of our stuff in my Dad's truck, to help us move in. As we were carrying boxes inside, we spotted two weird-looking guys. One was blond and pale, the other had a Robert Smith hairdo, teased out and dyed black. Both of them were dressed in all black. Valerie said that we should become friends with them. I told her that we would. She had played The Cure for me just a few weeks earlier and I didn't like it at all. I thought it was too poppy and too soft, but I was excited to meet this goth outcast duo regardless. I was excited about the prospects of meeting people in general. For the first time in my life, I felt like it was a real possibility. My parents left with Valerie. I kissed her goodbye and promised to pick her up at work the following Friday.

I was eager to introduce Joe to Matt, and Jim and I wanted to impress them with my new coolness, so we walked over to their house. We received a warm welcome. I tried to talk about all the cool local Louisville bands I'd been listening to with Jim, but he was preoccupied and upset.

"Green Day is playing at Twilligan's Tavern tonight," he explained. He could tell by the looks on our faces that we didn't know who Green Day was, and w"d never heard of Twilligan's. "Green Day is an awesome pop punk band from Berkeley and they are playing in Louisville tonight," he elaborated. He was so bummed he couldn't go.

"They suck," Matt said. "Don't worry about it."

I thought about it for a minute and said, "I have a car, we could go." Jim was excited and, after a small and hasty discussion about whether or not it was a good idea to go to a show the night before classes started, we rushed to my car without even going back to our room. There wasn't much time. It was a two-hour drive and the show started in two hours. We had to be quick, and my Mustang was the perfect car for that—it was fast and it didn't have a speedometer or a gas gauge. We raced through the dark hills and made it with time to spare. "This year is gonna be awesome," I thought.

The place was much smaller than I expected, and packed. We paid our $5 and squeezed in. I don't remember the names of any of the local bands that played, but I remember that one of them wore backpacks on stage. I laughed and Jim told me it was a straight edge thing. After the second band played, someone got on stage and announced that Green Day wasn't gonna make it. Apparently, their van had broken down in Evansville, Indiana. The crowd was bummed. Jim was bummed. The band setting up to play next was bummed. I would have been bummed if I had known then that Green Day would become one of my favorite bands. At the time though, I was blissfully unaware and happy enough to be at a real punk show. Most of the crowd left. Jim explained to us that it would really suck to be the next band and that we should stay and support them. I thought it was weird that a touring band all the way from California would be traveling in a crappy van and break down and miss their show. I had no idea how much of a reality this lifestyle would become for me—breaking down, missing shows, staying to "support" bands. This was my first show. I didn't think it would become my life.

We drove home with the heavy weight of Jim's disappointment. We got in late and barely had time to sleep before the alarm clock woke us up for the first day of classes. I couldn't sleep at all. I was too excited. The path I would soon follow was starting to reveal itself to me.

The evidence of the alternative explosion of 1991 was everywhere. During our first week that semester, we saw so many kids with brightly dyed hair and Nirvana shirts, and I made a vow to Joe that within two weeks, we were gonna know every freak on campus. He laughed, but I swore to him that I was serious. He asked me how I planned to pull it off.

"We'll just go up to people and talk to them," I explained. I was out of control. I exploded on the scene like a geek. I'm glad that most of the other freaks were just as naive and fresh as me. We were all young and dumb and new. We all came from dead end Indiana towns and we were all anxious to take advantage of our newfound freedom. There was so much energy in the air—at least I think there was. I can't be sure. It might have just been me. I was a power plant.

Our dorm room was on the second floor and overlooked the entrance to the building. During those first few weeks, we would sit and watch people coming and going, keeping an eye out for potential friends. One day, we saw a girl walking into the building carrying a rubber tree plant, or at least what we thought was a rubber tree plant. She was kind of a hippie and she was really pretty, so we decided that we should talk to her. I really wanted Joe to meet someone nice. I wanted him to have a girlfriend too, so I thought of a ridiculous plan to meet her.

Everyone in our dorm had a 4-digit phone number, and all the phone numbers on a floor started with the two numbers. For example, all of the numbers on our floor started with 90. All of the numbers on the third floor started with 91. All of the numbers on the first floor started with 89. The top two floors were boys only, so all we had to do was dial numbers that started with 89. We called around 15 different numbers and asked the same question each time: "Did you just walk in with a rubber tree plant?" Most of the girls laughed at us. Some hung up. Some got angry and accused us of being creeps, but we were not daunted. We kept dialing, and eventually we found her. She was sweet and she thought we were funny. We chatted for a while, and then I asked her if she wanted to hang out with us. She said yeah, and asked us what our room number was. She said she'd come right up. We were in shock.

We hastily cleaned up the room a little and tried to decide what music to put on. I can't remember what we settled on. She knocked on the door. We sat on the couch and talked for a while. Later, she suggested that we order some pizza. We did, and she paid for it. It was great. We hung out a while, and when she left, she said, "See you later." We were friends. After she was gone, Joe said he wasn't interested in her romantically—I think he said she was too much of a hippie or something—but despite my match making failure, I still felt great. We had made a new friend—who was a pretty girl—and we had eaten free pizza.

We met so many people so quickly. We met the Robert Smith lookalike and his shy roommate. We met Jeff, the blue haired boy. We met Derrick, the lanky guitar player. We met Eric Beaver, the kid with face piercings and a spiral buzzed into his hair. We met a guy named Ed who went by the nickname Jesus, because he looked like Jesus. It was great. Every day was a new adventure, and every day we met more people. Every new person introduced us to new music and new ideas. It was a flood. It was a blitzkrieg. We did our best to absorb it all.

Jenny, the heavy metal girl who I met at the end of the previous school year, lived on the ground floor of our building, just a few doors down from the rubber tree hippie. Joe and I hung out with her one night. She wasn't as interested in meeting people as we were. She kept to herself and did her school work. I don't know if she was proud of my progress or if she thought I was an idiot. I don't know if she had any idea of the tremendous influence she had on me. I wonder what would have happened if she hadn't taken pity on me that day and turned around and talked to me. Would I have ever found Danzig? She told us about a sexual assault that she had suffered and why she couldn't stand the color purple because of it. I was wearing my purple Dinosaur Jr. shirt, and it made me feel horrible. I had never thought about sexual assault as something that really happened to real people, but it happened, and it happened to this nice girl. I felt sick. Joe and I were in way over our heads. The floodgates were open, and we were getting washed away.

After lunch one day, we saw this longhaired kid playing an acoustic guitar. We walked over and watched him for a while. He was playing "Stairway To Heaven" by Led Zeppelin. At the time, I thought it was awesome, but now I know that if you hear someone playing that song, you should run the other way. When he was done, he introduced himself as Nate. We talked for a while and he asked us if we wanted to smoke out. We told him that we didn't smoke.

"No, I mean, smoke... out..." We still didn't get it. "Smoke pot! Do you guys want to go back to my apartment and smoke pot?"

We didn't say anything for a few seconds. I didn't know what to say. I had never met anyone who did drugs before. Just like sexual assault, I thought of drug use as something that happened in movies and TV shows. "Just Say No" popped into my head, but I didn't want to seem like a geek to this cool guy with his cool guitar—I mean, he could play "Stairway To Heaven"—so I thought it over as quickly as I could and said, "No thanks, we don't do drugs."

"That's cool, you guys could still come over and hang out." We promised him that we would sometime. We made some excuse and left. We didn't really talk about it. We just walked home.

Jim and Matt started a band with these two other guys, Thom and Ryan. Thom, the bass player, was tall and moody and didn't say much. Ryan, the lead singer, was scruffy and friendly, and I liked him right away. He had the same Dinosaur Jr. shirt as me. They called themselves Tree Frog. They were a mix of hardcore, metal, punk, and something else. I don't know how to describe them. They were probably horrible, but I loved them. They recorded a demo tape, then played their first show. It was a house show—my first—and I moshed and danced. People stage dove from the stairway. I got knocked around, beat up, and sweaty. It was great. I loved it. I wish I knew where that demo tape was now. We were a random collection of geeks and losers from all over Indiana, but we had a scene. I guess this was the first punk scene I was a part of. I didn't know it was a punk scene. I didn't know what it was. We called ourselves freaks because that's what the rednecks and the jocks called us, but, really, we were punks, goths, potheads, straight edgers, artists, poets, queers, and outcasts. We were all different, and all trying to figure out who we really were, but now we had a scene and a soundtrack. We all moshed together when Tree Frog played. We had a band to unite us.

Our dorm room became the hang out spot. Jesus came over almost every day to play Street Fighter II. He was good. I was pretty good too. He usually chose E. Honda and I always chose Chun Li. We ordered $4 pizzas every Monday night. We goofed off and wasted our weeks away. We met another Joe, Joe Stone. He was from Indianapolis and owned a really nice Fender Telecaster. He could play it, too. We started a horrendous improv band called S.P.A.W.N. The acronym stood for something, but I can't remember what. We were horrible. Joe Stone or Derrick would play guitar, anyone that happened to be in the room would play the maracas (usually out of time), and either Eric or I would sing. We were dumb. Our songs were either random nonsense or they were about dicks or pussies.

Jeff (the blue-haired boy), Joe, Ed/Jesus, Eric, and some other guy (in the back, with the hat).

Joe Stone, Me, and Eric.

My favorite line in one of Eric's songs had to do with the frequency with which the non-freaks on campus would harass him. You see, Eric stood out. He was short and small and had around 15 facial piercings—mostly safety pins that he put in himself. Jesus was a real artist with the hair clippers and would carve various designs into Eric's head. He was definitely the freakiest looking of all of us freaks. He'd get cornered and pushed up against walls and threatened at least once a week. They'd ask him why he wanted to fuck up his face like that and he'd say things like, "I like pain." They'd ask him if he was gay and he'd say, "Suck one dick and everyone thinks you're a faggot." That was the chorus of one of our songs. I thought it was really funny. We never knew Eric's sexual preference. He never talked about girls or boys. It didn't matter.

When I say that we started a band, I mean we recorded songs in our dorm room. I'm pretty glad that S.P.A.W.N. never made a public appearance. It's bad enough that I have a 60-minute tape to document our depravity. One of our last recording sessions ended with the R.A. knocking on our door and telling us that we needed to stop what we were doing. We left the recorder on while he scolded and reminded us that it was nearly 2 A.M. The song we were recording/writing when he interrupted us was about having a bald dick. It was some attempt at an inside joke about Joe's shaved head. We had a few songs about his head, and we even made a music video for "Hair Drying Mother Fucker," a song about the absurdity of Joe's use of a hair dryer on his non-existent hair. When the R.A. knocked on the door, Joe Stone was wailing on his telecaster, and I was singing "Bald dick, bald dick, I've got a bald dick" at the top of my lungs. It was pretty embarrassing. That night basically killed the band. We gave up.

There was a coffee shop in downtown Vincennes that was having an open mic and we all went. It was my first open mic. The place smelled like incense and Clove cigarettes. It was dark and there were people—older people, other freaks, and hippies—that we had never seen before. I saw a girl with bright red hair smoking a Clove cigarette, and I sat down in the booth with her and introduced myself. I can't remember her name. She asked me if I went to college.

I laughed at her joke and said, "Yeah, of course." She didn't laugh. "Do you go to college?" I asked, still thinking we were joking around.

"No way," she said. She was a local. I realized that a lot of the people at that open mic were locals, and I started to understand that Vincennes was a real town and not just a college. Ed surprised all of us when he got up and read some original poetry.

I need an army to follow me
to fight the people I want to be
  - Ed (aka, Jesus)

We walked home in a gang through the foggy streets. We talked about how cool it would be to play at the next open mic. We were excited and inspired. Suddenly, there was an outlet for our creativity, an audience for whatever we could pull together.

A few days later, we started a band, consisting of Derrick on guitar, Ed on the flute, Joe Stone on the maracas, and me singing. We settled on the name "Green Tea." I'd tried green tea for the first time a few days beforehand and I didn't really like it. This girl named B.C. gave it to me. B.C. was from Washington. She came to Vincennes on a bowling scholarship. She was tall and strong, and looked like a boy. I found her strangely attractive. So did Derrick. He drank green tea in her room before, too. She had broken his heart a few days prior and I was starting to develop a crush on her. It was a weird feeling. I had a girlfriend at home whom I saw every weekend and she loved me. She sent me letters and called me on the phone. I felt guilty about my feelings for B.C. and I felt weird about being attracted to such a manly girl, but she was easy to crush on. She had charisma, she was interesting, and she came from far away. We drank green tea and fell asleep together on her bed listening to Julian Cope.

So we called the band Green Tea. For Derrick, the name was about heartbreak. For me, it was about my crush and my guilt. We were so dramatic. We were so horrible. We wrote five songs and recorded a demo. The songs were metaphorical and romantic and terrible. The style was folk-funk. We didn't play at the next open mic. There wasn't another open mic. The coffee shop closed and I never saw the red-haired girl again.

Sometime before winter break, I caught Joe smoking. I didn't know that he smoked. We had talked about how dumb we thought smoking was, and it really hurt my feelings when I caught him. I realized he had been lying to me for two years. We were best friends. We spent so much time together. I couldn't believe that he'd hidden his smoking habit from me and lied about it. I felt betrayed. I thought about how many times he had insisted on driving down to the gas station alone. He was always making up excuses to do things without me, and suddenly I knew why. We had a real falling out, and Joe didn't come back after Christmas.

Joe Stone didn't come back after Christmas either. He came home with me one winter weekend and I introduced him to one of Valerie's friends, a hippie girl named Rachel. They hit it off, and he ending up getting arrested over Christmas break. It had something to do with Rachel and him vandalizing one of her ex-boyfriend's houses. I was pretty sad to hear that he wasn't coming back. I assumed I would see him at some point, since he was dating Valerie's friend, but I didn't see him again until about seven years later.

When I did see him again, it was at a show at my house on Madison Street. He walked into the kitchen, did a double take when he saw me, and said, "Are you Chris Johnston?"

"Yeah, are you Joe Stone?" I said. He looked different, but I recognized him right away.

"Yeah. What are you doing here?"

"I live here. What are you doing here?"

"I live in Bloomington too." It was great. We hung out and talked about our days at Vincennes… but that didn't happen until much later.

…

When I got back to school, I had the room to myself. It was cool. I was pretty bummed about losing my best friend, but I had so many new friends, I assumed that I'd be okay. I was still excited about my new life and I was still happy with my new face. I was starting to forget what it was like before, what it was like to be a monster.

A few new students showed up too. One of them was a cute artist girl whom I developed a huge crush on. I really liked her, and I thought that she liked me too. I decided it was time to break up with Valerie. I knew it was going to be hard, but she was my first girlfriend, and I didn't even think about whether or not I really liked her. She was the only girl I knew. There were so many more girls in the world. I was unleashed and I wanted to run free. At the very least, I wanted to kiss another girl. I went so long without kissing anyone and now there were so many people who might kiss me. I had to find out. The breakup was horrible and I handled it horribly. I tried to do it in person during my next weekend visit, but I couldn't work up the nerve. I tried to do it on the phone, but I chickened out.

I ended up sending her a breakup letter. It was so cowardly. I cried real tears when I wrote it. They dripped onto the paper and smeared the ink. I felt awful. I knew it was wrong, but I didn't know what else to do. The day I dropped the letter in the mailbox, I turned the ringer off on my phone. I knew that she would call and I knew that if I heard her voice I'd get back together with her. It was cruel and weak of me. I regret it. I'm sorry Valerie.

I was single. I tried to put the moves on my crush, but she shot me down. She said that she thought it would be better if we were just friends. I was destroyed. I felt so dumb and so heartbroken. I felt horrible for hurting Valerie and crushed by my first real rejection. The new Dinosaur Jr. album came out that week and I lay around my room feeling sorry for myself and listening to it on repeat.

I don't see you, I won't call you
I don't know enough to stall you
Is it me, or is it all you?
Guess, it's on and on
On a day, maybe I'd show you
But it's the least of all I go through
But the thing is I don't know you
And it's on and on

Trembling words Don't make my eyes close
And if anyone then you'd know
I can't find out 'cause it won't show
And it's on and on
Every dream is shot by daylight
And I pray that maybe you're right
But if you don't, maybe I might
'Cause it's on and on
        - Dinosaur Jr.

As the year rolled on, more and more people freaked out and quit school. Ryan, from Tree Frog, told us he was leaving sometime in early March. He wanted to have a farewell party at his house and he wanted a band to play. Tree Frog couldn't play, because they had kicked him out of the band and they had yet to find a new singer. I wanted to audition for the job, but I didn't want to disrespect Ryan, because I liked him so much. He suggested that we start a band and that we only play this one show. "It will be a one night stand," he said. He wanted to play drums, so I offered to sing, which he was excited about.

We asked Derrick, from Green Tea, to play guitar, and he said, "Groovy." We asked Thom, from Tree Frog, to play bass, and he quietly signed on. We spent an evening trying to come up with a good band name and decided on Beth, after the KISS song. None of us were KISS fans, but we all agreed that "Beth" was a great song. We listened to it numerous times on the jukebox in the student center.

Once the naming of the band was out of the way, I asked about band practice.

"We're not gonna practice. I hate practicing. We'll just get up there and jam," Ryan said. I protested and said that I needed to write lyrics. "Fuck that!" he said. "Just do what you do best, make shit up!" I was flattered more than I was frightened, so I agreed. Derrick was totally down for the jam performance. Thom seemed apprehensive, but didn't argue. He was a great bass player, so I knew he wasn't too worried.

At the time, I looked like Kurt Cobain. My hair was dyed blonde and hung down to my shoulders. The rednecks often called me Kurt when I walked past them. I didn't mind. I took it as a compliment, since I loved Nirvana, but after suffering my first breakup and my first rejection, I decided it was a time for a change. The day before our big show—our one night stand—I dyed my hair black and cut most of it off. I left it choppy and shaggy, with a long devil lock in front. It was liberating. I didn't even know about the cliché of cutting your hair after a break up—I think it's just human nature to try to change yourself after your life changes.

We were pretty bad. Ryan wasn't a very good singer and it was obvious why he was kicked out of Tree Frog, but he was even worse at drumming. Derrick was pretty good at guitar, but he'd only written a few riffs, and they were all funky. My lyrics were atrocious, and I sang in a deep, Eddy Vedder-like voice. Thom did his best to hold it all together with his strong and steady bass lines, but he was just washing the dishes on the Titanic.

Back then, I thought we were great. I drew all over myself with markers and wore my New Kids On The Block shirt to be ironic or something. We played for an hour or so, while people drank beer and wandered in and out of the room we were playing in. I didn't drink anything. At some point, I think I took my shirt off. I thought I was supposed to. The whole thing was caught on video. I can't bear to watch it. It's so embarrassing.

This new girl, who was one of our biggest fans, watched most of our first set and all of our second set (yes, we played a second set). Her name was Brandy, and she wasn't a student. She came to Vincennes to live with her boyfriend, who was a student. His name was Chris. He had thick glasses and a feline smile. Brandy had purple pigtails. They were both kind of goth, and they both loved our horrible band. We talked a lot at and after the show, and Brandy told me she was a Wiccan. I told her that I wrote my research paper on witchcraft. She was pretty impressed. We were flirting right in front of her boyfriend, but he didn't seem to mind.

A few days later, I went over to their house and hung out. They were weird, but I liked them. I'd never met anyone who claimed to be a witch, and I was intrigued. I asked a lot of questions and, though I was skeptical about the answers, I kept asking. I've always been interested in magic and the occult, and I believe in a lot of unbelievable things. I was turned off by the hippie aspects of her version of witchcraft, but that didn't stop me from hanging out with her, or having a crush on her.

A couple of days later, Thom and I were hanging out with the witch and her warlock boyfriend, and we started talking about haunted places and scary stuff. Thom told us about Stepp cemetery. He said it was a spooky cemetery in the woods near Bloomington, his hometown. We were lying on the carpet with all of the lights off when he told us the story.

"A young child was killed in an auto accident in the 1920's and, blaming herself, the little girl's mother would come to the cemetery to mourn at her grave. Distraught, she dug up her daughter's body so that she could hold it one last time. She was found the next day, having committed suicide. Her ghost still haunts the cemetery today. She sits on a tree stump near the unmarked grave of her daughter, watching over her."

We were all quiet. He told us about a glowing hook that appeared sometimes and chased people out of the graveyard. Then, in the same low, spooky tone, he said, "Do you guys want to go there right now?" There was silence, then we all said yes. The lights came on. We gathered our jackets and walked to Thom's car to make the two-hour drive to the haunted cemetery.

We got there after midnight. The park that the cemetery is in was closed, but the gate was open, so we drove in anyway. Thom assured us that the worst thing that could happen to us would be getting kicked out, but that seemed like the least of our worries as we walked down the dark trail from the car to the graveyard. The cemetery was small, with 20 or so stones placed randomly around the clearing. We found the stump and approached it slowly. Brandy said that she felt a chill. She said that she sensed the spirit. It was pretty spooky. We didn't see the grieving mother, but we were all scared, and we all heard noises in the surrounding woods. We lurked around in the dark for a while and decided to leave before a glowing hook, or something else, chased us out.

When we got back in the car, Thom asked if we wanted to get pizza.

"Yeah," I said, "but it's so late."

"That's fine, places in Bloomington stay open really late. We can go to my favorite pizza place, Rockit's Pizza," he said. We all agreed that pizza was a good idea, so Thom drove us to Bloomington. We got there around 2 A.M., and I was amazed to see so many people in the streets. I was still doubtful about a pizza place being open so late, but I was having fun, so I didn't care. We parked in a vacant gravel lot, and weaved in between drunken college students to the tiny pizza place. It was open, and doing great business. We waited a while for a table, but it went quickly, because there was so much to look at.

The walls were covered with framed, autographed band photos. There were a few guitars, a tuba, and various drum heads and cymbals, all scribbled on with markers. They said things like "Rockit's Pizza is the best!" and "Thanks for the 'za." Near the counter, there was a classic jukebox that played 7-inch records. Thom told us that it held a few local bands' records. The place was tiny. It was basically a hallway filled with tables and a counter at the far end. We lucked up and got the only window seat. Back then, Rockit's was kind of like a real restaurant. Our table had a gingham tablecloth and a candle burning on it. A waitress, who was also the owner, took our order. The pizza was great, and so were the breadsticks that Thom insisted we had to try. We ate pizza and watched people stagger around outside. We saw punks walk by or ride past the window on their bikes. We saw sorority girls in tiny dresses and high heels, shaking in the cold. We didn't want to drive back to boring old Vincennes.

Not long after that trip, things got weird with the witches and me. I told Brandy that I had a crush on her and that I felt bad about it. She said it was okay. She said that her and Chris weren't really dating anymore. She said that they just pretended to be dating to make their parents happy because they were both gay. Their parents didn't know and wouldn't understand, so they pretended to be straight. They were even considering getting married to cover up their secret. I felt confused. She said, "Normally I don't like boys, but I like you." I grew more confused.

...

Spring came, and things were still confusing. I wasn't the only one freaking out though. Eric Beaver stopped hanging out with all of us completely and when Derrick confronted him about it, he said, "I made some mistakes this year. I should have thought harder about the kind of people I wanted to be friends with." We were all pretty hurt by that. Matt and Jim stopped hanging out too. Everyone was being weird.

Thom and I were becoming good friends, and he asked me if I wanted to go to Bloomington with him to go to this outdoor music festival called Culture Shock. I said sure, and we went. It was great. The bands were good, and there we so many people there. We walked around Bloomington, and got huge sodas for 40¢ from this college convenience store called the Discount Den. Thom took me to the many used record shops on Kirkwood Avenue and I found some great music. We sat in People's Park and ate breadsticks, watching the weirdoes walk by. Thom told me he was moving into a house in Bloomington once school was over. He said there was an open room and he asked me if I wanted to move in with him. I said yes right away. I was already falling in love with this place. I asked him if he wanted to start a band. He said yes, then told me about some drummers and guitar players he knew. I was so excited! I just had to make it through six more weeks of school.

I started skipping classes, because they just didn't seem important to me anymore. I didn't want a degree. I didn't care about being there. I was ready to start living my life. I spent a lot of time hanging out with Brandy. One night, we went over to Thom's house together and ended up spending the night on his couch. Little did we know, Chris, Brandy's not-boyfriend, was freaking out and looking all over town for her. He ended up locking himself in a friend's bathroom with a bottle of aspirin and a handle of Jack Daniels. They had to break the door down. It was an obvious attention tactic, not a real suicide attempt, but it still stirred up a lot of drama, and I didn't like it. The rest of our friends didn't know about Chris and Brandy's secret, so I looked like a jerk, although I'm not really sure if I knew the truth about them either. I'd never been in a situation like that before. I didn't know how to handle it, so I just took a few steps back and stopped hanging out with Brandy.

A few days later, my phone rang. I assumed it would be Brandy, but it was Chris. He was crying. I apologized. "How could you do it?" he asked. I apologized and tried to explain that I didn't know that they were dating. I started to tell him what Brandy had told me and he interrupted me, still weeping, and said, "No, I mean, why did you chose her instead of me? I love you."

I didn't know what to say. I thought I had complicated drama before, but this was too much to even comprehend. I didn't say anything. I hung up the phone and turned off the ringer. I was used to having the ringer off anyway. I'd turned it off after I broke up with Valerie. She wouldn't stop calling me. She'd call my mom and ask about me. She'd write me letters. Thankfully, that was ages ago, before email and Facebook and cell phones. I could shut out the world with the flip of a switch.

Things stayed weird after that. I'd been skipping so many classes that I couldn't remember what time or what days my classes were. Brandy still wanted to hang out with me, but I wasn't sure if I still wanted to hang out with her. I avoided most people. I hung out with Thom a lot, and talked about the future that was waiting for us in Bloomington.

Around that time, I had completed a 30-day challenge that I took. This guy Big John bet me that I couldn't go for 30 days without eating meat. He was straight edge. He argued that eating meat was an addiction, and he dared me to try to live without it for a month. I took the dare, certain I could do it. It was hard at first, thinking of what to eat. Every meal I ate growing up was based around the meat. Vegetables were side dishes only, and usually the only vegetables on the plate were corn, potatoes, or peas. I had a lot to learn about eating vegetarian food. I survived on grilled cheese, peanut butter and jelly, french fries, and pizza. My month-long meat vacation was over a few days after my alarming phone call from Chris. I was lonely and confused and hungry, so I went to get a hamburger at Rally's. I loved Rally's. For some reason, there, and only there, I would eat my burgers plain, with no toppings or condiments.

I drove my Mustang into town, and ordered a burger and fries at the walk-up window. It was early spring, and the concrete benches were cold, but it was nice to be outside in the sun and out of my dreary dorm room with its muted phone, reminding me of my lurking troubles. I sank my teeth into the burger and savored the flavor. I thought about how horrible it would be to be a vegetarian. I thought about how I had proved John wrong. I wanted to tell him that I did it. I wanted to boast to him about how I had made it 30 days, but I couldn't, because he wasn't talking to me. He had taken Chris' side—had championed Chris' side—and he hated me. He told everyone that I was twisted and evil. He hung out with Chris and Brandy a lot, and he did his best to convince Brandy to stay away from me. It was just another log on the fire. I didn't have room in my brain to think about it. I ate my entire burger, but then I started thinking about it. I thought about the cow that my burger used to be, and I thought about how it had lived and suffered and died for me. I felt horrible. I thought about how I would never kill an animal with my own hands, and I realized the hypocrisy of my diet. I wiped the grease from my lips and felt sick. I decided not to eat meat ever again. That was 1992, and I haven't changed my mind since. John was a jerk to me, but I'll always be thankful for what he did.

On the way home, I thought about Valerie. I thought about that night nine months prior when I'd convinced her to give up on vegetarianism. Joe and I bombarded her and pressured her into eating Rally's hamburgers with us. I felt awful. I will always regret that night.

...

A few days later, I concluded that there was no way I was gonna pull myself together enough to finish the school year. It was a two-year college and I was three weeks away from my associate's degree, but I didn't care. I wanted to leave. My social life was a wreck and I didn't care about my degree or my transferable credits. I knew that I didn't want to transfer anywhere. I knew that I was done with school. I wanted to be a musician. I wanted to do great things and live a wild and free life. I was awake and ready, so I went to some office and told them that I wanted to withdraw. Someone told me that I should withdraw instead of quitting, that way it wouldn't hurt my GPA and I would get a partial refund from my meal plan or something. So there I was, trying to explain to some stranger that I wanted out. They asked me why. I said that it was personal. They tried to convince me to stay. I told them that I had to go. They asked me if something had happened to me and if I wanted to talk to a counselor. I told them that nothing had happened, I just had to go. Eventually, he let me sign the papers and leave.

I packed my stuff. I didn't say goodbye to anyone except Thom. We made plans to meet in front of the McDonalds on Kirkwood Avenue in Bloomington in around three weeks. I drove home on a Wednesday. My mom came out, surprised to see me, but then noticed all of the stuff in my car and asked me to explain. "Mom," I said. "I dropped out of school and I'm moving to Bloomington to start a band." She realized I was serious. She cried.

CHAPTER 2
INTERMISSION

I had time to kill. The Porno For Pyros album came out, so I went to Ear-X-Tacy and bought it. I brought it back to my parents' house and listened to it in my bedroom, which didn't feel like my bedroom anymore. It was such a let down. I had just recently fallen in love with Jane's Addiction, and I was so excited for this record to come out. Perry Farrell had really let me down. I wished that I had someone to talk to about it. I missed having friends around. Being back at my parents' house made me think about Joe and our falling out, but I didn't let it dull my fires. I had a lot to look forward to, and I wasn't gonna look back or let the past drag me down. I took advantage of my proximity to Louisville. I was eager to explore the scene I never knew existed. I didn't really know how to do it though. I'd go to the record stores and walk up and down Bardstown Road, looking for freaks to become friends with, but I quickly learned that the big city was a lot different than the microcosm of a tiny campus where everyone was bored and isolated. The Louisville punks were smug and elite. I didn't understand why. I was naive and unstoppable. I took a beating, but I kept getting up for more.

My dad convinced me to leave my Mustang in the garage in exchange for a Ford Escort. He said it would be cheaper to drive and to maintain. I was kind of getting sick of owning a hot rod, so I agreed, with the promise that I could have it back when I became financially responsible. He had gotten the Escort for $30 and had gotten it up and running for $15 worth of repairs. It was ugly and boring, but I was happy to make the trade. When you drive a 1964 ½ Mustang around, everyone wants to talk to you about it. Nearly every time I stopped for gas, someone would wander over and ask me questions like, "How much do you want for it?" and, "What kind of engine you got under that hood?" After a while, I started acting like a smart ass. I'd say things like, "Oh, a car engine." They'd walk away sighing and thinking, "What a waste." I didn't care. I liked letting them down. I was happy to trade it for a crappy little cracker box.

The day before I packed for Bloomington, I tried to solve the riddle of Louisville one last time. I didn't know when I'd be back, so I thought I should say goodbye to the fruitless streets of the city I wanted to know so badly. I wore my Dinosaur Jr. shirt and walked up and down the strip, making all the usual stops. Defeated, on the way back to my car, I spotted a girl with dyed copper hair, stapling daisies to telephone poles. I followed her for a while, then said, "Hello."

She was friendly, and stopped her flowering to talk to me. I asked her why she was putting flowers on the poles, and she said, "Well, there are so many ugly advertisements and posters on this street. I just wanted to try to make it look a little nicer." I smiled. She asked me if I wanted to walk with her. I held a handful of daisies and walked alongside her, pausing at every pole while she pinned one up. I summed up my life story to this stranger, and she was polite enough to listen. I told her that I was moving to Bloomington to start a band. She said she thought that was great. "Everyone should be brave," she said.

We walked back to her house and she invited me in. She had recently painted her bedroom, and was excited to show it off. It was red and orange and yellow, all mixed up and swirling. It looked like the sunset. Her name was Dawn. She kindly hinted that I should go, so I went.

...

My Mustang.

CHAPTER 3
BLOOMINGTON

I didn't really know how to get to Bloomington. I packed my tiny escort with everything I thought I might need, and just started driving. I knew that Bloomington was north of Paoli, and I knew how to get there because it was the halfway point between my parents' house and Vincennes, so I headed in that direction. When I got to town, I was way too excited. I saw a walking mailman wearing one of those safari style hats, and I stared long enough that he caught my gaze and waved cheerfully. I waved back with a smile and thought, "People here are so friendly." I was so caught up in the moment that I failed to notice my speed and the raised train tracks ahead of me. I'm pretty sure my front tires came off the ground. When I landed, all of my stuff went flying and bounced around the car. Various useless objects that I considered essential to my new life hit me in the head. I felt like such a dork. I parked downtown and put my feet on the ground of my new home. I felt the magic pulsing through my steel-toed Sears Die-hards. I didn't have much time until I was supposed to meet Thom, so I walked to McDonald's and got some fries (I didn't know that they were coated in beef at the time).

Thom didn't show up. I waited for an hour. I walked around and came back every few minutes to see if he was there. I got a 40¢ coke from the Den and brought it back to the patio in front of McDonald's, and waited some more. Finally, I saw Thom walking toward me.

"Hey Thom," I said. "Where have you been? You're two hours late." He looked surprised and asked me what I was doing there. I laughed.

"You're not supposed to be here until next Monday," he said. I laughed again, but he wasn't laughing. Apparently I had mixed the dates up and accidentally arrived a week early. He suggested I come back next Monday.

"No way, I'm not going back to my parents' house for another week. I've already packed my car and I'm here. I don't want to leave."

"Okay, okay, well, I'm squatting at my sister's old house out in Unionville. She moved out a few months ago and no one's bought it yet. It's empty. It still has power and water and stuff, just no furniture or anything else, but you can come stay with me there, I guess." I told him that I'd much rather do that than go home.

Thom filled me in on Vincennes gossip. Jeff, the blue haired boy, was robbed in his dorm room and stabbed in the butt. Derrick freaked out and left right after I did, for reasons unknown. B.C., the boyish girl, got a job as an erotic dancer. Then, with some reluctance, he said, "And, these druggie assholes stole my bass." He was so bummed.

"Did you get it back?" I asked.

"Nope, they skipped town. I bought a new one already." A lot had happened in the few weeks that I'd missed, but that was Vincennes and that was all behind me. I was in Bloomington now.

Unionville is only around 10 miles from Bloomington, so it wasn't that bad. The house was spooky though. It was in a wooded subdivision, and it was always dark and almost totally empty, except for a huge cache of canned food in the garage. We sorted out all the vegetarian stuff and that's what we lived on that week. Thom worked as a pizza delivery driver, and he stayed pretty late some nights. Those nights in that lonely house were scary. I tried to stay in town for as long as could, but I didn't know anyone, so it was hard.

My third day in town, I went to a show at Rhino's All Ages Club. Back then, it was a much smaller space on the corner of 4th and Walnut. A few local bands played. The only one I remember is this band called Pencil. I showed up at 7:30, since the flier said that the show started at 8 o'clock. I wanted to get there before it got crowded. I was the first one there. There wasn't anyone at the door. I wandered in and walked around. This guy came out of an office and asked me if I was there for the show.

"Yeah," I said.

"Well, it probably won't start for a while. You can hang around if you want to, or come back later," he said.

"Should I pay you now?" I asked. I'm pretty sure he thought I was weird.

"Sure," he said, and then he went and got a little cash box and took my money. I walked around a little and came back at 8 o'clock. There still wasn't anyone there, not even the bands. I walked around some more, and got lost for a while.

I came back at 9 as the first band was setting up. A few people had shown up too. The crowd I was trying to beat by arriving so early never even showed up. It was a very small show. I talked to a few girls outside in between bands. I told them my tale.

I told them that I came to Bloomington to start a band. I'm not sure if I impressed them or not, but they were nice to me. Pencil was good in a Dead Kennedys kind of way. I didn't know it that night, but this was my first date in a long-term relationship with Rhino's and Brad, the guy who took my $3 that night. I drove back to the empty house in the woods and cracked open a can of beans, a little disappointed with the lackluster evening.

The week in the woods passed quickly. We moved into our house on the corner of Atwater and Park. It was a great house. We had the entire first floor. There were four bedrooms, two living rooms, and a breakfast nook. It was furnished and the rent—$400 a month, total—included utilities. I had no idea how lucky we were, since I had no experience with renting. Thom knew this guy called Steve The Weave who wanted to move in, and for some reason Thom insisted on paying $200 a month himself, since his parents were paying his rent for the summer, so my share of the rent was only $100 a month. I had withdrawn everything I had in my savings account before leaving home. I had around $600 total. I decided it would be best if I just paid my rent for the summer, in full, in advance, so I gave Thom $400, leaving me $200 for the summer. Being completely inexperienced with supporting myself, I assumed it would be easy.

Me, my dad, and my new car outside of my new house a few days after moving in.

One of the first things we did together as housemates was buy a huge, six-foot-long Jane's Addiction poster. It was so cool. The image was the original cover of "Ritual De Lo Habitual," which depicts a paper-mache sex scene with a nude guy lying with two nude girls. A lot of stores refused to carry the album because of its "obscene" cover art, which lead to the band creating an alternate cover. The alternate cover is the first amendment in black ink on a white background, and on the back it says:

Hitler's syphilis-ridden dreams almost came true. How could it happen? By taking control of the media. An entire country was led by a lunatic... We must protect our First Amendment, before sick dreams become law. Nobody made fun of Hitler??!

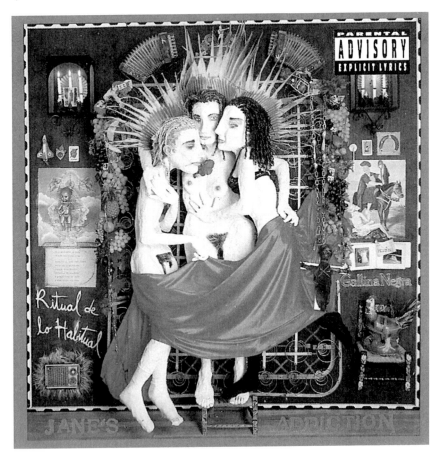

We hung it above the couch, and we couldn't wait for people to come over and see it.

The people living upstairs were musicians too. One of them, a ginger haired guy named Jason, was in a band called Tangleweed. Thom knew him from high school, which is how he had found out about the house. He talked to him and the rest of his floor about us playing music, and they were really cool with it. We made a deal: either floor was allowed to play music anytime they wanted. It was great. The deal also included letting one of them keep their drums in our music room and practice there sometimes, as long as we were also allowed to play the drums whenever we wanted to. The pieces of our plan were really coming together. All we needed to do was find a drummer and a guitar player. Thom had some ideas.

We went over to this guy's house. He was a friend of Thom's and he was a drummer. The plan was to talk about our ideas for a band and maybe set up a practice session. He lived in a shitty apartment complex on the north side. I said that I wanted to sound like Dinosaur Jr. and Thom said that he wanted to sound like the Smashing Pumpkins. This guy said that he wanted to sound like gansta' rap mixed with rock n' roll. He had a lot of ideas, which he fired at us one after another without pause or noticing that he was missing his mark. He said he wanted to call the band Bhudda Quest. He asked us if we smoked pot. We shook our heads. He kept going: "Here's what I think would be awesome. Imagine this, we make a huge joint out of paper or something and we hang it above the stage, then we get a smoke machine and hook it up so that smoke pours out of this fatty while we play. People will love that shit. Don't you think so?" I don't know what we said to that, but we left and we didn't call him back.

Thom and I spent a lot of time walking around or hanging out in the park downtown, and I would see all these cool-looking alterna-kids walking by and I'd ask him who they were. Sometimes he knew who they were but didn't really know them, or sometimes he had seen them around but had never met them. I suggested that we talk to them. He wasn't as enthusiastic as I was. I told him about how I had challenged myself at the beginning of the school year. I took the same challenge again that day. "In two weeks we're gonna know all the weirdoes in town," I said. He laughed and looked at me like I was an idiot, which I was, but I wasn't hurt. I was unhurtable. I wasn't afraid of being foolish. I'd show him.

On our way home that day, we bumped into a nerdy guy on a skateboard who happened to be another one of Thom's high school friends, named Marty. We talked for a while and told him about our encounter with the Buddha Quest guy. He asked me what instrument I played.

"I don't play an instrument, I sing," I said. There was a short and awkward pause. I had no clue why. I asked him if he played anything. He said that he played guitar. I told him that we were looking for a guitar player. He said something vague that I took as a maybe.

39

I asked him if he liked Dinosaur Jr. and he said, "Yeah." I had a good feeling about Marty.

The summer exploded. Every day was an adventure and every day I met someone new. I bumped into this girl whom I recognized from Vincennes.

"Hey did you go to Vincennes?" I asked.

"Yeah, I saw you there," she answered. I asked her what she was doing there. "I dropped out of school and moved here."

I laughed. "Me too." Her name was Christy. She was kind of a hippie. We clicked right away and started dating, and Thom started dating her housemate, another hippie named Pam. We'd go on double dates and stuff like that, but it didn't last very long. Me being straight edge didn't mix too well with her pot smoking. We argued a lot and eventually gave up. I was still moving very quickly. I didn't have time to worry or feel sad. I had so much to do.

I started hanging out with these high school punk girls who were always in the park. One of them, Miranda, had a huge crush on me, and would come over to my house every day. Sometimes she'd bring her friend Michelle and their gay friend Matt, who both tried to discourage Miranda's crush, because they liked to party and do drugs. They worried about me having an influence on her. I kept telling her that she was too young and that we couldn't date, but she wouldn't give up.

Marty and I became good friends. He introduced me to a lot of people. We'd go on adventures on the campus at night, sneaking into buildings and climbing onto rooftops. One night, I broke my foot jumping a gap, and I had to spend the next week in bed. It was a great week. All of my new friends knew that I was stuck in bed, so they'd come over after school and hang out with me. They'd bring me food and stuff too. It was really fun, despite the pain. Miranda came over almost every day and always brought me something. Eventually I decided that our age difference didn't matter, and we started dating. I dealt with the grief I got from people. After a while, everyone got over it and got used to it. We became inseparable. She quit doing drugs and smoking, and Matt and Michelle hated me for it.

Eventually, Thom and I grew apart. He didn't really like having people over all the time. He was too shy to deal with it, and he seemed jealous. He'd come home from work and go to his room with a pissed off look on his face. He didn't seem interested in starting a band with me, so I started playing with Marty, Marty's girlfriend named Molly, and a few other people. We sounded kind of like the Cure or R.E.M. I'm not really sure. We decided to start a band. We called ourselves Lost August. We played one show at Marty's brother's house, in the garage. I was so shy and so afraid of singing in front of people that I hid behind the bass amp. After the show, people kept asking Marty if the vocals were prerecorded. We never played again. I'm not sure why, but I think some of the other guys in the band thought that we sucked. Maybe we did. Again, I didn't care. I was too busy making up for my lost teenaged years to care. I was thoughtless and careless in those days.

Our housemate Steve was called Steve The Weave because when he came back to school after Christmas break, he had long dreadlocks. Before break, he had shaggy, shoulder-length hair. It was obvious to everyone that the dreads were fake, but he wouldn't admit it, so people called him Steve The Weave. He didn't seem to mind. Nothing really bothered him. He was a sweet guy, kind of like a puppy. He was cute, but he never paid his rent. When I say never, I mean never. One day, I found one of his dreads in the shower. It was wet and nasty. We kicked him out in July, but he never moved his stuff out. We'd catch him sneaking into the house every now and then, and eventually we had to start locking the doors and put his stuff out on the porch. A few weeks later, his ex-girlfriend and her mom showed up with a care package for him. They said that they were worried about him. We didn't tell them that we had kicked him out. We didn't tell them that we thought that he was living in his car. Instead, we promised to give him all the food and relay their messages of concern. When they left, we devoured the food they had brought for him. We were pretty poor and there was a lot of good stuff, like Cookie Crunch cereal and spaghetti and sodas. We thought it was an adequate revenge for his lack of rent-paying. It was one of the last things that Thom and I would ever do together. He was still dating Pam, and had started staying at her house. I almost never saw him again.

As August came to a close, I realized that my prepaid rent was running out and that I needed to figure out my living situation. I managed to catch Thom one day, and found out that he was moving to Colorado or something. I told him that he could keep the Jane's Addiction poster and asked him for the landlord's phone number.

I talked to a few of my new friends and got a group together to move into my house. They were so excited, since most of them had never lived away from their parents' houses, and since it was such a good deal. I called the landlord and said, "Hey, I think we're gonna keep the house."

"Who is this?" he asked. I told him who I was and what house I was talking about—I didn't even imagine that he owned more than one house. "Oh, you're the sub-leasers. You need to be out of there by tomorrow." I tried to explain that I didn't want to move and that I had found two other people to move in with me. "What are you talking about? That house has already been rented to someone else. They signed the lease in January. You need to be out of the house by tomorrow." I hung up the phone. I felt liked I'd been mugged. I didn't have a house. I had to pack my stuff. Thom was already out and I was on my own.

I spent the next month living in my car and occasionally staying with one of my few friends that didn't live with their parents. My friend Darin also ended up without a house that fall and moved into the Escort with me. It was pretty ridiculous, the two of us in my tiny car, my tiny car that I had spray painted with bright colors and had dozens of toys glued to the dash. We would sleep in "L" shapes, cramped and crowded, in the Bryan Park parking lot.

I met Darin through Marty, I think. He was the singer in a band called Yarn Marvins. I saw them play in the hallway of an apartment building downtown during my first few weeks in Bloomington. The show was an early show—it started at noon, I think—and some friends and I decided it would be better to stay up all night than to try to sleep and wake up "early" enough to make it to the show. I sat against a wall and tried to stay awake while they played. A few days later, I saw a really cute girl in a beret walking a bull dog down Kirkwood Avenue, and I waited anxiously for her to get closer so that I could get a good look at her. She came closer and I realized it was Darin. That's how handsome he is. He's a handsome man and a beautiful girl.

Months later, we were living in a car together. The plan was to live in the car until it got too cold, then we'd move into a house together somewhere. Darin got a job as a recess supervisor at an elementary school and I drove him to work, then picked him up an hour later, when his shift was over, five times a week. While he worked, I shoplifted at the mall or the grocery store. We both did what we could for our weird little family. He brought home a tiny paycheck and I got us food and books. We'd spend one night a week with his mom in her cabin in the woods and one night a week with our friend Eli, the guitar player of the Yarn Marvins. We'd spend the other five nights in the parking lot. It was a simple and happy life, but it got old. Darin decided to move back in with his dad while we saved our money and looked for a place to live. It was around this time that I met Sam.

CHAPTER 4
SAM

Marty graduated high school that year and decided to go to college. He managed to get a room in Collins, the cool dorm. We called it the cool dorm, some people called it the gay dorm. Collins was the place to be for the alterna-kids of the '90s. It was the place for bright blue, Manic Panic people. It was the place for skaters, punks, queers, freaks, and other non-sports fans. Hanging out there reminded me of the benches outside the dining hall back at Vincennes. It was a freak scene.

I spent a lot of time at Collins, and even slept in the common room there sometimes. No one seemed to notice—or they just didn't care—that I wasn't a college student. One morning, I woke up to find that someone had covered me with a blanket from their room. It was nice. A few weeks into the semester, Marty told me that I had to meet this guy Sam. We went downstairs and knocked on his door. He wasn't there. The door was unlocked, so we went in. There was a harmonica on the floor next to a Bob Dylan songbook. The room smelled like peanut butter. We continued our quest, and found him on the ground floor in Lisa's room.

Lisa plays a significant role in this story. She introduced me to some bands that became very influential—namely Fifteen, the punk rock hippies from Berkeley. My friendship with Lisa grew cold quickly with a few key events. One of them being the night, a year later, when she turned Sam and I onto the streets instead of letting us sleep on her floor. We hung out late in her room, drinking home-brewed root beer that exploded when you opened it. We assumed we'd crash on the floor since we had nowhere else to go. We assumed wrong. She had made a vow to her boyfriend, promising him that she would never allow a boy to sleep in her room. She kept her vow, and we slept outside that night. It was cold, but it was fine. The final nail in the coffin of our friendship happened years later, when Sam, looking rugged and wild, bumped into her. She asked him the standard questions people ask each other when it's been a while, then asked him if he was "going the Chris Johnston route." Sam asked her what that meant. She said something about me being jobless and wasting my life... We would turn this into one of our many catchphrases: "The Chris Johnston route."

Anyway, back to Collins. Marty told me that this guy Sam swore that he had spent five years in an alien prison on Deimos, one of the moons of Mars, so I was expecting someone really weird. I wasn't expecting the pin-stripped dress shirt or the huge, silver framed glasses. He had the math nerd look, but there was a spark in his eyes. I wouldn't say he had wild eyes back then, but you could see the fuse and the match. You could tell that sooner or later there would be an explosion.

We hung out all night, the four of us. We listened to pop punk, and Sam told me the story of his five years on Deimos, which he called Planet X. I didn't believe him, of course, but I could tell that, like me, he had recently escaped some form of imprisonment and he was excited to be free. He told us all about the persimmon festival in his hometown of Mitchell, Indiana, the home of Gus Grissom, the astronaut. We made plans to go. I had no clue how important this night would become to me.

Sam.

I really enjoyed my first fall in Bloomington; it was beautiful. I spent my mornings walking around campus or hanging out at the public library. Sometimes I would drive out to the strip mall wastelands and shoplift food, role-playing books, or gifts for my friends.

I'd spend my afternoons with Miranda and her friends when they got out of school. We'd go to Café Pizzeria and eat french fries in the "around the world room." It's not as fancy as it sounds—it's just a room with a mural on the wall of some people in a hot air balloon, based on the book by Jules Verne. Each booth has a different framed poster on the wall of some distant land: France, Germany, Greece, Italy, etc. My favorite booth, then and now, is France. It's in the front, by the window, so you can watch for people you know walking down Kirkwood. I'd eat my fries and dream about traveling around the world. I was sure that I would someday, but I didn't know how. I still love going to Café Pizzeria and eating fries or pizza—or both. I've been to all the places in the posters, so now, instead of imagining what they're like, I dream of going back. We'd eat fries and drink many refills of soda, then Miranda and I would sneak off somewhere to make out before her mom picked her up and took her home.

…

I made Sam a mixtape with the Misfits, Rancid, the Descendents, Green Day, Blatz, Operation Ivy, and stuff like that on it. Since the tape was mostly punk, I called it "a homosexual's young boy," which was one of the dictionary's definitions of the word "punk." I wrote that phrase on the side of the tape with a Sharpie. Sam loved it, and we quickly became friends.

One night in Collins, Sam stopped to check for strays in a pizza box that he spotted sticking out of trashcan. There were only a few pieces of crust, and Sam ate them immediately. He noticed a coupon printed on the top of the box. It read: "Collect 10 of these coupons and get a free 14-inch, one-topping pizza." Sam's eyes lit up. We knew what we had to do. We searched the trash on every floor of all three buildings that made up the Collins dorm complex. We didn't find enough coupons for a free pizza that night, but we knew that if we looked every day, we'd eat pizza soon enough.

The next day, when I found Sam, he showed me his bounty of coupons. Not only did he find enough to complete our set of 10, but he'd also found 10 more. He had 20 coupons! He had put extra effort into the hunt and searched outside of Collins. We were both surprised to figure out that almost no one cut their coupons out. That night, we would eat our first free pizza together. The deal was for pick-up only—they wouldn't deliver a free pizza—which was okay with me, and, since I was the only one with a car, I offered to drive. It made me feel like I was contributing to the pizza effort. We called in the order and went to find my car. I'd lose my car a lot back then. There were so many free parking places without time limits in those days, and I didn't drive that much, and since I didn't have a home, I'd just park my car somewhere and forget about it for days at a time. The pizza wasn't great, but the freeness of it was delicious. Marty and I got mushrooms and Sam and Lisa got pepperoni. It was the last time Sam ate meat. Years later, he'd tell me that he felt like such an idiot that night for eating meat in front of Marty and I.

We ate those first free pizzas in the parking lot, too excited to wait until we got back, and thus began our war with Mad Mushroom Pizza.

Sam, Marty (doing a cartwheel), and Miranda.

CHAPTER 5
COTTAGE GROVE

Sometime in November, Darin and I found a place to live. It was a one room sublet in a house with some random college dudes. The house was on Cottage Grove, which is only one block north of Collins, so it was perfect. We signed the lease without even meeting the guys who we were gonna be living with. We didn't really understand that we were moving into their house. We thought of it as renting a room, our room. We found a huge mattress by the dumpster of a furniture store and threw it on some milk crates. We put a deadbolt lock on our door while our new housemates watched from the couch. We didn't think we were being weird at all, but I'm sure they did. They were right.

One of the guys who lived there was a pothead and had an iguana named Iggy. He'd sit in the living room for hours, watching the fucked up TV. It was a black and white TV, and the picture was fuzzy on a good day. It had a red tint to it and if you watched it for too long, the world would seem bluer afterward. For the first few days, when either of us saw him, he'd ask us if we wanted to smoke weed. We'd tell him every time that we didn't do drugs. He was always surprised.

One of the guys who lived there was a bass player. He played along to Rush and Soundgarden on his upright bass for hours. From our room, all we could hear were the bass lines—the same bass lines—over and over. One of the only things I can remember him saying to me is this: "You ever try to get a girl to touch her elbows together behind her back?" I said no. "Try it," he said, so I tried it. He started laughing. I didn't get it. "See, it makes their tits stick out. Then you punch them in the tits." He left, laughing, without seeing my disgusted face. A few minutes later, I heard the bass lines thumping again.

The other guy lived in the mysterious upstairs bedroom. He was a drummer in a heavy metal band called Half Convulsion that practiced once a week in the cat-shit-filled basement. In between practices, he'd practice solo, for way too long. The drums were almost directly under our bedroom, and we'd have to listen to him trying to perfect some complicated fill for ages, attempting it again and again. We waited, hoping that he'd get it right. Bass coming through the walls and beats coming through the floor was the sound of our new home.

The smell of our new home was pretty bad too. The living room smelled like cigarettes and spilled beers with a hint of weed and a splash of bong water. The kitchen smelled like the rotting trash that was always piled high in the corner. The bathroom smelled like dry piss and mold, and the cat shit smell—rising from the basement—seeped into everything.

Despite the noise, the smell, and the weirdo housemates, we were happy to have a place to live, and we had a room of our own with a lock on the door. It was our sanctuary, and it sure beat living in a car or sleeping on whatever couch I could find.

I took a trip to my parents' house to pillage my cache of possessions. Along with all of the useless stuff I brought back to B-town, I grabbed a mini-fridge, a microwave, and my beloved toaster oven. With these items, our bedroom fortress was complete. We had no need, other than showering or pooping, to spend any time in the rest of the house (yes, we would pee in bottles in our room).

One day, on a rare occasion when our door was open, the drummer of Half Convulsion walked by our room. He stopped, said hello, and checked out our room. He spotted the micro-kitchen that we had created in the corner. He asked us if we were students. He asked us what we did. I told him that we played in bands. We talked about music for a while, and he suggested that we have a show sometime, in the basement, or, as we called it, the litter box. He looked at the mattress and asked if we both slept on it.

"Yes," we said. He didn't say anything else. The thought that it was weird for two friends to share a bed had never crossed our minds. I don't think he was a homophobe, and I'm pretty sure he thought we were way weirder than we were gay.

We lived self-sufficiently in our small bedroom. We had a "boog" (booger) ledge, a dart wall, and one bed. We locked our door when we left and we had a wide range of guests coming over all the time. He was right to think we were weird.

The three cats in the house belonged to the drummer. They were horrible. There was Clutch (named after the metal band), Beverly, and her son, Montana. Clutch was white and fluffy and spent most of his time in the bathroom. He liked to shit in the shower and unroll all of the toilet paper. Sometimes, instead of cleaning up the poop, I'd just run the shower for a few minutes until it dissolved enough to go down the drain, or, when I took showers, I'd just push the shit through the grate with my toes. It wasn't really that gross. Beverly was older and only had one eye. She was okay except for her general demeanor, which was crotchety, and her missing eye was kind of creepy. Montana was an asshole. He would knock over anything possible. His favorite things to knock over were ashtrays and beer bottles. He'd go for the bong too whenever he had the chance. Of course, we never let those furry bastards into our room.

This high school kid named Morley started hanging out with us a lot. He was really funny and we all loved his company. He said that he hung out with us because we didn't drink or do drugs. He was on probation and had to stay out of trouble. He'd come over after school and stick around all day, or we'd go over to Collins together and do something with Marty and Sam. One day he woke me up pretty early, on a school day, and said, "Hey Chris, we gotta go find Sam." I forced him to explain. "Little Caesar's has this crazy-ass deal and it's only for today."

I asked him what the deal was.

"You get two medium-one-topping pizzas for $4," he said. "I can't eat two pizzas all by myself. I need you guys to help me." I couldn't argue with his logic, but I didn't understand why he had to skip school and come right over. I asked him on our way to get Sam and he started laughing and said, "I don't know, I was just excited and I knew you guys would be too. I didn't want you to eat anything else. This is important." We found Sam and filled him in on the situation. Morley told him that he should skip his classes and eat pizza with us.

"Yeah, of course," Sam said. "Let's go."

Morley got a big kick out of the cats at our house. He renamed them all. Clutch became Shitty, for obvious reasons, Beverly became Cyclops, and Montana was rightfully known as Fucker from that day on. Me, Darin, and all of our friends adopted his names for the cats. We had to be careful when we talked about them, to make sure that the other housemates never heard us.

Especially the time Fucker got out and went missing. We felt bad and we didn't want his owner to hear us referring to him as Fucker. Morley grabbed one of the "missing cat" fliers, changed the name to Fucker, and hung it on the inside of our door. It became a game, to make sure no one was in the living room before we opened the door. We discovered a crack in our door, and we'd peer through it to spy on people in the living room and make sure that the coast was clear. We were weird, I know.

Our Mad Mushroom campaign was going great. We usually managed to get at least one free pizza a week, sometimes two, and occasionally three. One night, while feasting on our spoils, someone brought up the question: "Where do the coupons go after people turn them in?" We concluded that they must end up in the dumpster. We had never really checked their dumpster, since their pizza wasn't that great even when it was hot and fresh. There were so many other, more desirable dumpsters in town. We had no idea what we'd find. The thought of finding used coupons seemed too good to be true. We assumed that they must deface the coupons in some way, but it was worth another five minute drive to find out, so we finished our pizza and went back to Mad Mushroom.

We parked on the far side of the parking lot, out of sight of their front door. We were quiet and stealthy as we slipped behind the building. When we got to their dumpster, we noticed that their back door was open. Classic rock was blaring. We could smell fresh pizza coming from inside, and sour, rotting pizza coming from the dumpster. We didn't speak to each other. We exchanged looks with questioning eyes. Silently, we discussed our plan. Should we retreat? Should we push onward? Sam started moving toward the dumpster and slowly climbed in. A few minutes of digging and he threw a few bags out. Outside of the dumpster, we were nervous, with our eyes on the open door. The bags at our feet came from the front of the store, under the cash register; they had receipts and other odds and ends. A quick look into a hole that Sam had torn revealed a few bundles of cardboard coupons! We had found what we came for.

Sam was still digging. We pleaded with him, using our hands and our eyes, to get out of the dumpster. He handed me a few pizza boxes and climbed out. The boxes were heavy. We grabbed the bags and slipped away into the darkness. We found a hideout under a light and sorted though the trash. There we so many coupons. Most of them were bound with rubber bands into nice bundles of 10. We were frantic with joy! We were wolves with our prey in our teeth. We shook the bags, and the receipts scattered around us like feathers. When we had pulled all the meat from the bones, we walked back to the car, leaving the carnage for the pigeons. We sped home, listening to the Misfits. I asked Sam what was in the boxes. He opened them and showed me. There was a large order of cheesy sticks and a large cheese pizza! We had more free pizza and a huge pile of coupons.

We got home and I threw a few slices of our dumpster pizza into the toaster oven. After that, we started counting. We each made piles of 10. When all the piles were stacked nicely in a row, we added them up. There were 14 piles and a few strays.

We had found over 140 coupons!

I got my camera out and took a picture of our plunder. We couldn't stop laughing. We were so happy. I noticed the smell of burning pizza and remembered the pizza in the toaster oven. I got it out before the dripping cheese caught on fire. We ate pizza and laughed while we celebrated our great victory.

Sam and Marty with 140 coupons.

I started working for a temp agency. Having a place to live was great, but it also meant rent, and I needed money. Pizza couldn't pay my bills. A temp agency is a place that finds workers for companies that need people for a short period of time and don't want to worry about hiring them and doing all the paperwork themselves. Instead, the company calls a temp agency and tells them how many people they need and for how long. Then the temp agency picks some workers off of their list and calls them bright and early in the morning and offers them the job. You don't have to take the job offers, but the more you refuse, the lower you get bumped down on the list. The more jobs you accept, the better jobs you get. This was before cell phones. We had a landline and an answering machine with a mini-cassette. Randomly, it would ring sometimes at five or six in the morning and I'd let the machine get it, ignoring Darin's grunts of complaint. The tinny voice would say, "Hello Chris, this is Kelly from Manpower calling. I have a job for you if you want it, please call me back in the next 30 minutes if you're available." The 30 minutes after the call were terrible. I'd try to convince myself to get up or I'd try to convince myself that I didn't need the money, but I did need the money, so usually I'd get up and call Kelly back. "d worked at a temp agency for a while when I lived at my parents' house, and it was much worse down there than it was in Bloomington. There were lots of shitty factories near my parents' house, in the New Albany, Clarksville,

Jeffersonville area, and I had worked in several of them. A few examples:

- Assembling, testing, and disassembling riding lawnmowers from 6 A.M. to 6 P.M.. All of the other workers were on work release from prison. The sun rose and set while I was at work.
- Gluing the foam layer of an egg crate to the top of contour (as seen on TV) pillows, putting them into pillow cases, then plastic bags. The pillows built up static electricity and shocked me.
- Opening boxes which contained compact mirrors, removing each one of them from their protective bubble wrap, and stacking them in piles, near an assembly line of gossipy, middle aged women who put them into Winston cigarette packages, then back into boxes to be shipped to the cigarette factory somewhere else.

My jobs in Bloomington were usually much easier:

- Watching a conveyor belt in the General Electric factory for $8 an hour, waiting for it to jam up. When it jammed up, I was supposed to write down the time that the jam started, how long it took to fix, and whether it was a human error or a mechanical error. It only jammed once in a week. It was almost always human error. The line workers hated me and I quit.
- Folding clothes at Lazarus to make it look nice for the Christmas rush. We (the temps) came in at 5 A.M. and stayed until 9:30 A.M. We would arrange blue jeans, fold turtlenecks, and stuff like that. The store opened at 9 A.M. and, before we left for the day, we would witness all of the work we had done get destroyed. A full-time worker there never failed to say, "Early enough for you?"
- Using Elmer's glue to assemble the various cardboard chunks that fit inside boxes to keep their contents from moving. We never saw the contents, and rarely knew what they would be. We just rolled glue onto cardboard shapes and held them together for five minutes until they were dry. It sounds easy, but it wasn't. I had to stand around with middle-aged, redneck women and hold cardboard while they talked. I quit after discovering that the boss was a blatant racist. A few days into the job, he told us that he wouldn't need us anymore, then I got a call from him directly. He said that he had made a mistake and that he did need us. I went in the next day to find that me and the only other white temp had received his personal call. There were also two new temps there. While holding glue, I asked one of the women next to me what the deal was and she explained: "The boss can't really just call the temp agency and say, I don't want no niggers." I left my chunk of cardboard and went home. Later that day, I reported them to the temp agency.

The week before Christmas, I got a call from Kelly. She offered me a job doing janitorial work at a place called Stone Belt. I'd never heard of it, but I told her I'd take it. I needed money for gifts and I was bored out of my mind since so many of my friends had left town for family stuff. My house was empty. Sam was in Mitchell, Darin was usually at one of his parent's houses, and, since Miranda was out of school, I didn't see her very much either. I figured the job would be a good way to distract me from the miserable merriment of the holidays.

Stone Belt is a place for people with disabilities to work. It isn't so much for the money as it is for the experience of having a normal life and a healthy routine. They do a lot more than that too, but that's all that I understood at the time. I was filling in for a woman named Mary, who was on vacation. My job was to clean the bathrooms, empty the trashcans in the offices, and clean up the lunchroom. It was pretty dirty work since a lot of the disabled workers were very messy. I'd find huge piles of mac and cheese on the cafeteria floor, mop up what seemed to be entire bottles of spilled milk and juices, and deal with all the poop that didn't make it into the toilet for some reason. It was a really good experience. It taught me that nothing is really gross and that sometimes you just have to grin and bear the dirty work. It was strange though, and kind of surreal. I would spend six hours a day with the Stone Belt workers, some of whom would ask me every day who I was and what had happened to their beloved Mary, then I'd go home to a cold empty house and listen to The Afghan Whigs.

I smoke a pack a day
I hit the pipe sometimes
and drink my pay
Screw my friends
Understand my need to offend
Come home and smack the woman around
Tried to apologize
But she deserved it, that I know
Strangled with her pantyhose
What's with the flowers
Can't you smell me
I buried you and still you kill me
With all your crying, I can tell
That your disease will make me well
Twist your head so I can witness
Come and crawl inside my sickness
I'm hated

Undisguised
Never known why
Now I like it...
  - The Afghan Whigs

The Afghan Whigs were the soundtrack to my loneliness. A few days before Christmas and the end of my job there, I betrayed my brothers and used 10 coupons to get a pizza for myself after work. We had agreed to only use them together, but I couldn't help it—I was so sad. I ate my pizza and listened to the same album again and again. Now, whenever I hear that record, I taste Mad Mushroom pizza and feel a tingle of guilt for my treasonous act.

Eventually, the holidays were over and everything was back to normal. All of my friends came back. Sam told me that his dad had seen the mixtape that I had made him and freaked out. He wanted to know why it said "a homosexual's young boy." Sam tried to explain that it was a punk mix and that I had made it for him. His dad asked about me. "Who is this guy, Chris? Is he your homosexual sex master?" Sam said that he couldn't help but laugh, which just made his dad more irate. He grilled Sam about me, and Sam answered all of his questions. "Why would a 20 year old want to hang out with an 18 year old? What could you possibly have in common?" his dad asked.

My parents came up to visit, and my dad helped us build an awesome loft in our room. At last, we had our own beds. The loft was built in two sections in the corner, so that one bed was on each wall and we both had a storage space at the head of our bed, in the corner. It was a great loft. We went to a thrift store and found matching outer space mattresses too. Our room became so much cooler.

The boog ledge was getting full of boogers. It was disgusting.

Marty and I tried to start a band again. I brought my shitty electric guitar back to town and we got our friend Chris Dilts to play bass. We wrote a few songs and recorded them on a 4-track. We called ourselves Drowner. That's about as far as that band went.

I started hanging out with Sam a lot. He was so funny. One day, I was loitering around the Collins dining hall, hoping to get someone to sneak me in or bring me some food, when I saw Sam walking around like a cat with tape on its back, all low to the ground and freaked out. I watched him for a while. His arms were stretched out in front of him, feeling around. I called out to him. He looked in all the wrong directions. He couldn't see me. I walked over and asked him what was wrong.

"I lost my glasses," he said sadly. I asked him when he had last had them. "The night before." I offered to help. We searched his room with no luck. I asked him if they could be in the bathroom, and he said that he had already looked.

"How could you see them if they were there?" I asked. He shrugged. We went to the bathroom and there they were setting on the sink. He was so happy, and, as my reward, he snuck me into the dining hall and we ate cheesy pasta and he told me a crazy story about his bad vision.

He said that when he was in elementary school, his teachers all thought that he was learning disabled. They placed him in special classes. He told me that one of his classes consisted of doing jumping jacks in a basement room with a few other kids. Eventually, after a few years of being treated like that, one teacher asked him if he could see the chalkboard. He told her that he couldn't. She suggested that he have his vision checked. He got his vision checked and found out that he was legally blind. He got some glasses, was quickly put back into regular classes, then became the best student in the school. He stayed at the top of his class all the way through high school and won several awards. He got a college scholarship big enough to go anywhere. I asked him why he chose I.U. and he said that his dad talked him into it. He thought that it would be good for Sam to be so close to home.

It was pretty obvious that Sam was a genius, and it was clear that he had spent most of his life living in a very small and protective environment. He was born on the Fourth of July. When I found that out, I asked him if that was why he was named Sam. "No," he said. He told me that his dad said he had named him Sam after a little boy that had been run over and killed by a school bus. This little boy, Sam, dropped something in front of the bus and bent over to pick it up. The driver didn't see him and drove over him. His dad said that he thought it would be a good reminder of how dangerous the world is, and that hopefully it would teach him to always be careful when he's around cars. I worried that Sam might be a compulsive liar. Could his family really be that weird? It seemed too strange to be true, but I believed every word that came out of his mouth.

The free-pizza-club (Marty, Sam, and I) continued to be great. We went to the dumpster whenever we picked up our free pizza and sometimes we would find the coupons we had given them the day before. It was too good to be true. We would use the coupons we found in the trash to get free pizza, then re-dumpster the same coupons and use them again. It was like the circle of life or something. It was pizza paradise. We couldn't envision a better deal, but they started to get wise. We found fewer and fewer coupons and, eventually, our supply ran low.

One night, we were a few coupons shy of having enough for two pizzas. Miranda and her friend Corrine were hanging out, and a few other people were at the house, so we really wanted to get enough pizza for everyone.

"Do you think they really check the bundles of coupons?" Marty said. He had everyone's attention. "We could just cut a few pieces of cardboard and put them in the center of the stack, and wrap a rubber band around them."

"I've never seen them check," Sam added. Usually, when we turned in the coupons, they didn't even count them. If they did count them, they would do it by turning the stack on its side and counting the edges, not by unbinding it. It was a risky idea, but we were hungry people and we needed pizza. We decided to give it a shot. We divided the effort—Marty worked on the forgeries, Sam called in the order (using the name Hector), I would drive us over to pick them up, and Morley would go inside and make the trade. He wasn't happy about having to walk in and say, "Pick up for Hector," but he got over it pretty quickly, trying out various voices in the car on the way there. We kept telling him to use his normal voice, but he was in one of his funny moods and kept going. He thought it was really funny and he wouldn't stop laughing. We had to wait in the parking lot for him to calm down.

We always parked out of sight of the door so that the pizza workers wouldn't recognize my ridiculously painted car, which made the wait even more nerve-racking. We watched Morley walk toward the door. He walked inside. The seconds felt like hours as we waited for the door to open again, and when it did, we saw the pizza boxes in his hands! He played it cool and walked slowly toward the car, never looking over his shoulder. I kept the engine running so we could make a fast get away. Morley dove into the back and we left. We all started laughing and cheering. We raced home and busted into our sanctuary, careful to obscure the missing cat poster from my housemate who was sitting on the couch, watching the red TV. He said something about pizza. We laughed and stepped into the room. I locked the door behind us. We felt like heroes! We spread the boxes on the floor and everyone grabbed a slice.

From up on his bed, Darin said "Did you get a vegan one this time?" We didn't. I felt bad, but he didn't really care. He wasn't as into pizza as we were. He usually ate really healthy stuff. He went back to reading his book and we went back to relishing our moment of glory, which was quickly transformed into two greasy pizza boxes and a room full of happy people.

This was the first real pizza scam that we had pulled. Using dumpster coupons was a questionable action, but we weren't really scamming anyone. The coupons read: "Collect 10 of these coupons and get a free 14-inch, one-topping pizza" and that's what we did, we collected them (from the dumpster). This was different though. We were dishonest. We didn't give them 20 coupons for those two pizzas. We gave them 17 and a few rectangles of cardboard. We were bandits. I could sense that this was just the beginning.

The best thing about the Mad Mushroom coupon days was that when you got a free pizza, there was a coupon on the box that it came in. Every free pizza that we got came with 10% of what we needed to get the next one.

One night and several free pizzas later, Marty came over and we played guitar together. We had both kind of given up on Drowner, but we still wanted to start a band with each other.

"We should start a band where we all play an instrument that we don't know how to play," Marty said.

Darin popped his head over the side of his bed. "I'll play drums." We'd forgotten he was up there, which was something that happened a lot.

"I'll play bass, I've never done it before," Marty said.

"I guess I'll play guitar and try to sing at the same time. I've never been able to do that," I said. We all agreed, and we were excited. I don't know why this impractical line up seemed like the most likely attempt I had made since I had moved to Bloomington to start a band, but it did. It just felt right. Of course this was just talk. We had to find a drum set and a bass amp, and we all had to learn how to do our parts, but it seemed like a sure thing. We moved on to a more important issue, our name. We came up with what seemed like an endless supply, but we couldn't agree on one. Hours later, we somehow got to The Ted Danzig Machine. We all laughed and Marty tweaked it by suggesting The Ted Dancin' Machine. We didn't get it at first. We thought that he said The Ted Danson Machine. Ted Danson is the name of an actor who played a character named Sam on the TV show Cheers. The Ted Danzig Machine was a weird play on words, but it wasn't really a good band name, and The Ted Danson Machine was worse.

"Not Danson," Marty explained, "I said dancin'... like, dancing. Get it?" We got it and we all laughed, and it was obvious that we had a found our band name.

Spring was slowly approaching, and we started to push the limits of the coupon scam. One night, we used a single coupon and nine blanks, and it worked. We used the coupon on that box with nine blanks again and got another pizza the next night. The hardest part was finding pick-up people. We couldn't keep going in to pick up these orders with coupons. They would obviously get wise, so we had to induct other people into our free-pizza-club. Sometimes we would keep them in the dark. We'd just offer to share our pizza with them in exchange for them walking in and getting it. They suspected a scam, but we didn't go into the details. They were usually happy to get a free pizza. We realized that if everyone knew about our scam, they would do it too and it would be over. We had to protect our secret. The callers had to make up new names every time too. We tried to keep it simple: Matt, Mark, Brad, Brett, etc. but when Morley or Sam called in the order, it was always something atypical, like Boris or Nikolai or Ivan or something. They argued that it was more believable to have a unique name. The odd names were funny, but they sometimes created a problem with the pick-up person who would be hesitant to walk in and say "Pick up for Fritz." We kept pushing it.

One night, we decided to get two pizzas. The problem was that we only had one coupon. We considered binding 19 blanks to one original and hoping it worked, but we came up with something even dumber. The pizza boxes were printed with red ink, so we found a red, fine-tip Sharpie and drew a replica of the coupon. We made two bundles, one with nine blanks and a real coupon on top and one with nine blanks and our hand-drawn forgery on top, and it worked! It opened up so many new possibilities. Could we get a free pizza without a single real coupon?

We had leveled up. We got outright sloppy after that night. We grew foolish and rude. We concluded that they never looked at the coupons, and I decided to put our theory to a test. I made a fake bundle with a forgery on top, but this time my forgery read: "Collect 10 of these coupons and suck a 14-inch dick." I know it was dumb, and swear I was becoming a better person, really, but I still had a lot to learn. Anyway, Sam agreed to do the pick-up. They didn't look at the coupons. They just handed him the pizza and tossed the bundle in the trash as usual.

We had to take breaks periodically, not because we were over-scamming, and not because we feared getting caught, or due to dry spells in the dumpster, but we had to take breaks because the pizza sucked. The freeness was great, but after a few weeks, we had to give it a rest and eat dumpstered pizza from other places.

Darin found a few drums and Marty got all the bass gear that he needed, so we went into the basement and shoveled cat shit all day and made a practice corner. I shoplifted some air fresheners to try, in vain, to cover up the smell of Fucker, Shitty, and Cyclops. Darin decided to play the drums his own way, flipping the bass drum on its side and propping the open end up with a brick to let the sound out. He played it with a stick instead of a kick pedal. He didn't have cymbals or a hi-hat and it sounded pretty weird, but we didn't care. We played for hours with no idea of what direction we wanted to go in. Of course, even if we had known what we wanted to sound like, we didn't have the skills to do it anyway. We just played music and had fun.

Our musical influences were pretty different. Marty loved The Cure and The Smiths, Darin was really into R.E.M. and Pavement, and I listened to tons of Bad Religion, Green Day, and Operation Ivy. We all liked our collective influences, with a few exceptions, so it wasn't a problem. The only problem was deciding what we wanted to sound like and how to make those sounds. We didn't make much progress during that first practice, but we had a lot of fun and we learned the theme song to Cheers.

A month or so later, we decided that we were ready for our first show. I asked my high school friend, Ray, if his band Blister would drive up and play. He said that they would. We needed at least one more band, and my young punk friend, Austin Lucas, had just started a new band too, called The Dirtys, and he assured me that they kicked ass, so I asked them to play as well. We had a full bill! I got the okay from the other weirdoes who lived in my house to have the show in our basement, and we made a flier. It was the first flier I had ever made. I found a picture in an old '80s magazine of some break-dancers and I used the computers on campus to print out all of the text for the flier. I thought it was amazing that you could choose from so many different fonts. Like the dork that I was—like the dork that I am—I picked a different font for each band. There was a Kinko's Copy Center downtown, right next to People's Park, and I did all of my work there. I took my pieces there for assembly, cut out the band names, then glued them down with a free Kinko's glue stick over the image of the breakers posing. Then I took my masterpiece to the copy machine and ran off about a hundred copies. I was so excited. Sam and I hung them up all over town. I gave a huge stack to Marty too. I was certain that this show was going to be epic. Of course, we still needed to write more songs—we only had around three finished—but we had a few weeks before the show to get our act together.

Our songs were pretty bad. I couldn't play anything complicated and sing at the same time, and I couldn't play without looking at my hands. Darin's unique drum style didn't help much. He wasn't very loud, the drums got buried under the distortion from my amp, and he couldn't really play fast beats. Marty, on the other hand, was great. He wrote bouncy bass lines and helped me with my guitar parts. He really held us together. We had the framework for around six songs, but they needed work, and the fliers for our show were already hanging up on every pole in town. We had a deadline. We cracked down and practiced three or four times a week. We finished the songs and we were satisfied with the length of our set.

One night after practice, while eating a Mad Mushroom pizza, we started talking about our lyrics. They were a hodgepodge of random stuff that Marty and I had come up with together. They were vaguely about fictional romances and relationships. They were lyrics for lyric's sake. They were bad. I asked Marty and Darin how they would feel about changing them. I suggested that we make our songs about something. I didn't really know how to describe what I meant, so I said, "You know, like how Bad Religion songs are all about something."

"Do you mean political songs?" Marty asked.

"Yeah, I guess so," I answered. I wasn't really sure what that meant. We all agreed that it would be cool to have more meaningful lyrics, and I started re-writing all of our songs, with only a week or so to learn them before the show.

I took a break from song re-writing to go hang out with Sam. We were just goofing off with Marty and Lisa, when Sam asked, "Why don't people borrow sugar from their neighbors anymore?"

"I think they do," I said.

"No, they don't. Everyone is afraid of each other these days. No one relies on their communities anymore." He got up and left the room. He came back with a coffee can that he had found in the trash. With one raised eyebrow, he said "I'm gonna go and see how many people will lend me some sugar." Then he started taking off his clothes. We all protested when we realized that he was going to strip down, completely nude, but he ignored us and turned to face the corner. He was totally naked. He held the coffee can over his genitals and left the room. We had to follow him, to see what he was going to do. He walked down the hall and knocked on a random door. The dude that opened the door was shocked and laughed awkwardly when he saw Sam standing there.

"Hey, I was wondering if you would be so kind as to lend me a cup of sugar?" Sam asked. Then he used his free hand to point to the coffee can, to indicate that he could put the sugar in it.

The guy was speechless, then he laughed a little more and said, "I'm sorry, I don't have any sugar." He closed the door. Sam walked to the next door and did the same thing. We stayed back and watched, trying not to laugh too loud. No one gave him any sugar, which he said proved his point. He said that it was conclusive, people didn't help each other out anymore. I was starting to really understand how unique and beautiful and brave my new friend was.

With a few days to spare, I finished the new lyrics to all but one of our songs, which we decided was okay the way that it was. I felt good, our songs were about things now:

- "Television Head" was about people who watch TV and how dumb we thought they were.
- "Mellodrama" was about people who drink, and how dumb we thought they were.
- "Slim Fast" was about dieting and body image and magazines.
- "Thank You For Smoking" was about people who smoke and how dumb we thought they were.
- "Ball Park" was the one we left the same, about my transformation into a normal boy.

The big night finally came, and we were anxious for people to show up. We had spent all day cleaning the basement and getting things ready. Austin came over around 7 o'clock and told us that some of his band members had flaked and that they couldn't play. I was pretty bummed out. I was excited to see his band, and I thought that if they played, all the little park rats would come to the show. My friend Ray was supposed to show up early to hang out, but it was getting close to show time and he wasn't there. I called him, assuming his mom would answer and that she could tell me when he left for Bloomington, but, to my surprise, he answered! He told me the same story that Austin had told me. Our first show was starting to look less and less epic, but we didn't let it get us down. We waited and waited and eventually some people showed up.

We opened that first show, and every show that we ever played after that (all four), with The theme song from Cheers. Darin sang the first verse, since I couldn't play the guitar part and sing at the same time. He sang into a weird little clip-on mic that made his voice sound thin and tinny like it was coming through a telephone.

Making your way in the world today
takes everything you've got
Taking a break from all your worries
sure would help a lot

Wouldn't you like to get away

61

Sometimes you want to go

Where everybody knows your name
and they're always glad you came
You wanna be where you can see
our troubles are all the same
You wanna be where everybody knows
Your name

You wanna go where people know
people are all the same
You wanna go where everybody knows
your name
       - Gary Portnoy

Around 20 people came. I'm not sure how they managed to stay for our whole set, but they did. I think they were just being nice. We were a really bad band. We were also very alienating and somewhat offensive. Our lyrics were self righteous and aggressive. We were basically a straight edge pop punk band that didn't associate with other straight edge kids. We were only pop punk by default because I couldn't really play guitar. I just played distorted power chords. I said things like, "This song is called only rednecks drink beer."

"Hey, I drink beer," someone in the crowd said.

I looked right at them and replied, "Well, then you're a redneck," and we started the song.

During our song "Thank You For Smoking," Marty would say various insulting things about smokers, like, "The Surgeon General says, if you smoke, you're gonna die," but at this show, our first show, he said, "The Surgeon General says, if you smoke, fuck you." Darin and I laughed. We were very self-righteous, but we were just having fun. We didn't set out to offend people, but we thought it was funny when we did. We were ludicrous, fearless, and shameless.

Despite our opinionated lyrical assault, we weren't angry, we were just having a good time. We had so much fun that night. It was my first real show, and it was so much better than my last one. This time, I played guitar and didn't hide behind an amp. I loved it. I wanted to play again. We got some pizza and talked about our next show. We all agreed that we should try to play Rhino's All Ages Club and record a demo. I had moved to Bloomington to start a band, and I had been living there for nearly a year without doing it. At last, it was really happening.

My first spring in Bloomington was beautiful. We opened the windows in our room for the first time since we moved in. The breeze blew in and I was in love with my life. Miranda and Corrine came over after school one day and said that they wanted a pizza. I explained that we were nearly out of coupons and that I wasn't allowed to use them without the other guys. Miranda suggested that I do the forgery thing again. I was hesitant, but I gave in and started drawing. Miranda called in the order and Corrine agreed to be the pick-up person. Her name was Anna that day. I did a quick and sloppy job of the forgery while they cut out the nine blanks. We drove over and watched Corrine go in. A few seconds later, she came out with a pizza, smiling and laughing. A worker came out behind her and yelled at her. She started running toward the car!

The worker said something like, "Do you think this funny you little punks?" We laughed and he stopped chasing her. She threw the pizza into the car and jumped in. We sped off as if we had just robbed a bank. It was funny and fun, but it was bad too. The car had been compromised and the hand-drawn coupons were more than likely no longer an option. We had taken a serious blow that day, but we still got the pizza.

The spring semester was over, and the drummer told us that he wanted to move out of the house. He asked us if we knew anyone that might want to move in. This was great news, because if the drummer moved out, so would Fucker, Shitty, and Cyclops. If the cats moved out, we could clean up the cat shit one last time and it wouldn't come back! The drummer lived in a huge room upstairs that had a big walk in closet, so Darin and I decided that we would take over his room and try to find someone to move into our room. We planned to split the summer in half, and take turns living in the closet. We would both kind of have our own rooms.

Sam wasn't excited about going back to Mitchell for the summer, so he moved into our old room. Chris Dilts (former bass player of Drowner) moved in with him to split the rent. We had majority rule of the house now. There were four of us against the pothead and the bass player. It was great. We cleaned up the living room and the kitchen and started using the whole house. We even made house dinner a few times. One night we watched Texas Chainsaw Massacre on the red TV. Afterward, we decided to go out and look for trouble in the streets. When we stepped outside, everything was blue, and we were sure there had been a nuclear attack or something. Then I remembered what the pothead had told me once about the TV making everything seem bluer. It was amazing.

My one-year anniversary of living in Bloomington came, and I was having too much fun to notice. My second summer in my new hometown was great. I loved having Sam right downstairs, and if I ever got bored, or if I wanted to know anything, I just had to walk downstairs and hope that Sam was in his room. He kept us all entertained. One night, he came home with random stuff that he had dumpstered around town. The funniest item was an empty box that once contained a penis pump. The box claimed that the pump would increase your penis size by 50%. We asked him where he found it, and he said that he'd gotten it from the dumpster behind the adult bookstore. We all groaned with disgust!

"Did you really dumpster the adult book store?" I asked.

"Why wouldn't I?" he said with a sleazy smile. "It's not like people jerk off into it or anything," he added. He asked us not to tell his roommate Chris about it. He had a sinister look on his face, and we knew that he had some kind of prank in mind.

A few days later, Chris came to Darin and me and said, "I noticed this box sticking out of one of Sam's drawers and I looked at it. It's a penis pump!" We pretended to be surprised.

"Did you open the box?" I asked.

"No way!" he said. We somehow kept from laughing and we never let on that it was a joke. As far as I know, he still doesn't know that he was pranked.

In those days, color copies were pretty much inaccessible, and no one had a color printer in their house, so it was pretty exciting when Kinko's got new copy machines that could print in color. Well, they couldn't print in color, but they could print in a color. There was a blue machine, a green machine, and a red machine. It was a pretty useless feature, but at the time, it was exciting. Sam and I were messing around with them late one night and I got an idea. We went home and got a Mad Mushroom coupon. I made a copy on the red machine. It looked great. I made more copies, and then made a master sheet with as many coupons on it as possible. I made a few copies of the master sheet, stole a few glue sticks, and we went home. We glued the copies onto pieces of cardboard and cut them out. They looked great! We now had the means to manufacture our own coupons. We had unlimited pizza. We had free pizza for life.

We had to protect our new pizza scam more than the other ones. Anyone could do what we were doing, and if they did, we knew that eventually it would come to an end, so we didn't tell a soul. We tried to limit the free pizzas to two or three a week, with the occasional exception. When we went to Kinko's to make the copies, we made sure that no one saw us. We were like secret agents, but there was a leak. I think is was Corrine. She had been spending a lot of time hanging out with this new guy, Brad Baute, and one day I saw him at Kinko's making copies of the coupon. We thought that she must have told him. He swore that it wasn't her. He claimed that he just thought of it himself. I didn't trust him. I never trusted him. We came to an agreement that we would both be conservative in our use of the coupons, and we promised not to tell anyone else. It seemed okay, but I was still worried.

My friend Ray called me in June and asked me if The Ted Dancin' Machine would play his birthday party later that month. I said yes, of course. I was excited to play my first out-of-town show!

I met Ray in history class a few days before the end of my junior year. I hadn't made any friends at my new school and the year was almost over. I noticed Ray filling out a Dungeons and Dragons character sheet, and I approached him after class. It was so awkward. We were both cripplingly shy.

"Hey, I noticed you had a D&D character sheet. Do you play D&D?" I asked.

He shrugged. "Yeah, I play sometimes." I asked him what edition he played. He assumed the look of an expert, discussing his area of expertise. "I've played a lot of basic and AD&D, but these days I play second edition. I also play a lot of other systems like Palladium and Champion." I had no idea what he was talking about, but I knew he was cool. I told him about my weekly game, and I asked him if he wanted to join. "That could be cool. My group kind of fell apart. I haven't played for a while." A few days later, he came over and we made up his character. His character was a human fighter named Thalion Silversun who was a racist that hated all elves, which I thought was interesting, because my redneck friend Troy played an elf, and Troy was an actual racist. He became a regular player, and we became good friends. We hung out all summer. I met Joe the next year and the three of us teamed up to battle our geekish isolation.

Near the end of our senior year, Nirvana was on the radio and we all started getting into music together. Ray bought an electric guitar and a tiny amp. We played around, but never managed to make any music. I went to college then I moved to Bloomington, so I didn't see him very often. While I was away, he found some people to start a band with. They called themselves Blister. They were slightly grungy with a heavy Louisville hardcore influence. I think he felt really bad about having to cancel the show that they were supposed to play with us in Bloomington, which is why he invited us to play his birthday party. It was in his backyard and there was an above ground pool. His band and two other bands from the area were going to play too. It was going to be the first show for all of the bands except us. We were veterans. We had played one show already.

Sometime in mid-June, before Ray's birthday, a few of us wanted a pizza. I went into my secret stash and pulled out 10 of our homemade coupons. Sam called it in under the name Marcus. Everyone hanging out that day had picked up too many pizzas to do it again. Their faces were compromised. It was my turn. I put Morley behind the wheel. I don't even know if he had a license. We parked far from the front door, as usual.

I walked in and said, "Pick-up for Marcus."

The guy behind the counter said, "Okay, just a minute," then, to someone in the back, "Hey Alex, can you come up here?" I was getting nervous. This manager guy came up and took the coupons from the other guy.

He looked at them for a second, then looked back up at me. "We don't take photo copies." I pretended not to understand. I muttered something about them not being photocopies and then he held one up and peeled the paper off of the brown cardboard. I didn't know what to do.

"I didn't know that. My friend gave me those," I said, then I just stopped talking and walked out. I slowly walked back to the car, expecting them to chase me, but they didn't. I jumped into the car and told Morley to drive. We sped off into the night.

A few weeks later, Sam found a Mad Mushroom pizza box in the trash somewhere and brought it home to show us. He threw it on the coffee table and said, "Look, they changed it." It was different. The coupon now read: "Collect 15 of these coupons and get a free 12" pizza (limit one per costumer, per day)" We sat in unhappy sadness for a few seconds, then Sam said, "Doggamn it!" They had made it harder to get a smaller pizza. It almost wasn't worth it anymore. We couldn't make forgeries, and several of us couldn't show our faces there, so we tried regressing to our old tactics, but we rarely found anything in the dumpster. When we finally found coupons, they'd be marked with black marker to indicate that they had been used. The Mad Mushroom scam was over.

We took two carloads of people to Ray's birthday party. Steve The Weave drove his Oldsmobile and I drove my rainbow-colored Ford Escort. Sam, Miranda, Corrine, and Darin's girlfriend Madeline came with us. Ray lived in Greenville, Indiana, around 80 miles from Bloomington and only about two miles away from my parents' house. We stopped by to say hello to my mom and dad and to invite them to the show.

When we showed up to Ray's, the kids there treated us like rock stars. They seemed really impressed by the size of our entourage. One kid even said something to me about us being a real band. I laughed and told him it was only our second show and that he should wait until he's seen us play to decide whether or not we are a real band.

"But you guys have girls with you. How do you get those girls to come with you?" he said. I thought he was kidding, but he wasn't.

"They're our friends. They wanted to come," I said, then walked away. Our T-shirts also impressed the kids there. A few days before the show, we had two (yes, only two) T-shirts made at Kinko's. They were full color transfers. The design was a picture of Ted Danson holding up a huge mug of beer with the words "Ted Dancin' Machine" written in Sharpie above his head. Madeline was wearing one and Sam was wearing the other. I noticed one of the kids pointing at the shirt to show their friend. At first it felt nice to be treated like celebrities, but after a while it just felt weird.

Ray was happy to see me. He told me that their bass player refused to play the show, but that they were still going to play without him. There were two other bands—Doug, and The Latchkey Kids. They shared a common drummer who chickened out and bailed on the show too, so we were the only band with all of its members playing that day. Ray thought it would be best if we played last, and we didn't argue. The bands were terrible. We did our best to be polite and watch them, then we played.

My parents came, and I was kind of nervous to play in front of them, but I had to do it. We borrowed a hi-hat and some cymbals from Ray's drummer. It was crazy hearing real cymbals ringing behind us. We sounded so much better. A few people walked away when I said, "This song is about beer and how dumb you are if you drink it." A few people walked away when I said, "This song is about TV and all the stupid people that watch it."

We lost a few more when Marty said, "Surgeon General's warning says, 'If you smoke, you're gonna die,' ha ha ha." We loved it. It was so fun offending people.

As I watched people walk away, I thought, "We should make it our goal every time we play to clear the room." The people who stayed for our whole set loved us. They asked us if we had a tape (we didn't). They asked us if we had any more T-shirts for sale (we didn't). After the show, a few of Ray's friends threw him into the pool, and a few of our gang jumped in, wearing their clothes. We hung out for a while, then said our goodbyes and drove across the river to hang out in Louisville and go to Ear-X-Tacy.

When we got home, we decided it was time to record a demo tape. Our friend Tom Hoff offered to do it in exchange for some microphone stands that he needed. They cost $40 each. Sam said that he would pay for them and pay for the tapes. He had some money left over from his scholarship in the bank and he wanted to put it to good use. We recorded in Tom's house. It took around four hours to record six songs. Tom mixed them for us the next day, then gave us a master tape. We decided to only use four of the songs for the demo, to keep it short and interesting. Sam found a place to order custom-length blank tapes and he ordered 100 of them. They showed up a few days later, and we started working on the design for the tape case. We decided to title the tape Sam, since he was paying for it and we ended up using a picture of his face as the cover.

Someone took a photo of us at the recording session.
Me, Marty and Darin.

Sam and I went to Kinko's one night to make the covers. We were cutting and pasting and measuring things out when Sam asked, "Should we put a record label on the back?"

I shrugged. "Yeah sure, that would be cool." He smiled.

"What should we call it?" he asked.

"Maybe it should just be Sam records, since you're the one paying for it," I suggested. He frowned. "What about Deimos records?"

He frowned again and said, "That sounds too much like Demos records, no one knows about Deimos. Most people don't even know that Mars has moons, and I don't want to have to tell the story of my abduction and imprisonment every time someone asked about the name of the label." He started doodling on a scrap of paper. I kept working, and a few minutes later, he asked, "What about this?"

He slid the scrap of paper across the table. It was a lopsided planet with a huge "X"-shaped crack in the middle, and a Saturn-like ring surrounding it. A crooked radio tower stuck out of the topside, broadcasting something, and there was a small banner below the planet that read "Plan-It-X Records."

"Great, let's shrink it down and put it on the back," I said. I thought it would be cool to try to fool people into thinking that we were on a real record label.

Sam decided that he was going to sell the tapes for $1. I asked him how much they were going to cost to make. He said that the blank tapes were around 80¢ and the artwork and side-name labels would be around 10¢ more.

"You'll make 10¢ profit off of each tape?" I asked. He must have misunderstood what I meant, because he looked at me as if I had accused him of something horrible.

"I would sell them for 90¢ but I think it would be annoying having to carry around a bunch of dimes for change." he said. I laughed, and tried to explain that I meant 10¢ wasn't a very big profit. He was relieved. We both agreed that it would be cool to sell the tapes as cheap as possible. We both agreed that it was the punk rock thing to do. We were at Kinko's for hours, cutting, scoring, and folding. We walked home in the fog—the long way—past the pizza dumpsters.

We had managed to get The Ted Dancin' Machine added onto a show at Rhino's with a pop punk band from Chicago called The Bollweevils. We used the new, single-color machines to make the fliers. This time, I didn't use cheesy computer fonts—I drew the whole thing with Sharpie. We printed them on colored paper with colored ink. They looked great—yellow fliers with red print, light blue fliers with dark blue print, etc.

We were all really excited about the show, our first show at a real venue, and it was going to be our cassette release party too! We practiced a lot and worked on new songs. In between practicing and fliering, Sam and I dubbed tapes like crazy, breaking a few tape decks in the process. Our little, baby, joke of a record label was being born.

We wanted to be really good for our first show at Rhino's, and do something different, so we decided to do a cover of Danzig's "Mother." We thought it would be funny. A day before the show, my friend Brad Baute convinced me that we should do a Misfits cover instead. He argued that Danzig sucked and that a Misfits cover would be way better. I told him we would do both, if he agreed to be one of our dancers. We thought it would be cool to have a few dancers, since our band was called The Ted Dancin' Machine. He showed me the song, and I practiced it for a few hours. Later that night, at band practice, I told the other guys that we were gonna do it and they weren't happy.

"Well, if you're adding a cover of a band I don't really like, then I want to add a cover too," Darin said.

"We don't have time to learn another cover, the show is tomorrow!" I protested.

"Then let's not do any more covers," he said.

"Okay, what cover do you want to do?"

He was quiet for a minute, and said, "Wave Of Mutilation, by the Pixies." We argued for a little while, then I agreed, and he showed me how to play the song.

Marty was pretty neutral during our debate, but after we half-assedly learned the new covers, he said, "I want to pick a cover too."

I sighed, but I knew I had no grounds to resist. "What cover?"

"Stand, by R.E.M." Darin loved R.E.M., so I knew there was no hope in saying no. We were going to spend the day learning 3 new covers to play the next day. I wasn't worried. I knew the show was going to be great. I couldn't sleep that night.

The next day came, and Plan-It-X records was officially born. You can see the whole thing in Sam's hands.

We took 40 tapes and a pair of yellow, steel-toed Doc Martens (that you can see on the roof of my car) to sell at the show. The first Plan-It-X distro sold shoes! (one pair)

I convinced Sam and Steve The Weave to join my friend Brad on the stage with us as dancers. When we got to Rhino's, way too early, we found out that the Bollweevils had cancelled but that some of them were in another band called Oblivion and that they were gonna take Bollweevils' place. It seemed like we were cursed to play shows that the other bands didn't show up to, but it didn't matter. We were too excited to care. It was a big deal to play Rhino's. We played second, after some local band called Speed Luxury that I can't remember. Not many people came, but it was our third show and we didn't expect a huge crowd. We sounded so much different with the drums mic'd and with our

71

amps running through the P.A. system. We were so loud and so powerful. We were still sloppy, and we messed up at least a little bit in every song, especially the newly learned covers, but we had so much fun. Our dancers stripped down to their underwear. Sam wore dirty tighty-whiteys and danced as sexy as he could. The other guys tried to follow his moves. The crowd kept their distance. At one point, Sam started to pull his underwear down and Brad—the director of Rhino's Brad—ran up to the stage waving his hands and screaming, "No!"

Sam looked to me for advice. I nodded my head, implying that he should keep stripping. The other guys were ready to act too. We thought it was a statement to have all male dancers, acting sexy. We thought we were challenging people. Maybe we were, but Brad was freaking out and looking really mad, so Sam and the other guys kept their underwear on. After we finished the song we were playing, Brad explained that there was a strict no nudity policy at Rhino's and if it was violated, Rhino's might get shut down. We were still laughing and didn't really care about what he was saying. We wanted to keep playing. He told us that we had time for one more song. We had a few more left, including the Misfits cover and the anti-smoking song, and we didn't want to cut either one of them, so we decided that we'd try to play both. The plan was to play the Misfits song and then go right into the next song without stopping. We thought that he might not notice, and, even if he did, how could he stop us mid-song? We tried it, and a few seconds into the final song, the sound guy cut the power to the stage. Only the drums went on. We took it well, we didn't get angry. Brad walked up and explained that we had been playing for 45 minutes and our time was up. If I hadn't been so foolish and naive, I would've been ashamed of myself, but we weren't embarrassed or upset. We had just played our first show at Rhino's and it was great! We watched Oblivion play and hung out with them for a while after the show. They were nice to us, despite what they had watched us do earlier that night. After the show, about a dozen friends joined us at Denny's to celebrate.

A few days later, this local band called Slavic 747 called Marty and asked him about playing a show at our house. He told me about it, and we decided that it would be cool to play one more show at the Cottage Grove house before we moved out (the lease was almost up). I didn't know that it would be our last show ever.

This girl named Jenn Potts moved to Bloomington that summer. She was straight edge and had a shaved head. We all had a crush on her. She started dating one my friends, but they broke up after a while. One hot night, I found myself hanging out with her and a few friends. We decided that it was too hot to handle, so we walked to "the naked lady fountain" to splash around. It was a pretty common occurrence that summer and it was really fun. After everyone cooled down, we made plans to walk to Rockit's pizza and get some breadsticks. Jen said that she wanted to go home and change into some dry clothes. She asked me if I would go with her. I felt like I should have said no, but I said yes. We got to her house and she changed while I waited in the living room. She came out in dry clothes and asked me if I had ever seen the midget commit suicide in The Wizard of Oz. I laughed and said no.

"Come in my room, I'll show you," she said. She had a small TV with a built in VHS player at the foot of her bed. She put in the tape and pressed play. It was already cued up to the right spot. It was the scene in the woods, when the witch appears on the roof of a log cabin and there are all these weird looking, long-necked birds walking around. She got close to me and said, "Okay, here it comes. Watch over there." She pointed to the left side of the screen. Sure enough I saw what looked like a midget drop off of a chair and start swinging side to side. It was so creepy. I've never been able to find it again. We didn't go to Rockit's. We hung out in her room and she told me about her overly Christian grandmother who once ripped a Fugazi poster off of her wall because she said it was satanic. She showed me her 'zine and told me horror stories about growing up in Bedford. Later that night, we kissed, and I went home feeling guilty and excited.

The next day, I confessed my actions to Miranda. I told her that I kissed Jen and that I liked it. I told her I was sorry. I told her that I really liked Jen. I said, "I think we should break up."

"No! No way! We are not breaking up," she protested. We argued for hours. I tried to convince her that we should be friends instead of boyfriend and girlfriend. I tried to convince her that our relationship had lost its passion and that she was still too young for me. She cried and screamed and kept telling me no. I didn't know what to do. I tried to do the right thing. I confessed, apologized, and tried to end it. I thought that it wouldn't be up to me. I didn't have the nerve to hold my ground. I also couldn't just give up on the idea of being with Jen. She was cute and interesting and she liked me. I didn't know what to do. I was stuck.

Around that time, Sam had a run-in with this local lady whom we called Psycho Susan. She was a wingnut who frequented People's Park. She had dark rings around her eyes and long white fingernails. I had talked to her a few times. Once, she came up to me and a few other people and asked, "Do you guys have any spare change?"

We all shrugged and said, "No, sorry," then she dug into her pocket and pulled out a handful of change.

"Here you go," she said, as she passed out nickels and dimes to each of us.

Sam was drinking a 40¢ soda on the wall in front of the park when she came up and sat down beside him. She said hello. Sam said hello.

"Beware of cute girls with short red hair and two little curls," she said. She twirled her finger around in front of her ear when she said curls. Sam told me the story in a theatrical fashion, with a wild look in his eyes. He seemed genuinely afraid.

When he was done with his performance, he said, "Jen has short red hair and those little curly pieces by her ears. I think she's trouble."

The end of August was coming fast, and I didn't want to end up in the same situation I was in the year before, without a place to live, so I made plans to move into a house with Marty, Sam, and Chris Dilts. We saw a "For Rent" sign in the front yard of this legendary punk house on Henderson St. and a few days later we signed the lease. We didn't meet the landlord, only his maintenance guy named Gary. Gary was a hulking, grey-haired ex-hippie. When we gave him the deposit money in cash, he asked, "Is this drug money?" We were caught off guard and stood there stunned for a few seconds before assuring him that is wasn't drug money. He just laughed and said, "I'm just fucking with you guys, I wouldn't care if it was drug money, hell, I used to party pretty hard. Do you guys party at all?"

We shook our heads and I said, "Not really."

He laughed again. "Well, you guys can party all you want, as long as you invite me." He went on about party-related things for a while then explained that our landlord, Russ, was a very laid back guy and didn't care about much, but he hated it when the trash built up. Gary told us to make sure that, no matter what, we never let the trash get out of hand. We asked him for a receipt for the $1000.00 in cash that we had just given him. He made a joke about us not trusting him, but we didn't laugh. We left that meeting feeling pretty unsure of what we had just gotten ourselves into. It felt like we had made a deal with the devil.

Despite our fears though, we were excited about the house. It was in great location, it had a basement and it a punk rock history. The band With Authority had lived there before. They were a hardcore-punk band who had a pretty big following a few years before I moved to town. A few of them were still around, and I'd see them walking past the park sometimes. Their singer was kind of a celebrity. My friends always pointed him out: "There's Dave Tate, he's so cool," they'd say, or something like that. I always wondered why these cool, older punks didn't hang out in the park with the rest of us. Many years later, I would be the old punk guy walking past the park and not stopping to hang out. I wonder what the kids say about me.

We had a few weeks before we could move into our new house. We played the show with Slavic 747 and we played pretty well. We were getting more comfortable with playing in front of people. We even sold a few tapes.

I was broke again, so I got a job at this department store called Hills. I applied there because I heard that they paid their employees in cash, every Friday. I didn't have a bank account, so that sounded great to me. I filled out an application in the store, and when I turned it in, the lady asked me when I could start. She didn't even look at my application. I guess they were desperate. My job was stocking the shelves before the store opened. I had to be there at four A.M. and I think that's why they were so quick to hire me—the hours were terrible. I couldn't get to sleep early enough to make it worthwhile, so I would just stay up until it was time to go to work. My plan was to sleep when I got home at ten o'clock, but when I got home, people were waking up, so I hung out with them instead. Basically, I didn't sleep for three weeks, went crazy, fucked up my life, lost some friends, and killed The Ted Dancin' Machine.

Miranda wouldn't let me break up with her and Jen didn't want to wait for me to sort my shit out. I stopped sleeping. Instead, I put things on shelves in an empty store and listened to the same, one and a half hour loop of pop songs everyday. That meant I could hear Lisa Loeb's hit single at least three times a day. I really went crazy. I freaked out.

…

Nothing made sense.
My new bedroom (the closet) was so hot.
Miranda cried a lot.
I got Jen a job as a cashier and Brad a job as a stock person, like me.
I watched Family Matters in the break room.
Sam was worried about me.
"I'm more of a polka kinda guy." -Steve Urkle
We all talked about breaking the lease.
We all agreed we didn't want to live in that house.
We didn't trust the landlord.
Staff meeting with free donuts.
"Walmart is coming, we're doomed" - my boss.
Skipping work.
Leaving early.
Arguing and crying.
Never sleeping.
I lost it.
I left town secretly.
Cincinnati, Columbus, Pittsburgh, NYC, Amherst.
I didn't know there were punks out there.
I found J. Mascis' house.

I didn't knock on his door.
I found out that the lease could not be broken back home.
They moved in.
They were angry with me for leaving.
Dinosaur Jr. show in a small club in Northampton!
Dead broke.
Just enough gas money to come home.
I wasn't welcomed at the Henderson house.
I painted my rainbow colored car flat black.
I painted a Misfits skull on the hood.
Jen gives up and moves on.
Miranda doesn't, and is so angry about me leaving.
Lisa Loeb is burned into my brain:

So I turned the radio on, I turned the radio up,
and this woman was singing my song
lover's in love, and the other's run away
lover is crying 'cause the other won't stay.
    - Lisa Loeb

CHAPTER 6
RETREAT

So there I was, back at my parents' house. My bedroom was gone, so I moved into the basement. It was dark all the time down there. I traded my electric guitar for an acoustic. I went back to the temp agency and started working again. When I wasn't working, I was in the basement playing my new guitar and writing songs. I drove to Bloomington on the weekends to hang out with friends. Sam had to meet me somewhere, since I wasn't welcome at his house. I hung out with him, Miranda, and Corrine in the student union building or at Café Pizzeria. The girls and Sam would eventually go home and I would sleep in my car somewhere. Corrine told me that Sam was really depressed and had been skipping most of his classes. She said that he didn't really leave his room unless it was to hang out with me. She was really worried about him, and I was worried too.

I tried to talk to Marty, but he was so angry with me for leaving. I told him that I really cared about The Ted Dancin' Machine and that I didn't want us to break up. I apologized and said that I'd move into the house and pay all the bills that I had missed. He said that he didn't want me living there, that they had already found someone to replace me. He said that he wouldn't be in a band with me until I owned my own equipment—he had heard about me trading in my electric guitar. I was so sad. Marty was such a good friend and I felt so dumb for letting romance and sleep deprivation destroy that. The bridge was burned and I was sure we would never be friends again. I deserved it.

Miranda started hanging out with this tall, straight edge guy who had a long ponytail. He skateboarded and carried a gun. I didn't like him at all. She would insist that they were just friends, but I didn't care—I just wanted to break up. She didn't want to. Sometimes when I drove up on the weekends, she would be hanging out with him. It was weird, but I just found Sam or Corrine instead and I hoped that I would be free of our lingering relationship soon. I don't know why I couldn't just break up with her.

During the week, I didn't do much. I mostly just worked and stayed up late watching Nick-At-Night. Occasionally, I hung out with my old friends. I made up with Joe, but it wasn't the same as before. I didn't see him very much. I didn't dare call Valerie. I didn't need any more drama in my life. I still felt horrible about breaking her heart. She still called and talked to my mom sometimes. My mom would tell me all about it after they hung up. She told me that Valerie was dating some guy from Louisville and learning to play the drums. Joe knew this new guy and said that he was a weed dealer. I tried to explain to my mom that I didn't need to know about Valerie's life. I guess she didn't hear me, because she didn't stop telling me all the news. Ray told me that the Ted Dancin' Machine had made a big impression at his birthday party and that all of his friends loved us. They wanted to know if we had more tapes.

"How do they know about our tape?" I asked.

He told me that they had bought them from Ear-X-Tacy. I forgot that Marty had put five tapes on consignment there. We all assumed that they would be there forever, but apparently they had all sold and were in high demand. Ray was disappointed to find out that we had broken up, and assured me that his friends would be too. I asked him about his band. He said that they had played a few basement shows at this kid Roy's house. Roy was in one of the bands who played the birthday party. I asked Ray if his band had recorded anything yet. He said no, but that they really wanted to. I had an idea. I suggested that we should rent a 4-track from the Doo-Wop Shop in Louisville, this place that rents everything, and record his band and any other band that wanted to make a demo. He thought it was a great idea.

One of the other birthday party bands, The Latch Key Kids, heard about our plan and wanted to be a part of it. Their drummer, Tony Lincoln, was a big Ted Dancin' Machine fan and asked me if I was going to start a new band. He offered to play drums. It got me thinking that, if I was going to be recording bands and I was going to have a 4-track for a month, I should start a new band. I didn't want to lose the huge fan base that I had created with T.D.M. (by huge, I mean 10 to 20 people), so I thought that the new band name should have something to do with Cheers.

One night, I was hanging out with Ray, Tony, and Chris Lincoln—Tony's brother and the singer in Ray's band—in their practice space, trying to come up with names. We wrote the ideas on the wall with a big black Sharpie. Tony suggested "Carla's Got The Clap" and we all cringed. I came up with "The Norm Peterson Project" but no one liked it. We went through the cast of characters: "The Woodys" sounded wrong, "The Kirstie Alley Cats" was too rockabilly, and "Frasier And The Brains" wasn't funny at all, but then I came up with "The Cliff Clavin Operation" and no one groaned, which was a good sign.

Chris took the marker from me and said, "What about this?" as he drew some arrows to indicate a change in the word order to make my suggestion read, "Operation: Cliff Clavin." I liked it. We all liked it, so that was that.

I told Sam about my recording project plan the next time I went to Bloomington and he was excited. He suggested that I ask The Dirtys (Austin Lucas's band) to be a part of it. He also suggested that we make all of the demos into Plan-It-X records releases. I loved that idea. We walked downtown and got 40¢ Cokes from the Den, then we found Austin in the park and told him our plans. He liked them, and said to count The Dirtys in. We weren't sure what he would say, since we weren't really sure if he liked us. He was really punk back then and only liked traditional punk music. He made fun of me all the time for listening to pop punk. No matter what I was playing, he would ask me if it was Green Day. He also told me that only black T-shirts were punk. He said that if a band made a shirt that wasn't black, that meant they weren't punk. He was young and funny and we liked him a lot.

Austin and Sam, sitting on the wall in front of People's Park.

The next week, I went to the Doo-Wop Shop to rent the 4-track and a few mics. The guy showed me all my options and explained the differences in the machines. I picked out what I wanted and he started doing the paper work. He asked me where I worked.

"I don't really work, I work as a temp sometimes," I said.

He frowned and said "I'm sorry but we can't rent to you."

I was pretty confused and asked, "Why not?"

He explained that I had to have a full-time job.

"You're a music store that rents to musicians. Musicians don't have full time jobs, hopefully," I reasoned. "They are musicians, and that is their job." He wasn't impressed, and I walked out empty handed. I called Ray and he agreed to be the one to sign all the papers. He had a job, so he could do it.

When I finally got my hands on the 4-track, I realized that I had no idea how to use it. I messed around with it for days and didn't really learn a thing. Then it was time to start recording bands. Ray's band was up first. They had changed their name from Blister to Instinct. They showed up at my parents' house around noon and we went down into the basement. I thought that, since the 4-track had eight inputs, we could plug eight mics into it at once and record live. I was wrong. I thought that using the line-out on the back of their amps was a good idea. I thought I could just run a cable from the line-out on the amp into the line-in on the 4-track. I was wrong. I thought that it would sound good to use a normal mic for the bass drum, and plug that mic into the line-in too. I was wrong. I was wrong about a lot of things, but that didn't slow me down. The band had never recorded before, so they thought it sounded good. I wasn't happy with the recording, but I had no idea how to make it better.

Next up was the Latch Key Kids. They were pretty bad. Their biggest influence was Metallica—which isn't necessarily a bad thing, I liked Metallica a lot—but they had a long way to go. They had a song called "Jump On In" that was about mosh pits. Their singer, Scoot, wanted to call the song "Hardcore," but Tony managed to talk him out of it.

"Jump on in, jump on in
into my little mosh pit"
  - The Latch Key Kids

When they played the song live, Scoot sang "...into my fucking mosh pit," but he didn't want to have any cuss words on the recording, since his parents were going to hear it, so he changed it to "little." I did my best to make them sound good. I was as bad at using the 4-track as they were at playing music. Together we made an inedible pie.

Operation: Cliff Clavin didn't have a bass player, so I decided that I would play the bass on our demo. I had never played the bass before, but I figured it couldn't be that hard since there were only four strings. Tony wasn't very good at playing the drums, but he could play fast and he used all the drums, so he was a big improvement from Darin and his wacky drumming style. We were loud, at least. Despite weeks of practice, my recording skills had not improved, but, lucky for me, I didn't notice—I thought I was doing an okay job.

I packed all the gear into my flat, black Misfits mobile and drove to Bloomington to record The Dirtys. It was fun. It was great being out of my parents' basement and recording a band who knew how to play their instruments. The Dirtys were great and the recording went by quickly. Sam was there, and sang some back-ups on a song or two. Afterwards, Sam and I went looking for pizza. We found a few. They were old and gross. We ate them anyway and talked about the good old days.

I returned the 4-track, and, with the help of Sam, ordered some blank tapes in all the various lengths we needed. We started designing the artwork while we waited for them to come. There were two unreleased Ted Dancin' Machine songs, so we figured we should re-issue the demo with them on it. We called it "Son Of Sam." That brought us up to five new releases for Plan-It-X records. Of course, like our first release, we planned on selling the tapes for $1 each.

We decided that it would be fun to have a release show where all the bands played. Sam talked to Brad at Rhino's and booked a date in January.

For Instinct and The Latch Key Kids, this would be their first out-of-town show. They were excited and nervous. Scoot, looking very worried, asked me if there was a safe place at the club for him to set down his guitar. I didn't understand what he meant. He explained that he was worried about their song that he didn't play guitar on. He said that normally he just leaned his guitar up against his amp and grabbed the mic. I was still confused. "How high is the stage at Rhino's? Do you think people in the crowd will be able to reach my guitar? Is there security on the stage?"

I did my best not to laugh. I felt sorry for him. I tried to explain, without sounding condescending, that there would be no screaming fans or people trying to steal his guitar. I assured him that it would be safe against his amp, and I tried my best to gently shatter his rock star dreams. I figured it would better to crush him now than to see him get crushed on stage. Sam dubbed the show "The Return Of The Martian."

Tony found us a bass player, which was great, because we had a show to play and I wasn't going to do it without one. His name was Brett, but he wanted to be called "The Gooch." We all had nicknames—I was Blenderhead, named after a Bad Religion song, Tony was Warren Beatty, for some reason, and now we had The Gooch! We were a real band. The Gooch had a Beatle bass and he was pretty good at using it. We practiced a lot and he learned most of the songs. I felt confident about our Bloomington debut.

All the bands met at my parents' house and we figured out what equipment we would need and stuff like that. We piled into three cars and drove to Bloomington. For me it was a familiar drive and I knew what to expect when we got there. For the rest of the guys, it was a great adventure, their first out of town show, and their first show at a real venue. Their excitement was nice. I was excited too. I was excited to show Bloomington that I wasn't gonna give up that easy. I was excited to show my friends what I had been up to. I was excited to kick off my new band. I was excited to see Sam.

When we got to Rhino's, no one was there. I assured the guys that people were coming. I tried to explain punk time to them. Sam showed up with our tapes and we proudly set up the first Plan-It-X distro table. I had made a sign that said "all tapes = $1 cheap!" Miranda and Corrine came with a few home-made rockets and flying saucers and we hung them from the rafters. We set up our gear and did a sound check. No one was there. We stalled for as long as we could, then Brad told us that someone had to start.

Instinct offered to play first. A few people trickled in while they played, and by the end of their set, we had an okay crowd. It wasn't as big as I had hoped for, but it was okay. We played next. Brett—I mean, The Gooch—was really nervous. He had run off a few times before the show, and we had to track him down and convince him not to quit the band. He threw a roll of toilet paper into the crowd during our cover of "Where Eagles Dare." He made a bunch of strange jokes that no one laughed at, but he did okay. We did pretty badly overall and there is video footage to prove it. My guitar strap broke in the middle of a song and I dropped the guitar I was borrowing. Tony forgot to stop drumming at the end of a few songs and The Gooch was The Gooch. Lucky for me, not many of my Bloomington friends showed up to see my somewhat less than triumphant return to town.

The Dirtys showed up during our set, and Austin moshed a little bit. We couldn't tell if he was making fun of us or if he really liked the music. His whole crew rolled in with leather jackets, combat boots, and spikes. They laughed and slam-danced and acted like punks act in movies. It was fun, but I think it kinda scared my southern Indiana friends.

When The Latch Key Kids started, Sam told me that he had to run home to get something. A few songs later, he came back with a big bag of dried pinto beans and I knew why. They had a song called "Being Me" and it sounded a lot like they were saying bean me. So he thought it would be funny to throw beans at them during that song. He went around the room passing out ammunition and filling everyone in on the joke. I'm sure that Scoot was curious about why the crowd suddenly got so attentive. We waited anxiously for the song. They played "Jump On In" and we all moshed in the "fucking mosh pit," careful not to spill the beans. Finally, the moment came, and we gathered at the front of the stage. He said, "bean me" and we beaned him. I felt bad right away. He was barraged with beans. They hit him in the face and I think one or two went in his mouth, but he took it well and didn't waver. They finished the song and he managed to joke about it afterward.

The Dirtys played and, seemingly from out of nowhere, a few more of their friends showed up. They were probably waiting in the parking lot for the shitty bands to finish. The Dirtys really stole the show. They had full set and a few punk rock covers, like "Beef Bologna" by Fear, and "Jimmy and Johnny" by Rancid. We all moshed together and had fun. A few tapes were sold. We took down the rockets and flying saucers and packed up our gear. Most of the out-of-towners drove home after the show, but The Gooch stayed with me in Bloomington. We stayed in Sam's room. It was my first time in the Henderson house. I was so nervous that I'd see Marty and he would be mad that I was there, but Sam had talked to him about me being allowed to stay over. Sam had really taken a stand for me and threatened to move out if I remained banished. I was still afraid of seeing him. Miranda and Corrine stayed over too. We all slept on Sam's dirty floor, after I cleared a space big enough for us.

This was my first time seeing Sam's room. It scared me. He hadn't really unpacked any of his things. There were sealed boxes of clothes and books against the wall and his really nice stereo had never been set up. He slept on a small mattress on the floor. There were orange juice bottles filled with piss in the closet that he admitted to pissing in because he was sometimes too afraid to go to the bathroom. There were empty potato chip bags everywhere. The place smelled awful. The Gooch talked to himself all night and kept us up. It was really weird and it freaked us all out. It was nice to be with my friends though, and I realized that I had a huge crush on Corrine. She was so cool.

Roy was having another show in his basement and he asked Operation: Cliff Clavin to play. It was cool. The Gooch didn't want to do it, he was nervous about playing in front of people that he knew. We had to drive to his house and pick him up. We were starting to wonder if he was going to work out. Roy lived with his parents in the woods, but people came to his shows. There were around 30 or 40 people there. I played in a cowboy hat for some reason. During the show I decided that I should start a Plan-It-X records mailing list, so I announced it and told people to come see me to sign up. I found a scrap of paper and around 20 people signed it. Someone asked me what it was about, and I had to think a second before answering.

"We're gonna mail out monthly newsletters," I said.

"Cool," they said.

I didn't know what I was talking about and I had no idea what we would put in a monthly newsletter, but it seemed like a cool idea.

A few days later, we talked to The Gooch and told him that we were gonna look for a new bass player. We assumed he would be relieved since he never wanted to play show, but he seemed hurt. He referred to our talk as "kicking him out of the band." I felt bad about it, but I wasn't going to let anyone slow us down. Tony, once again, found someone to replace him. His name was Lewis. Tony gave him a demo tape with a lyric sheet and the bass lines that I had tabbed out. He knew all the songs at his first practice/audition a few days later. He was good. I liked him from the start and he had a long, black, devil lock, so I knew he was cool. A few days later, I was hanging out with him at a strip mall for some reason, and we saw this car with an American flag sticker on the bumper. An old guy got out of it, and Lewis stepped toward him, spit on him, then just walked away. He was definitely our guy. We had made a good choice.

Lewis.

I spent the rest of the winter working temp jobs and saving up money. It was too cold to sleep in my car, so I didn't go to Bloomington as much. I stayed in the basement watching Nick-At-Night and eating re-fried beans and salsa. Operation: Cliff Clavin practiced a lot and played a few shows in southern Indiana, but for the most part, it was pretty boring.

Sometime in the spring, just when it started to get warm, Sam called me and told me that he had been writing songs and drawing a lot, and wanted to make a 'zine. He was so excited about life. He told me about bands that he had read about in Maximumrocknroll and said that he wanted to start booking shows. It was great. We talked about me moving back to Bloomington. He said that he was going to talk to Marty and make another appeal for me. "See you soon buddy, I love you," Sam said just before he hung up, without waiting for me to say goodbye. A change was coming—I could feel it. The moon was waxing.

A few days later, I came home from work and my mom told me that Sam had called me around 15 times. She said that he sounded distressed and like he needed to talk to me. As she was explaining, the phone rang. I picked it up. It was Sam.

"Hey Sam, what's up?" I asked.

"Not much, I'm kinda freaked out," he mumbled.

"What's wrong, what happened?"

"I can't see, I think I might have gouged my eyes out..." I was starting to get really worried now.

"Sam, what are you talking about?" I asked. "Tell me what happened."

Eventually, he started explaining: "I was doing some magic—some black magic—then these tigers jumped out of the woodwork and tried to kill me. They attacked my eyes. They could sense my metal objects, so I took off my shoes, because of the eyelets, and my belt and my glasses. I threw them down. I threw down my metal and ran away. They chased me for a while, but I lost them..." I could hear cars passing by on his end of the phone and spring birds chirping.

"Where are you?" I asked.

"I don't know, I don't know!" he said. I told him to calm down and tell me what he could see around him. He told me that he couldn't see very well because his eyes were bleeding.

"Holy shit! Your eyes are bleeding? Really? If they are, you should hang up and call 911."

He was silent for a few seconds. "Maybe they aren't bleeding, they just hurt, and I don't have my glasses, so I can't see anything." I got him to describe everything he could see and to tell me where he was calling from. I figured out that he was at a gas station on Henderson Street, the street he lived on, but around two miles south. I convinced him that he could make it home if he just walked up the hill and stayed on the same street. He agreed to try it and to call me when he was safe at home, but he was worried about the tigers. I told him that there were no tigers.

The weekend came and I drove to Bloomington. I met Sam at the gazebo on campus—a common meeting place for us. I was worried about seeing him. I was worried about the state he would be in, but he walked up looking cheerful and excited. We sat in the gazebo and talked for a while. He tried to avoid talking about his freak out. I didn't push the matter. I figured that he would talk about it when he was ready. It was a great day. It was warm and sunny, and it seemed like winter was finally over. As we talked and laughed, Sam kept rubbing his chest. After a few times, I asked him why he was doing it. He got shy and said, "I kinda pierced my nipples." I assumed he was kidding and I asked him to let me see them. He slowly raised his shirt and showed the two huge safety pins sticking through his bloody nipples. It looked painful.

"Did it hurt?" I asked.

"Yeah, it hurt a lot," he said.

"Why did you do it?"

"I don't know, just for fun."

Later that day, I went to the Henderson house for a meeting to discuss me moving in. It was thorny. I was so afraid of talking to Marty, but he kept things very professional and stuck to the details of me moving in. We talked about how the rent would be broken down and who had what bills in his or her name. A few minutes later, it was done. I was moving in. I was moving back to Bloomington!

After the meeting, Sam and I went upstairs to his room, which would soon be our room, to start cleaning up and unpacking his stuff. We hooked up his stereo and put in a Fear CD. We could never figure out if they were gay or homophobic. Sam loved them though, and they were our soundtrack that day. I gathered the bottles of piss and dumped them into the backyard. We opened boxes of Sam's clothes and stacked them neatly onto the milk crate shelf that we had made and I helped him organize dozens of battle worn books. Sam was excited to see his things again. I couldn't believe that he had lived there for eight months without unpacking. When we were finished, we pried open the long-sealed windows and climbed out onto the roof to enjoy the sunshine.

"Let's have a war
So you can go and die!
Let's have a war!
We could all use the money!
Let's have a war!
We need the space!
Let's have a war!
Clean out this place!"
   - Fear

A drawing by Sam.

CHAPTER 7
DAYS OF CHAOS

I told the temp agency that I was no longer available and I told my mom that I was moving back to Bloomington. Once again, I filled my car with junk and headed home. It felt good. I was so happy to be out of the basement. I hoped that this would be the last time. I knew I wouldn't miss Dick Van Dyke or Bob Newhart. I could live my whole life without seeing either of them ever again.

After Sam helped me move in and I had my stuff sorted out a bit, he said "I've got a new pizza scam," then he showed me some coupons for a place called Mother Bears.

"How did you get them?" I asked. He told me that he just snuck into their office and looked through their drawers. He wasn't expecting to find coupons. He didn't even know that they had coupons. He was just snooping and hoping to find something worth stealing. We celebrated my return to town that night with Miranda, Corrine, and a free pizza. It was a good welcome. I could sense a storm coming. Sam's eyes were electric.

Sam's dad decided that it would be a good idea to give him a car, so for a while, Sam had what his dad called a Fuji green station wagon. We were all pretty worried about him driving, but he assured us that he could do it. He even got a job doing deliveries for this place called the Snow Lion. He said that he hardly ever crashed into anything, and it was usually just a curb or a telephone pole. I tried to talk him out of driving, but had no luck.

One day, he came home looking pale and frightened. He handed me a plastic bag with a metal chain inside. He asked me to hide it from him. He said that it was evil. I was familiar with the chain. We called it the devil chain. He got the idea for it in a dream. In the dream, Danzig came to him and told him to get a chain with 41 links, and to put heavy bolts through the last four links, then lock them on with nuts. He wrapped duct tape around the other end to make a handle. I took the bag out of his hand and asked him what had happened. He didn't want to tell me. I told him that I wouldn't hide the devil chain if he didn't tell me what the problem was. I said that I had to know for my own protection. I joked about him killing someone with it. He got angry and swore that he didn't kill anyone. "I almost did though...I was driving downtown and apparently I was going the wrong way down a one way street. This cop pulled me over. I didn't want to stop. I didn't want to talk to him. Before he got out of his car, I got out of mine. I had the chain in my hand. I started walking toward him. I thought about how I could just kill him and not have to deal with his bullshit. He saw the chain in my hand and asked me what it was. I asked him what the problem was and why he pulled me over. He told me to put the chain back in my car. I thought about it for a second. I could hear Danzig's voice in my head. He was telling me to kill this cop. I could feel the chain heating up in my hand. It wanted blood. I wanted blood. Somehow, I resisted its demands. I threw it back into the car."

I had been listening, speechless, not knowing if he was joking or not. He seemed very serious. I could feel the weight of the chain, in the bag that I was holding. It seemed heavier now. "What did the cop do?" I asked.

"Nothing, he just gave me a warning and told me to be more careful. He was pretty nice," he said.

"Well, it's a good thing you didn't kill him then." We both laughed. Later, when Sam was gone, I threw the chain into the far reaches of our insulation filled attic and I locked the door with a key-less pad lock that we had found somewhere. No one ever opened the door to the attic anyway. Now it was locked for good. Danzig's wicked weapon was gone.

A few days later, Sam slashed all four tires on his car and threw the keys into the storm drain. When I asked him why he did it, he said that he was sick of people asking him for rides and that cars were horrible. He suggested that I get rid of my car too. His dad came and called a tow truck to haul it away.

Sam didn't sleep much that spring. He was usually awake and out of the room before I woke up. One morning, he burst into the room and shouted, "Hey, Chris, I just checked the P.O. box and we got our first order!" We'd placed an ad in the classified section of Maximumrocknroll. It said something like:

Plan-It-X Records = $1 tapes
by the Ted Dancin' Machine,
Operation: Cliff Clavin, The Dirtys.
and more... P.O. BOX....

I sat up and rubbed my eyes and said, "That's great, who is it from?" He told me that it was from Alaska, from this guy named Moz who did a 'zine called Oi Punk. He told me that Moz mentioned that he would review the tape too. This was great news—our first order and our first review! Sam started digging though his bag for the letter. He couldn't find it. "What tape did he order?" I asked.

"It was Operation: Cliff Clavin," he said while frantically searching through his bag. He couldn't find the order. He never found the order. He had lost it somehow on his way home from the post office. Our first order ever, and it was lost in the streets somewhere. Sam was so upset about it. A few months later, Sam saw a review of Oi Punk in Maximumrocknroll, and Moz's address was listed, so we sent him his tape, along with a few extras and an apology for the long delay.

A lot of stuff happened before Moz got his tape.

We decided that Bloomington needed more punk shows with real punk bands. So we started trying to book shows. Sam was really good at making phone calls, and within a few minutes and a few phone calls, he could get anyone's number. He talked to Lawrence Livermore—the founder of Look-Out-Records—and Ian McKay, from Dischord Records, and told them about Plan-It-X. He kept making calls. He somehow found out that NOFX was touring in the summer and needed a show in Indiana. He called their booking agent to offer our help. I could only hear Sam's side of the conversation, it went like this: "Hi, my name is Sam, I run Plan-It-X records out here in Bloomington, Indiana. We also do show promotion and we'd really like to book NOFX this summer at our all ages club, Rhino's... Uh huh... Yeah... That date is fine with us... Uh huh... What's a guarantee? Well how much is it? What the fuck? Why? Are you kidding? We would have to pay them that much? Nevermind, fuck you." He gently hung up the phone with a confused and disappointed look on his face.

"What did they say?" I asked.

"She said that they had a guarantee of $1,200."

"What's a guarantee?"

"That's how much we have to pay them for playing." Needless to say, we didn't book a show for NOFX.

We didn't let NOFX stop us from trying. Sam had recently discovered a band called Black Fork. They were from the Bay Area and had one ex-member of the infamous Blatz. We were huge Blatz fans. Many of our nights of chaos were kicked off by chanting their lyrics: "Tonight we're gonna fuck shit up." We were really excited when we found out that they needed a show in our area. We decided that Bloomington wouldn't care enough about them, so we booked the show in Louisville at the Cardinal Inn. They had a few holes in their tour so they came to Bloomington a day early to stay at our house. I wasn't there. I was at my parents' house practicing with Operation: Cliff Clavin, since we were playing the show too—Lewis was a great bass player and we were slowly starting to sound like a real band.

On the day of the show, I got to the venue early to make sure things were okay. It was horrible. The show was outside on a huge stage, surrounded by beer banners. We set up our gear and did a short sound check. It sounded awful. A few hours later, Black Fork showed up in a rusty Suburban. Sam was with them. They poured out of the truck with their faded colored hair and dirty punk shirts. They seemed so cool. I think they were too cool to talk to us. I told Annie, the girl who was in Blatz, that I really loved their song on the "Can Of Pork" comp. She said "That's was our worst song, I hated that song." That was the end of the conversation.

Annie has a very high-pitched voice and usually sings a little off key, which I love, but the crowd didn't love it as much as I did. After the first song, someone yelled, "The vocals are way too loud, you should turn them down."

Annie looked at the guy and said, "Sorry, too bad," and they started the next song. They were so punk. There weren't many people there and I'm sure we didn't pay the band enough, but it was our first show. We did our best. After the show, they drove back to Bloomington to spend the night again. There was no other option, since I knew they couldn't stay at my parents' house.

When I got back to Bloomington, Sam told me everything that I missed. I guess Marty was really unhappy with Black Fork staying at our house, and he threw away one of their shoes. He had his reasons: The first night they were in town, they spray painted a stencil of their band name on Chris Dilts' skateboard and on the sidewalk in front of our house. Later that same night, Sam told the bass player, Rusty, about how he would steal cases of soda almost every night from the gas station down the street. They had stacks of them outside the shop. Sam would crouch down low and sneak up and grab one. The bass player said "Let's go get some soda," so they went. Only when they got there, Rusty didn't sneak at all. He just walked up and grabbed a case of soda right in front of the window. The guy working looked over and saw them with the soda. He shook his head "no" and wagged his finger, but Rusty just turned around and started walking away.

A few minutes later, back at the house, the cops showed up. They took Sam and the soda thief down to the gas station to be identified by the cashier, but when they got there the guy said that it wasn't them. As they were leaving, Sam said that the attendant smiled and winked at them. He was pretty sure that the he was flirting with them. They went home and drank their soda. The next night, when they got home after the show in Louisville, they found all the furniture out on the curb. Apparently Marty thought that if he threw away all the couches, then they wouldn't have anywhere to sleep and they wouldn't stay at the house. Sam and the Black Fork people just drug it all back inside and Marty didn't say anything. The next morning before they left town, the guy who's shoes got thrown away, found a newer pair of the same shoes, in his size, in the free box downtown.

One morning around 9 A.M., Sam came into the room holding a huge poster of a bloody fetus getting its head ripped off with a set of tongs. I had only been asleep for a few hours and I was tired. It was hard to understand what I was looking at. "What is that disgusting poster you're holding?" Sam seemed surprised to hear my voice. I guess he somehow thought that I might have slept through him slamming the door open and closed and stomping around.

He turned to me and said, "Oh, this is just something I took from the pro-lifers in front of planned parenthood. They were having some kind of protest against abortion, so I went up to talk to them. I told them they were fucking stupid and that they should stop what they were doing. They got really angry and threatened to call the police, so I just grabbed this thing and ran." It was so huge and disgusting. I noticed that his head was covered in duct tape.

"Why is your head covered in tape?"

"Oh, yeah. It was really cold when I woke up this morning and I wanted to put on a hat, but I couldn't because of my spikes." He had used wood glue a few days before, to spike up his hair. "So I used duct tape to make a hat," he said. I was still trying to wake up and I was having a hard time understanding what he was telling me. I thought that I was dreaming, then I noticed an army hat in his other hand. He saw me eyeing it and said, "I also joined the army today." I didn't believe him. "I was just walking by the recruiters office near Rhino's and a few of them were smoking out front. They saw me coming with this poster and my hair and they started laughing. I stopped and asked them what was so funny. They kept laughing and called me faggot and queer and told me to move along, so I told them I wanted to join the army. They laughed. I told them I was serious and I walked in. They spent the next few minutes berating me and calling me names. Then they looked me up using my social security number and found out that I was a math nerd with a full scholarship and they stopped laughing. They told me that I could go into engineering or cryptography. They said that if I joined, they could place me at a slightly higher rank than normal. I signed the papers just to prove a point. I'm not gonna join the army for real, don't worry." He threw down the hat and said, "I really need a nap." He laid down and closed his eyes. I tried to go back to sleep with no luck.

Sam found a shirt in the free box that said "killer" on the front, in big black letters. He took a marker and wrote the word "Christian" above it. He wore this shirt almost everyday for at least a month. He also used a wood-burning tool to engrave "Christian killer" into the handle of a huge sledgehammer that he had stolen from somewhere. He would walk around in his "Christian killer" shirt wielding his "Christian killer" war hammer and no one ever said a word to him.

One night, I was sitting in our living room playing Atari, when I heard a loud clank from far away. A few minutes later, I heard it again and it was closer. I went upstairs and onto the roof to get a better view of the streets. The sound rang out again, a few times in quick succession, and it was closer. I saw Sam with his hammer in hand, looking totally insane. He approached the intersection near our house and raised "Christian killer" above his head. Then, with maniacal strength, he slammed it into the stop sign on the corner, folding it in half. He raised the hammer again and struck it again, breaking it free from the pole. Sam crossed and walked into our house, never noticing me watching him from the roof.

Eventually, Sam told me more about the day the tigers attacked him. He told me that he was trying to put a curse on Corrine. He could tell that I had a crush on her and he didn't want any more trouble. He didn't want her to do damage to our weird little family, like Jen had done. He was trying to make her go away. He felt horrible about it. He regretted it. He started crying a little as he made his confession. I told him that it was okay and that he shouldn't feel bad, nothing had happened. I made him promise not to do any more black magic. We shook on it, then he got up and wrote it in Sharpie on our wall: "No More Black Magic."

My troubles refused to end. Miranda continued to hang out with the gun-loving straight edge guy and continued to insist that we were still dating. I just got used to it. I didn't care and I didn't argue. I devoted my time to more important things like music, Sam, pizza and scamming.

"I've heard that if you pick up a pay phone and tell them that you had just put in $3.50 to make a long distance call, and that the call never went through, the phone company will send you a check for the lost money," Sam said, in between gulps of soda. We were hanging out at Taco Bell, drinking free refills from a cup that we pulled out of the trash. We did it almost everyday. It was nice to sit in the air conditioning and drink for free. The workers never said a word.

"We should try it," I said.

"I've already done it around 10 times, I'm just waiting for the checks to come in." We talked about scams a lot, at first it was just talk, then we started trying them.

We were greenhorns. We started small, trying out all the things that we had heard about. One night we filled up some water bottles with salty water and went out with the hopes of coming back with pockets full of coins and backpacks full of soda. We stalked the streets, in search of soda machines with dollar bill slots. The first one was right down the street from our house, in front of a tiny grocery store. I was the lookout and Sam stepped up to the machine.

94

He took the bottle from his bag and popped open the squirt top. He squeezed water into the slot.

Nothing happened.

I whispered, "Try it again."

He squeezed the bottle again, emptying most of the bottle into the machine. There were a few sizzling noises and that was all. Sam started pushing buttons. "Doggamnit" he muttered. Then he pushed the coin return button and a few coins dropped out, clanking on the sidewalk. "Yes," we both whispered. But it was only a few coins and no more came, no matter how many times we mashed the button. We picked up our prize, 65¢. I pulled out my bottle and stepped over to the Snapple machine. I had no desire for Snapple since I heard they were owned by the K.K.K. and since soda was always my beverage of choice, but I wanted the treasure locked inside that lit up chest. I squeezed my bottle. There was a loud crackle and the lights went out. A small wisp of smoke came out from behind the machine and we took off running. We went home and refilled our bottles then went back out again, determined to pillage. We tried around 15 machines that night and got zilch to show for it. Maybe the saltwater scam used to work, but it didn't seem to work anymore.

A few days later, we tried a Coca-Cola machine in the basement of the student union. We salted it up and pushed the coin return, nothing happened. Then Sam started pushing the other buttons and a can fell out. Then another and another. We kept pushing they kept coming. They came so fast that they jammed up sometimes and we had to reach up inside the machine and break them free. We filled our backpacks. It jammed again and Sam had to put his arm in, up to his elbow. "I think I've got it" He said. Then he shook violently for a second and pulled his arm out.

"What happened?" I asked.

"I just got shocked."

"Holy shit, let's get out of here," I said as I offered my hand to help him up.

"No way, not yet," he said as he reached into the machine again. He cleared the jam and the cans were flowing again. When we had all that we could carry, we left. Our loot was heavy on our backs, but we were happy for the burden.

We got home and filled the fridge, then Sam said, "I bet the machine is still kicking out cans, we should go back." It seemed like a bad idea, but we went back and nearly filled up our bags again before it finally stopped working. We smuggled our second load of goods home and counted them. We got exactly 99 cans.

Another scam that Sam had heard about was this device called a "dialer" that allowed you to make free, long distance phone calls from pay phones. Anyone with the smallest degree of electronics knowledge could make one. You started with a gadget from Radio Shack called an "auto dialer," that you programmed all of your important numbers into. It was basically a speed-dialer. You programmed it, then used it by holding it up to the receiver of a telephone and pushing the number that you assigned to whatever phone number you wanted to dial. It was a pretty useless device, but if you took this thing and replaced its noise chip or something like that, you could make it duplicate the noise that a pay phone makes when you drop a quarter into it. You could order the parts needed to modify it from an electronics supply catalog. Sam made one.

It was great, we could call anyone for free. Every five minutes, the operator would come on and say "Please deposit an additional dollar for the next five minutes," then you would have to hold the dialer tightly to the receiver, to make sure no outside noise was picked up, and push the button four times slowly to make it seem believable that you were digging in your pockets and dropping quarters into the phone. Every now and then the operator would come on and say things like, "Please use real quarters," or they would say, "We know that you're using an illegal device and we know who you are, stay where you are." Of course they didn't know who we were and of course we didn't tell them. Keep in mind that there were no cell phones back then and no Internet really. It might sound ridiculous now, but the dialer was awesome and it saved us a lot of money.

Making phone calls was important to us. The phone was the only way to quickly reach people, so Sam was always looking for new ways to make free calls. The dialer was great, but you could only use it from payphones, which was sometimes inconvenient, and it was also annoying to use for lengthy calls, since you had to keep putting in more "money." Sam came home one day and said, "I got someone's calling card number today and it has a balance of $45."

"Great, how did you get it?" I asked.

"I just looked over this guy's shoulder when he was typing it in." He smiled.

"What is it?" I asked.

He thought for a second, then said, "It's 912-345-678 and the pin number is 0475." I asked him if he memorized it. "Yeah, I guess so," he said, proudly.

"You didn't write it down at all?"

"No, why would I?" We made lots of calls and we drained the balance to zero pretty quickly. A few weeks later, he somehow managed to get a corporate calling card number and it worked for nearly a year. We used it regularly and gave it out to friends whom we knew we could trust. It was great. It beat all the other phone scams by a long shot.

One day, out of the corner of my eye, I spotted our landlord, like a zombie, creeping up on me as I got my groceries out of the car. "Hey you! Do you live here?" he grunted, still moving toward me. I had never seen him this close up before. He was scary and I knew then why he was called "Liver Lips." I tried to pretend that I didn't hear him, but he kept coming. "Hey you, kid, I want to talk to you," he belched. I stopped and turned to face him. He was angry. He reached for me and I stepped back. "You dirty mother fuckers, I fuckin' told you to take care of your goddamn garbage! You live like pigs! I'll call the health department on you. You filthy sons of bitches!"

I ran into the house and locked the door behind me. He stayed in the yard for a minute, muttering to himself, then walked back over to his house, which was directly behind ours. I guess we should have heeded Gary's warning. Liver Lips was pissed. A few days later, someone from the health department showed up at our house and said that our landlord had called them. They told us that we had to clean up the trash and that we couldn't dump our old food out of the kitchen window. We thought that we could turn our landlord's attack back on him by showing the health inspector all the things that were wrong with the house. We showed him the hole in the kitchen ceiling where the shower leaked through. We showed him the broken windows and mold and everything else we could think of. He assured us that Liver Lips would have fix all of it. We were so proud of ourselves. We showed him, or so we thought, but the repairs were never made and the health inspector never came back. We could only assume that the rumors we had heard about old Liver Lips were true. Maybe he really was a well-connected slumlord that made bribes, dealt cocaine, forged art prints, and had connections in the mob.

There is this park in Bloomington called Cascades. It's really nice now and yuppies take their kids there, but back in 1995, it was kind of run down and not many people went there. It felt like a secret place. People would go there and meet their lovers. Bands sometimes practiced there, electrically and loudly, in the picnic pavilion. We'd go there late at night and climb trees and play games. I loved it. To get to the parking lot, you had to drive over this small stream where the water went across the road. It was really slippery, and just after the crossing area, there was a paved slope that created a natural slide. In the summer, it was fun to slide down it, into the stream. One hot night, Marty, Miranda, Sam, and I drove to the park to build a fire and roast veggie dogs. As we were leaving, I thought it would be funny to pretend to drive down the slope. As soon as I turned the wheels, we started sliding. It seemed like we were going to end up getting stuck in the creek. I couldn't get the car pointed in the right direction, because there wasn't any traction, so we all got out and tried to push it back into alignment with the road. When we did, we noticed that the cement was extra slippery, and we started sliding around on it for fun. We all ended up in the creek, soaked and laughing.

As Sam was attempting to climb back up the slope, his feet flew out from under him and his face smashed into the pavement. It sounded horrible. He made it to his feet and a stream of blood poured down from his chin. We were all in shock. He said, "I fuggin loss muh teef!" He smiled and showed us his broken front teeth. The three of us gasped in horror. Then Sam starting looking for his broken teeth pieces. He was on his hands and knees in the cold running water, feeling around for them. He picked up a pebble and said, "Uh tink uh fown it!" We cringed and told him that it wasn't his tooth. He tried to fit it into the gap anyway. We convinced him that he would never find his teeth and that even if he did, they couldn't put them back in. He gave up on his mission and let us examine his bloody chin. Apparently, he landed chin first and peeled off an oval of skin, then his teeth hit the pavement too. His chin wasn't cut open and there wasn't a flap of skin hanging off of it, but there was a missing piece the size of a quarter, dripping blood. We found some napkins in the car to stop the bleeding and drove him to the hospital. They stitched him up and he was fine.

A few days later, he went to the dentist to get his teeth fixed, and he came home looking as good as new. He thought his numbed face was really funny, and he kept trying to get me to punch him. I didn't do it. Then he said, "I don't want to waste this Novocain." He kept proposing ridiculous things that he should do, like picking a fight downtown or pulling out some other teeth that had cavities. I tried to get him to forget about it. He noticed the numbness encompassing his nose and said, "Maybe I should pierce my nose." I laughed. He dug around the room until he found a huge safety pin. He went into the bathroom and brought back a bottle of alcohol and "sterilized" it, then he put the point against his septum and pushed. I didn't think he would really do it, and the sound made me jump. I rushed over to see what he had done.

"I think I fucked up," he said. He had fucked up all right. He had pushed too hard and the pin went through his septum, and through the other side of his nose too, but he didn't care at all.

"Can you feel any pain?" I asked.

"No, not at all," he said, pulling it back a little and wiggling it so that he could clasp it shut. It looked hilarious. The pin was at least three inches long and he had pierced himself at an angle, so that it was lopsided. He still had the wood glue spiked hairdo too.

We were all broke that summer and we were always looking for ways to reduce our rent, so we decided to rent the breakfast nook. It was a tiny little room behind the kitchen. This kid named Justin Talley moved in. One day, we heard him calling out from his room: "Help me! Help me!" When we went to see what was wrong, we found him lying on his bed, looking really frightened.

"I can't move at all. I can't move my legs or my arms. I think I'm paralyzed," he said. We called his parents and they came and took him to the hospital. He came home later that night and he was fine. He said that he had an extreme potassium deficiency and that being vegan had nearly killed him. Justin is the only person I have known to ever have a health problem related to veganism. He was vegan for around a year when he moved in and he was really bummed about having to quit, but he said that the doctor told him that he'd have to eat around 12 bananas a day to keep his potassium at a safe level.

Justin wasn't safe in the breakfast nook. Vegan food nearly killed him again a few weeks later. You see, Sam had shoplifted some falafel mix and made it for Miranda, Corrine, and I. We stayed upstairs playing Uno while he cooked. He brought up an oily plate of burnt falafel chunks and we dipped them into ketchup. We had no idea how you were supposed to eat it. It was awful. A few minutes later, he said, "Oh shit!" and ran downstairs. While he was gone, we talked about how horrible it tasted. He came back up and calmly sat down on the floor beside me. He grabbed another crumbling clump and drowned it in ketchup. He ate it, adding a little more ketchup to his already messy face and said, "Guys, I think you should get out of the house." I played a "draw two" card and told Corrine to eat it. I noticed a burning smell.

"Sam, what's wrong?" I asked.

He ate another small piece of falafel and said, "The house is on fire." Sam was always funny. We all laughed, but he wasn't laughing. The smell got stronger. I asked him if he was serious.

"Yeah, the oil caught on fire and now the kitchen's on fire too, I'm sorry." I heard a scream from downstairs and I knew that this wasn't one of Sam's pranks—the house was on fire. Justin was in his tiny room behind the kitchen. I jumped up and ran downstairs. For some reason, we kept a mattress in the middle of the steps. We thought it was fun to bounce your way down. I grabbed it with the intent to smother the fire. When I got into the smoky kitchen, I found Justin holding a fire extinguisher, coughing. He had put the fire out. We opened windows and went outside to get out of the smoke. When we went back in, we could see the damage. The walls and the ceiling were blackened. There was melted cookware with dripping plastic handles on the stovetop. The cabinets above the stove were smoldering and charred. It looked horrible. Liver Lips was gonna kill us. Everyone was pretty angry. Sam's absentmindedness could have killed us all, so it was reasonable that we were upset. Sam didn't take it well. He became defensive, then indignant. I tried to keep everyone calm without looking like I was defending Sam too much. Eventually, everyone calmed down and Sam promised to clean up the kitchen. I offered to help. Chris Dilts was the most pissed off of everyone, because he kept his pots and pans in the cabinet that took the most damage. His stuff was ruined. I know that Sam secretly thought it was funny. Chris was the uptight roommate. He was the guy that collected our rent. He even started coming around a few days before the end of the month, trying to get the money. We took a stance against it. We held our ground and insisted that rent was due on the first of each month and that we wouldn't pay it a day sooner. He was the enemy—the roommate whom we declared the enemy anyway.

The clean up didn't work. The soot would not come off, no matter what we did. We decided it would be easier to paint over it. So I drove Sam to a hardware store and he walked out with two gallons of white paint that he didn't pay for. He just walked in, grabbed the cans and walked out. It was that easy. We painted coat after coat and the blackness still showed. We gave up after a while and decided that we would just tell Gary and Liver Lips that we painted the kitchen grey. It looked pretty cool really. The ceiling was dark grey and the walls were white at the bottom, fading into a dark grey at the top. Of course, no amount of paint could cover up the warped and cracked cabinet above the oven. There was nothing we could do about that.

Fifteen became my favorite band that summer. I loved them. I managed to overlook the songs that I didn't agree with, like the god songs and the overly hippie songs. Their other songs are great. I had written Jeff Ott, the only permanent member of the band, a few letters and I had sent him a Ted Dancin' Machine tape. I had also sent him a cover version of their song "Violation" that Jen (the girl I went crazy for) and I had recorded the summer before. He wrote me back and said that he loved the cover (he didn't mention the Ted Dancin' Machine) and that his wife really liked it and wanted to play it on her radio show. He asked me for permission. I wrote back and said, "You can do what ever you want with it, it's your song." He also mentioned that Fifteen was touring in the summer and asked me if I booked shows. Of course, I offered my services, so sometime in early May, we got a postcard from their drummer asking us to do a show for them in late July. We were so excited.

The exciting mail kept coming. Like most mornings, I woke up when Sam came back from his early adventures. "Look at this," he said, and threw some papers onto my bed. I picked them up and read them. It was from the university. It was about his withdrawal. He withdrew over winter break, before I moved in. I skimmed the letter, pretending to be interested and not knowing why he wanted me to look at it. Then I noticed the check. There was a check from I.U. It was a full refund for the semester's tuition.

"Whoa, that's a lot of money!" I said, surprised. Sam was smiling and started to laugh. "Yeah, we can use some of it to release your 7-inch," he said. He looked so proud. We had been talking about releasing an Operation: Cliff Clavin 7-inch, but we didn't have the money and our scamming income barely paid the rent. This check was big enough to pay for everything, even recording.

Then I thought about it and asked, "But you can't keep this money, can you? It's scholarship money. Won't they ask you to give it back?"

"I don't care, they can't make me give it back. It's the university's fault, they shouldn't have given me the check. Let them sort it out, I don't care, I'm not going back to college," he spat. We discussed it for a while and it seemed reasonable enough. Sam's plan was to deposit the check into his account and see what happened. Nothing happened. The check was good, so we booked recording time with a guy who had a studio in his basement. Sam started doing research on record pressing and I used the corporate calling card to tell Lewis and Tony, who still lived in southern Indiana, that we were going to have a real record soon!

Sam's research shed a lot of light onto the record business. We found out how cheap it was to make CDs and we were shocked that so many punk labels sold them for so much. It didn't make sense to us. We both agreed that punk should be cheap. Sam said, "If it ain't cheap, it ain't punk." I grabbed a marker and wrote it on our wall. We also couldn't figure out why bands relied on record labels to release their music. Of course, it made sense for a new band to get help from a label, but for established bands, it seemed so much smarter to release your own records. We talked about bands like Propagandhi and tried to understand why they would keep releasing albums on Fat Wreck Chords, a label who we were growing to hate. They were a well-known band and could easily press their own records and get them distributed everywhere. More importantly, if they self-released their music, they could sell it so much cheaper. Cheap was our main focus. For us, the best part about the punk scene was the fact that it was a community of friends. We both grew up without a sense of belonging. We spent our youth feeling like outcasts, then we discovered the underground music scene. It was wonderful and beautiful and it welcomed us. For the first time in our lives, we felt like we were part of something and it was so much better than the other groups that had rejected us. It was filled with creative, passionate people that wanted to change the world. We were proud of the new friends who we had made and we were excited to make more. The world was full of punks—making music, writing 'zines and raising hell. This is how we saw it then, and how I still see it today. The greatest thing about the punk scene are the friendships that it creates.

I was learning then, and I know now, that I will never be alone, I will never be stuck without a place to stay and I will never go hungry. I am part of a community who cares about me and I care dearly about it. We just couldn't understand why anyone would want to take advantage of this wonderful thing. Why would anyone want to make their friends give them so much money for music? Of course, we understood that we couldn't make records and give them away. Records cost money to make and making a small profit from selling them would allow us to release more music, but we could still do our best to sell them a cheap as possible. That's what we decided to do. Around that time, I bought the latest issue of Maximumrocknroll at the Book Corner and flipped through it at Little Caesars, getting pizza grease on the pages. I found an ad for Fifteen's summer tour and I was happy to see Bloomington, Indiana listed. The ad also announced the release of their new album, Extra Medium Kickball Star, and they were releasing it on their own label! I was so happy. I couldn't wait to tell Sam. Fifteen was already my favorite band, but this made it undeniable. They did what we wanted all bands to do. It felt like the universe was listening to us.

Sam found a curly, white-haired wig in the trash somewhere and he started wearing it everyday. It made him look like a founding father, kind of like a wild eyed, punk version of George Washington. He also got really into the idea of becoming primitive and instead of moving on from one costume to the next, he merged the two. He took an old pair of stained sweat pants and cut them up to make a loincloth. He "threw down his metal" again and stopped wearing his glasses and shoes. He was barefoot and blind with a white wig and a filthy blue loincloth. It lasted for around two weeks, until he finally lost the wig and got sick of us begging him to put some clothes on. During that time, a lot of funny stuff happened, starting with his visit to our neighbors. We were sitting on the porch eating some ill-gotten Mother Bears pizza and we saw a pizza delivery car stop in front of our neighbor's house. We were all out of pizza ourselves. Sam raised an eyebrow and asked, "should I go over there and see if they will lend us a slice?" We all laughed and that was enough to set him into motion.

He cautiously crossed the street, cursing every few seconds when he stepped on a sharp stone. He looked back when he got to their door, but he didn't look at us, since he was way too blind to see us. He couldn't tell if we were pleading for him to call it off or egging him on. He knocked anyway. The door opened and a dude answered. They chatted for a second, out of our earshot, then Sam went in. He was in there for about 10 minutes. When he came out, he waved a goodbye to the people inside and started his blind march through the minefield back to our porch. "What happened?" I asked.

"They were cool, they said I could have a piece but it had chicken on it, so I didn't eat any," he said.

Marty was there too, and he asked, "what were you doing in there then?"

Sam just pursed his lips and quietly said, "hanging out with my dudes." We all laughed. A few days later, Marty dared him to try the same type of stunt with the girls who lived in the upstairs apartment, catty cornered to us. We'd see them from time to time, drinking on their balcony, and Marty would joke about us crashing their party, but we never did. We didn't have the guts to do it, but George Washington—the cave man—was fearless. He accepted the dare and went right over there. A few minutes later, he was drinking a glass of water on their balcony. He looked in the general direction of our house and gave us a tiny wave. When he came home he said that they were boring. We asked him what he said to get into their house and he said, "I just told them that I was a weary traveler and I was dreadfully thirsty. I asked them for a glass of water. I played their Nintendo for a few minutes too, but I couldn't really see the TV."

Gary came over to collect the rent on the first of July. He asked us if we planned on staying another year. We said no. I didn't know where I was going when the lease ran out, but I knew I didn't want to live in that house. We sat anxiously waiting for him to leave, hoping that he didn't walk into the kitchen. Then he did.

"What the fuck happened in here?" he bellowed.

"We painted it," Sam said. Gary walked back into the living room looking very pissed.

"You'd didn't fuckin' paint it, you burned it. That's gonna come out of your damage deposit and then some." Someone said it was an accident. Gary didn't care. He stormed out of the house, and we could see him walking around back to report to Liver Lips.

We called a house meeting and discussed the idea of not paying the last month's rent. We had heard that if you were evicted, you were allowed 30 days to vacate the property, so we thought that it would be cool to just not pay the last months rent, then the landlord would take our damage deposit and we'd come out on top. Marty got the lease out and studied it. He found a section that pertained to eviction. The lease said that, if for any reason there is a disagreement between the landlord and the tenants, the landlord could end the lease and the tenants would be required to completely vacate the premises within three days. We didn't really read the lease on the day we signed it. We were all shocked to find out what it said, it was full of stuff like that. We had basically signed away all of our rights to old Liver Lips. We gave up on our renters revolt, we surrendered.

Chris Dilts changed the subject. "Does anyone know how my dishes ended up broken in the streets?" No one said a word, but Sam and I knew how his dishes got there, we put them there. We were sick of his attempts to manage the house. We were sick of his smugness.

One night, after we finished our pasta, Sam pretended to throw his plate through the open window. He laughed and smiled at me and asked, "Should I do it?"

"I dare you," I said.

He gave me a sly grin and said, "do you mean challenge me?"

"Sure."

We had defined the difference between the two terms the previous summer on some late night adventure with Marty. A dare is empty. It means nothing. You can always refuse a dare if you want to without losing face. A challenge is more serious. To refuse a challenge is to be cowardly, but to propose a challenge has its risks. If the person you challenge accepts your challenge and succeeds, you must do it too. Considering this, I said, "okay, yeah, I challenge you." Without a moment of hesitation and without any consideration for the possibility of passing cars, Sam launched his plate out the window. I didn't breathe until I heard it hit the street and shatter. No one screamed, no one slammed on their breaks, it was okay. Sam raised an eyebrow and smiled his sinister smile. I knew what I had to do. I forked the last few noodles into my mouth and sent my plate to join its sister in hell. I was lucky too, the coast was clear. We repeated this ritual every night until Chris ran out of plates. We were wicked young punks, careless and cruel.

Our 7-inch came out on Sam's birthday, the 4th of July. We decided that since no one liked Operation: Cliff Clavin in Bloomington, that we should have our record release party in southern Indiana, at Roy's house. The kids who came to shows at Roy's house really liked us, so it seemed like a good idea. This band from Louisville, called Out was playing the show too, so a few Louisville scenesters showed up. We were a little nervous to play in front of them, but most of them stayed outside while we played anyway. One of them was a guy named Greg Wells. He had a reputation for being an asshole because he did record reviews and was just a highly opinionated person in general. He came up to me after the show and introduced himself. He asked me about Plan-It-X records and I introduced him to Sam. He was really nice and really interested in our plans with the label. He told us that he had moved from Louisville to Lexington and had started his own record label called Small-town Records. He pulled a 7-inch out of his bag, it had a silk-screened cover. It was by a band called The Sally Strugglers. He told us all about them. He said it was his first release. We told him that we had just learned to silk screen and I showed him the patches that I had made. He asked us if we wanted to trade a few copies so that he could have some of our record for his distro. We didn't have a distro, but it seemed like a great idea to start one, so we agreed to the trade.

We talked about where we had our records pressed. We had both went through United in Nashville, which seemed like the place that all punks used. We talked about mastering and sticker manufacturing and where to get the best bags to put the records in. It was fun. This was my first time talking about boring record label stuff with someone else who ran a label. It wouldn't be my last. Years later, I would do it all the time, with young kids just starting out and with people like Var, from No Idea records who started way before me. Not many people understand the importance of tape, postage rates and packaging techniques. Whenever record label nerds get a chance to talk shop, they do, for way too long, then their band mates have to pull them apart. I didn't have too much to talk about with Greg that day, since Plan-It-X was still in its infancy, but it was fun. He asked me if we'd like to play a show in Lexington later that month with some band from Richmond, Virginia, called Action Patrol. I said yes without asking my band mates. I was excited to play somewhere so far away from home, it was like a mini-tour. Greg left with the Louisville band, then Chris Lincoln, from Instinct came up to me and said, "Were you just talking to Greg Wells?" I nodded.

"What did he say?" I told him that we traded records and that he asked us to play that show. He was shocked.

"Greg Wells is an asshole. He's a real jerk. He's probably just making fun of you."

"It didn't feel that way to me. I like him. He's nice." I really did like him. He seemed like an honest guy. Maybe that's why he was so hated by the scene, people don't like honesty if it insults them. I had a good feeling about Greg. I knew that we were going to become good friends.

Greg, years later in Houston, outside of a skatepark.

Sam and I were so excited about the Fifteen show. It was coming up fast, along with the end of summer and the end of our lease. I went home (to my parents' house) a few times to practice with the guys because I wanted us to be great when we played with my new favorite band. I don't think the practices helped much. We had a lot to learn.

When I got back to Bloomington, I noticed a "FOR RENT" sign in the front yard. It made me mad, even though I knew that we had told Gary that we weren't staying and I knew that they needed to find someone to rent that dump. I didn't want to live there, none of us did, but seeing that sign made me feel like we were getting kicked out. As much as I hated the house, I loved the times that I had within its cracking walls. It hit me for the first time that I was leaving and I felt sad. Sam must have felt the same way, because later that night he took a marker and changed the sign to read: "FORK TRENT."

The next day, Gary charged in and yelled, "Who the fuck is Trent?" We all started laughing. That made Gary even angrier. We assured him that none of us were Trent and that we didn't know anyone by that name. Luckily, Sam wasn't home. I'm not sure what he would have said. "I understand that some-one was trying to be funny, but they also changed the fucking phone number," Gary said, still pissed. "That's not funny, we need to rent this house and now I have to go buy a new sign." He stormed out of the house, slamming the door behind him. When we knew he was gone, we laughed again.

A few hours later, he came back with a new sign. I pretended not to be home and hid in my room. Sometime during the night, Sam changed the sign to read: "PORK BRENDA." The next morning we saw his handy work and we feared the inevitable visit from Gary. This time he was fuming. He demanded to know who Brenda was. Somehow we convinced him that we were being pranked by college students. We suggested that he tie the next sign onto the support beams on the porch, to keep it safe. I was proud of my housemates for not snitching on Sam. It was good to know that no matter how much they hat-ed us and no matter how much they loathed Sam's behavior, that they showed solidarity in the face of our common enemy.

Fifteen was on tour with Bisybackson, a band from Portland, Oregon. They showed up in one big van and spilled out into the Rhino's parking lot like clowns. They were dirty and wild looking. One of them was wearing a filthy rabbit suit. I could smell them from where I was standing, a few yards away. I didn't say hello, I was way too afraid to talk to them. We played first and we fucked up a lot. I was extremely nervous, we all were. My strap fell off again during one song and I dropped my guitar, Lewis got stage fright and didn't sing all of his back-up parts, but we made it through the set and we were all happy when it was over. Bisybackson played next. I didn't really watch them. I wanted them to hurry up and play, so that Fifteen could play. I was a kid on Christmas eve, waiting for the sun to rise.

While I was waiting in the parking lot, hanging out with people, one of the roadies came out and threw a bunch of patches into the air. He shouted, "Free patches!" and walked back inside. I didn't get one, but I looked at a friend's. It was a Bisybackson patch. The band I was rudely skipping. I felt bad, so I went in and watched their last few songs. They were good. I regretted missing most of their set. Years later, I would bump into them on tour and they would jump on our show, then we'd jump on their show the next night. We would eventually become good friends, but not that night. I didn't even speak to them. Hannah was there, she got one of the free patches. Her and her friends came down to loiter in the parking lot and flirt with punk boys. Of course, I didn't know her yet and I didn't meet her that night. A few years later, I would meet her and we'd fall in love and she would join Operation: Cliff Clavin and I would notice the Bisybackson patch pinned to her backpack.

Fifteen was great. They played all of my favorite songs and Jeff went on long political rants which Sam and I totally agreed with. Near the end of their set he said, "I still haven't met Chris yet. Where is Chris?" I wanted to run away, but people pointed to me. Still speaking into the mic he said, "Chris and his friend Jen sent me a cover of one of our songs a while back and I really liked it, so I decided to put it on our new record." My heart sank. For a second I was thrilled, then the reality of the situation hit me and I was devastated. Miranda was standing right beside me and I could feel her starting to boil. We never spoke of Jen. I never mentioned her name, no one did. It was our unspeakable secret which everyone knew about. It was horrible. One minute I was standing there, watching my favorite band and feeling great. The next minute the skeleton in my closet showed up and ruined everything. I knew there was no stopping the tidal wave of arguments that were coming.

I tried to stay calm and smile. I tried to keep up appearances. Jeff kept talking and Miranda stormed out. Corrine followed her and Sam stayed with me. Jeff bent over and picked up an LP, then put his mouth back in front of the mic and said, "We sold all of our records on tour, this is the last copy and I saved it for you." He held it out toward me. I reluctantly approached the stage and took the record.

"Thanks Jeff, it means a lot to me," I said. People clapped. I turned red. The rest of my night was spent fighting with Miranda for no reason. Our relationship was clearly over, but would not end. I couldn't even listen to the new Fifteen album. It was ruined for me. 16 years later, I played with my new favorite band, The Mountain Goats, on that same stage and it was perfect. John—of The Mountain Goats—played solo that night and broke a string, and he asked to borrow my guitar. It was the same magical feeling without any of the drama. I was so happy to listen to my favorite songs being played by my favorite musician on my guitar in a place that had become such a huge part of my life. I sat on the edge of the stage beside a girl that I was falling in love with and sang along to every song. I'm glad that music has been my life.

I had a long way to go before I got to that happy night in 2011. The lease was up. We had to move out. We tried to clean up the house, but it was pointless. We painted over the pentagram and the philosophies on our bedroom wall, but like the kitchen, no amount of paint would do the job. You could still see the "666" and Sam's sloppy scrawl: "PUNK ROCK IS ABOUT TOLERANCE." Marty and Chris had already figured out where they were going to live, but Sam and I didn't. We didn't really think about and we didn't have any money anyway. We intended to sleep outside as much as we could and try to find a new place to live before it got cold. We schemed new ways to get free pizza and concocted more moneymaking scams so that we could release more records and hopefully a CD soon. Sam told me about a magazine that the Maximumrocknroll people published, called Book Your Own Fucking Life. He said that is was filled with contacts from all around the country who would book shows for touring bands and pay them enough money for them to buy the gas they needed to get to the next town. It sounded great. We decided that Operation: Cliff Clavin should go on tour next summer.

I found a Walkman and I wore out my Fifteen tape, walking around at night, alone.

In 1492 Columbus sailed the ocean blue
for love of god and me and you, NO!
In 1941 we intervened to stop the spread of
world fascism, NO!

Listen up boys and girls
it's the history of the whole world
and you know it's true, NO!
6 million Jews they call it genocide
100 million native Americans what
an unfortunate price for today's quality of life

All people every person experiences violation
When told what is right and told what is wrong
And told what to do under the threat of violent intimidation

Virus kills us now virus kills us then
over and over and again and again
Sun goes down in my town
Berkeley CA sold me on too many dreams
of justice and brotherhood
Sun goes down in my town
Berkeley CA sold me on too many dreams
of peace on the earth in our time

In 1969 my forefathers said stop
this land is his and hers and yours and mine
In 1992 Rosebud sailed the sky so blue
she gave her life for me and you

All people...
Sun goes down in my town
I believe in me. I make my dreams real.
    - Fifteen

CHAPTER 8
EIGHT LONG MONTHS

The first few weeks of our homeless adventure were fun. We slept in parks and on rooftops and in various buildings on campus. We stayed up late in the computer labs, writing 'zines that never got published. We hung out in People's Park with the punks and made plans to smash the state. It started getting cold and our reputations as reckless punks had kind of ruined our chances of staying at anyone's house. I started going home to my parents' house sometimes, just to take a break. I'd take Sam with me once in a while, but he wasn't really welcomed at their house. He had done things that damned him, like puking in the hallway and staining the sheets with permanent marker. He was a dangerous houseguest. His hometown of Mitchell was in-between Bloomington and my hometown, so sometimes I would drop him off at home and pick him up on my way back to Bloomington. I was so bummed about not having a place to live again. I hated retreating to the basement. I felt defeated. I started staying at my parents' house for longer and longer periods at time. One of those times, I had dropped Sam off in Mitchell and he got into a fight with his dad about something, so he just walked out and walked the 33 miles back to Bloomington.

Sam got a job washing dishes in the student union and fell in love with a girl named Hazuki. One night they were sitting on the wall in front of People's Park in the rain. They were huddled together under one umbrella. It was the first time that they had been so close to each other. Hazuki had a shaved head and kind of looked like a boy. Back then, people used to cruise up and down Kirkwood avenue on the weekends. The street would be packed with rednecks from the small towns surrounding Bloomington. They would slowly drive back and forth, hoping to meet each other somehow. That rainy night, one of these cruisers in a truck crept by Sam and his new crush. Some idiot leaned out of the window and yelled, "Faggots!" thinking that Hazuki was a boy. Sam was so much more than a fag. He was a woman living in a man's body. That redneck had no clue. Neither did Sam. Sam told me all about that night. It was a sweet story. It never worked out between them though.

Greg Wells followed through with his offer to book us shows in Lexington and the punks there seemed to like us. The show with Action Patrol went really well, so Greg asked us to come back in October to play with Tilt. I loved Tilt, so I was really excited. I sold my Misfit's mobile and bought a huge green station wagon so that we could play these out of town shows. We needed a van, but I didn't have money and the station wagon was a super deal that my dad found for me. It handled like a boat, swaying from side to side down the road. We loaded our cargo and set sail for the south. The show was great, we played great and some people were there to see us! The next day Tony called me and said that he wanted to quit the band. He said, "I don't think it's worth it to drive for hours and play for 20 minutes." I was shocked. I felt completely different. I thought that we were really getting somewhere, we had a 7-inch and fans and people offering us shows. We were a real band. Tony didn't think so. He quit.

My friend Adam White, who played in a band called Four Rose Society, suggested that I ask his friend, Stan Doll, to take Tony's place. Stan worked at the other cool record store in Louisville. It was called Better Days Records, and there was a "punk" room in the back which only sold "punk" records. Stan worked in that room. I went there with Adam one day and he introduced us. Stan was familiar with our band and agreed to give it a try. His drums were in the basement of the record store and he said that we could practice there. We set up a practice for the following weekend since I had to give Lewis some advance notice. He had enrolled at Ball State University in Muncie, Indiana that fall, which is three hours north of Louisville. He was a trooper though, and didn't let the distance dampen his determination or his dedication to the band.

As soon as we started the first song we were in love with Stan. He was a real drummer. He knew how to play drums and he played fast. It was wonderful. He learned the songs quickly and added cool drum rolls and fills. We practically begged him to join the band. We told him about Plan-It-X Records and about the CD we wanted to release. We told him about the summer tour we were planning and he was totally into all of it. Stan joined the band. A few days later, he got a us a show in Louisville. It was in the basement of yet another cool record store in Louisville, called Ground Zero. It was a Halloween themed show, and Lewis and I decided that it would be cool to dress up like hair-metal-rockers. Stan wasn't into it at all and refused to wear the wig that we had bought for him. It was embarrassing, playing in silly costumes in front of snobby Louisville scenesters with our new drummer, in his normal clothes, but Stan played well and we were really excited about our new sound.

I drove Lewis back to Muncie after the show, then I drove to Bloomington, to find Sam. I couldn't find him anywhere. I asked around town and no one had seen him for a few days. I called his parents' house and his mom told me that he was there, but that he was asleep. At least he was okay, I thought. I figured I would pick him up the next time I was passing by....

Miranda was hanging out with a new guy. She was over the straight edge skater. He was gone, and I was glad, but when I called her house, she wasn't home, despite our plan to meet up. I called Corrine and found out that she was at this new guy's house. I knew his number, so I called and asked for her. She was really mad at me for calling. She said it was rude. She assured me that there was nothing going on and that I had nothing to worry about. She promised that she'd hang out with me the next day. I slept in my car that night and woke up freezing, and drove back to my parents' house, without seeing Miranda and without seeing anyone.

I didn't stop in Mitchell on my way home. I didn't want to see Sam. I didn't want to burden him with my misery. We were both down on our luck. As I passed by the turn that I would have made to go to his parents' house I thought about what Sam had done to the straight-edge-pony-tailed-gun-totting-skater, Miranda's first guy. He hated seeing me upset. He knew that Miranda and I shouldn't be dating, but he also knew that it made me sad when she spent the night at this dude's house. We both hated the guy. We didn't do drugs, but we didn't like straight edge kids and we really didn't like straight edge kids who carried guns, so this guy struck out on many different levels. One night Miranda and I had a big fight. I accused her of being in love with him and I tried to break up with her again. She swore that they were just friends and insisted that she loved me. It ended, hours later, with both of us crying and nothing resolved. Sam heard most of it and was really upset. When he had heard too much he left. He took his knife. He found the guy's car and slashed all of his tires. It freaked me out, but I knew it was Sam's way of telling me that he loved me. It meant a lot to me, even if I thought it was a bad idea. Everyone knew Sam did it. It was obvious. Miranda was really mad. Sam ended up leaving an anonymous letter in his mailbox with money to replace the tires. It wouldn't be the last time that Sam slashed tires for me.

That winter was harsh. Sam stayed at his parents' and slept. I stayed at my parents' and wrote songs in the basement, alone. We talked on the phone sometimes and made plans to go to Bloomington, but he would always cancel. I devoted all my energy to Operation: Cliff Clavin. I drove to Muncie to get Lewis, then to Louisville over and over so that we could practice. Then I drove Lewis home and I either went to Bloomington, or just drove back to my parents' house. It was bleak. We recorded a full-length album in Bloomington, during a snowstorm, with the same guy who recorded our 7-inch. We tried to get Sam to come and do back up vocals, but his mom said that he was asleep. After 10 hours of recording, I had to drive Lewis back to school and Stan back home, on the dark and icy roads. I drove so much that winter, and dreamed of the summer to come. The tour was my beacon of hope. I couldn't wait for summer to come. I'd sing Sam's song sometimes:

I love and respect you and I know that you do your best
This world is so fucked up, never let me take it out on my friends
And I know that it ain't all that bad
And sometimes I'm kind of glad
That I'm alive

And I know that Summer's gonna come
And all our plans might come together
At least we will survive

I love and respect you and I know you're gonna change the world
You've already made it a better place for me
to be

All we got it each other
All punks got is each other
    - Peanucle (Sam's acoustic band)

We couldn't start booking the tour until April 1st, because that's when Book Your Own Fucking Life came out. I had heard that it was useless to try to use the previous year's issue because punk venues and promoters come and go too quickly. The phone numbers would be disconnected. Places would have been shut down. We had to wait. In the meantime, I shoplifted an atlas to start planning our route. We agreed that we should tour for as long as possible and we settled on 60 days. We all wanted to go out west, but we also wanted to go see Greg Wells in his new home in Richmond, Virginia, so we plotted a path straight east, then through the south to New Orleans. From there we would turn west and go through Texas and then out to California. From there we'd go north, up the coast, then work our way back to the Midwest. None of us had been anywhere before and we were so excited. I couldn't wait to tell Sam. I knew that he was looking forward to the tour and I thought it would cheer him up when I updated him on the plan. I called and called but always got his mom or dad and they always said, "He's asleep." Miranda and I had worked some things out and asked if she could come on the tour. I wasn't sure it was such a good idea, but we were best friends and she had been a part of the band and a part of Plan-It-X from the start, so I talked it over with the guys and they were okay with it. Besides, if we didn't manage to get ahold of Sam, we'd need a roadie.

We started referring to the guy who recorded us as the "Fat Hippie" because he was pissing us off. He had also taken smoke breaks throughout our session to get high. We had mixed the album the day after we recorded it, and he told us it would take him a few days to make us a master CD that we could send off to the pressing plant. He promised to mail it to us as soon as it was done. A few days turned into a few weeks and then into a few months. According to the guy at the CD pressing plant, turnaround for a CD was four to six weeks. I had to ask him what "turn around" meant. He explained that it was how long it took to manufacture and ship out the finished product, once it had arrived in his hands. Our tour was starting in 7 weeks and it was beginning to look like we weren't gonna have a CD to take with us. We also had around 40 orders that we needed to mail out before we left for two months. The artwork was done, the patches were done, and the stickers were done. Everything was assembled and waiting for the CD to complete the package. We called the guy everyday and left messages on his machine. Then Lewis called and told him that he would come over and pick up the master in person. That got him motivated and he finally finished his job. We still owed him around $200 for the recording and we decided not to pay. At least, we decided not to pay until we got back from tour. We could use the money on the road, and we still didn't know if his laziness was gonna cost us the tragedy of not having a CD to sell on tour. We got the master and sent it off right away. We had 6 weeks to wait and hope.

While we waited, I looked for a tour van. We had been so focused on getting our album out on time that we kinda forgot about needing something to tour in. My dad is a handy man and part time mechanic, so he always knows a guy who knows a guy. I looked in the paper and cruised by a few car lots, but mostly I just badgered my dad and hoped that he found something and hoped that it would be cheap. Around three weeks before tour, he found our van. It was a blue 1984 Chevy, in pretty bad shape. I bought it for $600 and my dad did all the needed repairs for around $100 more. It was a gamble, taking it on a two-month tour, but it was a gamble that we had to take. We had no choice. It had cost us everything we had.

I spent the weeks before tour living with Stan at his dad's house in Clarksville, Indiana. His dad had some super good long distance deal and said that we could use the phone to make tour calls. We still needed to make a lot of calls. There was no other way to book shows back then. We called everyone listed in Book Your Own Fucking Life who lived in the places we were going, not just venues and promoters, we called everyone: bands, 'zinesters, people offering their houses as crash pads and everything else. Most of the numbers we useless. A common call went like this:

"Hey, is Seth there?"

"No, he moved out, I don't know where he is." said the random voice on the other end.

"Well, do you guys still have shows at your house?" I'd ask.

"Yeah sometimes." They'd say, usually unenthused.

"Would you want to do a show for my band? We're called Operation: Cliff Clavin. We're from Indiana..." Sometimes I could talk whoever answered the phone into booking our show. Then I had to get directions, since there was no other way to find their house, there were no GPS devices or internet map services. I wrote all the info down in our tour notebook and assumed that it was fact from that moment on. I'd flip the page and start working on the next day. I made tons of calls. Usually, no one answered. I just left message after message after message, hoping that some of them would call back.

We had a week to go and I had booked around 40 out of 60 shows. I felt pretty good about it, but we still didn't have CDs. We called the plant regularly and the guy assured us that he was doing his best. Of course, now I know that he didn't have anything to do with the actual making of the CDs. He was just a broker. All he did was take our stuff and send it to a huge factory somewhere in Singapore that made CDs for dirt-cheap. He doubled the price for us, so that he got a big cut and we still thought we were getting a good deal. It was a good deal for us, but it was a great deal for him. This is how it still works today for the most part, but I always make sure that the things I have pressed are made in places where the workers get a fair wage. I still have to go through a broker though, because huge manufacturing plants won't do business with small timers like me.

While I waited for the phone to ring, I reluctantly popped Forrest Gump into the VCR one day when Stan was at work. The movie was a huge hit the year before and everyone quoted it. They'd say, "Life is like a box of chocolates, you never know what you're gonna get." It made me sick. I didn't see the movie when it came out and I didn't see it when it was released on VHS. Everyone kept telling me it was so great. The more I was told that I had to see it, the more I didn't want to, but I was bored and I had to stay there. I had to answer the phone if it rang. I had to be there, because if I wasn't, and someone called us back about a show, they'd usually leave a vague message. They'd say something like, "This is Bobby in Bakersfield trying to reach Operation: Cliff Clavin, call me back." Click. Then I'd have to call back and I'd usually get a machine. It was horrible. No one ever left the message: "Hey guys, this is Mike. I'm just calling to say that I'll do your show for sure and here are the directions..." That would have been great, but it never happened, so we took turns waiting by the phone. It felt like imprisonment. It was so nice outside and I wanted to be doing something in sun. I wanted to go to Bloomington and hang out with my friends. Instead I was stuck in a suburban home in southern Indiana, waiting for the phone to ring, watching Forrest fucking Gump!

I loved it! It was such a great movie. I watched it again the next day, and one more time later that week. It inspired me. I was already excited about my summer adventure, but Gump made me even more excited!

Lewis's dad didn't want him to go on tour. He was really worried about his safety. When he found out about Book Your Own Fucking Life he said, "What if some serial killer put their name in there, to get you to come to his house, so he can kill you?" Lewis tried to convince him that wouldn't happen and that everything would be fine. His dad wouldn't give up. He said that he would cut Lewis off if he went on tour and wouldn't pay for his college tuition. Lewis took a stand! He told his dad that if that's how he felt, it was fine with him, but he was going on tour. His dad asked him how he would pay for college. Lewis said that he'd quit and move to Bloomington.

I called Sam's house everyday. I called early in the morning, in the afternoon and late at night. No matter when I called, his parents' said that he was sleeping. On my last day at Stan's house, I asked Sam's mom when the best time to call was. I asked when he was usually awake and she said, "Well, he's on a 24-hour sleeping schedule." She told me that she would tell him I called. I didn't know what to do. I really wanted Sam to go on the tour. It had been

116

our dream, but it didn't seem like he was in shape for it. A part of me thought that we should just show up at his house and kidnap him, just bust in and drag him out of bed and toss him in the van, but part of me worried that he might not want to go, or that he would sleep the whole time. I knew something was wrong with him, but I didn't know what it was. I decided that it would be better to leave him alone, let him rest, and then go get him after the tour was over. I'm still not sure if I made the right choice.

The CDs arrived at my parents' house the day we were leaving for tour. We quickly packaged them. We packaged all 1,000 of them and packed them into the van. We decided to bring them all on tour with us, because we couldn't guess how many we would sell. My mom helped. Then we drove to Blooming-ton for our tour kickoff show at Rhino's. We expected a warm welcome. We as-sumed that everyone would be just as excited for us as we were, but there were only around nine people there and we sold three CDs, which isn't bad really, it means that ⅓ of the crowd bought one. I felt let down by my hometown. I was so eager to show them what I had been doing.

Our first show of tour and our CD release party with Brian Munn, Brent, Amos, Corrine and Hazuki.

I was so proud of our CD, and it was a great deal too. It came with two vinyl stickers and a patch for $5. I couldn't wait to show it to Sam. It was so

117

punk and so cheap! The cover art was a drawing that I made of a wild looking guy burning the American flag. The original idea was to have a guy holding a gun to his head, which we thought would go well with the title Freedom Of Choice, but we concluded that suicide wasn't funny, no matter what, and went with the flag burner. We made shirts with the same design, which got kids kicked out of school years later.

The next morning we went to the post office and mailed out the forty pre-orders that we had received. It felt so cool, sending out so many of our CDs. We were thrilled that people had responded to our tiny add in M.R.R. and sent us $5.00 in the mail. This was the first time I stood in line with a ton of packages in the Bloomington post office. It would eventually become my life.

I said goodbye to a few people and we left town, to go on tour, without Sam.

Sam, after dying his hair black, in what some people called an attempt to be more like Marty.

CHAPTER 9
HOW I SPENT MY SUMMER VACATION

Our first out of town show was in Charlestown, West Virginia, and, since we had to drive passed my parents' house again, we stopped for a while and ate peanut butter and jelly sandwiches. My dad gave the van a final check. Before we left, my mom rushed out and said, "Let me get a picture of you guys sitting in the van." We opened the side door and posed awkwardly, unsure of the adventure which we were about to embark upon. I told her we were running late and that we had to go. We said goodbye and drove away. She took another picture as we were leaving, of the back of the van. I didn't know that she did it, of course, and I wouldn't know until I made it home again.

The first show would set the precedent for the whole tour: The promoter didn't show up, we didn't get paid, there were only a handful of people there, and we had to beg the crowd for a place to stay.

The next day, we drove through the mountains with the emergency brake on for three or four hours. Lucky for us, we figured it out before we did any real damage. The van ran much better after we took it off. We drove to Richmond to stay with Greg Wells for five days, before our show there. I had tried to book shows in-between West Virginia and Richmond, but nothing worked out. It was really nice of Greg to let us stay for so long. It seemed like we were there for a month. It was super hot and his place was small. I felt bad about making it so crowded. We tried to stay out of the house as much as we could, but we didn't have any money, so we just walked around for hours. Eventually, it was the day of the show.

The show was at this place called Twisters and, since it was on the last day of school, the show was an end of school celebration for the high school kids. All of the other bands who played were high school punk bands, and the only reason we got on the bill was because a previously booked band had broken up before the show. Greg pulled some strings and hooked us up with the open slot. It was great! There were around 400 people there and they all seemed to like us. People were stage diving and moshing. We played fast and tight! It was such a release of energy. We had been cooped up in Greg's place for almost a week after playing two sorry shows, and now we were on stage, playing our hearts out to a club full of sweaty teenagers. Greg did our merch, and when I finally made my way back to the table, he was ecstatic. He grabbed my shoulder and said, "You're never gonna believe this, kid. Guess how many CDs I just sold. Guess!" I was still buzzing from our performance and couldn't care less about our sales.

"I don't know," I said. "57?"

He smiled. "Nope, more like 25! I also sold around 6 shirts and a shit-ton of patches!" A kid stepped up to the table and Greg leaped into action, leaving me standing, sweaty and alone. A girl tapped me on the shoulder and said, "Can I get a hug? You guys are awesome." I didn't know what to say or what to do. I'm sure I blushed.

"I'm pretty sweaty," I said.

"So am I," she said. Then she grabbed me.

It was a free show, so we didn't get paid, but we made almost $200 from merch sales. It was such a relief. We were nearly broke and morale was dropping quickly. That show was just what we needed to raise our spirits and restore our hopes. We figured that if we only played one show that was as good every week, we'd do fine, but we didn't have any other shows as good as Richmond— it was the highlight of the tour. Had we known that then, we might have turned around and went home.

The next few days were rough. The south was hot and humid and the shows were smoky and small. In Columbia, we got framed for making long distance phone calls to Japan by this shitty pop punk band called Buglite. One of them made the calls and, after we left the next day, they told our host that they had heard one of us calling Japan. It took us years to clear our name.

In Killen, Alabama, a girl asked Lewis for a shirt, but she didn't have any money. She asked him if he would take a blowjob instead. He found me and told me about it and asked me what I thought. "Well, do you want a blow job from a stranger?" I asked.

He looked disgusted and said, "Not really, but it's pretty crazy. I'm sure she's serious." Lewis had a girlfriend and would have never done something like that. I thought it was really funny that he came to check with me first. We both agreed that we needed the $5 way more than he needed a blowjob and he went back over to the girl to break the bad news. The good part about that show was that The Grumpies, a squeaky pop punk band from Mississippi, played too. I was really excited when I found out that they were playing because I was super into their guitar player's old band, White Trash Superman. I sat with him on the edge of a fountain and we talked for a while. I asked him if the girl who was playing bass in The Grumpies was the same girl who was in White Trash Superman, and she said, "No, I was the girl in White Trash Superman..." He meant that he was the one with the high-pitched voice. I felt dumb. The Grumpies were great people and we became good friends, you'll see.

In Fayetteville, Arkansas, we pulled over so Lewis could drop a letter into a mailbox. The box was in front of the police station. On his way back to the van, he noticed a sign in the lawn that said "KEEP OFF THE GRASS." He pointed it out to us and smiled, then ran across their manicured yard. When he got to the van, he tried to jump into the open side door, in mock fear of the cops chasing him, and twisted his ankle. We all laughed at his silliness and I sped away quickly like a getaway driver, joining his game. We started driving south, toward New Orleans, but his ankle wouldn't stop hurting, so we decided to take him to the hospital. It turned out that he had fractured it. They put a temporary cast on his leg and told him to stay off of it for at least three weeks. For some reason, he didn't want them to give him crutches, despite the fact that he was still covered by his parents' insurance. He had heard that hospitals charge outrageous amounts for things like that and had insisted that he didn't want them, so Stan had to carry him to the van on his back. We sat in the parking lot for a while and tried to figure out what we should do. There was no way that Lewis could stay off his feet for three weeks. We had nearly six weeks of tour left. I asked him what he wanted to do. He seemed confused. I asked him if he wanted to go home. He looked shocked. "No way, why would I want to go home? I'll just sit on a chair when we play or something." My heart swelled with joy. I loved Lewis. He understood what we were doing. He was of my own heart. We pressed on.

In Houston, we met up with Moz, the guy who wrote Oi Punk, and the first person to order anything from Plan-It-X. We stayed in touch with him once we found his address, and I spoke with him on the phone a few times. He really wanted to join us on tour. He wanted to play second guitar. He had assured me that he was good and that he had good equipment. I told him that we'd have to wait until we met him to make any kind of decision. We arrived late at night, while Lewis was passed out on painkillers. Moz met us in a parking lot and we followed him to his mom's house. We were all dead tired from the daylong drive and we wanted to sleep, but Moz wanted to talk. He tried to keep us up. He tossed pennies at us in the dark. In the morning, his girlfriend came over and they had sex in the bed right beside us. We all had to sleep in his bedroom because he didn't tell his mom that we were coming. He said that she would freak out if she found out we were there, so we were all crammed into his small bedroom, pretending to be asleep while they had sex. It was awkward. The next day, we figured out that he didn't know how to play any of our songs all the way through, and that he only had a small guitar amp. He kept assuring us that it would be loud enough and that he really did know the songs. Later that night, at the show that he had managed to get us onto, his friends kept wishing him luck on tour and telling him to have fun. I felt really bad, because I knew that he couldn't come with us. This guy from the band Dig Dug went home and got a pair of crutches for Lewis, which was really nice. Stan didn't have to carry him around anymore. It was pretty funny though, watching him carry Lewis into the bathrooms at truck stops in Texas. The show was terrible and no one watched us. Afterward, we broke Moz's heart by telling him the bad news. He was really upset, and so were we. It made me feel horrible, but it seemed like the right thing to do. Stan was angry with us for not letting Moz come. They had hit it off, and Stan had hoped for an ally on tour. It was the beginning of a rift between us. We apologized to Moz and promised to stay in touch. We did stay in touch. Many years later he became a Buddhist.

Texas was killing us. We drove north to Denton a day early. We were broke and hot and out of ideas, so we went to K-Mart to hang out in the A/C. We walked the cool isles and looked at stuff that we weren't going to buy. It didn't keep us entertained for long and we ended up sitting on some benches by the door. We figured we'd just sit there until someone told us to leave. This nice-looking guy in a button-up shirt came over and gave Lewis a flier for a show coming up in a week or so. He left and we passed it around. The guy came back inside and said, "Hey, are you guys in a band?"

"Yes," we said.

"Are you in Operation: Cliff Clavin?" he asked.

"Yeah," we answered at the same time.

"Do you have a place to stay tonight? Do you need one? My name is Steven by the way." We humbly and eagerly accepted his offer, then he took us to his house. It was called "The Bonnie Brea House." It had a huge living room and several extra mattresses for travelers to sleep on. Everyone we met there was so nice to us. That night, Steven took us to a swanky apartment complex and we jumped the fence to swim in the pool. The next day, he took us to a huge playground before the show and we played tag, treating the ground as hot lava. We climbed and jumped around and watched in amazement as our host performed ninja-like acts of grace. We were all in love with Steven. Not only did he save us from another hot night in the van, take us swimming, and take us to an awesome playground, but he was also handsome, charming, and sweet. The show was great too. We played at a punk frat house. As soon as we took the stage, this guy came out of nowhere and asked us who we were. We told him and he started chanting our name and waving an Indiana University T-shirt around. He got the crowd to chant with him. It was amazing. During our set, people threw beer cans and balled up pages from a phone book. That show was more fun than any other show that we'd ever played, and I mean ever. We didn't want to leave the next day and they didn't want us to leave either, so we stayed another day and ended up playing another show at a house called "The Mansion," in one of the few basements in Texas. Denton was so good to us. We all missed it when we left. We promised to come back.

We drove for hours into the emptiness of west Texas, on our way to Albuquerque. Texas is huge; it took a day. We played in a gigantic, empty parking lot behind a video store with Scared Of Chaka. The few people who were there were sitting on their cars, 100 yards or so away from us. I asked them to move closer. They didn't. My voice echoed through the alleyways. The next day, there was a show at the guitar player of Scared Of Chaka's house. We went with hopes of jumping on the bill, but David, the guy in charge, told us that there were too many bands already. We got in for free though. He also let us use his phone to make some tour calls. We still had a lot of holes that needed filling and we didn't have directions to most of our shows. The touring bands playing that show were The Bananas and The Four Eyes, two three-piece pop punk bands from California. We loved them. After the show, I went up to one of The Bananas to see if they had a CD for sale. They didn't, they only had a 7-inch. We walked down to what is now my favorite thing about Albuquerque, a 24-hour restaurant called The Frontier, and got fries and sodas. We talked about how much of a bummer it was that they didn't have a CD. They were so good! Then the idea struck me that we could release their CD on Plan-It-X. Up to this point, I had never really considered releasing anything other than tapes for other bands, but it made sense. The Bananas were great and people needed to hear them and they needed someone to help them be heard. We went back to the house and I told them about Plan-It-X and made my proposal.

They were really excited and they said yes! I was so glad that they did. I had no clue that it would take them nearly two years to record and send me their songs. By the time they did, Stan and Lewis had quit the band and Miranda and I were finally and totally done, but that night, with the bats flying around in the clear desert sky above our heads, the four us were united by our love of The Bananas and thrilled by the prospect of Plan-It-X becoming a real record label. I couldn't wait to tell Sam.

Denton, Texas, with a beer can caught in mid-flight.

The Bananas in Albuquerque.

Lewis on crutches at the Grand Canyon.

We didn't make any friends for a while after that night. We drove through the Mojave desert and someone tried to break into our van while we were sleeping in it at a rest stop. They had their kid stick his arm through our slightly opened window. We made some noise and they ran away. The van overheated from time to time and we'd have to pull over and wait for it to cool down. The heat was horrible, but we still had California—where we had 10 shows booked,—to look forward to. When we finally made it to the first one, we found out that it was cancelled and that the club was closed. This wasn't the first closed venue we had encountered, and we had started to expect it. When we got to our second show in California, there was no show. The cops had come the week beforehand and told them, "NO MORE SHOWS!"

We decided to call ahead to the next few cities to make sure everything was still cool before we wasted the gas finding out. It was a good thing that we did, because all but one of our California shows were were canceled. We had seven days before our next one, in Arcata, so we decided to go to Berkeley and hang out. We were really excited about it. That night, we drove from some dismal southern California city straight up to the Bay.

The first thing we did was find 924 Gilman Street, the legendary punk club. It was just a building attached to a cannery in an industrial area. There were no punks on the curb to welcome us. The door was locked and the lights were off. We moved on, to People's Park. Our tiny People's Park in Bloomington was named after the one in Berkeley and I couldn't wait to see it. I had heard so much about it in Fifteen songs. I knew that the next day we could eat free food from Food Not Bombs and I was sure that all the cool punk kids hung out there. We parked in front of the bathrooms and were relieved to find them still open so late at night. It was hell finding a bathroom that night. I was buzzing. I couldn't believe that I had made it to Berkeley!

A guy sitting on a stump near the toilets smiled at me and motioned for me to come closer. I was certain then, that this was the greatest place on earth. "Do you want to buy some crack?" he asked. I laughed because I assumed he was joking. He wasn't. He held up plastic bag and waved it at me. I stopped laughing and politely declined. We got back in the van and drove away. We drove around looking for a 24-hour place and ended up in a Taco Bell. The next day, we went back to the park and it was much nicer. We ate delicious, free slop out of plastic buckets, courtesy of Food Not Bombs. It was great, eating free food and laying in the cool grass. It was also the Fourth of July.

These hippies brought a bunch of TVs into the park and smashed them with hammers, then burned some American flags and gave a rousing speech against the newly built volleyball courts in the corner of the park. Apparently, they were put there in an attempt to try to cut down on sleeping places for homeless people in the park, and to clean up its image by offering something for yuppies to do there. Before we knew it, we joined their mob and started ransacking the courts, which were surrounded by a wooden fence, a fence which we quickly tore to shreds. The nets were ripped off of their poles, then the poles were shaken until they were loose and pulled out of the ground. One of the hippies yelled something about ruining the sand and went back to the stage and started gathering up chunks of broken glass and TV parts. He threw them into the sand. Others joined him. The cops showed up pretty quickly, but they didn't enter the park. They just stood around on the sidewalk, surrounding it, with cameras and notepads, taking pictures and writing things down. A local explained that this was common behavior. He said that the cops were afraid to come into the park and that, instead, they just took notes and tried to bust people when they were alone, but we weren't afraid. We were inspired and fearless.

Later that day, I called Sam to wish him a happy birthday, but he was asleep. His dad promised to tell him that I had called.

It seemed weird to leave Berkley. Even though it didn't live up to my high expectations and punk rock fantasies, even though Aaron Cometbus wasn't hanging out at Blondie's Pizza, it was still really nice, and, after a week of hanging out on Telegraph and sleeping in the van, it felt like home, but we were on tour and we had a show to play. We headed north.

Arcata was great. The people were really nice and I tried nutritional yeast for the first time. I used way too much, but I liked it. We played with a crusty punk band from Canada called Submission Hold, and they were awesome. It was worth going on tour just to see them. Fifteen years later, I was playing a solo show in Berlin, and I bumped into a guy who had lived at that house. He remembered seeing us play. I asked him, "Didn't Arcata have a vegan-punk mayor back then?"

He laughed and said, "Yeah, they did, it was me."

The rest of the Northwest was okay, and the shows were okay too, but we were getting kind of tired of cancellations and sleeping in the van. The northwestern punks crossed their arms and looked bored when we played, but the scenery was great. We stopped a lot and swam in mountain streams or climbed around on rocks. We loved it. Lewis said, "This is the most beautiful place I've ever seen." We didn't argue.

We had three days to make it from Spokane, Washington to Chicago, with no shows in between. We decided to try to drive as quickly as possible so that we could hang out in Chicago. It seemed like a good idea. We made it in around 28 hours and regretted it right away. Chicago was too big and ugly and Midwestern. We weren't ready for it. We should have taken our time and eased out of the West. We tried to go swimming in the lake, but couldn't find anywhere to park that we could afford. I accidentally turned into a bike path and noticed my mistake right away. As I was backing up, a biker had to stop and wait for me to get out of his way. I leaned out and apologized very sincerely and told him that I felt like an idiot. He looked at me through his mirrored lenses and screamed, "Fucking Asshole!" I hated Chicago.

We decided to drive south, out of the city, and to kill time for the two days until our show. We didn't care where we went, as long as it was small town. We ended up in Kankakee for some reason and spent most of our time at the Denny's there. It was horrible and hot, not west coast hot or desert hot, but sticky, Midwest hot.

The show was really weird. We played with Strung Out and Diesel Boy. They were traveling in a real tour bus. The show was at The Fireside Bowl and it was sold out and packed. When we played, the punks stood back as far as the crowded venue allowed. After one song, someone yelled, "Play a fast one!"

Lewis said, "That was one of our fast ones." We were pretty sure they hated us, but after our set, Miranda told us that she'd sold around 30 CDs and a dozen T-shirts. One of the guys from Diesel Boy asked me how we could afford to sell our stuff so cheap. I explained that we made it all ourselves really cheaply.

He seemed confused and asked, "What about the shirts? Where do you get them printed?" I told him that we printed them ourselves. He looked amazed and sincerely said, "That's a great idea!" This was my first encounter with Fat Wreck Chords punks, and I couldn't wait to tell Sam about it.

We played a few more shows, then decided to skip Detroit and go home. None of us wanted to go to another big city. Chicago had weakened our grit. We were beat. We had to drive through Chicago again on our way home, and we stopped for a few minutes and sat by the lake. We had done what we set out to do, we toured. We were done.

I dropped everyone off and went to my parents' house for a few days to rest and watch TV and shower. Stan called and said, "I quit the band. I don't like touring and I know you guys want to tour a lot. I can't do it, sorry."

I called Lewis and told him. He was bummed. I asked him what he thought about tour. I asked if he wanted to quit too. "No way, this summer has been the best time of my life."

As awful as our tour was, I was in love. I couldn't wait to do it again.

I made a tour diary with one photo of each crowd we played for. Some of the photos are of a nearly empty room. It's a boring diary. The back cover was a breakdown of our tour:

MILES TRAVELED: 9,450

MONEY SPENT
GAS: $900.00
FOOD $1,000.00
LODGING: $0
REPAIRS: $114.00
TOTAL SPENT: $2014.00

MONEY EARNED
PAY: $536.00
CDs SOLD: 146 = $730.00
7"s SOLD: 23 = $67.00
SHIRTS SOLD: 19 = $95.00
PATCHES SOLD: 40 = $2.00
STICKERS SOLD: 30 = $7.50
OTHER STUFF: $168.00

So, subtracting what we earned from what we spent, the tour cost us $389.55 total. That's only $1.99 a day each, for a two month, 9,000 mile vacation.

Me, at the Grand Canyon. My first tour was rough, but I got to see the country.

CHAPTER 10
VAN LIFE

Tour was over, and I couldn't go back to the boring life in my parents' basement. I once again swore off the evils of late night TV, re-fried beans, chips and salsa, loneliness, and insomnia. I vowed to really make it work this time. I would stay in Bloomington no matter what. I had a van now, which was much better to live in than a car. I packed way less than I had ever packed when moving out before, and, once again, I moved to Bloomington.

Lewis' dad was serious about cutting him off, and refused to pay for his next year of school. He also told him that he had to move out or start paying rent, so Lewis and his girlfriend moved to Bloomington too. They rented an apartment in the Alpine Terrace, which was an ugly gray complex where the windows faced inward, toward the parking lot. It seems to me the nicer the name of an apartment complex, the uglier it is.

It was cool having Lewis in town and, once we found a new drummer in Bloomington, we would all be in the same place for once. It was an exciting thought, being able to practice without driving all over Indiana. All we had to do was find this drummer.

I lived in my van for around a month before some friends offered their garage to me. It was pretty cool, except I shared it with a beagle that shit all over the place. I re-arranged things and made a room that the dog couldn't get into. I built a loft in the rafters for my bed. It was nice. I felt sorry for the dog. His owner didn't let him in the house or play with him very often, so I was glad to be there with him, even if I had to pick up his shit. He was a sweet pup and it was a cool place to live.

I started hanging out with my straight edge friend Brian Munn a lot. He had opened a skate shop downtown and he was always there, easy to find. He secretly lived in the back room. Brian and Suzuki—Sam's old crush—started dating, and she was always around. One night, we started talking about Sam and how much we all missed him. I told them about my phone calls and about Sam's "24-hour" sleep schedule. They were rightfully freaked out. We all wanted to do something to get him back. When I was digging through my things trying to figure out what to bring to Bloomington, I found one of Sam's old notebooks from the Henderson house/days of chaos era. I remembered it being filled with random doodles, rants, essays, and some math equations. I was excited to show it to them, since we were having a serious Sam admiration session. I went out to the van and crawled under the loft with my mini-mag-light to look for it. When I found it and started flipping through the pages, I realized that Sam had torn out most of the interesting stuff. Around half of it was missing. I did find one page, hidden between some physics homework that was worth my search. This is what it said:

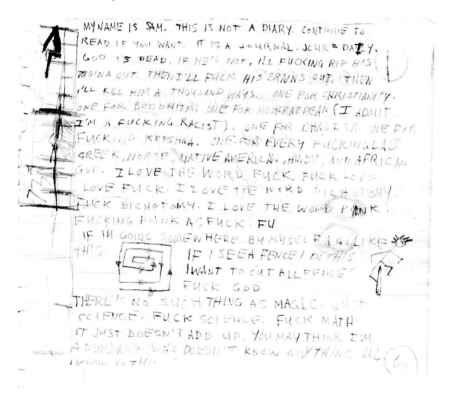

"My name is Sam. This is not a diary. Continue to read if you want. It is a Journal. Jour=daily. God is dead. If he's not, I'll fucking rip his vagina out. Then I'll kill him a thousand different ways. One for Christianity, one for Buddhism, one for Mohamaddean (I admit I'm a fucking racist), one for Dhaoism, one for fucking Krishna, one for every fucking last Greek, Norse, Native American, Hindu and African American god. I love the

word fuck. Fuck love. Love fuck. I love the word dichotomy. Fuck dichoto my. I love the word punk. Fucking punk and fuck. Fu... If I'm going some where by myself I go like this (see the next page) If I see a fence I do this (see the next page). I want to cut all fences. Fuck god. There is no such thing as magic. Just science. Fuck science. Fuck math. It just doesn't add up. You may think I'm a dumbass who doesn't know anything at all, I know this..."

The next page had been ripped out. "What did Sam know?" we wondered. We decided that this scrap of paper was meaningful and much more complex than it appeared at a casual glance. It challenged all religions as well as science and magic. It defied land ownership and tradition. We jokingly agreed that we would follow the philosophy of Sam and start our own religion around this one-page bible. We would become Samist. We would walk the streets in spirals and jump or cut fences when we came to them. We would love the word punk. We would love the word fuck. We worked ourselves into a frenzy that night with our fanatical new religion, and ended up making two different stencils of Sam. One was a silhouette of with a spiked mohawk and his name at the bottom. The other one was similar, but said "In Sam We Trust" at the bottom. We took to the streets, in spirals of course, and we spray painted the image of our beloved god throughout the alleyways of Bloomington. We agreed that if we did this kind of thing enough, our great leader would return. Of course, we knew without a doubt that he would hate our religion. We were sure he would say, "Fuck Samism!" but that was fine with us, because once Sam returned, we could disband. The need for our work would be over. The universe would be in order again. Sam would be back in town.

The fury of the night died down with the others, but I stayed devote. There were no more nights of fence hopping and vandalizing in the name of our de- ity, but our work lived on and helped to build the legend of Sam. People were talking about him. They wanted to know who this Sam guy was. My friends assumed that I was involved, of course. Some of them thought that Sam was secretly in town and had done the stencils himself. He would never do that. I got a job at the same dish room that Sam had worked at the year before. I liked the idea of doing the same thing that Sam had done. I would be washing the same dishes, in the same place, and I would be homeless, just like Sam was. I called it "walking the path of Sam."

Brian Munn, in People's Park, around the time I first met him.

Drawing, by Sam

We started looking for a drummer. At first we tried out a few of our friends, including Austin Lucas, but none of them could really play drums, and none of them were nearly as good as Stan, so we kept looking. We ended up making a flier:

We got two calls. The first one was from a 30-year-old guy who played in a death metal band. He said that he had never played punk music but had always wanted to give it a try. I told Lewis not to call him back. I didn't think that a death metal drummer would work out and, back then, I thought that 30 was really old. Now I'm 38 and frequently start bands with younger people, and I'm glad they don't discriminate against me the way I did him. The other call was from a local kid who was still in high school. Lewis said, "I think he's foreign or something, because he doesn't speak English very well." I asked Lewis to tell me everything that he had learned about him during their phone call. He said, "Well, he told me that he had just gotten back from Okinawa and that he loved our flier. He said that he ate meat and smoked cigarettes, but that's all, and he agreed with everything else on the flier and wanted to have a tryout." We talked it over and agreed that we should give him a chance.

A few days later, we met the kid downtown. He was wearing old man golfer pants and a white dress shirt. He had bleached blond hair, spiked straight up, and black eyeliner around his eyes. He was very short and didn't appear to be Japanese. After a few minutes of talking, I figured out why Lewis had thought that he didn't speak English. He had a thick stutter, but it got better as he started to feel more comfortable with us. His name was Frankie. He had spent the last two years living with his father on a military base in Okinawa, Japan. He told us that he knew how to play drums and would play any show, anytime, and that he would skip school if he needed to. We decided to see what he could do. We went to my garage, I picked up a few dog turds, then we starting playing. He was fast and he hit the drums really hard. We went over a few songs and he learned them right away. After around 20 minutes, I asked him if he would be ready to play a show in three days. You see, we had a show booked at a record store in Anderson, Indiana with J-Church, and we were assuming that we would have to cancel it since we had no drummer, but we really didn't want to. We were both really excited about playing with J-Church, so we just kept looking and hoping we'd find someone in time.

Three days wasn't much time, but Frankie said, "Yeah, for sure" without hesitation, which was a good sign. We practiced every day—after he got out of school—and he learned around 15 songs. We were a band again and it felt good.

The show with went well. We played fast and tight and really gave it our all. Lance, the main J-church guy, seemed to like us a lot. It was a good night. Later, Frankie went up to Lance and told him about Plan-It-X, which he had just learned about three days beforehand, and asked him if J-Church would be interested in doing a split 7-inch with us, on Plan-It-X. Lance said, "Yeah that would be cool." Frankie came over and told me about it. He was excited and stuttering. I was pretty angry. I couldn't understand why he would think that he had the right to make an offer like that, and he couldn't understand why I was angry. As time went by, I got used to Frankie doing this kind of stuff, but that night I was pissed. Despite his overstepping, Lewis and I both agreed that

135

he was a good drummer and had the attitude that we needed in the band. We decided to keep him.

Meanwhile, I was walking the path of Sam. I washed dishes three to four days a week, and all the money I made went into my wallet. I wasn't paying rent, I had no bills, and I ate free food for the most part. I got it from the pizza dumpsters, the dorm dining halls, the dish-room leftovers, the First United Methodist Church, and the shoplifter-friendly shelves of my local supermarkets. I worked, practiced, hung out downtown, then went home to sleep in my garage. It wasn't a bad life. I had a band again, I was saving up money for tour and recording, and Miranda and I had stopped fighting. We barely saw each other, but when we did it was friendly and fine. I did, however, miss Sam. I really missed Sam. No matter how good things were, there was something missing.

I started a letter writing campaign. I recruited the help of the other Samist slackers and we all wrote a letter to Sam, begging him to come home. None of us got anything back. I started to imagine what life in his house was like. He was in his room sleeping and the letters were probably just tossed on a desk or stacked in a pile somewhere. I doubted that he would ever notice them, so I got the idea to send something bigger and harder to miss. I wrote a letter that just said "Dear Sam, we all miss you, please come home. Love, Chris" and I put it in a huge cardboard box. I drew all over the outside of the box. I wrote things that only Sam would get - inside jokes and song lyrics—and I drew a chaos symbol in red ink. Nothing happened.

A few weeks later, I went to a thrift store and shoplifted a cute little stuffed rabbit. Sam loved rabbits. When I first met him, he had two beloved rabbit friends, Speedy and Rabbi. He had lost both of them when he was a homeless dishwasher and it broke his heart. He talked about it as if he had lost his children. He was filled with guilt about it. I had a plan to try to cheer him up and wake him from his slumber with a rabbit. I named it Gunther and I mailed it to him in a tiny box with a note, typed on the typewriter in the library. It said, "Dear Sam, my name is Gunther and I have no home and no one to care for me. I have heard that you are a rabbit lover and have been known to help rabbits in need. Can you help me?" I waited a few days and nothing happened. I was running out of ideas, then I thought of a new approach.

I tracked down Sam's brother, who had started going to the university, and told him about my concerns for Sam. I begged him to wake Sam up and make him open my mail. He said that he would when he went home that weekend. I didn't know if he would or not. I was worried that their dad had too much sway over him. I was worried that he thought that I was Sam's wicked homosexual sex master too. But it was something, and I had to keep my hopes up. If it didn't work, my next plan was to drive there and kidnap him.

A few days later, I was playing guitar in the garage when someone pounded on the door. It scared the shit out of me. I froze for a second, assuming it was someone who came over to complain about something, or an angry landlord that found out I was living in the garage. They pounded again and said, "Are there any punks in there?" It was Sam, I knew it. Well, I thought it was, but I didn't want to get my hopes up. I rushed outside, and there he was in all of his messy glory. He looked wild. His hair was long and ratty and his face had random patches of beard that he had missed while shaving. He had also nicked himself a few times, and there were spots of dried blood on his chin. He was wearing thin-framed John Lennon style glasses. I couldn't believe it was really him. I grabbed him and hugged him and couldn't stop laughing with joy! "How did you get here?" I asked.

"I rode this bike," he said, pointing to the bulky white cruiser he had leaned against the garage door. He had misunderstood my question. I noticed he was really out of breath.

"No, I mean, how did you get to Bloomington?"

"Oh, yeah, sorry, my brother gave me a ride this morning. I've been looking all over for you. Someone told me you were living in a garage by the mall, that's all I knew." I thought about the bike and asked him where he got it. He looked guilty and said, "I stole it from downtown, it was unlocked, how else could I get all the way out here to look for you?" I realized that he was really tired and took him into the house for some water. He looked crazy. I asked him about the 24-hour sleep schedule, and he confirmed that it was true. He told me that he really did sleep almost all day, everyday. He'd wake up every now and then and eat a can of re-fried beans, then go back to bed.

Sam said that he was tired and really hungry, so we walked to McDonalds, the closest place to get some fries and soda. Again, this was before we knew that they coated their fries in beef fat, not that we should have been eating at McDonalds anyway, but we needed fries and we needed fries quickly. I ordered us both a super-sized tub of fries and one large soda to split and refill until we were sick. Sam sat in a booth, looking really weak and pale, and waited for me.

When I came back to the table, I handed him the soda. He took a huge gulp and tried to set it down on the table, but he missed the table by around eight inches. He dropped it on the floor and it exploded. A grumpy old man gave us a dirty look and I met his glare with a furious vengeance. He had no right to look at Sam that way. I went and got us a refill and we moved to a drier part of the restaurant. After a few fries and half a soda, Sam got sick and had to go puke. He was loud and everyone in the place could hear him. I got more evil eyes. He came out with some vomit on his pants and finished his food.

Later that night, I gave him a haircut, and he shaved off the remnants of his beard. He started to look like Sam again. We went downtown to look for pizza and to see who was hanging out. Sam decided that he wanted popcorn, so he walked into the movie theater next to People's Park and got a huge popcorn bucket out of the trash. He took it straight to the counter and asked for a refill. They gave it to him and he came back, smiling, with a mouthful of popcorn.

"How did you get that?" I asked.

"I just walked in and asked for it," he said. The theater had a free refill policy, but obviously, it only applied to people who were seeing a movie and had bought popcorn there. Sam just walked past the ticket taker and the concession stand, into a theater, dug through the trash until he found the biggest bucket he could find, then took it right back to the counter and asked for a refill. Clearly, they knew what he had just done, the place was really small, but they didn't care, or they were too afraid of saying no to Sam. This kind of stuff happened all the time with Sam. He used to hang out in front of the ice cream shop and wait for people to come out with their cones. He'd step up to them and say, "Hey! Are you gonna eat all of that? Can I have it?" Most of the time, they would just step around him and walk away with a look of disgust or fear on their face, but around half the time, they would hand him their half-eaten ice cream cone. Of course, most people would be grossed out by the thought of licking someone's used cone, but Sam didn't mind.

We sat on the 'U' (a statue in the park) and ate popcorn while Sam told me about his year in bed. He told me that he didn't open the box with Gunther in it until 2 A.M. the night before. When he saw the rabbit and read the note he decided to get out of bed and stay out of bed. He took a shower and started shaving. His dad knocked on the bathroom door and Sam let him in. His dad was shocked to see him up.

"Why are you shaving?" he asked.

"Isn't it good that I'm out of bed? Isn't it good that I'm shaving?" His dad didn't want him to leave. He tried to convince him to just stay for a while and talk about it, but Sam was tired of him. He was tired of sleeping.

Sam was wide awake and ready to make up for lost time. We greatly increased our criminal activities. We broke into buildings on campus and stole random stuff, we shoplifted books from corporate stores and sold them to local stores, we stole food, we did coupon scams and return scams, and just about anything else we could think of. We were ruthless and relentless and we were living like kings. Like kings who lived in a dusty garage with a beagle. The leaves were turning red and yellow, and we had fire in our eyes that matched their colors.

One day, we were hanging out a friend's house and rooting through the random stuff—mostly old clothes and useless junk—that had been left in the basement by various past tenants over the years, when we found a checkbook. It was obviously outdated and we were sure that the account would be closed, but we took it, just for fun. Later that night, Sam suggested that we try to use the checkbook to get a pizza. "I'm sure that the driver won't make us show I.D., and there is no way the driver will know if the account is active or not," he said. I agreed that it was worth a shot. We walked to the student union to call in the order since we knew that it would be a bad idea to have it delivered to the house in front of my garage or to a friend's house. We didn't want them to be able to find us when they figured out that we were using bad checks. Sam called in the order from the free phone in the lobby. "Me and some friends are studying in the student union, can you deliver here?" he asked. "Great, thanks...Can I get two large pizzas with all the veggies and extra cheese?" He looked at me and raised and eyebrow. "Yeah, could we get a two liter of Doctor Pepper too? Thanks, okay, I'll be here." He hung up the phone, then all we had to do was wait and worry. We had no idea what the driver would say when Sam pulled out the checkbook. Would the driver ask for an I.D.? Would he or she demand it? We didn't know. We waited and hoped for pizza.

Thirty minutes later, the driver pulled up. I waited inside, out of sight. A few seconds later, Sam came through the revolving door with our prize!

"What happened?" I asked.

"Nothing," he said. "He just looked at the check to make sure it was the right amount and put it in his pocket." That pizza was great. We ate our fill and gave the rest to this homeless guy who was always hanging out in the union. We both thought it would be a bad idea to use the checkbook again.

A few days later, we figured that it would be safe try it again, as long as we called a different pizza place. It worked without a hitch. Again, the driver didn't care at all. The checkbook had six more checks in it, and we decided to use them all. It seemed too easy to do and too hard to get caught.

Greg Wells was happy to hear that Sam was back from the dead and came up to Bloomington to hang out with us. It was weird having a visitor when you don't really have a house, but Greg was gristly and didn't mind the Spartan accommodations. We went to the union and got a few pizzas to celebrate. It was Sunday night, so we ate our ill-gotten pizza and watched The Simpsons on the big TV. Greg hated all vegetables and was a Vegan, so we got breadsticks for him and a pizza with extra cheese for us. We always got extra cheese. It would be our downfall.

The next day, we were downtown hanging out with Miranda on the wall in front of the park. It was pretty warm for that time of year, so Sam and I got Den cokes. It felt good to be with old friends, downtown, sipping huge sodas. The sun felt nice on my face. I saw this girl that I had seen around town a few times and thought was cute. She came to an Operation: Cliff Clavin show at the radio station on campus once, but left before we played. I called her the blue backpack girl, since she had a shiny blue backpack. I pointed her out to Sam. She started walking toward us. I quietly said to Sam, "It looks like she's gonna do a walk by and smile." He laughed. She kept coming.

She stopped right in front of me and said, "Hi."

I said something, I'm not sure what.

Sam said "Hey how's it going? I'm Sam." He raised his hand to wave. She didn't notice. I saw his hand in the corner of my eye as it sadly sank in defeat.

"My name is Hannah," she said.

"Cool," I said. Greg and Miranda were just sitting silently, watching me try to talk to this girl.

"What's your name?" she asked. I realized that I was supposed to tell her my name after she told me hers, instead of saying, "Cool." I felt so dumb, but there was nothing I could do. I was helpless, but not in a trapped animal kind of way. I was helplessly enchanted by the blue backpack girl. I told her my name. She kept trying to keep some form of conversation flowing. She said "It's such a nice day today, so warm."

"Yeah," I said. She swayed about with school books in her arms, not willing to give up on me, no matter how horribly boring I must have seemed.

"Do you know of any good places to eat around here?" she asked.

I dumbly asked, "In Bloomington?" as if I was from out of town, or new to town.

"Yeah, in Bloomington."

I don't know what was wrong with me. "I'm not sure really…"

"Me either," she said, which made me think that she was new to town herself. I thought that she must be a new college student. She kept trying to get me to hang out with her. She said that she was going to go for walk and enjoy the day, no doubt hoping that I would ask to join her. I didn't. She told me that she lived close by and had food at home, and that she would probably just walk home and eat something. I didn't bite on that either. All I could think about was the fact that I had missed a patch of hair when I was shaving that morning. I wished that I had been more thorough. After all of those failures, she said goodbye and that she'd see me around.

I said, "Nice meeting you," and she walked away.

She was only around 10 feet away when Greg loudly asked, "What the fuck was that?" Miranda looked angry, but she knew that there was no reason to be, so she didn't say anything. Greg was furious though, he said, "I've never seen anything like that in my life and you just sat there like a chump. That girl was way into you. She was dropping all kinds of hints and you were being so cold. What's wrong, don't you think she's cute?" I told him that I wasn't worried about it. I admitted that I thought she was very cute and that I had a crush on her already. "Why didn't you talk to her then?" he asked.

"I don't know, I guess I'm just not worried about it. I'm sure I'll see her again, then I'll talk to her." I don't know why I was so confident in us meeting again, but I really believed it. I could feel a real connection with her right away, and I knew that I had no reason to be hasty. I knew that I'd see her again. Greg wouldn't drop it. He was sure that I had just missed a once in a lifetime chance.

A few days later, Lewis tracked me down. He was really excited. Some guy from Canada had called him and asked him if Operation: Cliff Clavin wanted to play with Propagandhi in Thunder Bay on the Fourth of December, which was less than a month away. He said that he told the guy yes already. I was worried. It was a long drive, and coming up too soon to book a tour to get us there and back. He told me not to worry and that he would pay for all the gas with his own money. He said that he didn't want to miss the chance to play with Propagandhi. I couldn't argue with that. I was excited too. I loved Propagandhi, and I imagined that playing with them in Canada would be great. I was also excited to leave the country for the first time in my life. I had never heard of Thunder Bay and had no clue what it would be like, but I couldn't wait to find out.

We started to feel guilty about our pizza crimes. Not guilty because we were ripping off corporate pizza places, but guilty because we felt selfish. We had so much pizza and so many other people had so little. We also felt bad about eating cheese, as we were both struggling vegans, but we couldn't resist cheese pizza when it was free. We justified it in our minds. Since we were stealing it from the evil companies, we considered it "even stevens" or as we came to call it, vegan stevens, but we wanted to do something good with our pizza power. Sam came up with the idea of ordering a bunch of vegan pizzas for the animal rights group that met on campus. Lewis worked at a snack bar in the building where they held their meetings, and there was a phone in his office that we used to call in the order. Sam ordered seven large, vegan pizzas with tons of toppings and a bunch of breadsticks. When they arrived, we carried everything upstairs and left it outside the door of the meeting room. We knocked on the door and ran away. One of our friends was a member of the group, and we asked him about it the next day. We were really disappointed when he told us that people were kind of freaked out about it.

"Did they think it was poisoned?" Sam asked.

"I don't know, they just thought it was weird," he said.

We dressed like rednecks or college students when we went shoplifting. I had a nice sweater that I dumpstered and called "the lady-killer" because I looked pretty good in it. Sam had a thick flannel jacket that made him look like a country boy, wholesome and harmless, and the jacket could hold a lot of loot too. On our way to the mall one day, we decided to stop at Fazoli's to eat free breadsticks and drink obscene amounts of free soda. Fazoli's is an Italian fast food place that has free breadsticks. We went there all the time. We'd go in and sit down at a dirty table, with dishes and cups still on it, and wait for the breadstick boy to come by. He knew we didn't buy any food, but he didn't care. He liked us. I think he had a soft spot for dirty punks, even when we were in disguise. He would bring a basket of breadsticks around and ask us how many we wanted. Most people said one or two, but we would say "six please." A lot of times he would just bring us a bagful without even asking us. We'd also take the cups left behind by the last people to sit at our table and we'd fill them with free soda. It was a golden age of free stuff. Of course we felt like buttery death by the time we left.

We decided to go all out this time, since we had so much extra cash. We decided to order a large plate of pasta to split. I got in line, looking good in my lady-killer, then I noticed Hannah there, working, and I felt weird. I didn't want her to see us in our shoplifting costumes. I stepped over to the longer line so that she wouldn't be the one to take my order, then Sam came out of the bathroom. I made him take my place so that I wouldn't even have to get close to her. I found a table in the corner that was out of the line of sight of the counter. I nervously waited for Sam to come back with our spaghetti. We ate and lay low, then she came out into the dining room. She was giving someone directions. She looked over at us and smiled. We were busted. Later, she would confess that she did it on purpose to get a look at us. We snuck out with bellies full of gluten, oil, and soda, and continued on our quest. At the mall, we stuffed our pants as full as our bellies.

Now that I knew where Hannah worked, I knew where I could find her. For the next few days, I got Sam to walk past Fazoli's with me, in hopes of seeing her. Sometimes we'd go in and use the bathroom just to see if she was working. She wasn't there. Three days went by until we saw her sitting on the hood of her red ford escort smoking. "Yuck," I thought, "smoking is gross." I chickened out. I didn't want to talk to her. I told Sam that we should abort the mission. We tried to swing wide through the parking lot and sneak past her, but she spotted us and yelled, "Hey guys, come here." We had to listen to her. We chatted awkwardly for a while. She talked about how happy she was that tomorrow was Thursday and that she didn't have to work. She asked me if I had any plans.

"No," I said. She said that she didn't have any plans either. I said that I'd probably just hang out downtown. She said that she would probably do the same thing when she got out of school. I found out that she was still in high school, but at least she was a senior. Her smoke filled my lungs and I tried not to cough. Her break was ending, and she had to go back to work. We said goodbye without exchanging numbers or making any solid plans to meet up.

The next day, I took a shower, shaved, and planned on hanging out downtown all day, starting at 3 P.M. Sam came with me to keep me company in case she didn't show up. Lewis walked by, and when we told him what we were up to, he joined us. He was certain that she wouldn't come. Sam bet him that she would. The wager was a Den coke. A few minutes later, I spotted the shiny blue backpack, walking down Kirkwood. She saw us from across the street and waved. She walked over to us and said, "Hi."

Sam looked at Lewis and said, "I think you owe me a coke." Lewis laughed, but Sam gave him a serious look and he realized that he was trying to leave us alone together.

"Okay, let's go," Lewis said. "Nice meeting you Hannah," he added as he walked away. Hannah laughed and I'm sure she thought we were all a bunch of weirdos.

We sat on the benches in front of Ben & Jerry's and talked until the sun started to set. She asked me if I had a job and I said, "No way, I don't have a job. Why would anyone want a job? Life's too short to have a job." She smiled. I decided before our meeting that I wasn't going to try to impress her. I was going to be myself and nothing more. She asked me what I did and I said, "I play music and I hang out with my friends." She asked me where I lived and how I afforded rent without a job. I told her that I'd been living in my van for a while, but that I just moved into a friend's garage, for free, and that I ate from dumpsters or got free food at the church.

"That's cool, you sound like you're living free. I've always wanted to live in a van." We hung out all night. We drove to the fire tower out in the woods and waited for the moon to show up, though it never did. We ended up in my van in the parking lot behind the park, making out until the sun came up again. In the morning, she went to school and I went back to my garage and crawled into bed next to Sam.

Sam's toenails fell off, all of them. We were both really freaked out about it. He went to the doctor and they told him that it was because of malnutrition. He told them that he stayed in bed for nearly a year and asked if that could have had anything to do with it. The doctor said that it most certainly did. He told Sam not to worry, that his toenails would grow back.

Miranda asked me about Hannah, and I told her everything. She didn't get upset. I told her that it was really over between us, and she didn't argue. She was hanging out with a guy from Indianapolis anyway and she had plans to spend her birthday with him. We were both ready to move on. It was good. We didn't see each other very much at all after that.

I hung out with Hannah as much as I could before our trip to Canada. Sam and I told her about our criminal activities and she wasn't freaked out. She ate scammed pizza with us in the student union. We started getting two or three pizzas every time and a few extra bottles of soda too, for the in-between times. We invited other people to come to our pizza parties. We told some of them what we were doing, but we kept most in the dark. We started tipping the drivers a lot. We realized that they got to keep the tip even after the checked turned out to be fraudulent. We thought it would be nice to help them out, and it made them a lot more agreeable to the idea of taking a check from someone without an I.D. when they saw the $10 extra on the check.

When we ran out of checks, Sam crossed a line that we had not crossed before. He grabbed an unattended backpack and looted it. He found a new checkbook and tossed the rest of this innocent person's stuff in a trashcan. We became real villains. We were bad guys. We didn't care. We considered the college kids to be our enemies. In fact, we considered most people to be our enemies. Sam didn't steal that person's stuff, he appropriated it. He liberated it. He took it from someone that didn't need it. That's what we thought, and that's how we justified it. We were mean and dumb. The backpack belonged to a girl, which was bad because the checks had her name on them. We didn't know if the drivers would take checks from us that obviously were not ours and we didn't want to get Hannah involved. We tried it out and it worked. A few times they would ask where Becky was, and Sam would say, "She's upstairs with our study group, do you want me to go get her?" and they always said no. Once or twice, Sam had to write his name and social security number on the check. He wrote: Steve Archer, 138-69-2323. It was his alias. He was Steve Archer and I was Matt Blue. This new checkbook was nearly full. It seemed like we'd be eating free pizza for many nights to come.

Lewis left a spooky message on our voicemail. He said that we should call him or come over right away, he had something important to tell us, so we went to his house that night. He told us that two police detectives came into his work that day and interrogated him about the seven pizzas that were ordered from the phone in his office. They accused him of being involved. They told him that only three other people had access to that phone. They tried to scare him, but he didn't crack. He swore to them that he didn't know what they were

144

talking about. They believed him for some reason, then went on to tell him details of the case. They told him they were looking for two people who used bad checks to order pizzas to the student union and occasionally to Collins dorm. They said that the crooks only ordered vegetarian pizzas and always got extra cheese. They knew which pizza places they ordered from and they were working with those places to catch the culprits. Lewis asked them what would happen to the people when they were caught, and the cops said they would be charged with forgery and potentially face many years in prison for each bad check that they wrote, but then they said that the chances of catching them were really slim. They said that because the pizza drivers didn't care, it was really hard to catch them in the act, and they had to be caught in the act of handing over the forged check. As the cops left, one of them said, "It's the best thing a thief can do with a check book."

We were pretty scared, but we also thought it was funny. We were grateful that Lewis hadn't sold us out and we were glad to know that we were wanted criminals. It was good to know that they were looking for us before they got us. Lewis said, "you guys should probably quit using those checks, before you get caught." We agreed. It was spooky, they knew that there was two of us and that they knew where were hung out and what kind of pizza we liked. We left and talked about it as we walked around town. At first, we totally agreed with one another that we should throw the checkbook away and not look for another one, but then we decided to keep it and just chill out for a while. We were going to Canada for a week anyway. It would be a good break and we'd be far away for a while. We could make our final decision when we got back. It also seemed that since we knew where they were looking and which pizza places they were working with, we could avoid being caught by changing our methods. We'd sleep on it.

It was a 24-hour drive to Thunder Bay. Sam and Christy (Lewis's girl-friend) came with us. I tried to convince Hannah to skip school and come too, but she wouldn't do it. We decided to go a few days early so we could hang out in Canada, because we thought it would be fun. The drive was horrible. It was long and cold and dark most of the time. When we got to the border, they asked us a lot of questions that we didn't expect them to ask. Lewis was driving because I thought he looked more clean-cut than me and Christy was sitting shotgun. "What are you guys planning on doing in Canada?" the guy asked.

"We're going to visit a friend," Lewis answered.

The border guard peered into the van. "You guys look young, are you still in school?" I don't know why Lewis lied, but he did.

"Yes," he said. "We all go to Indiana University, we're all students."

"But shouldn't you be in school right now?" he asked.

"No, we're on Thanksgiving break, it lasts for a few more days." Our interrogator was starting to look at us suspiciously.

"Still on break? But doesn't your Christmas break start soon?" he asked.

"Yeah..." Lewis said.

The guy changed the subject. "How much money do you have on you?"

Lewis looked surprised and asked, "Me, personally?"

"Yeah, you," the guy said, looking a little annoyed. Lewis pretended to calculate in his head and lied again for no reason.

"$4,000."

The guy told us to pull over for more questioning and searching. Other bands had warned us about Canada's strict policy, so we didn't bring music equipment, and we hid our CDs and T-shirts in the dash and door panels. We knew that if they found them, we'd be fined and denied entrance, we just had to hope they didn't find them. They questioned us one at a time in a tiny room, trying to catch us telling different stories. Somehow we all managed to give them the same answers. Luckily for us, they didn't ask Lewis where his $4,000 was and they didn't do a thorough search of the van. We were just about to be turned lose in their country when they asked us to empty our pockets and back packs. I wasn't too worried since I knew that none of us had anything illegal, then Sam tossed his phone dialer onto the table. I couldn't believe that he had it in his pocket. We all tried to stay calm.

The guy picked it up and asked, "What the heck is this?"

Sam looked nervous. "It's a phone dialer, it stores phone numbers." I stayed quiet and hoped that he had never heard of our payphone scamming gadget. He flipped it over in his hands, scrutinizing it. We waited for him to push the button and to hear that noise that mimics the sound a quarter being dropped in the slot. I hoped that Canadian payphones were different than U.S. ones, and that maybe they didn't make the same noise, maybe he wouldn't recognize it, even if he pushed the button.

After a few long seconds he asked, "What, do you guys put your weed in here?" We all laughed. He didn't. Then he slid the battery cover off and took out the batteries, which was great, because when you take the batteries out of a dialer, the device resets its self and has to be reprogrammed. Our secret was safe. They let us go, and I crossed my first invisible and meaningless border. I left the United States for the first time.

It started snowing. The roads were white and the sky was black. When we got to our host's house, we spotted an outdoor, public iceskating rink in the parking lot. I had never been iceskating, so I ran over to the ice and started sliding around. Everyone else came too. It was fun, but after around five minutes we all started to go numb. There was a bank clock/thermometer nearby and it read -19 degrees. We got our bags from the van and went to meet our host. He was shy but nice, and he welcomed us in. We were two days early for our show, and it was really nice of him to let us stay at his house. He made us spaghetti. He told us that he didn't know how to make vegan food, so he just bought all the ingredients and put them together. It was the worst spaghetti I'd ever eaten. The sauce was made of tomato paste with raw garlic and onion thrown in. When you lifted a forkful of noodles, the sauce slid completely off, leaving clean white pasta. We took turns covertly dumping our soupy sauce down the drain once our plain noodles were eaten up. I don't mean to sound ungrateful, I'm just amazed at how bad it was. I've been touring for over 15 years now and I've yet to encounter anything as awful. It's good to be the worst. It's like when a band is the worst band you've ever heard, at least you remember them. It's better to be the worst than the most mediocre.

While we were eating, he told us about his run-in with the cops. They came to his house, holding a flier for our show. They asked him if he was the one hanging them up. He told them that he was. They told him that he had to remove them all, or he would be arrested for hate crimes, or something like that. When he asked them to explain, they said "You can't hang up fliers that say anti-fascist and pro-gay." The flier that he made used the border from the latest Propagandhi album, "Less Talk, More Rock." Around the cover art, it reads "ANIMAL FRIENDLY, ANTI-FACIST, PRO-FEMINIST, GAY POSI-TIVE."

We asked him what he did. He said, "I had to take them all down." Thunder Bay wasn't making a very good first impression.

Our dreams of exploring the city faded quickly. We realized that there wasn't that much to see and that it was way too cold outside to do anything anyway. We surrendered to playing Kirby's Avalanche on Super Nintendo and eating peanut butter and jelly sandwiches. Frankie and our host started comparing our two countries. They went on and on and it got out of control. When Frankie asked, "How many classes did you have in high school?" Sam snapped.

"It doesn't matter! My high school had six classes and Chris' had seven. It varies from school to school. It's not a matter of national differences, and all of this is boring! Our countries are very similar. Let's just stop talking about it." Everyone was silent. Sam never looked away from the screen. He was deeply engaged in our game and was bombarding me with beans or pills or whatever they were. He went on to say, "From now on I declare open season on lying." Our host asked what he meant by that.

"I mean, if you ask me any questions about the U.S., I'm gonna lie. I suggest we all do, that way it will be more interesting." He still didn't take his eyes off the TV, and my side of the screen filled up, all the way to the top, defeated again. We were all really hooked on Kirby's Avalanche. Lewis took my controller to try his luck against the master. He was good, and after a few games, he brought Sam down and Frankie stepped in. Sam was bored, so he got wicked. He asked our host how he could afford to make fliers for punk shows anyway, going back to the story that he told us earlier about the cops making him take down the fliers.

"What do you mean?" he asked.

Sam's face was very serious. "Well, they are so expensive."

The guy looked really confused. "How much do you pay for fliers in the states?"

"They are around 75¢ a copy, if you go to the cheap place," Sam replied. Our host was shocked.

"Really? That's horrible. They're only 5-10¢ here."

Sam faked a surprise. "Wow! That's crazy. That's so cheap!"

"How do you afford it, what do you do?"

"Normally we silk screen all of our fliers, but it's a lot of work. It would be great to be able to run off copies for pennies."

"Shoot, well, you guys could mail me the master and I could make copies and mail them back to you. It would be cheap, even with postage." We all had to struggle to keep from laughing.

"That would be awesome," Sam said.

"Fuck!" Frankie yelped, as his screen filled with beans. He threw the controller down and Sam slid across the floor to reclaim his title. A few minutes later, he was slaughtering Lewis and taunting him by saying, "Somebody is about to kick the bucket" over and over. Then, he asked our Canadian ambassador if one could say those kind of things in Canada.

"What kind of things?" he asked.

"Idioms," Sam said. "You know, like, 'You're the apple of my eye' or 'You're the bees knees.'"

Looking confused, our host said, "Yeah, of course you can." Sam paused the game and looked very shocked.

"Really? That's crazy. In the states, some asshole named Steven Archer copyrighted all of them. You can't use any of the classic ones. If you're writing a book, you have to make up new ones. It's fucked up." It was so hard not to laugh. We assumed that Mr. Canada would see through this one, but he didn't, and the Avalanche went on. A little later, Sam pushed it. "Wait a minute," he said. "I just thought of something. Do Canadians believe that Elvis is dead?"

The guy said, "Yeah, of course, because he is."

Sam laughed out loud. "That's just a joke, he's not dead." We all laughed and the ambassador's face turned red. He was upset.

"You guys are hosing me!" Sam laughed even louder and, as a result, made us laugh even louder. Mr. Canada's face grew even redder. I felt bad, but I couldn't keep from laughing. He had fair warning after all.

The next day, we drove around the city and went into a store to see what they were like. They were just like our stores. We went to a fast food place to get fries. They were delicious and so much crispier than the fries back home. I decided to investigate the matter. I found an ingredients list hanging on the wall. The fries were fried in lard! When I got back to our table, everyone was nearly finished eating. I contemplated not telling them, but decided that I should. Everyone was really bummed. Suddenly, we could all feel the heavy oil in our tummies, churning around. The salt on my lips made me feel sick. I thought about the last burger I had eaten, years before. We refilled our sodas and went back out into the freezing day that was already coming to an early end. Lewis got sick on the way back to the house and we all agreed that Canada was a letdown.

Someone made us food at the show. It was a little better than the pasta, but nothing special. Propagandhi got tofu stir-fry though, and it looked great. We sat at the table next to them, eating our separate meals, but they were really nice to us. We talked after we ate and Todd remembered me from a letter I had written to his old band, I-spy. I felt cool. The show was much smaller than we imagined it would be. We played second and there were only around 60 people there. We thought it would be funny if we pretended not to know Sam so that he could heckle us from the crowd. When we got on stage Sam started yelling at us. "Go back to your own country!" he said. "Fuck you and your flag, you capitalist pigs. Why did you come here? We don't want you here!" We were laughing and trying to ignore him, but some of the people in the crowd took him seriously. A few of them told him to shut up, but much worse than that, a few of them agreed with him and clapped and laughed. Our plan wasn't really working. Sam kept it up all the way through our set and even spit on Lewis a few times. A couple of Canadian crusties spit on him too. We had made a terrible mistake that night, but we didn't care, it was pretty funny. Propagandhi was great, they played all of their best songs and we moshed our worries away. At the end of the night we got paid $100 Canadian dollars, which came out to around $50 U.S. dollars back then, which didn't come close to covering our gas. Lewis didn't care though, and reminded me that he would pay for all of it.

The next morning we went to a grocery store to stock up on snacks, since we planned on staying for a few more days with the hopes of doing something cool before we left. When we got back, our host said, "You guys might want to head out soon, unless you want to stay for a while, because a blizzard is coming." I asked him how bad it would be. "Last time, no one could drive for two weeks."

We all said, "Shit" at the same time. We packed our things as fast as we could. We apologized and thanked him for the show and for letting us stay, then we piled in the van and headed south. Kirby's Avalanche was fun, but not fun enough to stay in Thunder Bay for two more weeks. We had to get out of Canada! The roads were already pretty bad when we left. The only other vehicles we saw were logging trucks, and they slid back and forth across the white roads. We were all pretty sure that we were doomed. I thought we would at least end up stuck in a ditch, but we made it to the border safe and sound. We assumed that we would just drive through and the border guards would say, "Welcome home!" but we assumed wrong. They made us pull over and come into their office for interrogation. They asked us why we were in Canada and if we'd bought any drugs when we were there. I couldn't believe that our own country was harassing us at the border. They grilled us for a while, then let us in. We took turns driving and didn't stop until we made it home.

We got back to Bloomington at noon the next day. Sam and I wanted to get Den cokes, so we parked downtown, in front of People's Park. Lewis looked upset. He told me that he wanted to talk to Sam and me. He was shaking a little. We were all drained from the drive, we felt and looked like zombies. "I'm quitting the band," he said. I laughed. "No, really, I'm quitting the band." I realized that he was serious and I was really surprised, because he was so dedicated and loyal. I asked him why. He said that it was because Sam and I were too mean to Christy and that we made fun of him too much. He said that it was something that had been bothering him for a long time, and that this trip was our last chance to prove we could be better. We had failed. I tried to talk him out of it, suggesting that we talk about it later, after we all got some sleep. I apologized and promised to be better, but he didn't back down. He couldn't be swayed. "I quit," he said one last time, and I gave up. He walked home with Christy, and Sam and I got our huge sodas and joined Frankie on the wall in front of the park.

Frankie asked what we were going to do now. It really annoyed me. He wasn't really a part of the band yet, the Canadian show was only his third show with us. What did he mean, "What do we do now?"

I said, "Nothing, it's over. We can't do it without Lewis," while sipping my pop. It was way too cold to drink an icy 32-ounce soda outside, but compared to Canada, it was pretty nice, and, besides, where else would we go? We lived in an unheated, uninsulated garage filled with dog shit. Frankie stuttered a speech.

"We c-c-c-can't quit now! This is a great b-b-b-band and we have great songs that make a difference. We c-c-c-c-can't let Lewis c-c-crush that. This band is bigger than the people in it. We should find a new b-b-b-bass player and keep going. I love this band. This is the best thing I've ever d-d-d-done. I d-d-don't want to quit." My huge cup was empty and, somehow, Frankie had inspired me. I don't know how, I didn't really like him that much and I couldn't imagine the band without Lewis, but I couldn't imagine not being in the band, so I agreed to consider staying together and said that it would depend on whether or not we could find a bass player who could be as devoted to the band, and play as well as Lewis.

The next day, one of the straight edgers from the house came out to the garage and told me that I had to move out. They were pissed that Sam had moved in with me and that I didn't ask them first, and they accused me of borrowing their music equipment without permission. I figured out later that they meant their mic-stands, which we only used for practicing in the garage. I didn't care. The garage was cold, too far from town, and full of shit. I'd miss my little beagle friend, but that was the only thing I'd miss. I started packing right away. Before I left, I went into the house to use the bathroom, and they were smoking from a bong and watching James and the Giant Peach. I didn't say a word. I didn't say goodbye. I just left. I drove my van to my friend Brian Munn's skate shop and asked him if we could stay in his parking lot for a while. He was glad to have us. After all, he was a Samite.

I might have said that my luck had taken a turn for the worse, had it not been for Hannah. I was falling for her. We hung out almost every day. She would even come find me in my van sometimes. We'd hang out on campus or at her apartment, but her roommate didn't really like me, so we didn't do that very often. She didn't think Hannah should be hanging out with a homeless guy. Maybe she was right. I didn't care what her or anyone else thought of me. I wasn't worried about finding a bass player right away, and I wasn't worried about finding a place to live. I had Sam, I was finally out of my dead-end, drawn out relationship with Miranda, and I was hanging out with a nice girl who I really liked. Things were fine. I was cold, but I was okay. In fact, I felt like things were looking up.

We spent many nights that December playing Uno in the student union. We made up house rules, like cumulative draw 2's and apocalyptic 6's. Of course, we ate pizza too, paid for with Becky's checkbook. We invited Frankie and Hannah to share our plunder most of the time. We ate slices, drank soda, and did our best to get rid of all of our cards. It was a time of great luxury and indulgence, as well as a time of great risks and danger, since we knew that the detectives were on our trail.

Christmas came again, but this time I wasn't alone—I had Sam. Everyone else was busy with their families, but we stayed in town, and it was the same drill almost every night. We found a new place to have a pizza delivered, or we walked in and picked it up. They almost always took our bad checks, with a girl's name on them who wasn't there. The day before Christmas Eve, Bloomington was a ghost town, which meant we had nowhere to hang out other than the union,—until it closed—or my van. We spent most of our late evenings hanging out in the skate shop with Brian after hours, but he was gone too, so we picked up a pizza and took it to the Union to eat it. The place was empty, just us and a few other bums were there. We watched Rudolph the Red Nosed Reindeer (the stop motion animation one from 1964). It made us homesick, or time sick, maybe. We missed what Christmas once was to us. On the way out, we overheard "Let it Snow" and it got stuck in my head. I was singing it as we opened the doors to the cold outside world. It had started snowing while we were inside. There was an inch or so on the ground, and it was falling thick and fast while we walked home, to my van, singing the whole way.

"Oh the weather outside is frightful
But the fire is so delightful
And since we've no place to go
Let It Snow! Let It Snow! Let It Snow"
   - Sammy Cahn

We changed the words a little to fit our sad situation. We sang, "When you've got no place to go..." It was funny, we laughed like hell. When we got back to the van, I started it up to get the heater working. We did that a lot on cold nights, to warm the van up a little before we went to sleep. We'd put our pillows on the vents for a while too, otherwise they'd crackle when we went to bed. After a few minutes of futile heating, we went to sleep, snug in our beds, while visions of sugarplums danced in our heads.

I woke up freezing in the middle of the night because I heard something crack. "Sam, are you awake?" I asked.

"Yeah," he whispered.

"Did you hear that? I think someone is outside the van."

"No, it was my foot, it was frozen to the window and I just pulled it off." He wasn't joking. The next morning we found out that it had gotten down to -14° that night. We gave in and decided to go home for Christmas. I dropped Sam off in Mitchell at his parent's, and went down to my parents' house with plans to pick him up on my way back to Bloomington on Christmas day.

A few days later, we were all back in town and the holiday season was almost over again. Sam had managed to get on food stamps, and we celebrated by buying tons of food and vegan sweets. We bought four tubs of Tofutti ice cream, and took them over to the skate shop to share with Brian to thank him for letting us park in his parking lot and use his bathroom, which we could access any time we needed to. It was a Monday, and Sam kept saying, "Munnday," making a pun with Brian's last name.

Sam said, "I think we should do this every Munnday, I'll get us ice cream and we'll watch HBO." Brian and I both thought it was a good idea and from that night on, Mondays were Munndays and we ate vegan ice cream and watched whatever crap was on TV that night. It was a good tradition.

Frankie met a punk from Franklin, Indiana named Jason who had just moved to town and worked the graveyard shift at Steak 'n Shake. He told Frankie that he could hook him up with free food anytime after 2 A.M. and Frankie relayed the message to us, so we went to check it out that night. Sure enough, we ate whatever we wanted and it was all free. This worked well with our Freegan philosophy. We could eat all the cheese we wanted and not support the dairy industry. It meant we could get cheese fries, grilled cheese, milkshakes, and all the soda we could drink, and, even though we all got bellyaches, it was a wonderful night. Sam started calling Jason his "little vegan angel" which made no sense, but it stuck, and I started calling him that too.

Every night that he worked, we were there with Frankie, and sometimes Hannah too. Whenever Jason had a few minutes, he'd hang out and talk to us. He mentioned that he played bass and was looking for a band to join. Without considering talking about it with me first, Frankie blurted, "We're looking for a b-b-b-bass player!" Jason smiled. He was shy and humble and he seemed embarrassed by Frankie's forwardness. He asked us a few questions about the band and said that he'd love to tryout. It started to seem like maybe he was an angel who had come down from Franklin to bathe us in golden cheese and save our band.

We practiced at Frankie's mom's house in Ellettsville, around 10 miles from Bloomington, since I didn't have a house or a garage anymore. Jason showed up right on time and brought his own, nice equipment. It went well. He learned the songs quickly and we asked him to join the band. He said yes. He also said that Sam and I could stay at his house whenever it was too cold in the van. I wondered what else he was going to offer us. I felt like there had to be a catch. We joked that he was an undercover cop.

Sam's glasses were usually broken and taped together, but from time to time they were damaged beyond repair and he was forced to get new ones. His parents usually helped him out, but this time he didn't want to ask them. They weren't too happy about him dropping out of school and they didn't like the fact that he was homeless in Bloomington with me, his "homosexual sex master," so Sam hatched a bold plan to get the glasses without paying for them. "I'm gonna use the checkbook. I'm gonna say that she's my sister," he said.

I tried to talk him out of it. I was worried about them needing to do an eye exam or wanting to get some kind of medical records, but he assured me that it would be fine. He went to a fancy place that sold trendy frames and picked out a $200 pair.

Everything went smoothly, but when his glasses were ready, the lady came out and said, "Abe, your glasses are ready." Sam sat there, reading a magazine. She tried again, "Abe...Abe...Mr. Rosenbaum?" Sam kept reading. He forgot that he had given them a fake name. She had to come and tap him on the shoulder. He told me that she scared him and he jumped out of his seat. He was sure that they had figured him out, but she just thought he was weird. He walked up to the counter and pulled out the checkbook. He had already signed it, to make it seem like his sister had given him a signed check to use. They took it and he walked away with a beautiful pair of black, thick-framed glasses.

Munnday came again. This time, while we were at the store getting the Tofutti, I wandered into the video rental section. They had $1 rental deals, so I got Happy Gilmore. I knew it would be dumb, but dumb was okay for Munnday. It was a time to have fun and be silly. I loved it! We all loved it. We watched it again the next night and ate dumpstered pizza for a change. The next night, we bought microwavable popcorn with Sam's food stamps and invited Hannah and Frankie to come over to watch it again with us. We watched it a total of five times before I took it back. I still love it.

We were almost out of checks and we were running out of new pizza places to order from, so we decided to call it quits. We agreed that we had pushed our luck too far and it was time to end our check fraud days. Sam said, "Uno." He had one card left in his hand. I hadn't noticed that he was doing so well. None of us had anything in our hand to stop him, so he won the game on his next turn.

"Do you want to play again?" I asked.

"No, I'm getting sick of it," Sam said. "And I'm hungry," he added. It was late and freezing outside. We didn't feel like walking anywhere to get food. "Maybe we could call Pizza Hut, we've barely ever used them." We discussed it and concluded that it was a pretty safe bet.

"This really has to be the last time," I said. Sam nodded.

"Yeah, this is it, just one last time." I have since learned from my personal experiences—and from numerous crime movies—that you should never say, "one last time." If you do, you will get caught. It's the ultimate jinx. It's a black cat crossing your path. It's broken mirrors.

Sam made the call then came back and sat down. "How did it go?" I asked.

"It was fine," he said. He looked scared. He told me the total and I filled out the check, with a $10 tip for the driver. We alternated who wrote the checks, so that neither of us could ever get pegged with all of them. We thought it was a smart idea. Sam took the check and went downstairs to wait for the pizza. He never came back.

After 30 minutes, I went down to look for him. He wasn't there. I got nervous. I was worried that if he had gotten busted, the cops might still be around, looking for me. They knew that there were two of us. I went back upstairs and told Hannah what had happened. We waited for around an hour, hoping that it wasn't what it seemed. I theorized that maybe he had gotten a bad feeling and panicked and ran away. Maybe he saw a cop and took off. Maybe he just forgot what he was doing and wandered somewhere. You could never be sure with Sam, and I wasn't ready to assume the worst. After that long, worrisome hour, we left and walked to the van, hoping to find him there. He wasn't there. The lights were out in the skate shop, so I assumed he wasn't in there either. The van was cold and empty. I didn't sleep much that night.

The next day, Frankie found me and said, "Hey, I got a collect call from Sam, but I didn't accept the charges, the operator said that it would cost me $12 or something like that."

I felt my heart sink.

Drawing, by Sam.

155

CHAPTER 11
SAM'S IN JAIL

I had been holding onto the hope that everything was okay. I had been telling myself over and over that Sam was fine. I told Frankie what happened and told him to accept the call if it came again. I told him I'd pay for it. There was no way for Sam to call me and I knew that he wouldn't call anyone who didn't already know about our criminal activity, so Frankie was my only hope of hearing from him. I didn't dare call the jail, since I was worried that they might be looking for me too.

The next day I got that letter from Sam, the one that you read already.

I didn't know what to do. I was too afraid to go see him, and I didn't know how to go about getting him out of jail, if it was even possible. I had around $500 saved up to put out a split 7-inch with this band from Kentucky called The Connie Dungs. I didn't know if it would be enough to bail him out. I talked to a few of my friends and did some research. I told Frankie to go see him and try to figure out what we could do.

The next day I got another letter:

Jan 24, 1997. Letter #2

Dear Plan-It-X family,

Hello, this is Sam. Today is my second day in jail. It's seems like I'll be in here for a while and visiting hours/phone calls are gonna be few and far between, but I got plenty of time to write letters. Shit, so much funny stuff goes on here. Just now, everyone was freaking out about the front page of the newspaper missing while a guard made me get up and counted my blankets. I told Frankie the wrong times for visiting. I was really confused and nervous yesterday. I haven't seen anyone yet. He's got the real times now.

Here is my legal situation: $10,000 bond. April 3rd is my pre-trial hearing. That means that it would take $1,005 to get me out. They lowered it to a $5,000 bond once, but raised it again today. I'm charged with a class C felony: 2 yrs.

minimum sentence to a max. of 8, $0 to $10,000 in fines. Also, resisting arrest, a class A misdemeanor. I haven't talked to a public defender yet. The good news is my "psychological" problems might help me out. Someone from the mental health center is supposed to make an evaluation and give a report to the judge. Hopefully I'll get moved there and get out before summer.

The guys are trying to solve the missing front page mystery. They borrowed another one from cell block J, because they think that someone in our block stole it because they didn't want the other inmates to know why they were in here (e.g. child molester.)

Here is my material situation: I live in cell block 'I' (the guards call it Ida on the intercom.) on the second level, in a cot outside of Jeff Johnson's cell right next to the door to cell block 'J' (John), so I get to see all of the secret under the door deals and shit. Every couple of hours they lock everyone in their cells for two hours (lock-down). The guards don't usually come in here, except then. They pass out the food through a hole in the door. Uhh, I don't know how much detail you need. Sufficed to say, it's pretty ugly/concrete. The bathroom door doesn't close, so it's gonna be hard wankin' it. The lights go out at 12 and they wake you up at 6:00 a.m.

The food situation: The guards + stuff call me One-Shoe because I lost one shoe the first time I went to court. It was too big anyway. Now I have 2 shoes and someone even gave me some socks, I'm set up! But anyway, the nurse said "One-Shoe, so you're a vegetarian? Do you eat chicken or fish? No eggs? No dairy products? No beef?" I got a little slip of paper from her. "You must eat mostly beans, One-Shoe, beans and tofu." My eyes light up. "Sorry, no tofu in here." My first meal was iced tea, apple sauce and potato ships.

I can look out of the bathroom window and see the east side of the building: the corner of Washington and 7th street, Ace Pawn shop, etc.

The cops ate the pizza. The only cop joke made: "Hey man, you're eating the evidence." - Detective McClure.

I'm pretty sure my chest has gotten a lot hairier since I've been in here.

I have several library books here now. I don't think you guys can bring me books, it says in my handbook that the only type of books I can have are 1 bible and 5 religious books. The Christians run this fucking place.

A funny quote from the Inmate Handbook: "Borrowing a pack of cigarettes or a bag of cookies can quickly amount to $10 or more with inflated interest rates. Those who cannot pay are often assaulted physically or sexually. Those who ask for self protection because of debt are subject to disciplinary action.

Caffeine withdrawal sucks! I had migraine headaches and was puking and shit. Hey, I love all of you guys (especially my little vegan angel). Send me some progress reports on how things are going or just personal letters, or facts about Okinawa or animal rights or Chiapas. Whatever. Love, Sam.

On the outside, we tried to scrape together the $505 more dollars that we needed to bail him out. I called Greg Wells and he offered to send us some money, but we didn't know anything about bailing someone out of jail. I wanted to talk to Sam first, in case he was going to be transferred to the mental health center, or in case they lowered his bail again. While we waited for Greg's money to arrive, I shoplifted books and sold them, and I checked the P.O. box, hoping to get some orders. Sam sent Miranda a letter, which was how she found out that he was in jail. She didn't know, since her and I didn't see each other very much, and I didn't think that I should call her and tell her. Around a year later, I collected all of the letters that Sam sent and made a 'zine called "Sam's In Jail." This is the first letter that he sent her:

Jan 25, 1997. Letter #3

Dear Miranda,

Hello, this is Sam. I'm starting a tradition of writing letters every night at lock-down. I think traditions are going to be fairly important to keep me happy. Right now I am really happy, believe it or not. Hungry, but happy.

First off, I love you buddy. More importantly, I respect you a lot and I am really proud of you for what you are doing in your life. I think you are really intelligent and deserve a large community of friends who will give you affection, conversation and material support whenever you need it and for whom you would do the same. Also, I'm not sure if that makes any sense. But, no matter what, I'm happy to have you as part of my extended family (although my extended family is fairly tiny.) Whatever.

Whenever I get out of jail I'll get you some of that tofu that I promised you, in that bet. Speaking of tofu, I am finally getting some vegetarian (vegan) meals. Nothing worth eating yet, oatmeal, tomato soup, apple sauce and crackers. They fuck up every once in a while (I had to tell them that macaroni + cheese had cheese in it) (also, they gave me tartar sauce to put on my apple sauce one day.)

I saw an orangutan on TV yesterday. It was sad because it was going extinct. Or maybe it was sad because it was in a zoo. I don't watch much TV because it's usually on the wrong channels (TNN, race cars, ALWAYS cops, Rescue 911, or anything like that.) I always watch Seinfeld when it's on. I was trying to watch Millennium, but we were on lock-down, so I only saw the last 15 minutes. It didn't look too great. Lock-down is kinda like forced nap time.

A guard was talking about how on the weekends, this place loads up on domestic violence offenders. I got really mad about how I live in a fucked up culture that churns out problems instead of providing support. Culture (weekends, holidays, customs, etc.) is an artifact created by humans and it seems ridiculous that, even by accident, a culture could be built that leaves people feeling more

158

bored and scared and lonely than they started out. But it all makes sense when you figure in one thing: A lot of our culture was designed by very intelligent and precise advertising and PR men in a time after the great depression and World War II. A lot of people were really proud of what they were doing and how their country had turned around. Production seemed like the key to everything, but to keep production going, a steadily growing consumption rate had to be created. The nuclear family became the core of a rigid nightmare that was America. Loneliness was essential to keep the men, women and fully grown children hungry for more. Advertising doesn't work on the content. All the old forms of community had to be trivialized and bought and sold so that they were non-threatening to the American Dream: old-time religion turned into Christianity, jazz and blues turned into lonely commercial records, the comfort of bars turned into mass produced commercial beers. Cultures which could not be bought or sold were crushed: black communities, unions unwilling to sell their workers, communist, socialist and anarchist, all of these were swept under the rug unless they were willing to produce a marketable product or attitude that does little...

Umm, sorry sugar, I fell asleep for a few hours. I can't think of any reason I was filling your ears with anti-corporate propaganda. I was only going to write a paragraph or so. Oh well, just another sheet of paper wasted. But, I was thinking that maybe you could help me out with thinking of little changes we could make to our own culture (punk) which is not as financially straining and a hell of a lot more satisfying. Small changes that we can instantly put in to place are the best, because I think that practice is the most effective way of promoting any real social change: humans are still monkeys see, and monkey see, monkey do for the most part. Feel free to steal and modify ideas from other cultures, Americans especially, but also: Biafrans, the Mayans of Chiapas Mexico, the Navajo, and the flea circus of Mr. Charles Burton of Oklahoma City, Oklahoma. Also in almost every case of an American-commercial idea is a diluted version or a bloated version of a more natural tradition.

"While there is a lower class, I am in it. While there is a criminal element, I am of it. While there is a soul in prison, I am not free." -Eugene Debs.

The most selfish position of anthropologist is the belief that all cultures are equal and deserve to be preserved intact. Social scientists cannot make the same mistakes that chemists and physical scientists made when they pretended that their actions were only bringing humanity closer to total understanding of the universe, while they followed the agendas of industrialist and psychotic governments and brought us closer to total annihilation instead. Our American culture can no longer be aloud to strangle the well being of it's people and animals, or to wreak havoc on the bodies and minds of living beings all over the world. I may not be adverse to having one little Maybury like town filled with lonely fuckers, cleaning their guns and talking about hunting robotic animals.

I just kind of consider this whole business of being in jail to be a funny little episode in my TV show. Man it was nuts when I went to the library on Thursday. The guy in front of me looked just like this kid that I ate lunch with everyday in the 6th grade. Some guy on TV was talking about square dancing or something and this dude just goes "1, 2, 3, 4, 5, 6, 7, 8." Something to do with country music. The guy in front of me in line says "Thanks a lot, now we know how to fucking count." It reminded me exactly of the kind of thing that my friend Isaac would have said. Man, it was him! I asked him if he went to junior high in Mitchell, and he said yes. It took him a few minutes to figure out who I was, finally he said "Yeah, I remember you... You were real skinny, like you are now. We used to snort salt and throw pickles and shit, man, we were some stupid fuckers back then." I didn't have the heart to tell him that I still did shit like that, that I was still a stupid fucker. As far as I can tell, he's not Mr. brains either. We play connect 4 a lot, the only game we can both play. Hey, I'm running out of paper, so I leave you with a Kurt Vonnegut quote: "How do you find true love? Wear nice clothes, smile all the time and learn all the words to the latest songs." I think it's nice because it makes love sound simple + beautiful instead of complicated + messy + gross. Love, Sam.

We all wanted to see him, but we could only go on Mondays, Wednesdays, and Sundays, so we had to wait for the next visitation day to come. We also found out that we had to bring two forms of ID, which made me nervous, because I was worried that they were still looking for me. They knew that there were two of us, and if they had examined the handwriting on the checks, then they knew that Sam didn't write them all. Frankie talked to him on the phone and gave us an update. He said that Sam sounded good and seemed to be in high spirits. He told us that Sam made jokes and laughed a lot. He asked for someone to bring him underwear and stamps. He told Frankie that the underwear had to be brand new and that we had to write his name on them with permanent marker. I went to K-mart and shoplifted him some tighty-whiteys.

I was reckless on those missions. I didn't care if I got caught. I figured that if I got caught, I might get to go to jail too and see Sam. Jail didn't sound that bad. It seemed nicer than living in a van. I also felt bad that Sam had been the one to get busted, when it was both of our ideas, and I had eaten a ton of that pizza. Another thing I felt bad about was my happiness. While Sam was locked away, I was hanging out with Hannah more and more. We hung out almost every night, and she started skipping school and staying with me in the van. My band had a new bass player and we practiced at least three times a week at first, to teach him the songs. He was really good and it seemed like we were going to be able to get the split 7-inch recorded after all, despite the setback of losing Lewis. Things were going really well for me and really badly for Sam. We didn't get many orders back then, but whenever I went to the P.O. box, I found a letter from Sam:

Jan 26, 1997. Letter #4

Dear Chris,

Hello this is Sam. I was going to write someone else but my head really hurts tonight and it would be too much thinking and writing too. It's Sunday night, Superbowl Sunday. Doggamn! that was long and obnoxious. I just lied on my cot (I am not sure how to use the word lied, I think I should have said layed), and read Hocus Pocus, by Kurt Vonnegut, it's about a man's story he wrote in a prison library, which is kind of funny to read right now (not funny enough to make me laugh though so I don't know why I said it was funny). But, anyway I watched the Beavis and Butthead half-time thing, brings back memories of the good old days, back in the 60s. Beavis got arrested for being an illegal alien when he was saying "cornholio" and stuff so they shipped him to Mexico. If he had said Chiapas I would have had to wank it right there but as close as he got was Nicaragua. I had to use your strategy of talking about the Misfits with rednecks because this one guy was bugging me with a bunch of questions about what kind of music I liked and he knew about the Misfits.

Sometime soon I'm gonna start working on a 'zine called "Cell Block I" or something. "Pizza Scam" sounds better, I don't know. But you know, start with me and you and Marty, wondering down the halls of Collins, looking for left-overs, and riding around with Darren and Lisa asking pizza places for leftovers and me eating freegan pepperoni (you guys thought I was still a full meat eater then, but I just hadn't really said anything about wanting to become a vegetarian because I wanted to make sure that I wasn't going to wimp out when I saw my parents.) But, then I could move on to the Mad Mushroom Pizza Club...or the Free Pizza Club, whatever we called it, when we got serious about hunting down those fucking coupons, then the M.M.P.C. crumbles, then 1995, then the fraud explosion that summer with Mother Bear's burglaries and check fraud. The summer of 1995 was the best for me. I was happier than I have ever been in my whole life. I was also close to being the saddest I had ever been sometimes. For a while I felt like I could do anything if I got the chance. But, I'm a lot smarter now, or I understand a little bit more about how people act and shit. Whatever.

Everyone's a little too passive in here for me. The guard just came by and told these guys to clean up this area of he would shut down the TV for a day. I'm never watching TV again when I get out of here. Fuck them! Can they make it more obvious that TV is little more than a instrument of pacification? It's kind of funny to live in a community with little or no physical danger, but clear cut lines of exactly what the authority wants to do to you. But I'm running out of paper. Good night.

I love you, Sam.

P.S. If not a single monkey resists, who will ever want to be a monkey again?

The next day all I got was this poem:

Jan 27, 1997. Letter #5

A bright clean day and a summer dress
Nice clothes and a smiling lip
Half a smile and half a song
And a peck on the forehead

One dead flower that's not a rose
Make me half asleep and all along
Half in love and all alone
Half the night lying here awake

But I don't even like girls that much
And I sure as hell don't like you that much
I just have to have a reason to live
To see the sun again

(I'll be back in the summertime with a handful of flowers and a bottle of cheap wine) -Crimpshrine

Half a dream that half came true
Half a game of cards
Half a day that was half okay

But I don't ever write shit like this and I sure hope that if you ever see this, you will understand that I just really want to see my friend again, to see you shine again.

For some reason, just before Sam got arrested, he had started calling Jason by the name Otis, in addition to calling him his "little vegan angel." The next day, when I checked the P.O. box, I found a letter addressed to Otis and Abigail (which is what Jason called his bass guitar). Jason let us read it:

Jan 28, 1997. Letter #6

Dear Otis,
Hello, this is Sam. Give my regards to your good friend and girlfriend, Abigail. Are you guys still going to play in Operation: Cliff Clavin? Of course you are. It's long before my standard letter writing time, but I am bored and irritated. Not a good time to write maybe. Already, it's not coming out too good. Fuck it...

Dear Otis and Abigail,
Greetings from the planet Ida, my name is Sam and I believe that we have met, although I have only heard of Abigail from a friend of a friend. For the first time since childhood, I have been forced to go without underwear of any sort for almost a week now and I cannot say that I find the experience pleasant. However, once because of my political beliefs, I didn't commit laundry for an entire summer. Due to extreme conditions, I was forced to make due with a sweatshirt wrapped around my genitals as a loincloth, such as might be worn by the apes of Mexico. Sufficed to say, that was most uncomfortable and I borrowed some proper genital coverings, also known as briefs or tighty-whiteys or some such by the unlearned. On my current planet of habitation "borrowing" genital coverings without permission would be highly inappropriate or so I have gathered, since my previous attempts at swanking foot covering met with a slight failure when the individual from whom these socks were liberated...Please wait, while I close the door...Let me start again.

163

Dear Otis,

I am tired and I haven't slept very much, so instead of writing you a letter, you will have to make do with a series of words or phrases that will inspire you to remember stories of your own, since that is the reason I am writing you anyway, to coax some more tales from your sweet lips. Just tell me the best story that comes to mind.

1. A big yellow barn...
2. My step-aunt got lost at the zoo...
3. I got beaten up at the trailer park because...
4. Barbecued tofu...
5. Treblinka and Masada...
6. My stepson got sucked into cargo cults...
7. Tell me how the new version of Star Wars ends...
8. My friend Aaron was in Biafra...
9. Back in the 60s...
 10. Whatever.

Sorry buddy, next time I will send you something cooler. Love, Sam.

Wednesday came, and that meant we could finally visit Sam, but not until 6:30 P.M. I felt bad about him not having any underwear, even more so after I read Otis's letter, and I didn't want him to have to wait all day for them, so I dropped them off with some stamps right after I woke up that day. I was still too worried about getting caught to go see him, so Frankie, Hannah and Otis went instead. I waited in the van. When they came back, they said that it was awkward and sad. They said that despite his funny letters, he didn't seem to be having a good time in there. We all agreed that we should try and bail him out as quickly as possible.

The next day, I got letters for everyone:

Jan 29, 1997. Letter #7

Dear Chris,
Here is my mail. Will you be my postman to save stamps? If someone drops off money I'll be able to buy some, and peanut butter and crackers and pencils, but it's not necessary. Thanks a lot for everything. Read your letter carefully. I'm sure you'll get it.

Dear Plan-It-X
Hello, this is Sam. I'm in jail for pizza fraud, a class C felony. Because of this, the government wants to lock me up for 2-8 years for each pizza. Although I'm supposedly innocent until proven guilty, I'm going to have to sit in jail for 2 months, eating 3 vegan meals a day, obeying Christian-fascist totalitarian rules

and really missing my friends, until my court date finally comes. Whatever.

Contact with the outside world? That's a no-no, they don't want me fucking them up the ass.

My cell (also known as cold comfort cell or #6) is a 6X6 square with one corner cut out, also known as a pentagon. I've only just moved into it. There is some mysterious graffiti: Viva Chicango I Mexicano D.F. Dutos Gerge.

Anyone who would rather be in a George Orwellian world ought to be in here with me...Surveillance cameras, mean guards and plus you never have to do anything that you don't want to. Imagine if all of you guys where in here with me, they have Monopoly, Uno, Checkers and TV (although I'm sure we'd be losing our TV privilege all the time) and we could pull so many fucking stunts. There's nothing personal like lots of people have with their parents and the only thing they can do to punish you is lock you down. I don't really do anything funny because it would really piss off my block mates to lose their TV, and no one here has a good sense of humor.

FUCK OFF CHRISTIANS! KEEP YOUR FUCKING GIDEONS!

I've thought about making a little Gideons bonfire in here when it gets really cold. Okay, I don't know if I've answered all of your questions, but I'm gonna take a break and eat some PB&J. (I miss the sun, 40¢ cokes from the Den and Miranda.)

Shew, that break was longer than I planned. Isaac, my 6th grade buddy was reading from the bible and I had to talk to him and try to counteract the Christian propaganda. This is one of the places that they try to hit you when you're down and boy is this guy down...He's got to go to Bedford soon and face charges of attempted murder, theft and failure to appear. In junior high we used to sit together at lunch and snort salt and throw French fries. I think the most beautiful thing I can think of right now is ketchup and mustard swirled together. After school, my parents took me home to their paranoid-control-freak little world and he'd go out and smoke weed and drink and wish that he had a hot rod I guess. He dropped out of school and I stopped talking to anyone, because it was pretty embarrassing to be 15 and not be allowed to cross the street and have your dad accuse you of doing LSD at lunch. But now it's 10 years later, and we meet up again in jail and play Uno.

Oh, if anyone has been following these letters closely, the missing newspaper mystery was solved. A child molester was in here and he got moved to seclusion before he got beat down.

The only real good example of prison unique culture (besides tattoos) that I seen so far was some guys making a box out of playing card. It took exactly 52 cards.

One day a guard flipped out because she had misplaced her pen by putting it in the wrong pocket. She was worried that one of us had it. We aren't allowed to have pens??

Then our shiny dinnertime cook (what I call the cook) said "I've got some good shit for you today." And gave me peanut butter + carrots + celery. I told him it was good but that I liked PB&J sandwiches and vegetarian re-fried beans. He's been fixing me good stuff ever since. Food In jail: For one day I didn't eat anything but the other jailbirds noticed really quick and started bugging me about it. They wanted my food if I didn't. Finally I ate some cornflakes, but I didn't eat lunch or dinner. I threw up anyway that night because I was really nervous and I was going through caffeine withdrawal. But, the next day I played Monopoly with these guys, Zeke and Jeff. Jeff was vegetarian, so I told him I was too and that night at dinner a lot of people hooked me up with potatoes. Everyone is really nice in cold comfort Ida. The next day Zeke helped me get my diet slip, since then I've been getting some okay food.

Nicknames that I've been called in jail: Green Day, Rabbit-Ass, One-Shoe, People's Park, Green-Hair, Green-Bay, Dorsett, Leprechaun.

Names I've not been called: Sam.

Common hobbies in jail: TV + Games- brain eaters, fuckem...Origami, writing and drawing, reading, gambling, complaining, filling out grievances, smoking, trading, dreaming.

Books I've read so far: Kurt Vonnegut- Hocus Pocus, Palm Sunday, Wampeters, Foma and Grandfaloons; H.P. Lovecraft- At the Mountains of Madness; Stephen Hawking- Black Holes and Baby Universes; Jean-Francois- Treblinka; Robert Lewis Stevenson- Dr. Jekyll and Mr. Hyde. I get my books from the Monroe County Jail Library on Thursdays. Either that or out of the communal book pool. My favorites are the Kurt Vonnegut books, I am starting to consider him my best friend since I lost my stuffed rabbit.

I'm running out of space and I'm getting really sleepy. I didn't get to tell all of the stories that I wanted to tell, but thanks for listening my friends. I love all of you guys, especially Otis. -Sam

P.S. Sam ♥ *Frankie*
P.P.S. Fuck you, you tofu head.

Dear Miranda,
Chris will probably be by later to day to see me. I'm pretty excited. I thought I'd write you with a quick progress report. I have my own room now, with a desk, a window and a toilet. It's a little lonelier, but a lot cooler. Cook (just what I call the fat guy that brings my food) is trying hard to make me some good vegan shit. I think he noticed that I never eat my tomato soup. He's been fixing me rice and beans + salsa and PB+J and oatmeal and bean burritos. It's been fairly cool. I'm still getting headaches from no cola sometimes. Apparently, you get Coke on

Christmas and no other time. It's kind of like summer camp or something in here, except everyone is old criminals. Drunk frat boys and wife beaters wander in and out. Also, tell everyone that the time I do here in jail counts towards my sentence. My cell block is really mellow + nice. They all share a lot. They all smoked too much weed in their lives, they are too calm, I was hoping for something a little more exciting. I used your poker technique and won me some money, thanks for teaching me how to play. I feel like a rich person, sitting around and doing nothing all day. I tried writing some poetry, but it all sucked. I can't think of any tunes except county music. I wish I could listen to some real music doggamn it! Love you sugar, -Sam

Dear Frankie, Hannah and Otis
Hey! It's the day that I saw you guys. That fucking sucked, just made me lonelier,
but thanks for the effort, it's a nut house outside my cell block. Anyway, Everyone is probably getting letters today, it makes me feel better writing this all down. If anyone ever comes to visit me again, we should just play charades, it'd be funner. I mainly only wanted you guys to come to visitation so you could see me in my funny orange suit.

Sam included one of his poems, on another scrap of paper:

Now I may begin to fight

Thunder of spring
Arousing, moving upon
Gentle thigh,
Flexible bird of thigh

Thunder bends wood,
Wind slips inside foot
Flexible movement
Arousing Spring

I hold my freedom cupped gently in my palms
Stand before the sun and moon and earth
Reach out and release she to the sky
The once tightly shielded fledgling stirs
Stumbles and blinks and winces in the light
Proud and innocent she begins to fly

Nothing came the next day. I think having visitors must have bummed him out. I called Frankie to see if he had called, but he hadn't. Greg left me a message saying that some money was on the way. The following day, I was relived when I got more mail:

Jan 28, 1997. Letter #8

Dear Chris,

Thanks a lot for the letter. It cheered me up a lot, I had been lying in bed all day trying to get back to sleep after the nurse called me in to ask me about my depression. Legally, they don't have to grant me an evaluation until April 3rd, but she is speeding things up for me and I'll get to see a psychologist next Tuesday. She holds the belief that a real psychologist will prescribe medicine. This shouldn't be a problem, I know how to handle it.

I haven't spoken with my public defender yet, but right now I am only charged with one count of forgery. Since this is my first real criminal offense and considering the circumstances, I think I can ride it out. With any luck I'll be back in the summertime with a handful of flowers and a bottle of cheap wine. However, if more charges are filed it may be necessary to engage Mr. Ott as my attorney, if we can afford it. I don't know if I've told you or not, but each day I serve in here counts as two days towards my sentence, so I will have 140 days served by the time of my pre-trail. I'm fairly sure that I won't be able to get transferred to mental health at least not until after April 3rd, mainly because there is a schizophrenic man locked in his room 24/7 in my cell block. He is still a little bit functional but being locked in here is driving him nuts. Also, he's taking anti-psychotic medications and if you know anything about them, then you know that the side effects are often worse than the schizophrenia itself. He's all bunched up in a little knot.

I'm bored of talking about legal shit. I want to talk about my new friend, my little buddy Bob. He looks kind of like a skinny Danny Devito and he is constantly begging for cigarettes. He was arrested for sleeping in the federal repository law library (which we call the law building). According to him, it's a hang out for mobsters and he was arrested for interfering with a federal investigation. There was also something about a black van and crooked cops. Here are a few of my more interesting conversations with him, this is the first time I talked to him:

BOB: Hey you, Green-Hair!
SAM: Yes.
BOB: You from Florida?
SAM: No. I'm from around here.

BOB: In Florida they've got green hair. In Boulder it's flamingo pink.
SAM: Ahh. Are you from Boulder.
BOB: No. I just came from there though. I want to be buried there.
SAM: You like it there?
BOB: Yes. I like it a lot. There is this girl there, about this tall, red hair, beautiful. I want to be buried next to her.
SAM: Buried? Is she dead?
BOB: No, God no! (laughs nervously).
SAM: Ahh. Sorry. (trying to change the subject) Why did you come here?
BOB: The university. I'm friends with the president, staying at his home. Are you a student here?
SAM: Not anymore.
BOB: You can learn a lot of things here. You can study geology and biology and you can learn how to draw.
SAM: Really?
BOB: Yes, A lot of things, planets, trees, buildings, flowers, animals, people, they'll teach you how to draw about anything. Hey can you get me a cigarette?
SAM: I'll see if anyone has one that they can spare. Thanks for talking to me.
BOB: No problem man, thanks a lot. What's your name?
SAM: I'm Sam.
BOB: Okay, I'm Bob, Sam. See you around.

Hey, can you hold on to some of these letters for me? I'm pretty much sending you the raw materials for my 'zine. I wish I could photocopy certain things. There are a lot of funny little papers that would be cool. I'm gonna get a drink and eat my leftover PB&J, it's 3:00am.

This guy Bob, doesn't have anyone to look out for him on the outside. One time he gave me a # of some people on the outside and ask me to call them. He said that they owed him $200, but they wouldn't accept the call. But anyway, one day I was coming back from my 7 minute trip to the library (you have to be quick to find 6 entertaining books in 7 minutes) and Bob asked me if I wanted to play chess. He also asked me what books I was reading. I told him and he was really interested in my math book, Knotted Doughnuts, by Martin Gardner, on special order from the real library. We played a game of chess. He made 3 or 4 opening moves that were pretty normal, then he moved his bishop right next to my queen and called checkmate. I had to laugh, he wasn't going to play the oldest game of kings and queens by the white mans rules. Anyway, then we got out my math book and he said he would teach it to me. He looks at page 15 and says "F, E, D, C, B, A. The answer to that is 100111001." Then he flips to page 29 and tells me *that polycube # 4 fits in the maximum hole problem on page 35. He calls polycube #4 a sawed off shotgun and says that fentominoe #N on page 34 is also a gun. He went through all of this twice, with a 5 minute break in between, so I know it wasn't garbage to him. There must be some kind of logic in it. During the break, he turned to the I-ching section of the book on page 246. He knew a lot about the I-ching, like saying the lines of hexagrams are like questions and answers, solid questions and broken answers. He said there were 26 symbols with meanings at the top of the first page, arranged in order. Then he sang Que Sera, Sera. After that he turns to the drawings of knotted doughnuts on page 63. He points to the middle one and says "That is artwork, can you draw like that?" I tell him no and he slams the book shut. "Well, that's math! Need help with anything else?" I say no, but thanks for the help and I give him one of my extra blankets. He says god bless you, thanks for the blanket and then he wanders off, the end.*

You may want to check the book out for yourself and look at it. I strongly suggest that you do.

"In times of revolt there are questions of peace and balance- it's like breathing into the future, so you can understand the revolt and come from the present into peace."

Don't worry about my supply of cigs and cookies, I don't smoke or eat cookies and don't worry about me borrowing those things from other inmates, I won't. Also, everyone in my block is fairly nice, so it may be more irritating than scary. It's a misdemeanor block, only a couple of real criminals here. There is a guy here that worked as a manager at Mad Mushroom in 1994. He knew your old housemates from Cottage Grove and he knew Half Conniption. He's in here for growing weed. He talked to me for a minute when he found out that I was in here for pizza fraud. He knew about us and our coupon scams.

Man that freegan food sounds good, but don't promise me though, that's a bad habit. Promises don't always work out. Unless you don't mind breaking them. "Foma" you know, means lies meant to comfort. Like it's comforting to pretend that you're gonna get me out of here tomorrow somehow, but I know you're not. I'd rather see the Operation: Cliff Clavin/Connie Dungs split come out anyway. Right now, the thought of a freegan grilled cheese and a drink of Pepsi is enough to keep me alive, but when I get out, I'd settle for vegan food too, like crazy bread or a Subway or vagina or anything, but most of all, Pepsi.

They have a remarkable ability to prepare food in here which seems like it wouldn't be that bad but which taste, uh, substandard. I think it comes from really low quality ingredients. But, in theory the stuff I am eating is really good sometimes, PB&J at almost every meal, fries, bananas, beans+salsa, bean burritos and vegetables or all sorts. One of the cooks is a dick and makes me show him my vegetarian slip every time and acts amazed every time too. He always tries to give me chicken or whole eggs or some other shit.

Pigs coming! They searched my room last night and found my hoards of carrots and PB&Js. The guy was real nice though. He just told me that I wasn't allowed to stockpile food in my room, but he let me keep it. I had to eat it all quickly after that.

I gave up on the idea of this place being a hotel a long time ago. Of course I don't know much about staying at hotels and I've never done it. I've only considered doing it to sell secrets to the Soviets or make arms deals or visit a prostitute, but nothing like that goes on here, nothing exciting. This is not a hotel. Some of my more satisfying delusions are that I'm back in college, at summer camp, a visitor to an alien planet or distant country, a common man who was imprisoned in the tower of a castle for no apparent reason, an eccentric rich person, a leader in the struggle for the rights of indigenous peoples, or a citizen nestled inside a fierce totalitarian dictatorship, with imports of carrots, PB&J, bread, stamps, envelopes, paper, pencils and books and exports of letters, urine and shit. Usually it's entertaining enough to think that I'm in jail for stealing pizza with a couple of men that I can play Monopoly, Uno or Chess with and I get to listen to their funny stories about cocaine and stolen cars. "Guns and money Sam, that's all I want. Don't want them fools coming around my house bringing TVs or VCRs all that shit." Or I imagine that the government is spending thousands of dollars to try and punish me for trying to support myself by stealing $20 worth of pizza, and they are doing that by giving me food and shelter, medical care and legal counsel in the process. Ha ha ha ha. Man I miss you and I want to be out of here. The judge didn't lower my bond because he figured out that I didn't really have a place to stay. Once I get a public defender and a psychologist rooting for me, maybe I can get it lowered. Plus, the judge figured that it didn't really matter since I don't have any money anyway. Do you get it? If I can get my bail lowered to $100 or $200 or if I could convince the judge that I'd be better off staying with an old friend that I haven't talked to since before I starting getting into trouble, like Otis, I could get out and get a job and get back to my normal life. I could try and save up money to pay my fines and lawyers fees and rent and shit like that.

Man, I tried writing Peanucle songs a couple of times but my brain is too polluted with country music and they come out like shit. I wish they'd let me have a Walkman or something.

I've been reading about the Mayans and Chiapeneco art, it's mostly abstract symbols. I tried to make a border like in the book, but it's going pretty ugly. The Mayans used base 20 arithmetic because they counted with their fingers and toes and they invented the concept of a zero, as a useless placeholder based upon an especially fat and brainless ruler who held the throne until his nephew ascended and declared a sporting festival with Zero's head as the ball. The Mayans were a brutal people. Love, Sam.

Frankie found me the next day and said that Sam had called him and asked him to deliver a personal message to me. He said that he wanted me to get that book called Knotted Doughnuts and Other Mathematical Entertainment that he had told me about in the letter, from the library and to read it very carefully. He said that it contained a lot of interesting illusions. That night, I went and found the book. It was filled with old-time math puzzles. I had no clue what he wanted me to find. I didn't know if there was something special about the book or if he just wanted me to look at this nerdy math book. He knew that I sucked at math and had very little interest in it, but, in his defense, I loved puzzles. I flipped though the whole thing and didn't find any notes or scribbling in the margins. I was about to give up, but then I cracked open the spine and looked inside of the binding. There was a small piece of paper, folded really tightly. I pulled it out and got really excited when I realized it was the same kind of paper that Sam used to write his letters. I unrolled the secret letter:

To whom it may concern, I have created a code which we can use to communicate secret messages with each other in the letters that we exchange, since we know that our mail is read by the authorities. These secret messages will be disguised as borders around all future letters addressed to you. Please study the key below.

There was a key, which I have since lost, but here is an example of the code. It looks crazy, but it made sense. I couldn't wait to de-code my first secret message from Sam.

It was Groundhog Day, and a Sunday, which meant no mail that day. I would have to wait. I hated Sundays for that reason. Too many times, I've walked to the post office to check the P.O. box and found it empty, then remembered it was Sunday. Or even worse, I've ridden my bike there with a basket full of packages to send out and I'm thwarted by a religion that I'm not a part of. I'd have to wait at least one more day to see if Sam would send me any secret messages.

The next day I got a bundle of letters, for everyone except me:

Feb 1/2, 1997. Letter #9

Dear Hannah,
Thank you for writing me. It was like Christmas getting all of those letters. I

was trying to call your house when I got them on Friday night, but you have collect calls blocked, so I'll never be able to call you. It's okay, I'm trying to get used to thinking that I'm in a far away place and ignore the fact that I can look out my window and see downtown and know that my friends are out there somewhere. The collect calls cost a lot of money anyway, and they cut off automatically after fifteen minutes. I got cut off talking to Frankie once, it sucks. I don't know why they are like that.

I like getting read my rights, it makes me laugh like hell. It sucks making 'in' jokes when you are the only one that's gonna get them. Whenever I say "It makes me want to laugh like hell" I'm making a reference to character in "Hocus Pocus" the Kurt Vonnegut book. It's about an old guy in prison. "Jailbird" is better. Tell Chris that he might want to read "Knotted Doughnuts and Other Mathematical Entertainments" by Martin Gardner, I think he will like it. He might have to wait a few days for it to get back on the shelves of the real library. I don't know how long it takes to get from here to there. The part about coincidences is probably the most interesting.

I'm still about as nocturnal as before, I stay up until 4 or 5 then I take a nap. They wake me because they are Christian-fascist-morons. At 5:30 they yell into the intercom, then again at 6 and then again at 6:30, then breakfast comes at 6:45. I can sleep through everything except breakfast now that I have my own room. The first few nights that I was here, I was woken up by every little noise and I slept in cot in the hall, beside the door. The guards always slammed the door right by my head. Every two hours they made their rounds. They yelled into the intercom: "Ida-John 2, Ida-1" so that 'central' would open the door for them. Then the buzz. Then the Slam. It was impossible to sleep through. It's really high tech here, kind of neat actually, but not some place that I ever thought I'd live.

I don't really watch much TV, Seinfeld, Beavis + Butthead and Sunday night Foxx. I usually sleep and read all day. I share my leftover carrots with J.R. and Jeff. J.R. tells me funny stories and we make plans to rob banks and stuff. Everyone is really nice to me, even the ones that I've told to fuck off before, even the ones that I make fun of for liking country music, etc. As usual, everyone thinks that I'm their little brother or something.

I hate white people. I especially hate the upper-middle class white people. They act like little pricks.

This one scary biker dude, that watches TNN 3 hours a day is the only guy I've came close to getting into a fight with. He's got a rebel flag tattoo and I don't like him at all. One day he said something really racist and I just said "Whatever" and walked away, I was really mad. Also, before that, he got really mad at me because I won lots of money off of him playing poker. Every time he had good cards, I had one better. He was especially mad because he could tell that I didn't really know how to play poker. He would have been even madder if he known that my

173

strategy was just to throw down everything except hearts or pairs. But when he yelled at me, everyone else just laughed at him and he realized how ridiculous it was and we were cool after that.

Hey, I think I heard someone talking about the flag burning incident that you told me about in your letter, was that back in 1995? I'm sure it sucked, going in front of a judge is shitty. I hate it when I have to deal with authority. I wish I didn't, then I could be more of a smart-ass. See you soon, ♥ *Sam.*

Frankie,

Ya-yuh! I was hoping that you'd write me sometime with ridiculous questions about jail life. Thanks for being there for me and accepting those collect calls. I hope your mom doesn't get pissed off when the bill comes. I'm always afraid that she'll pick up the phone and interrogate me. I'd have to tell her some story about getting sexually abused.

All I keep thinking in here is that at least it's better than Ellitsville. I'm sorry that you've got to be there and go to that fascist high school.

Well, there's only one biker guy in here and he wants to buy me a beer when we get out, but I don't like him at all. I'm too socially maladjusted to be in here. I get too pissed off when someone says something sexist, racist or homophobic. I borrow people's socks without asking. Hey, I couldn't help it. I didn't bring mine upstairs with me, they were too dirty and the guy told me that they would bring some up for me, but they never did. It sucks man, I've never had to go so long without underwear. Once again, I was forced to make a loincloth out of a T-shirt. I borrowed it from my friend. He likes me because I'm a communist and I share all I got, even when all I've got is carrots. He sells rocks. One time he traded 4 rocks for a car. He's gonna quit selling them though, he doesn't like what it does to people. Whatever. Bye Frankie. Sorry if I spelled your name wrong. Tell me how things are going, hope like the new Star Wars. -Sam

Dear friends,

Books Thru Bars?
Books I'd like to have:
1. *The Illuminati Trilogy- Robert Wilson & Mr. Shea*
2. *Feet of Clay or Seargent of Arms- Terry Pratchett*
3. *Journey Into the Center of the Night- Celine*
4. *Anything- Bakunin (not Bukqnon)*
5. *Anything- Martin Gardner or Nietzche*
6. *Almost Anything- Upton Sinclair*
7. *Anything about the Mayans, especially mythology*

8. *Any non-Christian mythology books*
9. *Anything about Liberia or Africa in general*
10. *Anything with lots of cool addresses to write to*
11. *Try slipping in a copy of MRR*
12. *Anything the Miranda recommends*
13. *Anything at all!*

Paperbacks are better, anything you bring will be rationalized by the jail. I'm not allowed to have much personal property. That's okay by me as long as someone else gets to read them.

Non-book stuff:
1. *Long johns*
2. *Fresh tofu*
3. *Letters (colorful is good)*

Sorry it's taken me so long to get this list to you, it's hard to work up the nerve to ask for help. Don't try too hard with the books, I can get a lot of stuff myself, from the library.

Dear Mr. Van + the rest of Plan-It-X

Good news! The jail is overcrowded and they are letting people out left and right. jesus fucking vagina, you guys are sappy, I've only been gone for a day or something. Your letters are so dramatic. Chris goes to his parents house for longer than that every fucking week. But, anyway after my psych evaluation I'm gonna write a letter to the judge and try to get out of here before the weekend comes and brings in all the wife beaters and drunks. I have to make up a good story about who I'm staying with. I want to get the hell out of here. I'm getting sick of it. I just slept for 2 days straight basically + I'm still tired. I try to keep busy so I don't go crazy. I'm already sick of these stupid books. I've been in here forever!

I'm just kidding. I'm having a lot of fun in here. I get hundreds of carrots for dinner! I just read this really funny "National Lampoons" books, blah blah blah. I bet you really want to hear about it right? Well fuck you! Where the hell is Gunther? Gunther, fuck where are you, goddamn it, you doggamn bunny? I need you here. There is a hole where you used to be, a cold and empty hole. I'm sorry I didn't take care of you. I did my best.

Dear Miranda,

Hey you little fucker, thanks for writing me, I love you too. People make some funny vegan comments in here: "You eat beans? I thought you were vegetarian, beans are meat, peanut butter, nuts, tofu, that's all meat. I don't care if it came out of the ground or not, potatoes come out of the ground too and it doesn't matter if they are never alive, they are still all meat." & "Green Day doesn't drink milk because he likes cows. Don't eat nothing that comes out of an animal cuz he likes animals. I like cows too, but I've gotta drink milk." I guess that's all of the funny ones. Hold on a minute, I've gotta go tap on my wall.

It's cold outside again, isn't it? Did you finally get to see Star Wars? Just kidding, I don't care. Frankie said that he camped out for it, what the hell is he talking about? It must have been really crowded. I was writing him a letter earlier and someone ask me if I was writing my old lady. Ha ha ha.

That circle thing in your letter confused me. I thought that the upside down writing was Swahili, but I figured it out. That paper was cool, but it reminded me too much of the Chinos. Bye, -Sam

P.S. I don't like monkeys, I was making fun of them, especially hairless ones that think they are cool just because they can read + write and watch TV. Don't take it personally, just joking around, you are alright for a human.

P.P.S. "This one's as stupid as, uh, garbanzo beans." -? I am munchkin! I am muchkin? I maim chunk? You can tell I'm pretty bored huh? But that's fucking funny.

The next day, I got a letter. It had a code border. I deciphered it before reading the anything else. I was excited. It was mostly silly stuff and inside jokes with a few lines about running away to Berkeley if it seemed like serious prison time was certain. After de-coding the secret message I read the rest:

Feb 3/4, 1997 Letter #10

Dear Chris Clavin,

I'm getting bored of writing jail stories, so instead I'm gonna tell you some more things that my friend Bob has said. I'll draw you a picture of him someday, but for now, just imagine a short Italian guy without much hair. Today he told be that he was supposed to be out of here by last Friday, he was kind of upset about it. "I'm just trying to stamp out injustice" he said "I want to stop them from torturing the mentally ill, the homeless and the poor." I used to think he was just lying when he talked about all the stuff that he claims to know a lot about, *but sometimes he proves me wrong. For example, once he was talking about being an accomplished jazz musician or something, and he showed this fucking Christian a bunch of guitar tablature and proved it, of course a Christian will believe anything, so I'll think of a better example and tell you later. Anyway Bob was locked in his cell because he smarted off to judge Todd (who is my judge too). Excuse me if this doesn't make any sense, I don't have a very good memory for exact quotations and it's hard to piece together complex arguments. He accused judge Todd of soliciting cocaine and destroying the society of Bloomington. He explained this elaborate theory to me about how money from arrests goes into the court system, then back to drug dealers on the streets. This is a huge simplification of Bob's theory, which also involves the Pentagon. Sometime later I will interview him again and get the full story. Basically he gave judge Todd a big fuck you in front of everyone. It's fairly interesting, since I have heard several rumors that the Todd really does cocaine and possibly sells it. I don't think Bob will be turned lose anytime soon.*

I forgot to tell you the most important thing about his appearance, his eyes, they are brown and sunken deep inside his head. His face is twisted and has deep creases and his eyes usually never move. He doesn't really get excited about much, except cigarettes. He talks very politely. If someone gives him a cigarette though, he jumps around, straight up and down for around 5 minutes. Sometimes I collect butts out of the ashtrays for him so he can smoke the leftovers. He wants to smoke a lot, I understand, he's locked in his cold comfort cell for 22 hours a day with nothing to do.

(This paragraph is boring) During lock-down I read about Treblinka and thought about what Bob was saying. At Treblinka, each prisoner, or slave, or laborer, or patient had 1000 deaths of his fellow Jews on his hands each day, and yet they still held on to their identity and rose up again. Now the Jews have a treasure that so few others in the world really have, a powerful set of legends that relate to modern times with heroes and demons. All it takes for any fairly normal human with a moral code to become a hero is to have some demons to do battle with. I'm definitely not saying that the extermination of 6 million people was worth it for a couple of stories, especially since these stories haven't even come close to stopping genocide, and the nation of Israel, created basically by the fact that these powerful stories went along with the interests of the world's rulers, has come doggamn close to committing genocide. But who knows? Racism doesn't have much intellectual credibility anymore. Before WWII is was an accepted fact that anyone that didn't look like you was inferior. Now only high school cheerleaders and egomaniacs believe that, and all intelligent people with half a conscious have to remember the Holocaust, even if they can manage to forget about slavery or the genocide of the Indians. It didn't have to be like this. The world could have ignored 6 million corpses. We ignored 30 million in the USSR.

But, with the Jewish people that survived, so survived their stories, stories about monsters and beautiful girls and dying children and humans that did their best. I'm wasting paper though, I talked to Bob more after we got out of lock-down:

"So what if there is nothing left after you stamp out injustice?" I said. "It isn't the stamping out of injustice that matters, but the process of revolt, of creating a desire to move forward, into the future. It is like a potato ship, it consumes you, even as you consume it. The stampers become unjust. I only want to create peace. I used to drive a delivery truck in Rochester, NY, delivering potato chips. We had all kinds, mostly Jay's. It was great man, potato chips bring peace. Hey, do you like potato chips? How about when I get out of here, I come a visit you guys? I'll bring you some potato chips and some Pepsi and a couple of cartons of cigarettes. You'd like that wouldn't you? Judge Todd still owes me $315 dollars. How much Pepsi do you think I'd need for all of you guys? 20 liters and 2 cartons of cigarettes?

Do you remember the voice mail that I left on our machine that was on there the night that I got arrested? I was afraid that you would think it was from me after I disappeared. Really it was from when Frankie dropped you off at your parents' house on the way to see Weezer in Louisville. I was calling from the free phone outside of Collins at 2:08 AM. It was raining and I was really tired. I thought that I would call you and tell you where I was, since you were coming back soon, but then I realized that I didn't know where I'd be once I hung up. It was too cold to wait there. That's why the message was so confusing. Maybe you didn't even hear that message, I don't know.

In other news, the magic necklace didn't really break. It just came off, I can put it on and take it off now.

Anyway, the person from mental health came today and diagnosed me with bipolar disorder type II and wants to get me on a treatment program, get me on more medication. I told them that jail was driving me crazy and that my old friend Otis (I used his real name) told me that I could stay with him and get straightened out and apply for disability. He and everyone else seem to think that I shouldn't worry too much. Everyone says that I probably won't get in too much trouble and I won't get sent to the farm. Sorry you bit your lip on Hannah's trampoline, but you may have gotten lucky. Once when I banged my knee against my chin, it chipped one of my teeth. Oh yeah, I forgot about another mental disease that I have, the old disability doctor diagnosed me with: antisocial disorder type I or something like that. It means, humans make me really nervous.

I don't really need you to come in here and see me. I don't like visitation anyway, because I have to leave my cell block. The last time, I had to wait for 20 minutes in a tiny room with a big ex-con who told me that I reminded him of a fishing-bait that he used once. He yelled about how he was going to kill the social worker that accused him of molesting an 8 year-old girl. He was trying to be *friendly, but it was one of the scariest experiences that I had since the night that I got arrested. I usually like talking to people. But I prefer the class warriors a lot better than the violent offenders. But anyway, then I go into this other room and the other guys are yelling as loud as they can into these little drive through-like windows. The gang thought that I was deaf, but really there were just tons of people yelling: PELICAN BRIEF! /JURY! /TRIAL! /MAXIMUM! /PROBATION! /BATTERY! so you're not missing much, and I understand why you would be afraid to come here. I really don't like leaving the comfort of my cold comfort cell block anyway. But, if someone else wants to come by, I wouldn't mind giving it another try.*

You know that guy Zeke that helped me get my vegetarian slip, well he's gone now. Do you remember that other Zeke, that was always at our house on Henderson, painting miniatures and drinking 40s. Remember my mouse that I had there, Titler? That one time...fuck! I'm gonna have to waste another sheet of paper! How about I just write more later, my back hurts anyway. See you, -Sam

P.S. No, I can't have a guitar in here, sorry.
P.P.S. I just got your letter buddy, was it ripped when you sent it?
Tell Otis to use my real name on the outside of the envelope.
Also, nobody draw any pictures of fags butt-fucking or anything unless you want to (on the outside of the envelope I mean, well they get ripped open any-way). Draw whatever you want on the inside, except don't draw me. I see me enough already.

On the inside flap of the envelope, Sam scrawled:

! Hey the jail is overcrowded! I might get out soon, I'll get evaluated + write some letters to get my bail lowered...Hopefully, I'll be out there soon eating potato ships with you guys!

Dear Chris,
How many vegans does it take to bake a Christian cake? Fuck. Bye, -Sam

Speaking of potato chips, this wasn't Sam's first run-in with the law. Dur-ing the days of chaos, when we lived in the Henderson house, he got busted for stealing CDs at Street Side Records. He was using a technique that he discov-ered during his research. We tired a lot of new stuff that summer and we were always trying to network with other crooks to learn as much as we could. We heard rumors and we tested them. We sought out rare books about scamming. Sam read about how alarm gates worked and theorized that aluminum foil would prevent them from sounding, so he tested it at the library by wrapping a book in foil. It worked! Obviously, he couldn't wrap CDs in foil in the store, and it was summer, so he couldn't wear a jacket or a coat with foil-lined pockets, which meant he had to think of something else. He went into a store with a bag of potato chips. As soon as he walked in, he asked the clerk if it was okay to eat chips in the store, which was his idea of nullifying any suspicions that might arise, then he walked around the store, casually dropping CDs into the bag of chips. The first time he did it, he came home with six CDs! The next day, he went back and added a 40¢ Coke to his disguise and came back with six more CDs.

Having no control and being totally fearless, he went back the day after that and they caught him. While he was waiting for the police to arrive, he "accidentally" spilled his huge coke all over their counter and a rack full of CDs. The clerk was really pissed. The cops came, filled out forms, gave him a court date, and banned him from the store for life. A few days later, Sam noticed a stack of boxes on their steps. It was a delivery in progress from UPS. He grabbed a huge box and ran away with it. He brought it home and rushed into our room, out of breath. "I think they were chasing me," he said. "I heard those fuckers yelling at me!" he continued, before asking me for my knife to open the box to see what he had nabbed. He sliced and ripped. It was 30 copies of the same CD: monks chanting Christmas songs. "Doggamnit!" Sam yelled. "The joke's on me I guess, fuck!" He tossed the box into the closet.

…

We still didn't have enough money to pay Sam's bail and, after what he'd told us in his latest letter, I was hopeful that he would get out. A few days passed with no mail and no phone calls. We were all worried. Then:

Feb 6, 1997. Letter #11

Dear Chris,
Hello this is Sam. Sorry I missed a day. I wrote a letter but didn't send it. It was concerned with nothing but underwear and my need for them, I've used or lost my other ones. I wasn't very happy. However, today is library day, so I am getting new books, I hope. Here is something I wrote yesterday, so you'll have something from every day.

Here is what I can see from my room, sorry it's glued with toothpaste, they don't let us have glue, please re-glue it.

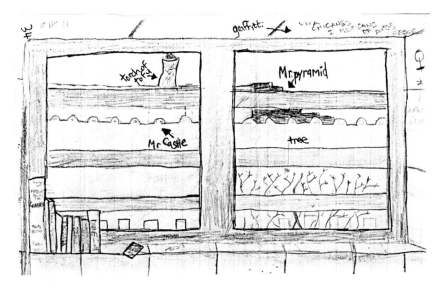

Feb 5, 1997.

I have a mission for anyone that wants it: find out what Mr. Pyramid is. Also what are the mystery flags? As always, lies are totally acceptable. For a long time I wondered what the billboard was, behind the 3 identical apartment buildings. I was pretty disappointed when I found out. Whatever.

Anyway, I notice if it's cold or warm outside by feeling my window. I like it better when it's warm. I like thinking about you guys, out there, having fun. Sorry you busted your lip. Did I tell you about the time that I chipped my tooth on my knee? It's okay that you don't want to come here, stay away, it's funny. No, you can't have a guitar in here unless you make it out of banana peels, pencils, celery and lint. You could also use old toothpaste containers, and use the toothpaste as glue. I think the guards would be really mad when they found it under my cot and I'd lose my cell. It would be weeks before I got my own cell back.

Man, I kinda think this is fun sometimes. I felt like I was cheated out of having a long letter writing campaign when I was living in Mitchell, you know? But I just couldn't stand it there, once I was really awake, I had to get out. My dad yelled at me every time I moved and would ask me what I was doing.

I wish me and you would have gotten our ministers credentials. That would have been worth the $15 and I bet you could come and see me, as my religious advisor.

This Indian guy scribbled all over my paper today. His relatives left him $15 on commissary and he ask me if I would put it in my name instead, so that he wouldn't have to pay back his jail medical bills. He bought what he wanted and let me spend the leftovers on stamps and envelopes.

There is only one song on TNN that I like. It's by Deanna Carter and it's about Mexican music. It's nice, although she has a stupid name. It was just on.

I just found out that I won't be able to go to the library for a while, maybe a month or so. I'm ready to get out of here now! I think it's time to have Frankie and Otis start a campaign of telephone harassment to get my public defender in here. I'll start writing letters. Some harassment from the outside might help other things too, but it's hard to decide. Everything has to be perfect. I'm playing a dangerous balancing game with 2 or 3 terrible outcomes and all I've got to work with is my guts, my brains and you guys. I don't want to go to prison and I don't want to get institutionalized, mainly because I don't want to be forced to take drugs, I also don't want to go crazy. But they don't really want to do either of the first things to me, just the third. I'm supposed to be taking Depressol to treat my depression. But isn't jail supposed to make you feel sad and guilty and isolated and lonely? It seems like they would give you drugs if you weren't depressed because you'd be a psychopath if you were locked up in here having a great time, reading tons of cool books, playing games and thinking about how funny everything is and never having to worry about what you're going to eat or where you are going to sleep or who you are going to irritate when you stay over at their house.

I just think of it as if I'm playing Monopoly, I've been landing on "chance" every day for a long time and I finally hit "go directly to jail," but that was fine with me, because all the properties are bought and covered with houses and hotels and I don't have any money to pay rent. The jackpot has $1500 in it and I might as well just sit in here and hope for doubles.

I finished Hocus Pocus, it was good. It's about a guy in prison for starting an insurrection (is that a sexual word or something?) In his prison, the convicts have to watch TV shows that are 10 years old so they don't get excited about what's going on outside.

When I first got here I kept hearing funny coincidences on TV that drove me crazy. I kept hearing about a Gregory Wells that got burned to death in a chemical fire and a Christopher Johnston that got arrested for robbery or something, it wasn't you, or Greg, just people with the same names.

Doggamn it! I wish I could relax for a minute in here. The fire alarm just went off. I think I can smell smoke. I hope that we don't have to go outside. How can this place burn, its all metal and concrete? I don't feel any explosions, so I don't think it's a jailbreak or anything, if it is I hope I can go outside. Never mind, it's over. What was I talking about before?

I'm reading another K.V. book now. It's called "Galapagos." I've only got 90 pages left and it's gotta last until my next library trip. I wish they would let me go, no never mind, I don't want to waste a wish on that. I didn't think I would like it at first, but it's really good. I've been practicing writing with my teeth (it's a forgery technique) and it's really hard, my jaw hurts now.

I made a little buddy out of lint. He doesn't have a name, but he looks neat.

Did I tell you that I really need clean underwear, not long johns, but I wouldn't mind one pair of long johns & 3 pair of clean underwear. I keep calling Frankie and telling him to bring me some, but I guess he keeps forgetting. I hate calling there, but it's the only place I can call. I'm always worried that his mom will answer.

I have had only one dream that I remember: I'm sitting in a room and there is bald fat man sitting behind an oak desk. The room is a library/study type room and the man is wearing a suit. I am really nervous. There is woman standing beside him. She hands him files from a cabinet and then he shows them to me. I'm not handcuffed or anything but I am not free either. He wants something else from me. The files are filled with facts about my friends, like where they are at 3:20 PM and stuff, it's really scary. Lewis' file said "He is easily manipulated by the combination of mild punishment followed by acceptance and respect." For some reason, in this dream, I thought it was written by the girl who was his boss at the snack bar and I wanted to kill her. But I still didn't say anything to the man, I couldn't give up. It was awful. My "friends" didn't include you, just people that I didn't really talk to anymore but wouldn't want to see any harm come to. Michelle and Morley were in there. It wasn't much fun.

Are you going to watch Dante's Peak? Have you heard the theme song of Treblinka? Get your very own FASCIST STATE MODEL TRAIN SET TODAY!

I continued my reckless quest to steal enough stuff to bail Sam out. It was slow going, but I considered it honorable to take these risks and to walk the path of Sam. I'd steal $40-80 worth of books a day and sell them for ¼ of their retail price, so on my best days I only made $20. I missed Sam, so I went through some of his things in the van and found several IDs and credit cards that didn't belong to him. I wondered how many backpacks he had stolen and didn't tell me about. I also wondered if the credit cards would still work. I figured that they would at least work for pizza, since a lot of the pizza places used the old style carbon copy credit card system, which wouldn't tell them if the card had been cancelled right away. I hoped every day that Sam would just show up and knock on the van and say, "Are there any punks in there?" but he didn't come, only his letters, and this time there were three of them:

Feb 7, 1997. Letter #12

Hey I just found out that my public defender won't come see me until I go to court in April. So, I need you guys to help me out. Tell him my story please! I'll write some letters too. Some public defenders work on 200 cases at a time, so he'll probably say that he doesn't have time. Tell him that judge Todd raised my *bail when he found out that I couldn't pay $500, which seems really unfair, now that I could (you could). Also you should try to pick up my disability paperwork, I listed you as contact or something, so they should let you have it. It would look good for my case if I had those papers. I can't call them. They won't even let me call 1-800 #s! These bastards definitely read the mail you guys send me. They ripped the letter from you with the picture of Chiapas. I drew my own. Thanks for dropping off the money. I can't use it until Thursday (commissary day.) Thursday is also library day. I'll make you a schedule.*

NEWS: My bond is just $5,000, so it's only $505 to get me out! Maybe I could get it lowered more. Anyway, I guess it's not that bad, I'll have clean underwear! I'll have a much underwear as I want! Yeah!

Feb 7, 1997.

Dear Plan-It-X
This is Sam. It's 8:00 and I just spent a minute trying to get through to Frankie's. My bond is only $5,000. I was mistaken this whole time. He said that he was going to raise it to $10,000 but he didn't really do it and I never ask. I'm so happy, now I can leave whenever I want, $505 isn't that bad. Since I'm happy and I'll hopefully be out of here tomorrow, I'll tell you some jail stories.
After 9:30 lock-down I sit around with J.R., Estep and Flipper and they tell me stories about real prison. J.R. used to sell rock cocaine, he's a black man. Estep is an alcoholic Indian and Flipper is a scam artist and a white man. They are all burglars and they help me eat my carrots. I read to J.R. I think he is illiterate.
Jailhouse tattoos: I've seen some really well done ones and some really shitty ones. My friend J.R.'s are well done. Usually the subject matter sucks. The coolest one was this guy with a chain around his wrist. He is a child molester, the one from the missing page mystery, the one that said I reminded him of a fishing-bait that he used one. He was really tough, and mean.

MONDAY: free popcorn
TUESDAY: laundry
WEDNESDAY: visits
THURSDAY: order commissary + library
FRIDAY: get commissary + free popcorn
SATURDAY: nothing
SUNDAY: nothing

Why I can't write in pen:

I think they are afraid that we would give ourselves jailhouse tattoos. That one time when the guard misplaced her pen, they yelled at us for 20 minutes and searched everyone's room before she found it, in her pocket.

My Schedule:

- *5:30 First wake up- they open the doors and yell over the intercom. Now it's easy as pie to sleep through anything. If I get caught skipping my medicine, I get locked in my cell for 30 days.*
- *6:00 Medicine. I fake taking Prozac.*
- *6:40 Breakfast. Oatmeal, juice and coffee. I don't drink the coffee. I stagger out, eat breakfast then it's back to bed.*
- *8:00 Lock-down. We get locked in our rooms.*
- *9:00 Razors. They call over the intercom and say "press call button for a razor." Then if you pressed the button, a guard slides a razor through a slot in your door. When you're done, you have to pass it back through.*
- *12:40 Lunch. Usually PB+J and a ton of carrots. From 12 to 3 Jeff (a baker guy, kinda) watches TNN. It sucks. I stay in my room. I used to play chess during this time with a guy named Roger, but he got out. Sometimes the Jewel video for "Save my Soul" comes on and I crawl out of bed to watch it. When it's not TNN it's horny dudes watching "The Grind" on MTV.*
- *3:30 Another lock-down. Why? Don't ask me.*
- *6:40 Dinner. Oops. Sorry for that drool spot. I'm eating tomato soup and crackers. I usually only eat the crackers, you know how I feel about tomatoes. The good cook is gone, the new one is a redneck fucker. I hate him.*
- *7:00 The mail comes.*
- *7:30 Seinfeld.*
- *8:00 Last lock-down. This one causes me to miss most of the TV that I might actually watch. We get out again at 9:30.*
- *11:30 Bedtime. Back to our rooms. I read a write till 4:00 a.m.*

Man, people are telling J.R. racist jokes. It's fucking rude. I think he's getting mad. Someone just said "What do you call a black..." He interrupted and said "You're mama motherfucker!" He's mad now. I'm mad now. It's over now. I hate white people. I'm locked in my room again.

If you're ever in jail or prison, never say that you are a "punk," say "punk-

rocker" instead.

I had an argument about homophobia one time. It wasn't very rational. All J.R. would say is "I see where you are coming from, but I'm not gonna fuck a girl in the booty. I ain't doing none of that shit."

"Punk" is a homosexual's young boy, or "a person that takes it up the ass in prison." to quote Charlie Manson. Racism is real. Homophobia is real. Sexism is real. Classism is real. "I'm just joking man, I didn't mean it. I thought you were laughing." Charlie Manson is this old fucker's nickname in here. "Just playing with you girl, you know I respect you." The only one laughing is the upper-class hetrosexual white man, 'cause he's running the motherfucking show. All I can say is that I'm glad that I'm not a motherfucking part of this shit.

If you want to go someplace where black men are in charge and homosexuality is sort of accepted, you can go to prison. Of course, white guards can beat you up or yell at you whenever they want. Love, Sam

Feb 7, 1997.

Dear Chris,

Hello, I am kind of nervous, there was almost a race war earlier and the whites are being really racist and telling redneck jokes. I'm just a skinny little punk, but I can't sit down, I know what side I'm on when it comes to the race war.

Anyway, thanks for the ongoing story. I hope I'm out of here before it's over. I've got a migraine headache. I haven't been eating much. J.R. has been really worried about me and he's making me eat his chips and drink his lemonade. I'm not even hungry.

Anyway, I've been reading this book "Strange Tales of Foreign Lands" by Felix Krull, it's got some cool stuff in it. There is an article about an architect in Russia who designed a lot of impressive Soviet buildings in Moscow. As a reward, the party told him that he could build a home for himself and place it anywhere he wants in the Soviet Union and build it out of any materials. They didn't exactly tell him that because they knew that this guy was an Idealist. He knew his country wasn't perfect, but he believed that if everyone worked at it, it could be closer to perfect, and he loved the people. He wasn't much different than the good patriots here. So instead, they offered him the job of designing the residence for the Master Architect of the Soviet Union, so that he could do his work in a comfortable environment and one that inspired him.

Like his country, he wasn't perfect, he was a dreamer and he was proud of his work. He accepted the job. The architect had, since the death of his wife, lived in a single apartment in Kiev. When the young men and women woke up to go to their dismal jobs in the factory, he arose and went to his office. He tolerated no less from his comrades. At night he ate in the common refectory, saying the pres-

186

ence of others helped digestion. "The man that eats alone, sleeps with heartburn," he liked to say. Maybe it was true, but it wasn't why he ate in the refectory. Or maybe it was. Who am I to know, I just read about him. But I suspect that it made him feel rooted in his people. He often said that it was his greatest ambition to create a building that was as strong, persistent and noble as the Soviet worker. Of course he was no fool, and almost all of his buildings are still standing. Many of the Soviet workers that he based his designs upon were dead within a decade. Accidents happen.

Now he was faced with the difficult task, to design a building that could "inspire" the architects of the future and be a standing monument to his work as well as his home. He was not sure if it was possible. Of course he hoped that all of his creations inspired but his home had always been a simple place.

There was another problem. He, himself was not inspired at all. He had not taken on a new project in 2 years. Each day he still arose with his people at dawn and stared at a blank sketch sheet in his office. Each night he returned home with a handful of doodles of beautiful women and he ate dinner with his "strong and persistent" people. But, his strong and persistent people were sinking, in fear, in depression, in vodka. It was not so easy to be strong and persistent anymore. Maybe it never was. Maybe it didn't matter. He didn't consider himself either strong or persistent. He couldn't take much more of the fear or depression or vodka.

The architect was an old man. He had been hired to design his own epitaph. They considered him a fool. They considered him a tool. They were wrong, he was a dreamer.

He couldn't decide what materials he would use to build his home/tombstone. He spent a lot of time in the library reading about what others had done. He was no king or prince, his tomb would not be made of granite or marble or alabaster. In fact, he was against stone, he was a man of ideas.

He didn't spend much time in the office anymore. Instead of drawing young women in their summer dresses, he watched them. He fed ducks in the park. He left the blueprints to his underlings. I mean comrades, I am sorry.

Blueprints...

The old man designed a crypt made of blueprints.

It was actually constructed of blueprints. The party was really impressed by it's novelty although they were astonished by this sign of flippancy in someone so stable. They assigned a young man to be the architect's friend. This man wasn't a patriot but was a professional friend. He looked after people for money and made sure that they didn't get into trouble. If they did, he got them help.

When the old man moved into his new home (his crypt) his friend ate meals with him, to avoid indigestion. His friend kept him from drinking at least. His friend made a knot in his stomach. The old man was done dreaming about buildings. He only wished for one thing; that he could be persistent and strong like his comrades. He wished that he could die.

The old man never made anything, he said, other than a clipper ship in a bottle and a lot of drawings. It was the people who made the buildings. The state, the state made nothing but headaches and ulcers.

It was 3 whole months before the old man's friend got him help. He spent a whole summer in the house made of paper by the pond where the ducks swam. There was a patch of blue grass where the rain washed out the gutters. They tried to get the old man to move into a home for the mentally disabled. The old man didn't want to go. He wanted to go to work camp with his comrades. The old man's professional friend had to shoot him in the back of the head. That's what friends are for.

They took apart the blueprint house and filed the blueprints away. They are probably still inside the Kremlin now. I don't know for sure, this book was written before the Soviet Union broke up. But I wouldn't doubt it. Some things usually stay the same. If you could find them, you would see what inspired the architect while he fed the ducks and looked at his old drawings and so on. There were blueprints for a factory in Kiev that assembled chairs for Armenian school children. There were blueprints for a factory in Armenia that disassembled chairs for shipment to Kiev. There were blueprints from every part of the top secret Soviet space program.

The Soviet space program contributed a lot to science. Now we know that humans don't explode when subjected to a vacuum. We also learned how to deliver projectiles across intercontinental distances.

In addition, he had blueprints from corresponding industries in America. No one knows how he got them. For every Chernobyl, he had a 3-mile island. It must be assumed that in the end he learned to admire the strength and persistence of the American worker as well, or that we are all ONE people. A lot of old mean and young workers received bullets in the back of the head trying to figure out how he did it. When his professional friend asked him, he only gave one answer: "I spent a lot of time in the library finding out how people designed crypts. I decided that I wanted them all."

We bailed Sam out the next day. I was still too afraid to sign my name on any official papers, or to be seen in the jail, so Otis did the paperwork and I gave him the $505 he needed to bring Sam back to us. He looked frightened when I hugged him. He was pale and nervous. He was acting like a wild rabbit, scared and alert. I told him that everything was gonna be okay and that I had a surprise for him. We went to Collins and Hannah called in a pizza order. She said, "Can I pay with my credit card?" Then she gave them the number on the card that I had found in Sam's bag. They asked her for a name. She said, "Anna

188

White" and a new character was born in our alias family of scammers. Sam didn't know what we were doing, we had left him waiting in a common room with Otis and Frankie, and when we came back he asked me what we were up to.

"We ordered a pizza. Anna White ordered it, I mean," I said. I was so excited. I wanted to show him that we weren't gonna be scared straight. I wanted to say something cliché about getting back on the horse. I didn't, because he turned ghost white and started to panic.

"Do you think this is a good idea?" he asked.

"Yeah," I assured him, "don't worry. We used the credit card and it worked." He looked worried. We asked him questions about jail while we waited. The pizza came and everything went smoothly. It was "the big cheese" from Pizza Express. It's a great pizza, with four cheeses and pecans on top. We got an extra large and a full order of breadsticks, and sodas of course. Once the exchange was over and Sam had a slice of pizza in his hand, he cheered up and started acting like himself. "Do you think they are gonna send you to prison in April?" I asked.

"No, I doubt it, but if it looks bad at my pre-trial, I might have to go to Berkeley. Don't worry, I'll pay you guys the money back if I jump bail," he said.

"Don't worry about it. I don't want to see you in prison for two years." We all agreed that Sam wouldn't do well in prison and that it would be easy to jump bail and hide out in the underground scene. We slept at Otis' house that night and Sam didn't hear anyone shouting anything over the intercom in the morning.

We went to the P.O. box together the next morning. It was good to have Sam back. There was a letter for Otis, from Sam, written the day before he got out:

Feb 8, 1997. Letter #13

Dear Otis,
(By the way, everything in this letter may or may not be fictional. fuck off)
-Sam
Hello, this is Sam. Thanks for the story. Cops and prosecutors are full of shit, they do their best to scare the hell out of you. If you offer up any kind of resistance at all, they are likely to just give up. Here, if you just threaten to fill out a grievance form, the guards roll over like dogs, they are just bullies.
How about if today, I just tell you about a job I had at Eigenmann hall as a janitor. It's the longest I've ever kept a job. Eigenmann hall is a dorm full of graduate students. Lots of foreigners live there. Also they have different confer-

ences and workshops for high school students. There is a floor for only Japanese students, a floor for only Korean students and a floor for only Chinese students. Only, the students weren't really from those countries, they were just learning the languages. Frankie wants to learn/is learning Japanese so he can talk to Japanese girls. There are a lot of Japanese girls in this story, so you might want to share it with him.

Anyway, I didn't really consider it a job. I considered it a treasure hunt. It was our job to clean out these fuckers' dorm rooms after they went back to foreign lands. Lots of these rooms were hell holes, it looked like no one lived in them, but zombies, rotting food, layers of dust, tons of oriental coins and fans and calendars. These rooms were the best, man. Once I found a diamond. It was a big as my fist, made of glass. I think I gave it to Chris and told him to give it Miranda. One lady found 300,000 yen, or $300. I had a whole collection of little foreign coins, but never found any real money. This stupid kid found a VCR once. He left it out in the hall, unattended. I found it out there and took it and hid it in a bush and rode home with it on my bike after work.

I worked in a crew with Mahmood from Afghanistan, this girl from England who was a graduate student and Matt Blue, a Christian. I used to log onto Matt's email and read his messages, and I kept a little book with facts about him, his SS # and his birthday and stuff like that. I was a wicked fucker, he thought we were best buddies, but I was just gathering information on my enemy, he never seemed to notice that I never talked about myself unless I was lying.

Mahmood was the coolest man. He didn't speak English very well, everything that he said was a direct quote from MTV or commercials. He always said things like, "If you need help, call 1-800-MAH-MOOD." That translates to meaning, "If you need help, just ask me." We would clean out a couple of rooms, then goof off for the rest of the day. We usually only cleaned roughly two rooms a day, but sometimes we'd do 20. If we weren't doing anything, I go around searching the empty/unlocked rooms for loot, or I would make prank phone calls. No matter what, I made at least one prank a day. I would call 1-800-MAH-MOOD to entertain Mahmood. The number belonged to a seller of wholesale vegetable produce. I called and ordered huge shipments of parsley and stuff like that. Mr. Mahmood got pretty sick of it. Since I was able to make untraceable calls from unoccupied rooms, I made some great prank calls. I called the motherfucking FBI and stuff, it was fun.

One day Mahmood bought a new car and drove it to work. He doesn't (or didn't) have a driver's license. He didn't care at all. He said "In my country if you are caught driving without papers, you would be shot. Here you just get tickets, they are nothing." He loved America. He loved MTV, Salt n' Peppa, Aerosmith (mainly the girl from the Aerosmith video.) I rode home with him from work one day, a year later, after he got his license. He was just taking me home to get my

190

glasses, it was cool. When we got back, he parked in a handicapped spot. I asked him if he knew it was a handicapped spot and he said "Yaas, I'm handicap." I asked him how and he twirled his finger around his ear and said "Crazy, I'm crazy." He really had a handicapped sticker.

Partway though the summer we traded the English girl (Goddamn, I can't remember her name. All I can think of calling her is Jamaica...She was vegetarian and cool, that was way before everyone knew about vegetarians and punks and stuff, so she was the only one who thought there wasn't anything wrong with me having pink hair) for Fedora, Mahmood's cousin. I wished that we could have traded Matt Blue instead, so that there weren't any white people on team Mahmood. But, Matt loved Mahmood too, so it was okay. Fedora (that was really his name, but he went by Fred) said that Mahmood didn't make any more sense in his own language than he does in English. He said that Mahmood was crazy! One day we had to help this guy carry his stuff out of storage and he gave us a $3 tip. Me and Mahmood went straight across the street to the V.P. and got a 2-liter of Pepsi and some vegan cookies. I guess that's not very entertaining but, I'm dying for a cola and it's fun thinking about sharing a Pepsi with Mahmood back in the 60s. I hope I get out tomorrow!

I liked pretending like I was real working class, I had this tin lunchbox like a factory worker would use and I stocked it with coke, PB&J, fruit and potato ships. The fruit always tasted kind of rusty. The chips fell out of their baggie sometimes and then they tasted rusty too. The coke was Big K, the chips were cost cutter, generic. This is way before I knew about all the ways to get cooler food for free. Back then I bought my food, so I bought the cheap stuff. But anyway, for a while I'd just come home from work and relax while Chris told me about all the work that he'd been doing at home, cleaning the bathroom and stuff like that. It was cool. It was like he was my housewife. Eventually though, I ran out of Big K and that was bad. I went for a week without cola of any sort. By the end, I could smell it from really far away. One night after work we went and watched "The Crow." Marty was really excited about it because of the soundtrack. The movie kinda sucked, but all I could think about was the smell of the cola all around me. It felt good to be there. Man, I must had some other reason other than being broke, because I paid to get into that movie. I didn't know you could sneak in back then. Oh yeah, I remember. That Friday was my first payday. It took like 4 weeks to get your first check. I did get coke, I bought 2 cans of name brand Pepsi! It was so fucking great. I can't believe I didn't even go to Taco Bell or anything. I could have gotten unlimited refills. I guess it was because I was really against fast food. I still am now, it's just that back then it was easier to make a big deal out of everything. I was also really nervous about eating in restaurants. I was scared of Americans and embarrassed about being a messy eater. I usually hid when I was eating.

That was all during one week when Miranda was on a school trip or some-

thing. Chris started going insane from hanging out with me too much, mumbling and thinking illogically, or not really illogically, but twisted logic, and speaking my funny language or whatever. That was just after 4 days or something. Now he's insane too, so it doesn't mater anymore. But back then, he was really glad when he could hang out with some humans.

I liked exploring the dorm too, there was so much crazy stuff. There was this huge sub-basement full of junk. I stole a bunch of blueprints from it one time. There was a huge boiler room and a laundry room where the laundry shoot came to its end. There was one room that I called the dirt room because it was filled with dirt, there was a huge pile of dirt in the middle of the floor. There were rooms filled with broken equipment and old mattresses, dirty laundry and old chairs. It was cool, I loved it.

One day on an adventure, I climbed down the laundry shoot. It was a little metal tube around 2 to 3 feet in diameter that went from the 14th floor to the dungeon. I was going to climb from the 10th floor down to the 9th. The 10th floor was Korea and the 9th was Japan. Matt Blue stood guard on the 10th floor and Alex (this kid that loved The Beatles and wanted to join the peace core) stood on the 9th. On the 9th floor it was illegal to speak English. There was a beautiful half-Japanese girl with a shaved head and skater clothes that lived there. She always smiled at me, but I could never talk to her, since she was of a different social class and I wasn't allowed to speak English, so I just smiled. I was stationed in "Japan" at the time, cleaning bathrooms and sweeping floors. I talked to her eventually...maybe I'll tell the story later.

Anyway, the tube had all these jagged edges and it was really slick. I kept from falling by bracing my knees on the sides. I think the shoot was aluminum because it was really thin and buckled a lot when I put my weight on it. I shuffled down by keeping one knee wedged and moving the other one up and down. I had to move fast, if someone dropped a dirty blanket in the shoot above me, it would have really sucked. If someone dropped a load of heavy laundry into the shoot, I might had fell into the dungeon. Sorry, there is no exciting climax. I made it safely to Japan. But then Matt Blue tried it and slipped and I had to grab his arm. I had to get someone help me pull him out. If he would have fallen, the jagged edges would have ripped him apart. Of course he made a really big deal out of it and says that I saved his life. Whatever.

Every day at lunch time I would scrounge all the couches for change. I could make $2 a day doing that. It was fun. One day this Japanese lady asked me what I was doing. It was the first floor lounge, so I was permitted to answer. I told her and she thought it was really funny. Her name was Jihan or something. It stared with a 'J'. She turned out to be the shaved-headed skater girl's teacher. For a while she taught me Japanese in the lounge but the only thing I can remember is konichiwa.

Anyway, one time, me and Matt Blue got a clean out order for the 9th floor, Japanese territory. Matt Blue unlocks the skater girl's room by mistake. "Whoops!" Christians, who need em? By this time Matt had figured out that I was a vegetarian. He bugged me about it constantly. He said that real vegetarians didn't eat milk, cheese or eggs. I told him that I was trying to do that, but I messed up every once and a while. He made jokes about it all the time and it was really irritating, but it worked to my advantage once because my crush heard him making fun of me and she thought I was cool. One day I was hanging out on the wall in front of People's Park and she walked by twice. She asked me where to get lotion for a cut on her leg. It was such a lame attempt to talk to me. Anyway, I was really nervous at first but we got to be friends, then summer came to an end and she grew up and I can't stand her anymore. I might have been in love with her. She thinks I'm a moron now. Whatever. I tried to hang out with her little sister too, but she grew up and I think that she thinks that I'm a moron too. Whatever.

Anyway, that's enough for today. I am hoping you guys bail me out, but if you don't that's okay. I don't really miss you that much, but you were pretty funny. It was cool hanging out with you and I liked your letter. It was a lot easier to understand than hearing the story over the phone or through the drive-thru window visitation hole. See ya later, -Sam.

Drawing, by Sam.

193

Of course, I didn't read that letter until almost a year later. That cold February day at the post office, he snatched it out of my hands and said, "You don't want to read that, I talk about the Chino sisters and how they broke my heart." I didn't pressure him. I knew I'd get to read it someday, when he put it in his "Pizza Bandits" 'zine. We went to the library to look for some good movies to watch later that night with Brian Munn, since it was Munnday and we couldn't always count on HBO. We grabbed some comedy, I think, and got some random stuff to read, then went upstairs to find a hidden table to loiter at for a few hours. It was still freezing outside, and we were still homeless.

On the way, Sam spotted a copy of Alas Babylon by Pat Frank. "Hey, did you have to read this in high school?" he asked, holding the copy up. I hadn't thought about that book in years. I didn't like reading when I was high school and I usually just didn't do it, but I had read Alas Babylon. I couldn't help but read it. It was terrifying. It's about a nuclear war and a handful of people who try to survive it. It was the first book of it's kind. Keep in mind this was the 80s, when we were all told that the threat of nuclear war was very, very real. We all lived in fear of it. Every time the sky would turn a funny shade of green, I thought they'd dropped the bomb. It was scary to be a kid in the 80s. I can't believe they made high school kids read a book about nuclear apocalypse. Sam held on to the book, and we sat down near a window with a view of Kirkwood. He thumbed through the book for while then looked up and said, "Do you remember the code word thing?" I wasn't sure. "The brothers in the book had a code word," he continued. "They used it to warn each other when something bad was about to happen. One of them sends the other one a telegram that says to meet him somewhere and uses the code word. The code word was 'Alas Babylon.'" It was coming back to me. One of the brothers was in the air force or something.

"Yeah, I remember," I said. We decided that day that we would do the same thing. If we ever needed each other, or if we ever thought something horrible was about to happen, we would send a letter or leave a voice mail message and we would use the same code: Alas Babylon. We agreed to meet in People's Park in Berkeley, not Bloomington, at 3 P.M. as soon as we could get there. We shook on it. We swore to never use it unless it was serious. We never did.

Sam tried to use it once in 2005 to save me from my sorrows, but a Greyhound bus driver ruined it all. You see, in 2005, Sam was living in Oakland and he had figured out that he was really a woman. I was stuck in an unhappy romantic puzzle back in Bloomington and I went on my first-ever solo tour to try to get away from my heartache for a while. I was miserable. I went to Berkeley on the tour and hung out with Samantha for a while. It was great. I was so happy to see my best friend, but she could tell I was really sad. A few days after I left, she got on a Greyhound headed for Indiana. Her plan was to buy a can of spray-paint, find my house, and spray paint "ALAS BABYLON" in huge letters on my wall. Then, when I got home from tour, back to my problems, my headlights would have lit up Sam's message, and, without a doubt, I would have to turn around and drive back to the West Coast. I wish she would have made it, but instead the fucking bus driver accused her of being drunk or on drugs and not only kicked her off of the bus, but banned her from the station too. She wasn't on drugs or drunk, she was just Sam —wild and wonderful and not like the other humans. Her confrontation with the driver really freaked her out. She decided that it was a bad idea and gave up on her mission.

We had all kinds of secrets and codes. We both carried a ticket stub from some casino that neither of us had ever been to called PAIR-A-DICE. Sam had found them somewhere on the ground one day and given me one. He said, "Hold on to this, it has a date on the bottom. Save it in your wallet, that way if we ever get lost in time, we can find each other by going to this place on this date." I thought it was a good idea. I tucked it away and agreed that if some kind of time travel mishap occurred, I'd meet him at the PAIR-A-DICE casino on April 23rd, 1996.

Drawing, by Sam.

CHAPTER 12
WAITING FOR JUDGMENT

Sam was technically free, but he was chained by a creeping sense of dread as the days moved slowly toward his trial. A friend recommended a cool lawyer and Sam hired him. He was an animal rights activist and rode a motorcycle. He seemed pretty confident that as long as Sam cleaned up his act and stayed out of trouble, he would get off without serving any prison time. We all liked the sound of that.

Of course, staying out of trouble was hard for Sam. A few weeks after getting out of jail, he tried to use the stolen credit card with Hannah in the mall to buy some CDs while I was at band practice. The card was denied and the clerk asked them to wait for a few minutes and talk to the manager. They bolted and made it safely out of the mall. I like to imagine that when they told me about it, I was pissed and that I scolded Sam for being so reckless, but I didn't. I was just as foolish as he was, and I was proud of him for not letting "The Man" keep him down. We were criminals, despicable and vile.

Sam's disability application was rejected, but he reapplied right away and felt more confident that he would get it this time, after they learned about his arrest and the diagnoses he had received. It would take a few months to find out. Another thing to wait for.

Operation: Cliff Clavin had a 10-day tour booked in late February and I asked Sam to come with us. I thought it would be good for him to get out of town for a while, and we were heading south, so it would be a nice break from the cold winter. Besides, Sam lived in the van with me or stayed with Otis, and both of us were going on the tour. Greg Wells signed up to come too. He was excited to see Sam and really wanted to tour with us, despite the fact that he claimed to not like our band at all. He always said, "I don't really like your music, but I like the way you do things." He kind of glorified us as the hardest working DIY band on the road. Maybe we were. I doubt it.

We went to Starkville, Mississippi and played with The Grumpies. The show was in a house shaped like an octagon. I was so excited to see The Grumpies again and I was excited for Sam, Greg, and Hannah to see them too. They were so great, everyone was impressed. After the show, Jason Grumpie and I went to a gas station to get some soda. While we were waiting in line, he told me about Daniel Johnston. "I think you'll really like him, Chris. He's kinda a crazy guy that sings in a high-pitch voice. He records tons of music in his basement and puts it out on tapes," he said, in his sweet, slow, Mississippi accent. I didn't take his advice for many years, but I wish I had listened to him. I didn't hear Daniel Johnston until 2004 on my second European tour with my folk punk band Ghost Mice. We were leaving Paris and my friend Pascal gave me a Mix CD and a Daniel Johnston tape called "Yip Jump Music." I loved it. We listened to it as we made our way across Belgium and I thought about that night in Starkville and The Grumpies.

Anyway, when we got back to the house that night, Amy Grumpie made us pasta and put walnuts in it. Back then I was a picky eater and I was really worried that it would be weird. I had a bite. It was delicious and I've put walnuts in my pasta almost every time I've made it since then. We played strip poker, but no one got naked, because we didn't have time. Before we could get that far, some asshole kicked the door down, insisting that we had taken their beer and that we were hiding it from them. When they busted in, they found us playing cards in a circle, in various states of undress, and decided that the other touring band must have taken their beer. The other band was also from Indiana, but that was the first time we had met them. They were called The Mixelpricks, and they were from Lafayette, Indiana, as was Axle Rose, Izzy Stradlin, and Shannon Hoon—the singer of Blind Melon. The Mixelpricks left after the show to drive somewhere, which, in the drunken minds of the beer-less assholes, proved their guilt. "They must have loaded up on our beer and took off!" one yelled, then they all piled in a car and drove off, drunk, into the night, after them. We gave up on our card game and Amy decided to gather up all the beer cans and count them. When she did, she found 48 cans, which was how many beers the dudes had bought that night. They drank all of their own beers.

Jason told me a funny story about Shannon Hoon. Besides Shannon, all of the other guys in Blind Melon were from Mississippi and went to school in Starkville, so Jason knew all of them. One day, Jason was playing guitar and the Blind Melon guitar player came in and asked him what he was playing. "I just made it up," he said. The guy asked him to teach it to him. Jason did. A few years later, the riff was on MTV when the Blind Melon's song "No Rain" became an alterna-hit. I asked Jason if he was mad about it and he said, "No way man, they made it up to me. When they toured with Guns N' Roses, I got to come along for five days and I had a full VIP pass. It was cool. I got to hang out with all those guys. Man, Slash is really cool." Jason kind of looked like Slash, with his curly black afro. He almost played guitar as well as Slash too. He was great! He didn't get into punk until he was 30 years old. He said, "I just listened to rock and country, then someone played some punk for me and I really liked it, so I found some guys to start a band." I fell in love with him, we all did. He's a great person.

Jason and Sam, taped together.

The next morning, I woke up to Greg Wells' voice. "Kid! Wake up! Your boy has got the van stuck." I had no clue what he was talking about.

"Whose van?" I asked.

"Your van, the tour van." I reached for my keys. They were gone. I got up and went outside to find the van stuck in a dip at the end of the driveway. Otis was standing there, looking guilty.

"What the fuck?" I asked. He explained that he had stayed up all night talking to this girl Darlene and that he was going to take her to work in the van. I walked away. I got in the van and wiggled it out of the ditch, impressing Greg and Otis, who had both tried and failed. I walked toward the house to go back to sleep and Otis asked, "Can I use the van?" I was pissed.

"No..." I answered and went back inside. I noticed a pair of underwear lying on the driveway. They had been run over by various cars, and were pressed flat. I was eager to leave the octagon house. Later that morning, when we were all awake and getting ready to go, I noticed that they were missing. When we got in the van I asked Sam about it. "Sam, did you find some underwear in the driveway?" I asked. He was shocked and embarrassed.

"How did you know?" he asked. We all either laughed or groaned with disgust.

"How could you put on some one's dirty underwear?" Frankie asked.

Sam shifted to angry and said, "Fuck you Frankie."

...

Otis started getting weird. He spent most of his time sleeping. The van was packed, so he would sleep on the floor, against the sliding door, in what we called "the gutter." I talked to him and asked him if he was upset about the van thing. I asked him if he was mad at me. He assured me that he wasn't mad or upset, just feeling down.

A few nights later, after a terrible show somewhere, we decided that it would be cool to drive along the Florida coast from Pensacola on our way to Gainesville. It was a horrible idea. It was a twisted path and the roads were filled with stoplights. After a few hours, we decided to try to find a nice beach for a quick swim, but it was impossible, because we were surrounded by condos and private property. Every time we turned off of the main road, toward the ocean, we ran into a gate. We gave up and started heading back toward the interstate, but a cop was following us. He followed us for around 10 miles before pulling us over. Since none of us drank or did drugs and we didn't have any warrants out for our arrests or anything, we weren't worried. The cop was a huge asshole right away. "Do you know why I pulled you over?" he asked. I said no. "Well someone in a van has been shooting a BB gun at the McDonalds." I told him that it wasn't us and that we didn't have a BB gun in the van. He took our IDs and left. Two more cop cars showed up. One of them was the K-9 unit.

"Do you mind if we search the van?" he asked.

"We've been driving for hours and have a lot more left to go, I'd rather keep moving," I answered, keeping eye contact the whole time. He kept his light in my face.

"Why don't you want us to search your van?" he asked.

"Because we don't have drugs or guns or anything illegal in the van and we didn't shoot at the McDonalds," I responded. They said that they were gonna walk the dog around the van and, if he smelled anything, they would search us. The dog was a cute little beagle. They got really mad when we tried to pet it. The dog-cop smelled something, so they searched us.

The first funny thing that happened during the search was a cop holding up a jar of peanut butter and asking, "What's in here?" It was hard not to answer without sounding like a smart ass.

"Peanut butter," I said. He unscrewed the top and checked for himself. The next best part of the search happened when they opened up our camp stove. They found an oily zip-lock bag with something small wrapped in aluminum foil inside of it.

"Here we go!" the cop yelled, and took the baggie to show his cop friends. We started laughing. They opened it up and unrolled the aluminum foil and found our matches.

"Why do you keep these matches in this baggie?" they asked.

"To keep them dry," I said without laughing, somehow. They gave up on finding drugs, but they didn't admit that there weren't drugs in the van. They said that was it was probably too small of an amount to worry about. Then they searched our bags.

They were shocked when they found out that Sam didn't bring any clothes with him, only a shoulder bag. We all laughed. I tried to tell them about the underwear in the driveway, but they didn't want to hear our funny stories. They found the IDs in Sam's bag. I didn't know he still had them. He had the driver's license that belonged to the girl whose credit card he had tried to use at the mall with Hannah and a few other random IDs and cards. The girl was from Georgia and we were from Indiana and in Florida. It looked bad, like we robbed a girl on our way down south. They took Sam away for questioning and put him in the back of a cop car. They took Otis for some reason too, and put him the back of a different cop car.

They questioned all of us and caught us lying. We all told them different stories about where I lived and where Sam lived. They knew we were lying. They seemed too dumb to do what they did, but somehow they figured out that Sam and Hannah had tried to use the credit card in the mall. They pulled classic moves that none of us were prepared to handle. They told Hannah that Sam had admitted to trying to use the card and they told Sam that Hannah had told them the same thing. They told us that the two of them had come clean and were in big trouble. We pretended not to know what they were talking about, which was easy for Greg, Jason, and Frankie, since they really didn't know. The whole thing took around two hours, and we assumed that they were gonna haul Sam and Hannah off to jail. I was so worried. I was really worried about what this would do for Sam's pending case. This wasn't good. Then, to our surprise, the cops brought them back to the van and let us go. "What happened?" I asked. They said that the cops just made them sign some papers admitting guilt. They both signed them. They had admitted to being in possession of stolen property. Apparently, the wonder-cops called the Bloomington sheriff's department and found out that this girl had reported her backpack stolen. They also found out that it was a guy and a girl who had tried to use the credit card in the mall, because the manager of the music store had reported it. Of course, there was no way that they knew Hannah was involved, they were just guessing, but we didn't care. They didn't get arrested so it didn't seem to matter. We drove away, happy to be moving again.

The rest of the tour was okay and we didn't run into any more cops. When we got home we realized that we still had some money in the gas money bag. We had $90! We had money! We had made money on tour! I couldn't believe it.

April came and Sam finally met his lawyer and went to his pre-trial hearing. It went pretty well, despite the fact that Judge Todd called him a parasite of humanity. His lawyer assured him that he would be okay, but Sam wasn't so sure. He was still worried and he would have to wait again. His trial was three months away.

We recorded our side of the split 7-inch with Connie Dungs and, a few days later, Jason (Otis) said that he was going to quit the band and move back to Franklin. We assumed that it was because he was a Christian. We hadn't known he was Christian when he joined the band, we found out on tour. Sam came right out and asked, "Are you quitting the band because they are militantly anti-Christian and you're Christian?"

"No, it's not that. I just miss my ex-girlfriend and my friends back home."

Sam's face got serious. "But if you move back to Franklin, what about Steak 'n Shake? What about my little vegan angel and the free cheese?" Jason laughed, assuming Sam was kidding. I was bummed. Jason was a really good bass player and I was really getting sick of lineup changes. I didn't want to be one of those bands with only one original member who everyone made fun of. I was starting to think that I was an asshole or something. Why wouldn't people stay in a band with me? I never considered the fact that not everyone is into driving thousands of miles, barely getting paid, and sleeping on floors.

I didn't want to look for a new bass player and I didn't want to advertise with fliers again. I considered ending the band again, then I got an idea: Hannah. She was a violinist and could play acoustic guitar, so she could learn bass easily. I asked her if she was interested. "It seems like you're gonna go on all of the tours with me right? Then why not play bass?" I asked. She agreed, and wanted to give it a shot, but we needed a bass. We found one at a pawn show in New Albany, Indiana and Hannah wiped out her savings account to buy it. A few weeks later, she played her first show and she was great.

Hannah quit going to school, because she had enough credits to graduate or something like that, and she basically moved in with us. It was too crowded with three people living in one van, so Sam decided to move into a house. Besides, he thought, it would look a lot better when he went to court if he had an address, and with Otis gone, his fake address was no longer an option. He moved into a house on West 6th Street, which was great, because we could park the van in front of it and use the bathroom and stuff.

Later that spring, we were on tour out east. Sam came with us and we picked up Greg in Richmond. Somewhere in Massachusetts, we got pulled over. This time, we really weren't worried. I had a talk with Sam before we left and made sure that he wasn't carrying any stolen property or ID cards. We were all squeaky clean. They came and took our IDs and my registration and went back to their car. We joked about busting out a deck of cards while we waited (we had a table in the van and the front chairs swiveled to face it) and we thought it would be really funny if, when they came back to the van, we were relaxing, unafraid, playing cards. We didn't do it. No need to press our luck we decided.

I heard the door slam on the cop car and saw their flashlights coming back toward us. Before I knew it, there was a gun in my face. Greg was riding shotgun and he had a gun in his face too. "Please put your hands on the dash!" they yelled.

"What's going on?" I asked.

"Hannah Jones and Sam Dorsett, please step out of the van, you are under arrest!" one of them yelled, like a robot. I tried to talk to them.

"Why are they being arrested?" I asked. They didn't answer. The next thing I knew, Sam and Hannah we being pushed into one of the cop cars. I yelled back to the cop and asked where they were taking them.

"To the station," he said. "You can follow me." They flashed their lights and pulled out, into speeding traffic. We tried to follow, but we lost them. I was so angry. It all happened so fast. I spotted another cop car sitting in a parking lot and I pulled in, way too fast.

I rolled down my window and asked, "Can you please tell me where the police station is?" He told me and we sped off.

When we walked into the station and approached the bulletproof glass, the first thing the guy at the counter said to me was, "You can't have that in here." I didn't know what he meant.

"What?" I asked. He pointed to my wrist, I was wearing a pyramid stud bracelet.

"That's a weapon, you could hurt someone with that," he said. I laughed.

"They aren't sharp," I said. "They can't hurt anyone." I rubbed the bracelet hard against my face and eyes, to demonstrate. "Besides," I said, "you're behind bulletproof glass." Surprisingly, he dropped it and asked why we were there. We told him, then asked him what we could do to get our friends out.

"There is nothing you can do," he said. "They are going to be driven back to Indiana by a sheriff to face charges. They'll be billed for all the gas the sheriff uses to get there and for his meals and hotel rooms too." We were all angry.

"What are the charges?" I asked. "Why were they arrested?" He mentioned possession of stolen property and we all knew what had happened. Those papers that they signed in Florida, on the side of the highway, in the middle of the night, months ago, had come back to bite them. "Are you telling me that there is nothing we can do?" I asked.

"Nope," he said. He was a smug asshole. We were about to leave, when a cop standing further back said "Unless of course the judge decides not to..." Then the other cop interrupted him and gave him a dirty look. We all went back up to the glass.

"What?" I asked. "What were you going to say?" He didn't speak, he just shook his head and walked away. We badgered the mean cop for a while but all we got him to tell us was that they would go to court in the morning, in Salem, Massachusetts.

We sulked our way back to the van and sat in the parking lot trying to figure out what to do. We still had a week's worth of shows to play and we were dead broke. None of us had any money and I didn't even know how we would afford the gas to get home. We decided that we'd go to court in the morning

203

and, even if they didn't get out, at least we could say goodbye. We weren't in a hurry anyway. If we didn't have shows, and Sam and Hannah were going to jail, we figured we might as well take our time getting home. Greg said, "Great, sounds like a plan. I'm gonna go take a shit in those bushes." He jumped out of the van.

"What are you going to use for toilet paper?" I asked.

He laughed. "I'm vegan, I don't need toilet paper. If you quit eating cheese, you wouldn't need it either." I laughed, but I then realized that he wasn't kidding.

"No way, I'm sure you have sticky poops sometimes."

"Nope, not since I became a vegan. My shit slides right out and I can stick my finger up there as far as I can reach and when I pull it out, it's clean, spotless." My face twisted in disgust as he disappeared behind a bush beside the police station. I hoped that they didn't have cameras, I didn't want Greg to get arrested for shitting.

While he was away, Frankie said, "It's like you said in that interview, t-t-t-tour sure is a roller coaster." It made me really mad.

"Fuck you Frankie, that's not what I meant. They took Hannah and Sam!" Then Greg came back and asked me if I wanted to inspect his asshole.

We drove to Salem to look for somewhere near the courthouse to sleep in the van. We found a nice spot, parked the van, and made some peanut butter and jelly sandwiches. We noticed a small white pick-up truck circling the block. They passed us three times, slowly. On the fourth pass, they parked in front of us, and a middle-aged guy got out. He walked back to our van and popped his head into the open side door. He looked at all of us, then all around the van. For a second, we were too stunned to talk, then Greg asked, "Can I help you with something?"

The guy shook his head and said, "Nope," then walked back to his truck. He left, but he continued to circle the block. We were pretty creeped out, so we decided to look for a better place to sleep. We found a nice park and I got out to piss in some bushes, then the white truck came back. I made eye contact with the creep. We all got back in the van and drove away to look for another place. We ended up parking in an alley downtown. I'm sure we weren't allowed to park there, but I applied my theory that if you do something obviously illegal, people will assume that you must have some special permission to do it, and leave you alone. Besides, we were hidden from the street and from our stalker, and that was all that mattered. I figured that if a cop woke us up, I would tell him that we were hiding from the white truck killer. Court started early, and we didn't get much sleep.

We woke up, without a ticket on the windshield, and stumbled out of the van and wandered around, looking for the right courtroom. We settled in and waited. There were a lot of people to sort through, including a guy who got arrested for shooting a shotgun at a house and a Haitian crack dealer who swore he was only selling crack so that he could send money back to his family. Eventually, Sam and Hannah were brought in. They were chained together with a few other people. When it was their turn to be tried, the judge said "State of Massachusetts...blah... blah...blah....Hannah Jones..blah...blah...Sam Dorsett..charged with...blah...blah... blah... Dismissed," then he whacked his little hammer.

I turned to Greg and asked, "What did he say? What just happened?" We all heard the word "dismissed" and that seemed like a good word to hear. We had to wait until everyone was processed before we could get any answers. At last, we found out that they were getting out! We waited in a lobby, and an hour later, they came out holding some papers. Sam looked really freaked out. I felt bad for him, he had spent enough time in jail. They told us that they were released on their own behalf with instructions to report to a judge in Indiana as soon as possible. It wasn't great news, since they were still in trouble, but at least they weren't being driven back to Indiana by a sheriff and at least they were free, for now. We all worried what this would mean for Sam and his existing trouble.

We talked about what we should do. We decided that, instead of canceling tour and driving home and Sam and Hannah turning themselves in, we should finish the tour. We played a show that night. It was pretty small and people didn't really care about us, but we didn't mind. We were just happy to be together. Later that night, when we spread out our sleeping bags on that dirty punk house floor to go to sleep, I thought about how lucky I was to have such good friends and I how happy I was to be there with them.

When the tour was over, Hannah and Sam faced the music. Sam was really mad at his lawyer, who should have known that a warrant had been issued for him. His lawyer said that the new charges shouldn't affect his case too negatively, since the crimes were committed at roughly the same time, but Sam wasn't happy with his lawyer's casual/worry-free attitude. I went to court with Hannah. She had Judge Todd too. I felt like I knew him from Sam's stories, but this was the first time I had ever seen him. He was gnomish, with a thin brown mullet, and he was such a jerk. He asked her how much money she had. She tried to ask him a question about what he meant exactly and he cut her off and said, "It's a simple question, how much money DO-YOU-HAVE? In your wallet, in the bank, buried in your back yard, anywhere. Just add it all up in your head and tell me." I wanted to tell him to fuck off, but I didn't say anything. My face was red with anger.

Hannah ended up getting off pretty easy, she had to pay some fines and got put on probation for a year. Sam said that his lawyer and the judge worked out some kind of deal in which the new charges would be lumped in with his existing case and his punishment would be figured out at his upcoming trial. We didn't know if that was a good thing or a bad thing. His lawyer assured him that it was a good thing. Sam asked him if he should dress nice for his court date. His lawyer said, "No, don't worry about it, just don't come to court with your dick hanging out of your pants and you'll be fine."

At last, summer arrived. We had another west coast tour planned, and Sam's court date finally came. I woke him up that morning. I asked him what he was gonna wear and if he was gonna clean up. That's when he told me what his lawyer had said, about his dick. I disagreed. I forced him to get up and take a shower. While he did that, I got a razor and borrowed some hair clippers. We shaved his head and face, and he put on an older pair of glasses with big, thick lenses. We went to Salvation Army and found some nice slacks and a striped white dress shirt. He changed in the bathroom there, and came out looking like the math nerd from Mitchell whom I met years before. He was nervous, but he was also looking forward to the end of his long wait to be punished. We walked to the courthouse and joked about me sending him a cake in prison, a cake that secretly held a supply of tofu and potato chips.

As soon as the judge looked at him, he said, "Well Sam, looks like you really turned your life around. I see you've been staying out of trouble." Sam's lawyer and the judge did most of the talking, and they quickly settled on a pretty minimal sentence: two years probation, 80 hours of community service, and around $2,000 in fines that could be paid in installments over the next two years. We were all so happy! Sam wasn't going to prison, or going to have to run away from it.

He did all 80 hours of his community service at the Community Kitchen in two weeks time. He ate there often, and had always wanted to volunteer there anyway. He really enjoyed his "punishment" and he wasn't too worried about paying his fines, because he was pretty certain that he was going to get approved for disability this time. If he did, his first check would be around $1,500 and then he'd get $500 a month after that. He just had to hope that they deemed him "crazy," and he was pretty sure they would. He thought it was hilarious that he was most likely gonna pay his fines with money that the government gave him. "I'll just be giving them back their own money," he said. The only thing that really worried him was the probation. He wasn't sure if he could stay out of trouble for two whole years and was worried that he would be stuck in Bloomington the whole time.

A few weeks later, some traveling punks showed up in town and ended up staying at Sam's house. I never really met them, but I saw them coming and going. One of them, a girl named Jess, fell in love with Sam. It was cute. They were always together and I caught them holding hands once. I was so happy for Sam. He was unburdened by the law and he was in love. It seemed like it was going to be a great summer.

We stayed in touch with Otis, and through him we met a bunch of other punk kids from Franklin, Indiana. One of them was a kid named Jasin, who spelled his name with an 'I,' not an 'O.' He played in a band called The Ataris. The other kids were in this sloppy punk band called Biscuit Head. We played a few shows together and became friends. Jasin had a falling out with the other members of The Ataris and told me that he was moving to Goleta, California to live in the drummer of Lagwagon's house for free. He said that we should come too.

"We?" I asked.

"Yeah, the whole band. He has a huge house and he's rich. He's not even in the band anymore, but he gets royalty checks from Fat Wreck Chords once a year for $30,000. He's gonna let me live there for free."

"But would he let all 3 of us live there, and maybe Sam too?" I asked.

"I think he would, he's really cool. I'll ask him." A few days later, Jasin left a message on our voicemail.

"Hey, I talked to Derrick and he said it was cool! Call me back," I told Hannah and Frankie about it, and we talked it over. We were all into the idea. We concluded that we would check out the house and the city when we were in California on tour, and then make our final decision, but we were really excited about it. Jasin left for Goleta few days later. We made plans to meet him there in six weeks.

Tour was only a few weeks away and we were still trying to figure out if Sam could leave the state or not. He talked to his lawyer and found out that he could, as long as he stayed in touch and checked in with him. This was great news. Greg Wells wanted to come too. It would be the whole gang, together again. Things were going good. Sam was unleashed, we had a free place to live in California, we had around 15 new songs, and I was about to go on a huge tour again with my best friends.

A week or so before we set out, I found a note under the windshield wiper of my van. It was written in calligraphy on really nice paper. I couldn't guess who would leave me a note like this and I was worried that it was from a neighbor, someone angry with me for living in my van on their street, so I looked at the bottom of the page first. It said, "Love, your best friend, -Sam." I couldn't believe it was from Sam. His handwriting was always pretty horrible and this note was impeccable. I sat down on the curb and read it. It was a perfect day, with just the right amount of sun in the sky and the birds provided a soundtrack to it all.

Dear Chris,

This Is Sam. I'm so happy that summer is here. The world is such a beautiful place and I'm happy to be a part of it. I'm happy to be free and I'm happy to be your friend. As unlikely as it may seem, I think I am falling in love with Jess. She asked me to go west with her. I think I'm going to do it. I've slept for so long and I missed so much and I don't want to miss this. I'm going to take my chances. I'm sorry, but this means that I can't go on tour with you. Hopefully we will cross paths on the west coast. ♥ your best friend - Sam

I was a little sad that Sam wasn't going to come on the tour, but I was happy for him. I thought it would be good for him to do something without me, to go on an adventure that was all his own. I was looking forward to meeting up again and hearing his stories. I was curious to see how it would work out with Jess. From what I knew about Sam, he didn't like girls. He had occasionally had crushes on girls and sometimes made out with them, but he had never really been in love with a girl. He left the next day to start hitching to the west coast. I was sad to see him go, but I was also a little relieved. It was hard sometimes. Sam was a lot to worry about. He was intelligent, funny, and selfless, but he was also clumsy, confrontational, and unpredictable. It was kind of nice to know that I wouldn't have to worry about him on tour. I wouldn't have to find him when he got lost at a truck stop. I wouldn't have to clean up after him at the places we stayed. Instead, I would worry about him hitchhiking across the country with a strange girl.

CHAPTER 13
ON THE ROAD (AGAIN)

We started the tour by heading south and meeting up with The Grumpies. We were going to tour from Mississippi to southern California together, and I was really excited about seeing them every night for three weeks. When we got there, we found out that their drummer didn't want to tour and was quitting the band. I never really got to know their drummer. He was a short little guy with a Grateful Dead tattoo. We were so bummed, and I was really worried about having to call all the promoters to tell them that The Grumpies couldn't make it. Their drummer played the show in Starkville, then quit the band. Afterward, we talked about how sad we were that they weren't coming, and tried to convince them to come with us anyway, just for fun, then Frankie offered to play drums for them. It seemed crazy, since we had a show the next day in New Orleans, but Jason and Amy were willing to give Frankie a try. They were really excited by the chance of being able to do the tour. The next day, The Grumpies practiced in Jason's parents' barn with Frankie for hours. Around 3 o'clock, they came out in a hurry and Jason said, "Well, Chris, I guess we need to pack our stuff up, we're coming on tour!"

The next two weeks were great. We toured the south and through Texas. In Houston, Moz booked us a show at a skate park and his band played with us. It was good to see him again, and to see him playing in a band. He was really sad that Sam wasn't with us, they had became regular pen pals. The show was pretty bad. The woman who owned the skate park was the one who made the flyer.

In Denton, we played the Bonnie Brea house. I was excited to be back there and to see those guys again. Just like the first time, they treated us great and welcomed us warmly. The show was really fun. Marty and Darin, from the Ted Dancin' Machine, had started a new band called The Panoply Academy Glee Club and they played the show too. It was so good to see old friends on tour and I was glad that our tours had crossed paths. Two days later, just like my first time in Denton, we came back and played a second, unplanned show. The first Denton show was great, the second show was crazy. Almost everyone in the crowd and on "stage" was naked. There's a video to prove it. When it was all over, Greg realized that he was wearing someone else's underwear.

Jason and Amy drove their tiny car on tour, since we would be splitting up in California and they would need a way back. They argued a lot, and, to get a break from each other, they started taking turns riding in the van. One of them would drive their car and one of us (usually Frankie) would ride with them. Whoever rode with us in the van would complain about the other one the whole way. It was comical and got more comical as the miles went on. Somewhere in west Texas Jason said, "Hey man, Amy is driving me crazy. I think I might just move into that house with you in Goleta, would that be okay?" We said sure, the more the merrier.

A few days later, Amy was in the van and she said, "Jason is killing me. I need to get away from him. How would you guys feel about me moving to California with you?" We laughed (she didn't know why) and said that it was a great idea. None of us wanted to see The Grumpies break up, or Jason and Amy break up, so we figured that if they both moved to California with us, everything would be okay. We just wouldn't tell them about each other's secret plans.

In Tucson we played at a record store called Toxic Shock. We were all really excited about this show because we were playing with a new Anna Joy band, called Cypher In The Snow. Anna Joy was in Blatz, and we were all Blatz fans. Well, I doubt Greg was, but I seldom worried about his musical tastes. They were cool. One of them gave a hateful speech about G.G. Allen and how he was a fucked up rapist, which I totally agreed with. They demanded that the record store owner take his shirt off of the wall before they played. I admired that. I hated G.G. Allen and I've never understood why anyone wouldn't. Things were cool until after the show, then they got weird. When Greg went to the promoter and asked about getting paid, he said "Well, Cypher In The Snow gets 80% of the door and the store takes 20%, so there isn't really any money for you guys. Sorry." Greg was furious and didn't roll over. He argued for a while and we ended up getting a measly 30 bucks for both of our bands to split. Then I tried to trade 7-inches with Anna. She said, "Yeah, I'd love to trade, but I need to get at least $1.75 for our record, since that's how much we paid to get them."

I thought she was joking. She wasn't. I wondered if she thought that we somehow got our records made for free. I was so let down. This was my first disenchanting experience with meeting a musician whom I looked up to. I didn't trade with her because I really couldn't afford it, especially after playing a show and only getting paid $15. Maybe she just didn't like our band and didn't want to tell me. I don't know. Regardless, I usually skip "Lullaby" when I listen to Blatz now, because I don't like her voice as much anymore.

This nice kid at the show invited us to stay with him. On the way to his house a huge pick-up truck crossed the centerline and was headed right for us. I swerved just in time to avoid a head on collision. He still hit us. Glass flew into my face. I heard metal crunching and tires screeching. We lost a tire. We were spinning. I stabilized us and steered toward the side of the road. Then I thought about The Grumpies. They were right behind us! Then I heard a crash. I heard glass breaking. If you've never heard a car crash before, you might be surprised at how dull they sound, I was. It was deep resounding, not like in the moves. It sounded horrible. I heard Greg scream, "HOLY FUCKIN' SHIT!" He was on the loft.

"Are you hurt?" I yelled back to him.

"No, but look at this!"

I looked back and I could see the street, the side of the van was missing! I jumped out to check on The Grumpies. It wasn't them that got crunched. A car had gotten in between us, which was lucky for The Grumpies, but not so lucky for the car. It was a little gold car all smashed up against the front of the wayward truck. The guy in the car was smooshed against his airbag and had blood on his face. I ran up to the car. "Are you okay?" I yelled.

"I think so," he said. Then I turned to look at the truck driver. He was unconscious and had hit his head on the windshield, but seemed okay. Then the cops showed up. I remembered that I swallowed some glass. The paramedic told me not to worry about it. They asked us if we wanted them to call a tow truck. We said no. We didn't want our van, full of equipment, with one side missing, to be towed anywhere. We told them that we wanted to change the tire and see if the axle was damaged. One of the cops on the scene helped us change it. While we were working, a lady came out of her house and brought us some waters and sodas. When she found out that we were musicians on tour, she offered to let us put our stuff in her garage until we figured out what we were doing. We did it.

When we got the wheel on, we drove around a little to test things out. The van drove fine, so we filled out the insurance paperwork and then found a 24-hour store and bought a tarp and some duct tape. We taped up the hole and eventually made it to the kid's house—who was probably thinking that he was in way over his head. He was nice and he said we could stay as long as we needed to. I had a lot of trouble sleeping that night. I assumed that tour was over, and I had no idea how we were going to get our stuff, and ourselves back to Indiana.

The next day, we had to do some more paperwork at the police station, and we found out that the guy in the truck was drunk. A fucking drunk driver! I was so mad. The cop assured us that drunk drivers always lose and that his insurance company would do whatever we wanted them to. He told us not to worry, but I was worried. We had shows to play and no way to get to them. We called his insurance company and complained and told them that we were missing shows. We lied and said that every show that we missed meant that we lost $100 or more. They gave us a rental van to use while we waited for the paperwork to be processed. It didn't do us much good since we had to come back to Tucson, but we managed to play two shows in Arizona while we waited.

It was starting to look like we were never gonna make it to California, and like we were never gonna see our potential home there, so I called Jasin to tell him the bad news (I called the house in Goleta. Remember, no one had cell phones in 1997). The guy who answered the phone said that he wasn't there. I asked them if he had moved in yet. They said that he did, but that he had moved out already. I was confused. I hung up and called my voicemail to see if there was any news about our insurance settlement. There was a message from Jasin. He told me to call him and he gave me a phone number. I called the number. I told him what happened.

"Are you still in Arizona?" he asked.

"Yeah, we're stuck here for a while," I said.

"I'm in Arizona too, in Tuscon with my cousin."

"We're in Tucson too!" He invited us to stay with him at his cousin's house. When we got there, he told us why he had moved out of the house in California. He said that there were tons of people staying there and that they were doing heroin. He said that he was never going back. He apologized. We were all looking forward to checking out Goleta and maybe moving there, it was another blow below the belt. This tour was taking a turn for the worst, it was determined to knock us out. Everyone was miserable and we felt like we were just waiting to go home.

The insurance guy came to look at our van. He filled out some papers and handed them to me to sign. I noticed that he had lied a lot and had said that our van had new tires, a new CD player, custom seats, and "bay windows." I realized he was trying to help us by making the van seem more valuable than it was. Then I looked down at the bottom and saw that we were going to get $1,800 for the van. It was great, I only paid $600 for the van when I bought it. Then he explained "salvage" to me. He said that either they could have the van towed away to a junkyard, or we could salvage it for $200. Basically, we would be buying our van back from them. We decided to salvage it. I figured that we could just tape it up really well and drive home. It seemed like our best option. He did some more paper work and handed me a check for $1,600.

We had a check, but we didn't have a van. We had a few options: We could buy a new van as quickly as possible and hope it turned out to be reliable, tape our van up and drive home with our tail between our legs—defeated by the road—or, try to repair the gaping hole and finish the tour. I didn't want to give up on Mr. Van.

I called my dad and asked him for advice. He told me to ask the people we were staying with if they knew a mechanic. He said that anyone with the right tools and a little bit of skill could easily rivet on a piece of sheet metal over the huge hole in the side of the van. I asked the kids at the house, and found out that one of the guys had an uncle who was a race car driver, which was great because most race car drivers build their car bodies out of sheet metal. It was perfect. We called and talked to the uncle. He was excited to help us out. He told me where to get sheet metal and which kind to get, and gave me directions to his house out in the desert. The next day we got the metal and drove out there. He was really good and knew what he was doing. It was done in less than an hour. I offered to pay him but he wouldn't take it. On the way back to the house we stopped and bought some blue spray-paint and painted the shiny new side of our van in the parking lot. I was so happy that we didn't have to go home. I was also happy that Mr. Van was going to finish the tour. I didn't care how it looked. In fact, I liked how it looked. We looked like real road warriors.

When we got back to the house, I told everyone to pack their things and hurry up so that we could make it to our next show in time. They were excited. We were a band on tour again. After a quick stop at the nice lady's house to get our gear, we headed westward to California.

The next day, we mailed our huge insurance check home. I had no idea how to cash a check that big on the road, and I didn't want to lose 10% or whatever at a check cashing place, so we just mailed it home. We decided to use the money to release our next album. The wreck was starting to seem like a blessing more than a curse. We still had our van, we were still on tour, and now we had enough money to record and release our next record, waiting for us at home.

When we said goodbye to The Grumpies in L.A., it was sad. I really hoped that they would work out their differences and stay together. We promised to stay in touch and tour together again. They stayed there and we headed north, up the coast.

Much like my last trip to California, most of our shows fell through. Seven of our shows were cancelled, and we spent the week in Berkeley again, but this time I was with all new people. I loved the new people (well, not Frankie), but I missed the old people too. I planned the tour so that we would be in Berkeley on the Fourth of July again, and I told Sam to try to meet us there if he could. When we arrived, we noticed that all of the parking meters around Telegraph Avenue and People's Park were missing. In their place, atop the poles, were baskets filled with toothpick American flags with matches taped to them. If you struck the match, it would set the tiny flag aflame. I loved Berkeley. Thanks to the hippies, would could park anywhere we wanted and for free. It was great, since we had a week with no shows. We went to the park and looked for Sam.

He wasn't there. I called the voicemail from a payphone and we left him a birthday message, again, from the same phone as the year before, hoping that he would check it sometime.

That night, we heard crazy noises coming from campus around 10 o'clock. We went to investigate, and found a drum circle made up of homeless people beating on trashcans and buckets. One of them offered me a bucket and some sticks. I took them and joined the chaos. Everyone did. It was great. We banged for hours and scared the kids walking home from the bars when they passed us.

The next day, we played a show at Gilman with the Groovie Ghoulies and the Crumbs. I was so excited to play a show at such a legendary place. The place where Blatz came from, where Operation Ivy, Crimpshrine, Green Day, and so many other bands got their start. The show was fun, and the people there were really nice to us.

We hung out at the drum circle every night and made friends with the regulars there. They were really interesting and seemed to have created their own social structure. We found out about it when Hannah asked a guy if she could pet his puppy. He said, "Say fuck you first." She laughed and told him that she didn't want to. He said, "Then you can't pet my dog. I can't trust you unless you say fuck you, or unless you tell me that you hate me."

Hannah laughed again and eventually said, "Fuck you." He told her that she could pet his dog then she asked "What's its name?"

The guy laughed. "Do you really want to waste one of your questions on that?" He could tell that she didn't understand, so he explained that you only get to ask three questions, ever. "Don't waste them on dumb stuff like that."

Over the next few days, we witnessed a lot of these guys adhering to these rules. When a new person walked up, they would say, "Fuck you," and everyone else would say "Fuck you too." They told us that it was the only way to be honest. They insisted that humans were horrible people who didn't care about anyone except themselves, so to be polite, or to act interested in someone else, is to be a liar. It may sound weird, but it was nice hanging out with them. There was one older man who looked like a wizard, with a long white beard, who wore bright colors and layers of charm necklaces. I called him the King Of Berkeley because he seemed to be highly respected by the others, and he looked like a fucking wizard. People would walk up to him and say, "Fuck you, give me a cigarette!" and he would give them one. One time he got into an argument with the guy who had the puppy and as soon as they started arguing, they leaned against each other, shoulder to shoulder. Afterward, he explained it to us. "When you're arguing with someone, you should push against them, so that they feel you, and they understand you." When it was time to leave Berkeley, I was sad. I knew that I would miss the "negative cult" or whatever they might have called themselves, I never wasted one of my questions by asking them.

In Colorado Springs, we played a show with Bisybackson, the band who was on tour with Fifteen when we played with them in Bloomington. Hannah showed them their patch on her backpack and we talked about how we were both at their show, and didn't know each other. They didn't have a show the next day, so we got them onto our show in Fort Collins. It was great hanging out with them and getting to know them. They told us they had met one of our friends, named Sam, and that he was in Portland, their hometown, a few weeks before. I asked them how he was doing.

They told me that he seemed pretty crazy. They said that he got drunk on a six-pack of Little Kings and that he was hitting on one of their friends inappropriately. I was sure that it was a different Sam. I told them that he didn't drink, didn't really like girls, and that he never hit on anyone. I made them describe him to me. They did, and I concluded that it must have been Sam. I still thought that they were joking and I kept asking them if they were messing with me or if Sam had told them to tell us that story to freak us out, but they all swore that they were telling the truth. They probably couldn't imagine why I was so freaked out, but they obviously didn't know Sam well enough to know how weird their story sounded. I asked about Jess and they said that she wasn't with him. They said that he was alone and that he had lost his backpack. I was really worried and upset. I kept telling myself that it was some misunderstanding. I kept telling myself that it was some other Sam from Indiana with thick glasses and a chipped front tooth. I really wanted to talk to Sam, but there was no way to do it. I called the voicemail to see if there were any messages from him... but nothing.

The rest of the tour was okay. Nothing special happened. When we got home, Sam wasn't there. He hadn't made it back yet. I was really worried about him. I spent the rest of my summer living in my van and going back and forth between Hannah's parents' and my parents' houses, and I was getting tired of this kind of life. I was getting sick of living in a van, but I didn't want to pay rent and I couldn't afford to either. I wanted Sam to come home.

Sometime in late August, he left a message on the voicemail: "Hey Chris, this is Sam. I'm having trouble getting home. I'm traveling with these Indian businessmen now, they have huge knives strapped under their suit jackets. Last night they got really mad at me because I ate some of their Doritos. They threw the rest of the bag away and told me to never touch their food, because I am unclean..." CLICK. That was the end of the message. I didn't hear from him again for two weeks, when he left another message that said he had found

217

a ride and was on his way home.

When he got home, he looked really worn out. We went to Café Pizzeria and got fries and an endless pitcher of Dr. Pepper. I asked him about Portland and what had happened to Jess. He told me that he caught her smoking crack with some guy who gave them a ride. He said that they got into a fight over it and that she left the next day and took his wallet with her. He didn't know what to do, so he decided to keep going west.

When he was alone at a truck stop in Wyoming somewhere, a trucker picked him up and said that he would take him all the way to Portland, but that he would have to drive some of the way. Sam told him that he didn't really know how to drive a car, much less a huge truck. The guy told him that it was easy, and he taught him how. During his driving lesson, Sam realized that the trucker was really drunk, and still drinking. Somewhere in the mountains, Sam took over and drove the giant truck—pulling a heavy trailer full of some unknown cargo—through the night. I thought he was kidding. I interrupted and asked, "Was it a real semi-truck, like the kind with 18 wheels and tons of gears?" He nodded and said that it was. "But wasn't it really hard to drive?" I asked.

"Yeah, I thought I was gonna die for sure. I didn't really care though. I thought it would be kind of funny to be found dead with a drunken trucker in the mountains of Wyoming behind the wheel of a big rig." We both laughed and refilled our cups. I slid the empty pitcher to the edge of the table so that the waitress would see it and fill it back up. She knew us well enough to know that we were far from finished drinking soda. I worked up the nerve to ask him about Portland. He confessed that it was true. He got drunk for the first time that night.

"I also bought a pack of cigarettes and smoked them one after another on a rooftop," he said.

"Why?" I asked, disgusted at the thought.

"I thought that if I did, I might die. I thought I could overdose on nicotine or something."

"Why would you want to die?"

"I don't know, I was really sad. I left my backpack in the truck when I got out and I was really upset about what had happened with Jess. I didn't have my wallet or my ID, I didn't have much money left, and I didn't have anywhere to go, or a home to come home to," he said. "I spent the last of my money on beer and smokes," he added. I didn't know what to say. I told him that I was glad that he was home. I told him not to worry about any of it. After a few more sodas, I asked him about the girl he was hitting on in Portland. He had no clue what I was talking about. He didn't remember meeting the Bisybackson guys either. "I was out of my mind," he said.

218

Later that night, he told me what happened to him in Arizona. A trucker picked him up and it seemed like he was gonna give him a ride all the way to Kentucky, but then the guy started making comments about sleeping in the cab together later that night. Sam told him that he would just sleep outside. The guy said, "No, you're riding with me, you're sleeping with me." Sam ignored him and figured that he would just get out when they stopped, but he couldn't deal with all the fucked up racist stuff that the trucker said. Finally, Sam snapped and said, "I'm not sleeping in the cab with you, and I'm sick of your bigotry, let me out at the next stop please." The guy got really mad and stopped the truck.

"Get out!" he screamed. Sam got out. The truck drove off and Sam realized that he was in the middle of the desert with no lights in sight. He didn't care, and he didn't even try to hitchhike in the dark. Instead, he just crawled under a bush and went to sleep. He woke up really early, when the sun came up, and realized that he had left his water bottle in the truck. He was dehydrated and stuck in the desert. No one would pick him up, because he looked like a freak, and they were going too fast to see him in time to stop anyway. He thought that he was going to die in the heat. He said that he thought it would also be a funny way to die, but that he really wanted to go home, so he kept trying to get a ride.

Eventually, he made a sign that said "I NEED WATER" and a hippie stopped and picked him up. He took him north to Flagstaff, and the cool mountain air made everything better. A few days later, he decided to get moving again. He got a ride from another lusty trucker that said he would take him all the way back to Indiana and that he would even drop him off in Bloomington if Sam would be "his little buddy." I asked him what he did.

"I was his little buddy," he said. I laughed. Sam didn't.

"What do you mean you were his little buddy?" I asked.

"I sucked his dick," Sam said, with no concern for the other people in earshot. I laughed again. Sam didn't. I realized that he wasn't kidding. "I just really wanted to get home and it wasn't that bad. Sucking dick isn't that bad."

A few days later, Sam's disability application was approved and he got a check for almost $2,000. He told me that he was sick of living in the van too, and he made a joke about how he had gotten arrested deliberately so that he could get away from me and Hannah and have a room of his own for a while. We both wanted more than a house though. We wanted to get out of the van, but we wanted to do something cool.

Drawing, by Sam.

CHAPTER 14
PLAN-IT-X RECORDS

After hours of brainstorming and gallons of Dr. Pepper, we decided to open a record store. We found a place for rent in a strip mall on 17th street for $375 a month. I signed a three-year lease with no reservations. I didn't care about breaking leases. Our plan was to secretly live in the store, all three of us; Hannah, Sam and me.

We built elaborate cabinets with secret doors and we put mattresses inside of them. We thought it was a great idea. We put latches on the inside, so that no one could catch us sleeping. We had no idea how to run a business or a record store, but we needed a place to live and a record store seemed like a cool business to open. We figured that we could have "in-store" performances too, which was just a fancy way of explaining having shows to our landlord. We didn't think it would be very hard running a record store and selling enough records to pay our rent. The rent was really cheap, and Sam was going to be getting $500 a month for the rest of his life, so even if we had a bad month and didn't make enough for rent, Sam could pay it (with the government's money) and he'd still have a lot left over. We got an old couch and a TV, and hooked up my Super Nintendo with a note on it that said "PLAY ME." I raided my parents' house and got the mini-fridge and toaster oven that Darin and I had used in our room at the Cottage Grove house. We covered the front windows with posters so that no one could see in. We set it up really nice. We had everything we needed, except for records. The shelves were empty, but we didn't let that stop of from having a grand opening.

The problems with our plan became evident very quickly. The first night that we slept in the store, in our coffin like beds, we woke up to the sound of the phone ringing in the chiropractor's office next door. I assumed that he had a really loud phone, then he picked up and we could hear his whole conversation, every word, loud and clear. That meant that he could hear us too. That meant that we had to be really quiet getting up. We couldn't talk until someone snuck out and came back in, to pretend that they we just arriving to

221

open the store for the day. It also meant that we couldn't really play music at all, until he left at five o'clock. I was sure that people lying on a chiropractor's table, getting their spine aligned, wouldn't want to hear Fifteen or Propagandhi coming through the walls. The walls were so thin! We knew that he could hear anything that we said, so when our friends came over, we had to make sure that they didn't say anything about us living in the store. Basically we had to be really quiet until he left. The weekends were great, we could do whatever we wanted.

We needed some records. We did some research and figured out how to contact the big distributors. It was disheartening. We assumed that the people who sold punk records would be punks, instead we found out that they were businessmen. They told us we needed to set up an account with them. We said okay. They said that we needed to fill out an application and that we needed a bank account and they would prefer that we had a credit card too. Sam did most of the phone calls. We made the calls from the payphone down the street. I'd stand beside him in the cold and listen to his half of the conversation. He'd say things like, "Can't we just send you some money and get some music?" then, "Well, what is the minimum order? Wow, that's a lot of money, we don't have that much to invest right now. Is there any way we could make a smaller order to get us started?" He'd look at me with a disgusted face and say something like, "Well, okay, thanks for nothing" and hang up the phone.

We really wanted to carry a lot of Lookout Records releases, so we tried to bypass their distributor and call the label directly. The person that answered was friendly and asked all kinds of questions about the store and about us. Sam mentioned that Hannah and I were in Operation: Cliff Clavin and the guy laughed. He asked Sam how old we were. Sam told him, and he was surprised. He said that he thought we were 15. "Well, they're not 15. We are all adults and we've got a real record store, can we order some records?" Sam started shaking his head and said, "Thanks for nothing." Click. He told me that the guy told him to contact their distributor. We called Fat Wreck Chords too, despite our growing dislike for the kind of people that listened to their bands and our eye-opening experience of trying to book that NOFX show. We expected them to be assholes. We kind of hoped that they would be, so we could tell everyone about it, but they were great. They were really stoked about our store and let us order exactly what we wanted. We got all the Propagandhi stuff that they carried, and a bunch of other cool records. When the order came, it came with a ton of free stuff: stickers, posters, and sampler comps. I felt a little bit bad about the patches I had made the summer before that, which had said "FAT WRECK CHORDS SUCK$."

We had a few shows. Not too many people came, because it was winter and we were kind of far away from downtown. Not everyone in Bloomington drives a car, and we were too far away to walk or ride your bike in the middle of winter. The day after our second show, the landlord stopped by to talk to us about it. He said that one of the other tenants in the strip-mall drove by and saw a bunch of people standing around outside late at night and they were worried about their businesses. We argued with them and reminded them that we told them that we'd be having "in-store" performances from time to time and that they had to be late at night so that we didn't disturb the other businesses. They said that they would talk to the other tenants and that as long as it was only once in a blue moon, it would be okay. We weren't happy about that. We wanted to have regular shows, and we were looking forward to summer and planned on trying to become the main place for punk shows in town. Things were looking bad for Plan-It-X Records; We had to be silent until five o'clock and we could only have shows "once in a blue moon."

One day I was "working" alone in the store. Sam was downtown and Hannah was with her parents somewhere. A young girl came in and walked up to the counter. She asked, "Is this place a real record store, or a front for some kind of illegal operation?"

I laughed and said "It's a real record store, I assure you. We're just starting up, that's why we don't have many records. We're trying." She smiled and laughed.

"That's what I told my mom. I knew you weren't doing anything shady. She wanted me to come in and ask." Then she handed me a little metal charm. I didn't know what it was, so I asked. She said, "It's a zodiac charm. It's Leo." Then she started looking through the T-shirts. I was freaked out.

"I'm a Leo, did you know that?" I asked. She didn't look at me. She laughed and said, "Yeah, I know. I am too."

Then her mom opened the door and popped her head in and said, "Hey, let's go." The girl said goodbye to me and left. I had never seen her before and I never saw her again. It was really weird.

A few days later, the landlord came back and asked us to take the posters out of the windows. They said we could have some posters, but that we couldn't cover the windows completely. They said that some of the other tenants were curious what we were doing inside. I said that the other tenants were more than welcome to come in and look around. They laughed, but said that we had to remove the posters. I said that the sun was blinding us in the afternoon and they said we could have blinds. So we took down the posters and put up blinds. Our days were numbered. It wasn't very fun running a record store. It meant

223

that one of us had to be there all the time. When we wanted to go eat fries, someone had to stay at the store. When something was going on during the day, someone had to miss it. When Operation: Cliff Clavin had a show out of town, Sam had to stay and run the store all alone. If we stayed away overnight, he would have to crawl under the CD rack, into his secret bedroom and latch himself in, all alone in an ugly strip-mall. It wasn't fun. Sometimes, we would just leave and put a note on the door. We assumed that no one would come when we were gone, but they always did. We'd bump into someone and they'd tell us that they walked up to the store, but we weren't there. It was hard.

We lasted for around three months. Then the landlord came again. This time he told us that some of the other tenants thought that we were living in the store. I feigned surprise. "Why would we want to live in this tiny shop?" I asked. "And how could we?" I added.

The guy laughed and said, "I don't know, I guess it's just that your van is always parked out back and you seem to be here late at night, every night." I lied about how there was never parking on my street and I gave him a fake address for my apartment on 13th street. He said that he just had to come and check with me about it. I'm pretty sure he didn't believe me when I told him that we just liked to work late and that we would practice in the store, after hours sometimes. He smiled and nodded, trying to avoid confrontation. I kept up my charade of innocence. He apologized and left.

That night we all talked about how much we hated running a record store and how obvious it was that we were going to get busted soon enough. Of course, we had the option of moving out and keeping the store going, but we didn't think it was worth it. The store sucked and we sucked at running it. None of us wanted to, or could afford to pay rent on a house and on the store, and we didn't want to move back into the van. We decided to try and get out of the lease. I wrote a letter to the landlord that said that we were really offended by the attitude of our neighbors. We felt like they were not willing to give us a chance. We did our best to be friendly to them and they never came in to see what we were all about, instead they made assumptions and accusations. I said that we didn't mix well with them and we didn't know what to do. At the end of the letter I said that we were willing to move out if they were willing to let us break the lease. I think they were really glad to get my letter. They stopped in a few days later and said that they were fine with terminating the lease and they would even give us our damage deposit back. I think they were just as eager for us to leave as we were. We shook hands and I promised them that we would be out by the end of the month.

I learned a valuable lesson that helped me form a theory that I always share with my friends when they tell me that they want to start a record store or a restaurant or whatever. I say "No, you don't want to start a vegan diner, you want to go to a vegan diner, don't get those ideas mixed up." Of course, it was a good experience and I learned a lot about record labels and distributors and I had a warm place to sleep for most of the winter. We closed as gently as we opened. No one really noticed.

CHAPTER 15
MR. DUPLEX

I hauled most of my stuff back down to my parents' house again. I was getting tired of this lifestyle. I wondered when I would settle down a little and stop being so weird. I'm still wondering, eleven years later.

We spent a few weeks floating around town and in-between our parents' houses before we found a place to live. It was a tiny, ugly duplex on West 6th Street, just a few houses down from the place that Sam had lived the summer before. It was ugly, but it was cheap and there were two bedrooms. Most of all, we could live there, like normal people and make food and watch movies and make noise. It was such a relief. Sam called it Mr. Duplex.

Frankie got a job at Papa John's Pizza. Obviously, we were excited about this and started scheming right away. It was the same Papa John's that we had written so many bad checks to the year before. They were one of the places that were working with the detectives too. This was our chance to get our revenge, or whatever. Most of all, we just wanted pizza.

Frankie was really into the idea of helping, and eating free pizza, which was great. We had never had an inside man before, and we were excited to explore the possibilities it would create. We launched our first attack a few days after Secretary's Day. Frankie came over with a handful of coupons good for a free small pizza. They were handed out to secretaries in appreciation of their work or something. He had around 10 of them, and he brought more whenever he managed to steal a stack. We used them relentlessly and without caution. If the pizza man ever questioned us, we said, "My mom works at I.U." It was enough to satisfy them and there were no rules on the coupon that said that the secretaries had to use the coupon themselves. There were also no rules against giving your coupon to someone else. This lasted a while, I think we got at least 30 or 40 pizzas this way, and Frankie was giving them to a few other people too. Eventually the manager figured it out and started ripping them in half, and our supply dried up. Luckily they didn't know who was smuggling the coupons out. Frankie's position was safe. We still had an inside man.

Our next plan was simple. We called in orders for pizzas and we never came to get them. At the end of the night, the workers got to take home the unclaimed pizzas. Frankie would bring them over when he got out of work. There were a few problems with this plan. The first problem was that sometimes the other workers wanted the pizza and Frankie didn't get it. Or, the workers ate the pizza at work, as a snack. The other problem was that he didn't get off of work until really late, which left us waiting like Schrodinger waited to see if his cat was dead of not, wondering if we had a pizza coming or if the pizza was being eaten by our enemies. Our pizza existed in two realities, in one, it was on a shelf waiting to come to our hungry mouths, in the other, some stoner was devouring it. We didn't find out until around midnight when Frankie showed up, either bearing a great gift, or empty handed. It drove us crazy waiting.

Sam took to superstitious rituals to improve our luck and the outcome of the evening. He had a small statuette of a golden cat that he called his lucky road cat. He had found it somewhere out west on his big journey. He would rub it and ask me to rub it too. He'd say, "Hey Chris, will you stroke my lucky road cat, to help us get some pizza?" I usually did it. Both of us got really crazy as the night grew late. Minutes before midnight we would turn off the music so that we could listen for Frankie's car. Hannah thought we were nuts, and she was right. If Frankie showed up with nothing, Sam was angry and wouldn't hang out with him. He could be cruel sometimes, and thankless. If Frankie showed up with pizza, he was our best friend. We'd sit around the open box and listen to his work stories. We'd pour him a cup of Big K soda and thank him over and over. Pizza made us so happy.

Frankie also gave us inside info on what happened to pizzas that were being thrown out. He told us that they stayed on the shelf, inside the store, until morning and the prep crew threw them out when they got there at eleven o'clock. He said it was a safety issue. They didn't open the back door late at night to avoid being robbed. It was a good thing to know, it helped us out a lot on the days that Frankie didn't work. We would call in pizzas and go look for them the next day, often finding other pizzas that we didn't even call in. It was great and it helped us dumpster at other pizza places too. No more staying up late, waiting for places to close so we could look for our pizzas. Instead, we called in pizzas all night and gathered them up in the morning. It took planning and patience, but it paid off. We had more pizza than we could eat. We ate it anyway.

For some reason, Papa John's never caught on that Frankie was involved in the fake orders, and he kept bringing us pizza and we kept pushing our luck. We started calling in five to ten pizzas a night. Frankie told us what the other workers didn't like, so we could assure that they didn't eat our pizzas, or take them home. Sometimes he would bring every pizza we ordered over at the end of the night. It was out of control. He even started calling the orders in himself. He would stop by our house whenever he was on a delivery in our neighborhood and use our phone to call in a pizza. He loved doing it. He loved acting, and he thought it was fun creating characters and coming up with different accents and deceiving his co-workers. He even called the orders in from the office in the pizza shop sometimes. There were a few phone lines and as long as he pushed *67 before he dialed, the number didn't show up on the caller ID. He was an excellent ally in our war on the Papa. We were back in the pizza scamming business and this time, it didn't seem like there was any chance of anyone going to jail. The worst thing that could happen would be Frankie getting fired.

One night, along with the usual spoils of our war, Frankie brought over a 20-pound bag of mozzarella. It was better than any Christmas or birthday gift that I had ever gotten. We walked to Kroger and I shoplifted a loaf of Italian bread while Sam waited outside. When we got home, we made thick grilled cheese sandwiches. It had been so long since either of us had eaten a grilled cheese, since you couldn't find them in a dumpster and they were hard to scam. Don't forget that we didn't buy cheese ever, and we were militant freegans—if we couldn't get our cheese for free, we didn't eat it. When we bought food, we always bought vegan food because we didn't want to support the industry that tortured and killed animals. Grilled cheese was almost as treasured as pizza, maybe more so since it was so much harder to acquire. The cheese wasn't that good, but we loved it anyway. When we were done with round one, we made more and we put pickles or jalapenos in them. We used tons of margarine and drowned them in ketchup, with potato ships on the side.

Speaking of margarine, let me stray from the story a little bit to tell you about Sam and the margarine-eating contest. I'm not sure where this story fits in, but it happened. Sam loved margarine and would put tons of it on anything he could get away with putting it on. Spaghetti got a huge spoonful, or half a stick if we had sticks. Rice swam in yellow oil. Toast was soggy with the stuff. Someone once asked Sam how much margarine he could eat and someone else said that we should have a contest, so we booked the contest as an act at Rhino's with bands playing too. Sam made fliers seeking challengers. I wasn't surprised that no one replied right away.

Eventually a challenger stepped up. It was a 14-year-old local girl named Corinna who had recently started coming to shows. Everyone loved her and tried to pretend that they didn't have a crush on her. She told me that she wanted to sign up for the contest. I laughed and she got really mad. She asked me why I was laughing. I didn't know what to say. I was afraid of looking like a jerk. I said something about how Sam was disgusting and I warned her about how much he loved margarine. She assured me that she was very serious about signing up and I said, "okay, sorry." I guess I laughed because she was shy and cute and the thought of her on stage beside Sam stuffing margarine into her face was absurd. Then I thought about how funny it would look and I realized that it was a great idea. I knew that everyone else would be just as shocked as me when they found out that Corinna had challenged Sam. It was great.

We decided to get tub margarine instead of sticks, and we figured that one huge tub each would be enough. No one else signed up. It was just Sam and Corinna on stage, each holding a huge tub of generic buttery spread (vegan of course). I didn't think about how the contest would work until they were up there waiting to start. Corinna asked if it would be timed or if it was a contest to see who could finish the tub first. I hadn't thought about it. We had to figure it out quick because there was a room full of people eagerly awaiting the grossness to start. A few of us on the side of the stage discussed it and agreed that it should be timed, for sake of the attention span of the crowd and because there were bands waiting to play. Sam was furious.

"I didn't agree to a timed contest!" he shouted. I tried to explain why it made sense. He didn't agree at all. Someone asked what happens if they puke.

"They lose," I said. After some arguing with Sam, we started the contest with a five-minute limit. It was so gross, they shoved their hands into the tubs and shoveled marg into their mouths. The crowd either groaned in disgust or gasped in disbelief at what they were seeing.

Some weird girl in the front row, who none of us knew, kept saying, "Yeah, that's it. Eat that shit like a sloppy pussy." We told her to shut up or leave. I found out later that she made someone else in the crowd so sick that they had to go outside and puke. Sam was doing great, taking little handfuls and swallowing them quickly, without chewing. Corinna was having some trouble because she had too much in her mouth to deal with. She gagged and spit up a huge clump into a dirty cooler that I had found in Rhino's and put on the stage in case someone needed to puke. It still had a few inches of old cooler water in the bottom. When she spit out the clump, the crowd went wild. "She's out!" someone yelled. "She puked, that's it!" Corinna wasn't ready to lose. She reached into the cooler and grabbed the soggy chunk that she had spit out. It was dripping with stale water. She shoved it back into her mouth and we all gagged. I checked the cooler and saw that she had gotten it all out, so she was still in the game. The timer sounded, the contest was over. We took the margarine tubs away from them and tried pushing the remaining marg down and flattened it out to see who had won. It was too close to tell. Sam was still angry.

"I won, I know I did. And besides, it wasn't fair. I never agreed to a timed contest." We really couldn't tell who won, so we put the lids on the tubs and said that we would weigh them later and announce the winner. I took them home that night and put them in the freezer for some reason. I never weighed them, but I'm pretty sure Corinna won. I didn't want to upset Sam.

Anyway, back to Mr. Duplex and our huge bag of free cheese. We ate one or two grilled cheese sandwiches every day, and we usually got at least one pizza a night. We were cheese crazy and eventually we were punished, well, Sam was (again). He came to me and said "I can't poop." I asked him how long it had been. "At least 5 days, and my stomach hurts really bad," he said, as he raised his shirt to show me his swollen tummy. I suggested that we go to Kroger and get some laxatives. Sam waited outside while I stole them. He took a triple dose that day and nothing happened. The next day he took another triple dose and nothing happened. While we waited, we calculated what all was inside of him. We figured out that he had 5 large extra cheese pizzas and 7 grilled cheese sandwiches as well as some potato chips and at least two orders of fries.

"You must feel awful" I said. He looked so sad.

"I do."

The next day we were on our way to a show in Louisville and it happened. "Please pull over right now! I need to go!" he cried. There was a gas station nearby and I pulled in. He limped out of the van and made his way inside. We were all really worried that he had already shit himself. Around 10 minutes later, he came out, white as a ghost.

"How did it go?" I asked.

"It was horrible. The men's room was out of order, so I had to use the ladies and the door didn't lock. People kept trying to get in. My ass exploded like a volcano and it smelled really bad. I puked in my mouth. It just kept coming too, it filled the bowl and piled up like a shit mountain. I had to stand up so that it didn't touch my butt. When I was done, the mountain peak was high above the toilet seat. I didn't even try to flush." he said. We started driving again, and he went on and on about his terrible shit. "There were a few people waiting to use the bathrooms. I was going to try and explain what had happened and tell them not to go in, but I felt too bad and I didn't know what to say, so I just walked past them and said sorry," he concluded.

Despite the free pizzas and the bag of cheese, Sam became depressed. He started sleeping all day and all night. I was beginning to understand what his parents meant by the 24-hour sleeping schedule, and how hard it was to wake him up. I would go into his room and do my best to get him out of bed. He wouldn't budge. He'd try to convince me that he was sick or just really tired. He'd promise me that he would get up soon. This went on for weeks and weeks. Then one day, me and Hannah were walking home from downtown, it was a beautiful day and it was the first nice day of the year. Everyone was outside walking around and enjoying the sunshine. I saw Sam walking toward us, smiling. We stopped on the corner of Kirkwood and Rogers and talked for a few minutes. I asked him where he was going.

"I'm just going for a walk, it's a beautiful day isn't it?" he said.

"Yeah," I agreed. I was so happy to see him up and on his feet. The sun was setting and we all had golden faces. It was so nice.

Then he said, "Well, goodbye guys," and walked away, giving us an awkward wave. It was weird and seemed overly emotional, but since he had been sleeping for weeks I didn't think about it too much and I didn't ask him to explain himself. I didn't want to ruin the moment. He didn't come home that night.

Around two in the morning, Sam's brother called. He told me Sam was in the hospital. "Why? What happened?" I asked. I assumed that he got hit by a car or something, he was horrible at crossing the street. He told me that Sam had tried to kill himself by cutting his wrists with a knife. I felt sick. I didn't say anything for a minute. I thought about Sam's goodbye earlier that day and realized that he was saying goodbye for good. "Where is he?" I asked.

"He's okay. He's at the hospital. He went there on his own." I hung up the phone and went to see him. They told me that he was on 24-hour suicide watch and that no one could see him until it was over. I was so mad. I argued with them for a while, then went home. I didn't know what to do with myself, so I went into Sam's room and looked through his stuff. I couldn't believe that he had tried to kill himself. I couldn't imagine what it would be like to live without him. I felt scared and horrible. I examined his possessions like I was on a archaeological dig. I went through everything. I cleaned his room and gathered up his filthy laundry to wash and took the sheets off of his bed. I vacuumed, I arranged his new stuffed rabbits, then I found his suicide letter:

Dear Chris,
This is Sam. You are going to hear some awful things about me, but they are not true. Whatever you do, don't believe what people tell you. I had to go underground. I can't live this way anymore. There are really important things that I need to do, and I have to be underground to do them. I'm really sorry but I'll never see you again. I can't, but just know that I'm out there, doing really important stuff and that I love you, and that I miss you. You can have all of my stuff, I don't need it. I love you buddy. - Sam

I couldn't believe that he wrote a funny suicide note. I was so mad, but I was laughing too. It was such a Sam thing to do. Then I found a few other drafts that weren't as funny and were only half finished. I also found a bunch of unsent letters to some of our mutual friends and drawings and songs that he had written. I collected everything I could find and carefully put it all in a folder. I don't know why. I guess it was all I could do while I waited for them to let me see him. Those scraps of paper were treasures to me, they were like artifacts, or sacred scrolls.

DEAR PAPA,

HELLO, I HAVEN'T HAD A CHANCE TO CALL YOU ON THE PHONE FOR A WHILE. I JUST MOVED INTO A NEW APARTMENT ON 6TH STREET, 1020 W. 6th STREET IS THE ADRESS. I AM SORRY I HAVEN'T GOTTEN A CHANCE TO READ ALL THE E-MAIL YOU SEND ME BUT I DON'T REALLY HAVE ACCESS TO A COMPUTER, INSTEAD I WILL SEND YOU A GOOD OLD FASHIONED LETTER.

I USED TO THINK COMPUTERS LINKED TOGETHER COULD PROVIDE NOW THE WORLD WITH SOLUTIONS TO ALL ITS PROBLEMS BUT NOW WHAT ONCE WAS JUST SCIENCE FICTION IS TURNING INTO REALITY AS HUMAN BEINGS ARE CLONED, ORGANS ARE STOLEN AND SOLD, AND THE FEAR OF STARVATION AND THE ELEMENTS KEEPS PEOPLE ALL OVER THE WORLD WORKING FOR MULTINATIONAL CORPORATIONS INSTEAD OF FEEDING THEMSELVES AND FULFILLING THEIR DREAMS. THE MYTH OF THE RESPONSIBLE CORPORATION CAN BE EXPOSED BY LOOKING AT THEIR TRACK RECORD IN ALMOST ANY AREA WHERE THE PEOPLE ARE NOT PROTECTED BY LAW AND ACTIVE MONITORING GROUPS. THIS IS A LITTLE OFF THE POINT WHICH WAS THAT A GENUINE SMILE CONTAINS A LOT MORE INFORMATION THAN A MEGABYTE OR ALL THE MEGABYTES IN THE WORLD.

I WAS REALLY GLAD TO SEE YOU AT CHRISTMAS AND THANKSGIVING AND I WAS GLAD TO SEE MOM. YOU SEEM TO BE DOING REALLY WELL. I'M SORRY THAT I HADN'T SEEN YOU FOR A LONG TIME, IT SEEMED LIKE THE ONLY WAY I COULD GET BACK INTO THINGS WAS JUST TO RUN AWAY.

I was afraid to walk into his hospital room. I was afraid to see him. He looked embarrassed and worried when I came in. We made small talk for a while and eventually he told me what had happened. He said that he just felt really sad and that his brain was messed up. He thought it would be nice to just die. "Do you still feel that way?" I asked.

"No, I feel better now. Do you want to see my arm?" Reluctantly, I nodded and he pulled back his bandage to show me the 30-something stitches on his wrist. He had cut himself at least 10 times, all on the same arm. It looked horrible and made me feel sick. He told me that he used his survival knife and then he laughed. I made a confused face and he said, "I thought it was funny, using a survival knife to kill myself." I didn't laugh at first, then I chuckled a little to keep him in the oddly-good mood he seemed to be in. I told him that I was glad that he didn't die. He said that he was too. I asked him how he pulled it off, and he told me that every time he cut himself, the blood clotted and the wound stopped bleeding. After 10 tries, he decided to give up and walk to the emergency room. He told me that once he started walking, the bleeding increased and he was dripping blood on the ground. As he got closer to the hospital, he realized that he really didn't want to die, but he was bleeding so much that he thought he was going to anyway. He told them that it was an accident, hoping that they wouldn't lock him up, but obviously, they knew what he had done. He said that he would have to stay in the hospital for at least a week.

On the way out, I noticed a few drops of blood on the sidewalk by the door. I looked for more and I found them. I followed the trail of blood back to where he had tried to kill himself. The path led me to the roof of a battery shop on 6th street. There was a pool of dried blood in the gutter. I felt sick, thinking about him sitting on the roof cutting his wrist, hoping to die. Then, I thought about the time when he was sleeping all day, for months at his parents house, and I got the same job that he had and I was homeless like he was, and I called it "walking the path of Sam." This path was much more gruesome.

I burned the suicide note. I didn't want it to exist in my world. I burned it and buried the ashes. I took the rest of the stuff that I stole from his room and made a 'zine called "Samzine." I made around 20 copies and gave them to Sam's closest friends. I included a few of his unsent letters, and I mailed a copy of the 'zine to each of the unknowing recipients, so that they would finally get their letter from Sam. I showed it to him in the hospital. He was embarrassed and a little angry, but agreed with me that it was fair play after what he had done. I told him that I did it to celebrate him. He told me to shut the fuck up.

Summer was still coming, despite this horror, and that meant it was time to start thinking about tour again. We had just released our second full-length album, Paradise Lost, (with the money that we got from the drunk driver's insurance company) and we were excited about taking the new songs on the road. I decided it was time to retire Mr. Van and my dad sold it for me to some guy he knew for $300, which was pretty good considering it had a sheet metal side and I only paid $600 for it. I bought a new van for $800, and my dad and I went to a junkyard and found a camper top for it. We attached it and then we cut a huge hole through the roof of the van. I put a mattress on top, and we built a loft below it, making it a double-lofted van with room to comfortably sleep five people. We called it "Super Van," obviously.

This time we were gonna take Sam for sure. I wasn't going to let him out of my sight. Sam had still never been on a full sized tour with us. This time he had to come. I called Greg Wells to tell him about the new van and fill him in on the tour dates. He told me that he couldn't do it. I was so sad, Greg was practically a member of the band. He was always with us and he was great as his job. When he wasn't on tour with us, he was a mover, so he never complained about carrying our amps or drums and he was really good at selling our stuff and dealing with promoters when they tried to rip us off. He was the best roadie on the road. I didn't know how we were gonna live without him. We needed a roadie, and I didn't consider Sam to be a roadie—he was too unpredictable and he wasn't good at working the merch table. I wanted him to come, but we needed someone else too, so I placed an ad in Maximumrocknroll that said something like: "Operation: Cliff Clavin needs a roadie for a two month tour all across the USA." It went on, much like the flier that we made when we were looking for a drummer, listing the idealistic political requirements that

234

the applicant must meet.

We only got two calls. The first one came from a kid in New York state. He said that he'd been having a rough life and had attempted suicide recently. He saw the ad and took it as a sign. He thought it might be good for him to go traveling and see the world. We thought about it and talked it over, and came to the conclusion that although it could be a life changing experience for him and set him down a better path, it could also be stressful and difficult and might send him further down the dark path. We didn't want to take a chance like that. We didn't feel qualified and we were already bringing one suicidal person on tour. One was enough. We turned him down.

Then a guy named Dave called and left a message on our voicemail. He sounded desperate and we decided that it was a bad idea to take some random person on tour with us. We didn't call him back. We thought that was the last we'd hear about Dave.

CHAPTER 16
THE DOCTOR

A year or so later, we were living with Dave, the guy whom we tried not to take on tour, and Sam had started calling him "The Doctor" because he always had boxes of mouthwash and medicine, which he shared with all of us. Sam would just knock on his door and say, "Doctor, I need some Neosporin," or, "I need a bandage," and he usually had it, whatever it was. He got the stuff from some relative who had some sort of job where you can get things like that, but The Doctor wasn't Dave's only nickname. Somewhere during his high school years, he got the name "Dooms Dave."

He explained it to me one day—he said that he was cursed and everyone back home knew it. It happened in a graveyard somewhere in Rockford, Illinois one night. This graveyard had a legend, like all graveyards have legends, and this one involved a witch's tombstone. The legend was, if you touched the tombstone, you'd be cursed for seven years. Dave, who didn't believe in such stupid crap and was riding high on life at the time, thought that it would be funny and maybe earn him some street cred with his friends if he went up and spit on the tombstone. After hearing the mixture of gasps and cheers from his friends, he took it a step further and kicked the thing over. Since that day, Dave will tell you, his life has been total shit. It all started with him losing his car in some sibling rivalry. He had a cool car, and that was a big part of why he got the respect that he got at school. After losing the car, he started taking the bus again, and maybe because of losing the car, he lost his girlfriend too. She dumped him. She was his first real love and it really hurt him. He was cursed, and it kept getting worse. Anyway, now that you know a little bit about Dave, let's go back to the spring of 1998. We don't know him yet and we're getting ready for tour. He's at home. He's miserable.

Dave was fed up with his shitty life in Rockford and decided that he couldn't take it there anymore, and he had found just what he needed to escape—our ad in Maximumrocknroll. He took it as sign, just like the kid from

New York did. He called us and left that desperate message on our voicemail system, and, like I said, we didn't call him back. A few days later, I got a message from his mom. She was freaking out and wanted to know if we knew where her son was. She said that he ran away from home, and that she knew that he called our number. She sounded really worried, so I called her back and told her that I didn't know Dave at all and that I had no clue where he might be. We considered ourselves lucky to have avoided harboring a runaway teenager with a pissed off parent, and we were sure then that we wouldn't be calling anyone back about the roadie job. The ad was a big mistake.

A few weeks before the tour, Sam got arrested for getting naked downtown. He called Mr. Duplex, because we finally had a phone! The robot voice said, "You are receiving a collect call from an inmate at Monroe county jail. Do you accept the charges?" I knew it had to be about Sam, so I said yes. It was, and he was pissed off.

All he said was, "Can you come bail me out? It's only $200..." I asked him what happened. "It doesn't matter. Just come get me." I asked him if he would pay me back when his next check came, because I only had a little over $200 and I still had to spend some money on the van, getting it ready for tour. He was raging mad, he said, "Don't worry, you'll get your fucking money. Just come and get me!" I told him that I'd get him out as quick as possible.

When they finally let him go and I got to see him, he looked crazy. I asked him what happened. He told me that he got naked and tried to kiss a cop. "Why?" I asked.

"I don't fucking know. I don't care," he said without making eye contact with me. I asked him about the money again, since tour was coming up so soon, and he got really mad. He tried to run away from me. I grabbed him and he twisted out of my hands violently. I told him to calm down and he screamed at me and told me to fuck off. I tried to grab him again, but he ran away. I chased him for a while, but I couldn't keep up. I begged him to come home. He kept running. I went home, frightened by the look I had seen in Sam's eyes. A few hours later, I got a call from the hospital. He was there again—he drank half a bottle of toilet bowl cleaner and had almost died.

I went to see him the next day. His parents were there when I got there. They looked so worried. I could tell that they really loved him, even if they were bad at it. We chatted for a while, then they left. Sam apologized. I told him that he didn't have to. He told me that he would pay me back before I left for tour. I told him not to worry about it.

"I'm sorry," he said. "I was going to sneak off into the woods somewhere and do it, so you would have never known what happened. You would have thought I was just missing or that I ran away or something." My heart sank. I felt so horrible. It was an awful thought, the idea of Sam wanting to die, but not wanting to trouble us with his death, and the thought of him in the woods somewhere trying to hide his corpse. Again, I asked him if he still wanted to die.

"No way, I really don't want to," he said. We talked for a while and he told me that he had meant to get Drano, but accidentally bought the wrong thing. If he had bought the Drano he would have been dead for sure—that stuff turns your stomach into a volcano of black sludge that erupts out of your mouth. I was so glad that Sam didn't get the right thing, although toilet bowl cleaner was still poison.

"How much did you drink?" I asked.

"I drank around half the bottle and it was about this big," he said, holding up his hands to show me. My eyes focused on the I.V. in his arm. He said that the doctor told him he was lucky to be alive, that drinking that much should have killed him, that he would probably need a new stomach, and, more than likely, he would get cancer in five years. I felt like throwing up. Then Sam changed the subject and said, "I guess I can't go on tour with you guys." I told him not to worry about it, and suggested that maybe when they let him out, he could meet us somewhere. He smiled and said that he might.

The day before the tour, I get a call from Greg Wells. I was really excited to hear his voice and the first thing I said was, "I hope you're calling to tell me that you've changed your mind about the tour."

"Sorry kid, I can't do it this time. I've got too many projects to do here." Then I told him about Sam. He was really upset, he loved Sam almost as much as I did. We talked about it for a while, then Greg told me why he called. He said that he had a kid staying at his house who wanted to be our roadie. I asked him who it was and he said, "it's this guy named Dave, from Rockford." After many doubtful questions, he convinced me that it was the same Dave who called me.

It turns out that he was offered a ride to Richmond, and since we had never returned his call, he took it. This still didn't explain what he was doing at Greg's house. I asked for an explanation. Greg told me that he found him on the streets, "looking like a lost puppy," he said. Dave didn't know anything about Richmond and had no friends there. He didn't have a plan. He just had a free ride and he took it. Greg felt sorry for the pup and asked him where he was from and what he was doing. Dave started talking about his summer plans to be a roadie falling though. He mentioned Operation: Cliff Clavin, and chaos took its course. I told Greg the runaway story, but he assured me that Dave was no teenager. He told me that he was 21 years old.

After a lot of explaining, I eventually agreed to talk to Dave on the phone.

He told me that his parents were really fucked up and very overprotective and that they didn't want him to leave home. He assured me again that he was not a runaway, and swore that he was 21, even offering to show Greg his driver's license. After a while, I decided he was probably telling the truth, and maybe we should have given him a chance, but it didn't really matter since we were starting the tour in southern Indiana the next day and he was in Richmond, Virginia. I told him it was too late, unless he could find a way to meet up with us. He asked me if our first show was anywhere near I-64. I told him that I-64 runs right by my parents' house and was only a few miles away from our first show. He got really excited and told me that these girls he had met were driving from Richmond to St. Louis. They were leaving really early the next morning, which would get him there in time. I told him that we needed to talk it over and that I'd call him back.

At this point, I decided that Chaos was trying Her best to get Dave into our van, and that fighting Her will would be useless, and/or dangerous. We talked it over and decided to give him a shot. I called Greg back and told him that we were probably going take him, but before breaking the news to Dave, I asked Greg what he thought of the guy. He said that he was all right, a little shy, but all right. That was enough for me. Four weeks later, we broke down in the blazing Arizona heat and I called Greg to tell him how bad things were going, and he asked me how Dave was doing. I started to tell him about all the awkward moments and the weird things that he did, and Greg starts laughing and says, "That kid is a freak." He goes on to admit that he only vouched for him to get him out of his house. It was his version of a prank. I was so mad. Anyway, Dave was happy when I told him that he could be our roadie. We had a lot of miles between home and Arizona. Dave was in Richmond, we were in Indiana.

I told him to meet us at this gas station just off of I-64. It was right down the road from my parents' house and we had planned to stop at my parents' house anyway on our way to the show. I told him to wait there for us and we would pick him up. We got there and we didn't see him. We searched the place, but he wasn't there. Everyone was a little relieved. It was looking like we wouldn't have to have a random roadie after all. I checked the voicemail at my parents' house in case he had called. He didn't, but I got a message from my friend Chris Lincoln who used to be in Instinct (one of the first Plan-It-X bands). He was in a new band now, called Left Out, and they were playing the show with us that night. He lived really close by. His message said, "We've got your roadie with us." That's all it said. We ate peanut butter and jelly sandwiches, then we headed out to play our first show of a long summer tour, and to meet our new roadie.

When we got the show, I found Chris right away to figure out what he was talking it about and it turns out that Dave got dropped off at the wrong exit and the wrong gas station. He was just hopelessly waiting there for us at the wrong place, with no way of knowing. Chris and the rest of Left Out stopped to get gas and saw a sorry looking punk sitting on the curb. They ask ed him what he was doing and he told them his tale. They told him who they were and where they were going, and said, "Get in the van."

After all of that, I knew that for better or worse, Dave was a part of our fucked up family and that was that. Chaos had its way. I met him and told him that he could come with us, but that he had to work. I told him that it wasn't just a free ride. His first words were, "I need a toothbrush and a blanket, and I don't have any money."

CHAPTER 17
STARTS AND ENDS

The tour was hard and filled with gaps, like a boxer's mouth. The gas tank was always hungry, and so were we. Our daily meal was one pound of pasta and one jar of pasta sauce, cooked in parking lots on a camp stove, often outside of a Taco Bell or Burger King, so we could fill up our travel mugs with free soda. In Portland, we played with Bisybackson again and stayed at their house. They were a great band, and really great people too. The next morning I walked down to Safeway and bought some fireworks. I thought Sam would like getting fireworks in the mail for his birthday, since it's illegal to mail them. I caught a punk girl eating candy out of the bulk bins. She was wearing camouflage pants and a football jersey with the number 55 on it. We smiled at each other and I carried on with my task, thinking that I should have talked to her.

A week or so later, in Berkeley, we were playing at Gilman Street and I saw her there. She was wearing a boy scout shirt this time. I went up and said hello.

"Hey, I think I saw you in Portland," was my opening line.

"Yeah, that was me," she said.

"Do you live here... or there? What are you doing?"

"I've got a Greyhound pass for the summer. I'm just traveling around. I'm from Pittsburgh, but my dad lives in Oakland." I don't know what I said in response.

She told me that she saw us play the previous summer in Ft. Collins, Colorado with Bisybackson. I told her that we just played with them in Portland. We talked for a minute or two, then I left to return to our merch table. I told Hannah and Frankie about my encounter and suggested that we ask her to join our tour. They both liked the idea. Of course, Frankie only liked it because of his lecherous nature. I found her again and asked her name.

"I'm Ali," she said.

"I'm Chris," I replied. "Do you want to come on tour with us?" I asked.

"Yeah," she answered without hesitation.

"Cool." She said she had to hang out with her dad for a few days but could meet up with us in a week or so. I checked our schedule and we settled on Albuquerque. Dave was not happy about this plan.

Ali, a year or so later, playing in The Sissies.

On the way to Phoenix, the van stopped running. We broke down in the blazing heat on a small highway just north of a town aptly named Nothing, Arizona. Dave and Frankie hitched a ride into "town" and found out that one of the four people who lived in Nothing happened to be a tow truck driver. He looked a lot like Santa Claus. He loaded up our van, with us in it. His truck was one of the flat bed kinds, so we were sitting pretty high up and feared for our lives on those windy mountain roads. We just had to hope that he had hooked us down good. Ten minutes later, we pulled into the town square of Nothing.

It was a dusty gravel parking lot surrounded by collapsing sheds and junked cars. There was a small house and a general store perched on the edge of a steep slope above a scrap heap. Santa Claus went into the house and said he'd be back in a few minutes.

A few minutes passed, and it was way too hot in the van, so we climbed out to explore the wonders of Nothing. There was a box outside the store with a hinged lid that read, in hand painted letters, "see baby rattlers." Frankie opened the lid and laughed. I reluctantly walked over in looked down to see an assortment of plastic baby rattles. There was another box that read, "see the albino bat." It held a small baseball bat, painted white. It seemed that Santa's plan was to leave us sweating in the van until we got thirsty enough to patronize his shop. His plan worked. We bought drinks and snacks for the ride.

Our plan was to get towed directly to the show in Phoenix. It was less than 100 miles away, so it would be covered by Hannah's Triple A plus card. Santa wasn't happy about having to make such a long trip, and he decided to bring his kids along for company, meaning all four of us would have to ride in the van, praying that the chains held tight. On the way he made a few strange turns. We consulted the map and concluded that he was trying to tack miles onto the trip, so that not all of it would be covered by Triple A. We honked the horn and tried to get his attention, but he wouldn't stop. We made it to the show a little late, but confident that we weren't too late to play. Everyone was outside smoking and cooling off between bands. They all watched us climb out of the van and down off of the tow truck. Then they watched our dead van roll down the ramp and us push it into a parking spot and start unloading our gear. It was a pretty punk entrance. Santa turned out to be a real scrooge and tried to make us pay $90, but we argued and talked him down to $45. He left in a huff and we rushed to set up our gear. We were on next.

After the show, the van started up fine and we drove it to the house we were staying at. I called Greg that night, and that's when he told me his true opinion about Dave. The next morning we made some calls and considered taking the van to a garage, but we decided to risk the drive to Flagstaff instead. We made it and we didn't speak of the van's troubles, so we wouldn't jinx it. I'm pretty superstitious, and I enforce my beliefs on everyone I travel with. We pretended that the breakdown never happened.

The next day, on the way to Albuquerque, the van died again and wouldn't start. We got towed to the nearest town, since we were way too far away from Albuquerque to get towed all the way there. It was Holbrook, Arizona, and it wasn't much nicer than Nothing. It was Sunday and all the garages were closed, so we had to spend the night. Our show in Albuquerque wasn't until the next day, so we weren't too worried about it. We slept in the van even though the town was filled with cheap hotels advertising COOL A/C & HBO for $15. That's how cheap we were. We wouldn't pay $15 to sleep in the cool A/C.

When we woke up, Dave was gone. He came back with some breakfast snacks and told us that he was going home. He said that he was worried about the van and about all of us running out of money. He didn't want to get stuck somewhere and he was also worried about how things would work when Ali joined the tour. He didn't want to be useless. I asked how he planned to get home, and he confessed that he had called his dad and that he had sent him money through Western Union for a bus ticket. He had already bought the ticket. There was no talking him out of it. He was leaving.

The garage opened and we waited for the van to get fixed. It was the fuel pump, and it was gonna cost us everything we had. Dave treated us all to fast food fries and soda, then gathered his things and walked to the Greyhound station. I didn't know if I would ever see him again.

The next day we met Ali at The Frontier in Albuquerque. We ate fries and told her about Dave jumping ship. Just like that, we had a new roadie, and we all liked her a lot. I didn't miss Dave yet and I would have never guessed that I would. Ali was great. The show was okay, and we got paid enough to press on and to start recovering from the fuel pump replacement. Ali breathed new life into our dismal tour, but we were excited to get home. We had big plans after the tour, and I missed Sam. I told Ali stories about him as we drove through west Texas. I told her about the time he tried to join the Canadian Navy.

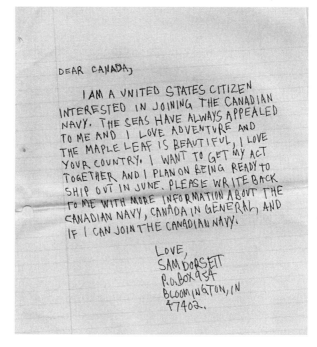

DEAR CANADA,

I AM A UNITED STATES CITIZEN INTERESTED IN JOINING THE CANADIAN NAVY. THE SEAS HAVE ALWAYS APPEALED TO ME AND I LOVE ADVENTURE AND THE MAPLE LEAF IS BEAUTIFUL, I LOVE YOUR COUNTRY. I WANT TO GET MY ACT TOGETHER AND I PLAN ON BEING READY TO SHIP OUT IN JUNE. PLEASE WRITE BACK TO ME WITH MORE INFORMATION ABOUT THE CANADIAN NAVY, CANADA IN GENERAL, AND IF I CAN JOIN THE CANADIAN NAVY.

LOVE,
SAM DORSETT
P.O.BOX 954
BLOOMINGTON, IN
47402.

CHAPTER 18
THE MADISON

At the end of this huge tour we were going to move into a real house. We had already signed the lease. No more van life. No more secretly living in a strip mall. No more tiny duplex. It was pretty exciting to think about coming home from tour and being able to get out of the van. The last few tours were weird for me. It was like two or three other people invaded my home, the van, for several weeks. They made messes, they slept on my bed and they took up all of my space. Then, I'd get home and drop them off at their houses and I'd get my home back. This time, I would pull the van into the driveway and get out, I was eager to set up my new room, it had been so long since I had a real room. We already had so many plans! The house had a small basement, accessible by a trapdoor on the back porch, and we were gonna have shows and potlucks and movie nights and other stuff, but I was mostly excited about cooking good food. That's pretty hard to do when you're living in a van or a record store, and during our months at Mr. Duplex, we mostly ate free pizza. It was great, but I was ready to start making good food.

The house was on Madison Street, so we decided to call it "The Madison." We thought it sounded classy, like a fancy hotel. I couldn't wait to get home, but we still had a long road ahead of us. We struggled on through Texas and the south, always running on empty, always pumping the last of our dollars into the tank. We took refuge in Gainesville for a while, then had an unexpected weeklong break in Bloomington before heading east to do the last three weeks of the tour. Our new roadie and friend, Ali, came with us. We surprised Sam when we busted in, four weeks early. Mr. Duplex was a disaster, but we still had around half of the bag of cheese from Papa John's, so we ate grilled cheese and drank Big K. We tried not to think about the days ahead. I didn't want to leave Bloomington.

Sam told me about his time in the hospital and why he had to stay so long. His IV had gotten infected and he got really sick. He almost died. He said he would have been really mad if he died that way. I told him that I would have been really mad too. I asked him how his stomach was. He said it was fine, but that he would never be able to eat big meals again, he would have to snack all day, forever. He told me that the doctor was sure that his stomach was ruined and that he would have to get a goat's stomach put in, but somehow it healed really well and he got to keep it. We were both glad that he didn't have to get the goat's stomach, but Sam joked about how he kinda wished that he did, because then he could eat cans and stuff. I asked him if he wanted to finish the tour with us. He said that he couldn't, he had appointments with his doctor. I told him not to worry about it. I told him that we'd be home soon, and reminded him that we'd be moving into a real house when we got back.

We weren't even sure if Frankie was gonna go on the next leg of the tour, because he wasn't speaking to us, so we didn't know if we were even going. We didn't talk to him at all during our break. It all started in Valdosta, Georgia, when we showed up at our show one month late. We were sitting on the curb outside the closed venue and a guy showed up with a guitar. We asked him about the show. He told us that there wasn't anything booked that night. We were pissed. He asked us what band we in. We told him and he said, "Oh, I remember that show. That was June 23rd, not July 23rd. You're a month late." It was pretty funny.

The tour wasn't supposed to have a break. We were supposed to just keep working our way up, and all over the East Coast, but the next six or seven shows were still up in the air. We were trying to jump on a bunch of shows with The Grumpies and F.Y.P. but it didn't seem like it was going to happen. We were beat and broke, so we went to Little Caesars and got crazy bread. We started discussing the plan to go home for a week. Frankie quit talking. We asked him what he thought we should do. He didn't answer. We asked him what was wrong. He didn't answer. I freaked out a little. I told him that I couldn't take any more weird shit. I threatened to put his bags on the curb and drive off. He still wouldn't say anything, so Hannah, Ali, and I decided that we'd go to Bloomington and take a break. We got in the van and started the 13-hour drive home. When we began seeing the signs for Macon, we adapted the lyrics of some song that we didn't really know, We sang it for hundreds of miles until we were all crazy as hell: "we're going to Macon after all." Hours and hours flew by, and ounces and ounces of scammed soda refills kept us awake. We sang, and Frankie sat in silence.

The day before we were supposed to leave for tour again, Frankie came over and said, "Do you guys want to practice?" He'd dyed his hair red and was wearing a cowboy hat.

"Are you okay?" I asked. "What's up with you? Do you remember not talking to us?" He said that he was just going through some rough stuff, but that he was okay now. "Are you sure you want to go on tour?" I asked.

"Of course I do," he said, smiling. We practiced, and the next day I said goodbye to Sam, then we got back in the van to continue this shambolic tour.

Some time later, we got a voicemail from Jasin—the Jasin from Franklin, the one who was in The Ataris—the one we were going to live with in Goleta. He and his girlfriend Sherry were going to move into the house with us in August. His message said to call him, so I called him. I assumed it was bad news, I thought he was going to back out of moving in with us. But, I was wrong. He told me that he wanted to get more involved with Plan-It-X records. I told him that sounded great. He wanted to release a 7-inch for his friends from Franklin who played in a sloppy punk band called the Wyld Stallions. We knew them. They were the same people who were in Biscuit Head. I was into the idea, and said we'd talk about it when I got home. He was excited. I was excited too. I didn't know Jasin very well, despite the fact that I almost moved to California with him and he was moving into my house, but he seemed like a pretty cool person, and I loved his enthusiasm. I really couldn't wait for this tour to end.

The East Coast leg of the tour was a mess, but we were having fun, and Hannah and I both fell in love with Ali. It was hard to say goodbye to her at whatever Greyhound station we left her at. She had to get all the way back out west, to Portland, to start classes at Reed College. It was sad. We promised we'd come visit her as soon as we could, and we made plans to start a band called The Sissies. She would write the songs and send us tapes so that we could learn them. It was sad when she left.

After what seemed like years, the tour was over.

It felt good to pull into the driveway of our new house. Everyone else had moved in while we were gone. Sam moved in first, then Jasin and Sherry, a few days before we got home. Sam had the place all to himself for over a week before they got there, and he had managed to get it pretty messy. He could wreck anything in a lot less time, so I could tell he was trying to keep it nice for our arrival. He may have even cleaned up that morning. I'm sure Jason and Sherry were worried about what living with Sam was going to be like, and I was eager to assure them that we'd keep the house clean and keep Sam in check. I found Sam in the kitchen making pasta. He seemed nervous. Jasin walked in and said, "What do you think?" pointing at his leg. I looked down and saw a fresh tattoo. It was the Plan-It-X logo. It was pretty strange, since I hadn't known him very long and Plan-It-X only had a few releases. He explained that, "bands come and go, but friends are forever." I was flattered, but I felt weird about it.

A few weeks later, Jasin handed me a record. It was the Wyld Stallions 7-inch. It was finished, meaning it must have already been at the pressing plant when he proposed the idea of releasing it. I flipped it over and saw the Plan-It-X logo. He explained that before I listened to it, to keep in mind that they were very satirical, like Propagandhi. I immediately noticed the song title "Feminist Are Chauvinist." I took the record to Sam's room and listened to it with him.

"Twats are for fucking, get back in the kitchen" was the chorus to "Feminists Are Chauvinists." It was hard to listen to. They also did an Operation: Cliff Clavin cover. It was our song "Coffee Houses," which added to my sickening feeling. I didn't want my band to be associated with this band, and I really didn't want our record label associated with them. They had an anti-hippie song with lyrics about how girls should shave their legs and armpits, which I hated, because I love hairy arm pits on girls. I hated the record. I took the needle off and went to face Jasin. I told him what I thought of it. I told him that it wasn't satire and that it wasn't funny. I told him that I couldn't put it in the Plan-It-X catalog or distribute it at shows. I confessed that I hated it and that I was offended by it and that he should have waited until I got home. He was heartbroken. Our friendship never recovered. He and Sherry kept to themselves, and pretty much and stayed in their room. I felt horrible, but that record was fucking terrible and offensive. There was nothing else I could do.

It was nice having a house. We cleaned up the basement, painted it yellow, and decorated it with crucified baby dolls and Christmas lights. We booked shows, had really great open mics, potlucks, movie nights, and we cooked big vegan meals. Frankie moved away to become an actor or something, and this guy whom we had met on tour that summer named Jared (aka JRD) moved into a weird little room in our basement and took Frankie's place as the drummer for Operation: Cliff Clavin. It was a nice change. Frankie was loud and lusty and a total ham. Jared was shy and awkward. Hannah and Jared and I went to Portland to visit Ali sometime in October. She decided to drop out of college and move to Bloomington. She moved in on New Year's Eve of 1998. Then 1999 came the next day, and we all knew we were running out of time before the end of the world, so we moved quickly. We recorded a Sissies album and a new Operation: Cliff Clavin E.P. that winter, and both bands went on a West Coast tour only a few weeks later. A few months later, in Chicago at the Fireside Bowl, I decided that Operation: Cliff Clavin should break up. It just wasn't the same. As much as I didn't miss Frankie's annoying habits, I did miss his drumming and his stage presence. I didn't want to kick JRD out of the band, I didn't want to beg Frankie to return and I didn't want to endure another line-up change—there had been too many already—so on the way home, I told my bandmates it was over, and it was over.

Hannah and I made plans to go to Europe. We'd be classic backpackers. I remembered reading the title of some book once that said something about Europe on $10 a day. It sounded easy and cheap to travel around Europe, but I didn't read that book. I've never even opened it and it was written in the 60s. We thought that if we were going, we should stay for a while and we agreed on 3 months, starting in May of 2000, assuming the world didn't end. Based on my awareness of that book, that I had never read, and without taking into account 30-something years of inflation, I calculated that we'd need around $900 each and plane tickets. We had to make a lot of money somehow. We had about a year to do it.

CHAPTER 19
GET A JOB

Sam and I had made a vow to never work for anyone other than our friends or ourselves. No gods, no managers. After living in the van for two years, I figured out that not having anything wasn't so bad. It's very liberating to be on the bottom. You realize that no matter how much they take from you, you still have yourself. We can all be free if we chose to be, most people don't. Most people chain themselves with their wants and what they think they need. Despite these bold discoveries and idealistic claims, I decided that I should get a job. I had rent to pay and money to save, so I had to. Sam didn't have to worry about money, since the government paid him to be crazy.

Also, Hannah was going on tour with The Sissies and I wasn't going. I wasn't in the band anymore. I wasn't in any bands anymore. I figured out that I couldn't really play the drums. I couldn't, and still can't, separate my right hand and my foot, they always do the same thing, so I stepped down and JRD took over, which was good for him, since he moved to Bloomington to play drums in Operation: Cliff Clavin, and I had broken up the band. I knew that I would be lost without Hannah around the house and I knew I'd get sad, so I decided to get a job. This went against my beliefs, but I thought as long as I didn't take it seriously and as long as I knew it was only temporary and that I didn't need it, it would be okay. I was also dead broke and for the first time in around two years, I had a house and that meant rent and bills to pay. I also needed to save money for the Europe trip. I guess this is how we build our cages. It's nice being wild and free, then you start wanting things. Then you need a job. But, having a house was nice, and it was worth it, for the most part. It meant being able to practice in our own basement and it meant we could have shows and cook real food. I liked the domestic life. I needed money and I needed to occupy my time, so I would get a job. I made that decision, but I didn't make any real effort to find a job, I waited for one to find me.

Sam's stomach healed really well and he could eat as much as he used to of whatever he wanted. The doctor said it was a miracle. I started thinking that Sam was invincible. He was doing really well mentally too, he had started taking some kind of mood suppressant that kept him stable. I was really against him taking drugs. I was against anyone taking drugs, but this one really helped it. It was good seeing him acting so "normal" and he seemed happy. He started going back to school again.

Dooms Dave came down to visit. This was the first time I'd seen him, or really talked to him since he left the tour. He told me the rest of the story of his tour breakdown. When he called home, his dad told him that his ex-girlfriend was really worried about him and wanted to talk to him. Dave called her, and she told him that she missed him and wanted to see him. She said that she wanted to get back together. So, Dave left us and got on the bus for 42 hours. When he got home to Rockford, he found out that it was all a lie. His dad convinced his ex-girlfriend to participate by telling her that Dave ran away with a punk band and was starving and broke. Maybe she was really worried about him, or maybe she was just evil. Dave was crushed and trapped at home again. He was miserable. He was working a shitty job that his asshole dad got for him and he hated life. His curse was evident.

Jasin and Sherry had moved out, back to Franklin, with almost no notice, so we had an empty room that we needed to fill. We offered it to Dave, and he took it. He went home and filled his purple Toyota min-van full of stuff and came straight back to Bloomington, with the full disapproval of his father of course. Once again, chaos had put Dooms Dave back into our lives.

He settled in and started looking for a job. He was looking for weeks. We were getting worried about what would happen when he ran out of money. One day, I was asking him about it, and he told me how hard he was trying, and how hard it was to find something. I suggested the grocery store down the street. He insisted that he had applied there and done everything he could do to get the job. To prove a point, I walked down to the store with a 7 o'clock shadow and a Crimpshrine shirt on. I filled out an application at the customer service counter and handed it in. I lied on every line except my name, address and phone number. I said that I had worked for six years at a local grocery store that had shut down recently. When I handed in my application, I didn't let go when the lady behind the counter grabbed it. We played tug of war. I told her that my roommates were horrible at giving me my messages and I was worried that I would miss their call. I asked for an interview, on the spot. She made a call and I was sent up to the office. The manger looked over my application and said she was afraid they couldn't offer me any position equivalent to what I had held at my "past job." I told her that was okay, as long as there was room for advancement. She smiled, we worked out some details, and I was officially a bag boy when I walked out the door. I went home and showed Dave my name badge and my cool purple work shirt. A few days later, I put in a good word for him and he got hired too.

The worst part was: I got the job. Even though I had decided to get a job and I knew I needed one, it was horrible. Putting groceries into hundreds of plastic bags is a terrible way to spend your time. Occasionally, I got relief when I was told to go and gather the carts. Gathering carts is pretty fun. There was this tool for keeping them from separating when you were pushing them back to their homes. It was a canvas strap, around 20 feet long, with a metal hook on the end. I took it upon myself to become a master of the cart hook. I would gather the carts, and then, instead of hooking the hook on the front cart by hand, I would sling the thing like a grappling hook from the rear end of my cart train. It was fun practicing my art. I had to be really careful not to hook a passerby or hit a car. Cart wrangling was the highlight of my night, and of the job.

Two cool things happened when I was a bag boy. Both happened in the parking lot, of course. Once, while gathering carts, I found a forgotten bag of groceries. It was a small bag and I assumed I wouldn't be willing to eat whatever was in it, but it was someone's quesadilla kit: flour tortillas, shredded cheese and taco sauce. Oh, happy day! The second coolest thing that happened was pretty funny. I was gathering carts, and I looked over my shoulder before slinging my cart hook, to make sure I wasn't gonna kill anyone. I saw a middle-aged couple pushing a giant shopping cart! I was literally in awe for a few seconds before I figured out that the cart was of average size and that the couple were both dwarves. It's pretty rare to see a dwarf, and I had never seen a dwarf couple dressed in nice clothes pushing a cart. I laughed out loud at how dumb my brain had been. It was really funny, at least it was to me. Those were the highlights of the job.

Despite those two encouraging moments at the grocery store, I grew tired of being a bag boy pretty quickly. After two weeks or so, I called it quits. I told them that I was having a personal emergency and wouldn't be able to come back to work. I apologized and promised to bring my uniform back, I didn't. I took a few days to relax before thinking about getting another job.

I heard a rumor that Rockit's Pizza had changed hands, and that the new owners were planning to completely change the menu. These rumors spoke of organic ingredients, whole wheat crusts and veggie meat options, it sounded cool, it made sense, it seemed like a good place to work if you loved free pizza, so I rode my bike down there.

CHAPTER 20
ROCKIT'S PIZZA

My interview at Rockit's was pretty funny. The guy at the counter, who would later break in after hours, rob the cash box and take the time to make himself a few pizzas to-go, told me to take a seat and said that the owner would be right out. That's when I met my sweet prince, Paul. Paul was clearly once a real rock 'n roller. He wore all black. His dark brown hair was pulled back in a long ponytail. His apron was black. He had the snake eyes of an old cowboy. I was a little frightened. He sat down and shook my hand and introduced himself.

"You've made pizza before?" he asked.

"Not really," I said. I thought it would be fun to try a completely opposite approach to this interview. Instead of lying, I'd be totally truthful.

"What kind of experience do you have? What kind of jobs have you had?" he asked.

"I'm a musician, and I run my own record label," I said.

"Great," he said, with a big smile slowly cracking its way across his face. "You can make pizza. If you can play music, you can make pizza." He was sure of this. He went on to tell me that he only wanted to hire musicians and he wanted to have live music and make Rockit's great. He took my number and said he'd let me know something in a few days. I walked out with no idea what would happen. He seemed like a wild man. My number on a piece of paper that he folded up and shoved in his pocket, that's all I had to hope on.

A few days later, I got a call from Alan, the guy who was working the counter the day I applied. He told me that he was making the schedule for the next week, and needed to know which days I could work.

"So, I got the job?" I asked.

"You're on the schedule."

"Okay," I thought, "I guess I got the job." I told him I could work every day, and he put me down for most of them. I was going to start the following Monday.

Excited about the prospect of being an "inside man" and providing our family with free pizza, I told Sam and Dave the good news. Instantly, they started plotting. I told them to slow down, I didn't want to fuck up my first night. I made them promise that they wouldn't do anything, but I could see the sinister look in Sam's eyes.

I showed up on time, and was thrown right into the job. I expected some sort of training, but I quickly realized that there wasn't gonna be any. I recognized one of the other workers. His name was Chris Resnick, and he was from Bedford, Indiana, roughly 20 miles or so south of Bloomington. I met him at least once in person, in line at a Green Day concert in Indianapolis. I was there with Jen Potts, my long-ago summer love affair. Jen and Chris used to date. I think Chris might have been her first real boyfriend. She told me that he was her only ex-boyfriend whom she still spoke to. She said he was a really sweet guy. When I met him that day in Indianapolis, we said hello and stood awkwardly in line together, and that was that.

Jen and I didn't last long. She broke my heart, and caused some serious damage to my social life in Bloomington. I taught her how to ride a bike. The day we broke up, I was living at my parents' house, after a failed attempt to move to Amherst, Massachusetts. Jen was living with her overly religious grandmother in Bedford, and we rarely saw each other. We had made plans for her to come down to visit me, and to stay for a while. She was running late. I waited by the phone, classically, and I answered it every time it rang.

My aunt Mary called, and I was disappointed that it wasn't Jen, but I liked my aunt Mary, she was a good person. She went back to school after her kids were old enough to leave home, and she got a teaching degree. That might not sound like much, but it was a big achievement in my family, and I was really proud of her. When she called that day, she asked for my mom, who wasn't home. She could tell I was bummed out and asked me how things were going. I admitted that things were pretty bad. I told her that I was stuck back at my parents' house and my friends in Bloomington were all mad at me. There was a pause, then she said, "Well, you know what they say: life's a bitch and then you die." We said goodbye. I told her that I'd tell my mom that she called.

An hour or so later, Jen called and explained that she couldn't come because she was working on her 'zine. I protested, but only halfheartedly, because I knew this was the end. I never saw her again. Years later, I found out she had become a Christian punk and had moved to Chicago to live in a co-op house called Jesus People USA.

An hour or so later, the phone rang again. My mom picked up and I waited nervously to see if it was for me. I thought that maybe it would be Jen, that maybe she had changed her mind, but it was my uncle or someone calling to say that my aunt Mary had drove off of the road and crashed into a tree. My aunt Mary was dead.

Years later, in the tiny hot kitchen of Rockit's, on my first night there, while learning how to make dough balls, I asked, "Is your name Chris Resnick?" He said yes without really looking up, and I told him that we met once, through Jen, at a Green Day concert.

"Yeah, I remember you," he said, and that was it. We made more balls.

Eventually, Paul (the owner) came in and started "working." He noticed that I was doing next to nothing, and he asked me why. I told him that I just started and had no clue how do anything. At first, he was surprised. I think that he thought I had been working there for a while. He was pissed that no one else had taught me anything, and he took it upon himself to show me how to make pizzas. He was messy and frantic. He stretched out a sloppy circle of dough, showed me the tool that puts little holes in it, then splashed sauce around. While doing this, he assured me that we'd never have to wear uniforms or stupid hats. He said that I could wear anything I wanted to work, except tie-dye. "Tie-dye freaks me out," he said with a very serious look in his eye. He pulled himself back together and told me that the sauce was what made Rockit's great—it was a homemade recipe. They took canned tomato paste and added their own blend of spices to make it special. Then they baked the sauce to meld the flavors together. As I watched him make the pizza, I noticed that there wasn't a hint of organic ingredients anywhere, or even whole-wheat crust—there were only cheap, food service basics, and bleached-white Pills-bury flour.

I watched as he put the cheese on, and listened as he explained that they used the second-most expensive pizza cheese you can buy. The cheese did look good. It was moist, rich, and it looked like real cheese. He was making a pie, to sell by the slice—a "slice pie," he called it—so he kept it simple and just made it a pepperoni. He taught me how the conveyor oven worked. He put in the pizza and we waited six minutes. Six minutes at 600 degrees, and our pepperoni pizza started to peek out the other end of the oven. He grabbed the pizza shovel, like a dwarf grabbing his battle axe, and told me to stand back. He was explaining the technique of moving the pizza from the oven to the cutting table, when the newborn pizza started to slide off of his shovel. He tried to save it, but ended up throwing it against the wall. I did my best not to laugh at the ridiculous image of the pizza sliding down the wall. Paul was enraged and cursing himself. He sheathed the shovel and stormed off.

A little later that night, someone decided that I should be a delivery driver. I didn't protest. I thought it would be nice to get away from the chaos of that small kitchen, and all I had been doing was washing dishes a little. I mostly stood around feeling useless. I was excited to get out of there for a while.

It was hard at first. I had never done delivery before, and I quickly found out how horrible college kids are. There was one guy who was a few cents short and got really angry with me for not giving him his breadsticks. I tried to point out that not only was he supposed to pay for his food, he was supposed to tip too. It sucked. When I got back, Paul told me that I was gonna give some kid who worked next door a ride home. He said that he told the kid to tip me, and I agreed, since it meant leaving again and not even having to deal with pizza transactions. I recognized the kid, but I didn't know him. He had a Disarm patch, which was one of my older, short-lived bands, sewn onto his hoodie. I wanted to say something about it, but I didn't. This was my first time acting like a taxi driver. I took him home, and he tipped me $5. This time, when I got back, Paul had a delivery for me, and a few drunken college kids to take home on my way. They tipped me $10. It was a pretty short ride, so I felt good about this taxi service idea.

For the rest of the night, I struggled with pizza making, did dishes, and drove drunk people home. Around 2 A.M., Paul noticed that I looked tired, and asked me when I came in. He thought that I came in at 10, when he was supposed to come in (he was usually an hour or two late). He was shocked when he found out that I had been there since 4 o'clock, and told me to go home. He apologized, and assured me that it would never happen again. He then asked, "How much money did you make in tips?"

I thought, "Here it is, the catch to this to-good-to-be-true deal." I was sure he was gonna ask for a cut of my tip money. I stuck to my honesty policy, and told him that I made around $40. He smiled and said, "Great! That's fuckin' great. We're gonna do this every night. We're gonna put a sign in the window that says, Rockit's taxi service."

Someone else in the kitchen said, "Paul, we can't do that, it's illegal."

I went home, covered in flour, with cash in my pocket. When I got there, Sam and Dave were waiting for me and wanted to know everything. They asked me if I brought home any pizza. I didn't. They were disappointed. They asked me if I noticed any unclaimed pizzas. I didn't. I suspected they had done something, but I'd worry about it later. I had just worked a 10-hour shift and I was beat.

The next day, I went in at 4 o'clock again. It was pretty slow. Mostly we did prep work for the busier night shift. I was slowly learning that pretty much all of Rockit's business happened after 10 o'clock. Paul had an evil brother named Bob, and Bob was all business. Bob came in a few minutes after me and didn't seem to notice that I was new. Bob was the square brother of a rock star. I could imagine them growing up together. I could imagine Bob giving Paul shit for his long hair. I could imagine Paul smoking weed out back in the tool-shed and hiding it from Bob. As he told us things that we should and shouldn't do, I started to hate him. I knew he was going to be the thorn. A little later, he noticed that there were five pizzas in warming bags, leftover from the night before. They were supposed to be picked up, but never were. He asked us to explain. We didn't have much to say on the matter. He read the names on the pizzas. Most of them were average, but then he got to Hector and I knew the game. Hector was a name we used a lot for stand-ups. I knew this was the work of Sam and Dave. I couldn't believe that they would pull a stunt like that on my first night, but I also kind of knew that they would try something. It was in Sam's nature—there was no way he could stop himself. Bob seemed to understand what had happened too. He turned and said, "Somebody's fucking with us!" but he didn't catch on that it was an inside job. He thought it was a simple prank. He had no idea that the intention was for me to bring the unclaimed pizzas home to my pizza-crazed cohorts. The night slugged on, and I got off before Paul came in. I made myself a pizza to take home, with green olives and extra cheese. I didn't ask for permission and no one said a word.

When I got home, I shared my spoils and told Sam the story of Bob's discovery. He laughed deeply and loudly and kept repeating what Bob had said: "Somebody's fucking with us!" I didn't know it that night, but it would become a catchphrase that would last a long, long time. From then on, whenever something went wrong, or whenever something broke, Sam would twist his face up like an angry ogre and say, "Somebody's fucking with me!"

When I turned up to work on my third day, there was a note on the door that said "CLOSED FOR REPAIRS." I stood around for a few minutes, then Bob pulled up in a truck. There was a heat-lamp pizza box on the back, and he asked me to help unload it. Apparently, we were gonna start selling pizza on the street in front of the building, in an attempt to ensnare the drunks walking by. The drunks don't always have what it takes to walk 20 feet from the front door to the counter, then stand in line and order something, but if you put it out there on the street in a lighted box where they can see it, they can't resist. That was the theory anyway.

Bob informed me that the health inspector came by and that we got shut down. He said that the problems were minor and that we should be open the next day. I'm sure he didn't know my name. I rode home and broke the bad news to Sam. There was no chance of getting free pizza that night.

The weekend came and I was working the late shift. I went in at 10, and business was already picking up. The newly acquired slice box was on the sidewalk and this ginger haired hippie was working it. I said hello. He said hello. His name was Ben. He brought his bongos to work with him. I went right to work and made a few deliveries. I got lost a lot. I made a few pizzas too, and they came out pretty good. At some point, I realized that the other workers were doing whatever they wanted and eating pizza at will, so I called Sam and told him to come down. Sam's walk from our house on Madison Street to Rockit's would be an important one, because two things happened that night: 1.) Sam got the first slice of authentic free pizza from Rockit's, and 2.) He walked past Ted's Army/Navy store, which had recently closed. There was a "FOR RENT" sign in the window, and Sam noticed it. His gears started turning.

A little while after Sam and I had enjoyed our first free slices together, Paul came in. He was wearing all black and wearing dark sunglasses. His first order of business was to say hello to everybody. He came in like a mob boss in a movie, saying hello and passing out pats on the shoulder, even if you didn't want one. His second order of business was to find the dimmer switch and lower the lights so much that people stopped chewing to look around and see what was happening. Paul was happening. He then lit candles and brought them to every table, including Sam's table. This was the first meeting of two of my favorite people in the world. Imagine an ancient mural on a wall in a ruined city. Imagine the figure of Paul, a dark-clad warrior with long flowing hair; in one hand he holds a blade. The blade is wide and square-shaped and has a long wooden handle. In the other hand he holds a flame. Sam is a wizard sitting at a table. The table cannot be seen, because it's covered with pizza and tankards of Dr. Pepper. In this cracked painting, the mighty warrior is greeting the wizard and bringing him a magic flame. A union is being made. A pact is being written. An empire is erupting. This is what happened that night at the booth closest to the drink machine. It was magical. (Sam always sat as close to the drink machine as possible).

I loved the disorder of Rockit's, but I got tired of being a driver pretty quickly. I would take a few pizzas out and come back and notice that the orders that were hanging up when I left, were still hanging up, unmade. The first time it happened, I found Ben, the ginger haired bongo boy, and asked him about it. With a whoa dude kinda face, he said, "What orders?" I decided I'd rather be making pizzas, with my back against the oven in that tiny kitchen, than depend on these people to prepare the packages that I'm supposed to deliver. A pizza delivery boy is only as good as the cooks in the kitchen.

A few days later, I accidentally ran a red light on a delivery and sideswiped a Buick. I had one more pizza to deliver, growing cold on the floorboard after its short flight from the shotgun seat. It cooled as the cops guided us through the forms that I needed filled out. There were no cell phones around back then to check in with home base, or to alert the poor person waiting on their tragically injured pizza that it was gonna be late. The guy I hit was really nice.

I apologized over and over, and he kept saying it was cool. It was pretty weird. The cold, tardy pizza in the car was a vegetarian soy cheese pizza, which made me feel worse about being so late with it. I felt so bad, so I drove it to the address scribbled on the tiny yellow slip. I was greeted by a very friendly hippie woman and I explained that I was in a car wreck and that I was gonna go back to the shop and make her another pizza. I showed her the crumpled mess in the box and told her that she could have it, if she wanted it. I promised her that I would be right back, and she wouldn't have to pay for either pizza. She was so nice and concerned for me. She insisted that I didn't need to make another pie, and she insisted on paying and tipping. I crept back into the darkness of the Rockit's dining room, expecting to get scolded or at least questioned, but this was Rockit's—no one even noticed that I was late. I was gone for over an hour. There were pizza orders hanging, unmade, and the phone was ringing. Ben was playing the bongos by the slice machine, the walk-in smelled like weed, and I went back to work. It was almost like nothing had happened. Then I remembered that I'd have to tell Hannah that I wrecked her car. It wasn't that bad, but it was still wrecked and down one headlight and one turn signal. She took it pretty well. Her mom, who paid for the insurance, didn't take it quite as well. This officially ended my delivery days, since there was no way I was gonna deliver pizzas in my tour van, and I had lost my car privileges.

Staying in the kitchen was fine by me. I decided that I would become the center of the chaos. I would become the axle. The disorder would spin around me and I would stand strong in the eye of the storm. Rockit's was a mess. The workers were misfits and fuck-ups. I knew that I could at least make sure that one thing worked, the most important thing, the pizza. I took pride in my pies. I made the orders as soon as they came in, or as soon as I walked up and tore them out of the order pad, when the counter person forgot to give them to me in the kitchen. No matter how dysfunctional Rockit's was, I was determined to make sure the pizzas were made with haste and perfection. It was fun.

Chris Resnick warmed up after a few weeks. We talked about Jen and how she went Christian. He told me that she had a kid now and was married. I got him hooked on Bright Eyes. We wore out my tape of Fevers and Mirrors and Letting Off The Happiness. Conor's voice reminded us that life is beautiful and painful, and we should look forward to living it after we got off work. Of course, it was hard to really live life when you get out of work at 4 A.M. Even the night owls start winding down at that hour. The lightweights are snoring. The nerds have been dreaming for hours. The ones that are still raging are the ones I don't really like to hangout with.

Staggering out at closing time was always fun. I felt like I survived something. A few random drunk kids lingered in the quite streets, but the chaos was gone. The order of morning was on its way with newspaper trucks and chirping birds. My hands smelled like bleach. My clothes smelled like several days of caked on rotting flour. I'd ride my bike home with the plan of going straight to sleep, so that I could get up at a reasonable hour and get something done and live some of this life that I would think about at work. But the sandman refused to show up. It was impossible to shut down so quickly. I'd usually end up staying up a few more hours, doing nothing. I would wait for the sky to start lighting as my final warning to get into bed. I would put on some music and turn off my brain. In those days it was usually Neutral Milk Hotel or Bright Eyes. I dreamed of Anne Frank and heartbreak. I woke up in the P.M.

Paul's idea of only hiring musicians was obviously horrible. Musicians always want off on the weekends. Either they are playing a show or they want to go to a show or they just want to party, and they're not known for their good work ethic. They are often drunks, and/or potheads. They usually think of jobs as temporary, as I sure do. Most employers avoid hiring musicians for these reasons. Paul was not like other bosses. Paul was rock 'n roll. Paul was the kinda of person whom other employers avoided hiring, and now he had his own pizza place—his own clubhouse, his own pirate ship—and he manned it with the most dysfunctional crew he could shanghai or lure into service with promises of adventure and fame. He was a real captain. In other lives I'm sure he was a swashbuckler, a train robbing outlaw, or a member of Robin's merry men. He had that look and that kind of charisma. He had cowboy eyes. There was a Polaroid of him and Steven Segal pinned up behind the counter. Paul had his hat off in the picture. He was holding it to his chest and looked so proud, but for all of Paul's charms, he was still a fool for hiring a band of fuck-ups to run his business, and I guess I was a fool for coming on board.

A few weeks in and I was already getting fed up. One night I was slammed with orders. Our driver was slow and we had pizzas cooling on the rack. We had hungry people waiting in their houses, waiting for our pizzas. I was the only one in the restaurant, so I went out to investigate. I found Ben and some forgettable other guy outside working the slice machine. Well, the forgettable one was working the slice machine and Ben was playing bongos. I asked him where Sumi, the counter person had went.

"She went to the bar," he said.

"But she's only 18," I protested.

"Dude, she doesn't need to show I.D.," he said while simultaneously doing sign language for "big tits."

"Where's Paul?" I asked, trying to move past his disgusting gesture as fast as I could.

"I don't know," he replied, as he started back into his beat. I told him I needed help in the kitchen. I told him how many orders that I had to make.

He told me that Paul said he could play his bongos. He said that Paul thought it would help to attract customers. I started to walk back inside, then I turned and said, "you can't play bongos, I need help, and Paul is crazy. Come on, get in the kitchen."

It worked. This was the first time I took charge of the sinking ship that was Rockit's, it wouldn't be the last. We pulled through, Sumi came back, Paul eventually came back and acted like he was never gone. Luckily, Ben didn't last too long. He was the first to go. I never missed him or his bongos.

The second person to go was Alan, the guy who put me on the schedule, and he went with a bang. I didn't know much about Alan, other than the fact that he was the one that hired me. We rarely worked together since he mostly worked days. He did prep work and the ordering of supplies and stuff. The few times we did work together were pretty funny. One night we ran out of Alfredo sauce and he encouraged me to use ranch dressing instead. He insisted that they wouldn't know the difference. I did it, and they didn't complain, but I'm not convinced that they didn't know the difference.

We made the pizza sauce in 10-gallon buckets. We usually made two buckets at a time and they would last a few days. Alan had an idea one day and brought in a 55-gallon trashcan. He said it would save time. He called it "the super sauce" or something like that. We spent hours roasting the spices and mixing can after can of tomato paste with an electric drill affixed with a mixing bit. It was a lot of sauce—it was enough sauce to drown in. Then we tried to move it into the walk-in and realized there was no way that this vat of "super sauce" was going anywhere, so there it sat, right by the oven, all day and all night. Alan said that we shouldn't worry. We could use it all day, then move it into the walk-in, later, during the night, when it was lighter. We used it all day and it was still way too heavy to move. When I came in to work the next night, it was still there by the oven, still too heavy to move. Later that night, we slid it into the fridge with great effort. It lasted a few days before it went bad. On its last day, Alan fought for it. He insisted that the fermenting smell would cook out and that since the pizza oven is 600 degrees, there was nothing to worry about. We made a new batch of sauce and the 30 or more gallons of rot-sauce sat in the walk-in, in everyone's way for days, until I decided to throw it out. The problem was, how do you throw out 30-something gallons of sauce?

I waited until after closing and dragged it into the street. I dumped it into the storm drain. It was 4 A.M. and I was dragging a half full trashcan of fermented pizza sauce around. I pushed it over and tried to look casual as the cop drove by, hoping the stinking mess went quickly into the underworld. A few days later, Rockit's was robbed. The culprit made some pizza during the robbery and took some cash. The point of entry was alleged to be a small vented window above the make table, but it was pretty clear to everyone that this was an inside job. No one climbed through that tiny window. It was obvious that someone had used their key and thought that breaking a few louvers would cover their tracks. Only a few people had keys. Alan was the main suspect and Paul let him have it. Later, we found out that he was fired from Café Pizzeria under the same suspicion. I found it hard to believe that anyone could betray our loving king. Paul trusted us and loved us. Rockit's may have been a chaotic kingdom, but to steal from its coffers was a dishonor.

Things started to get really great, a few nights later, when Paul made me stop stretching out the pizza I was working on to come up front for a minute. I'd soon learn that this was gonna be a normal part of my workday. Later, I'd learn to say, "fuck you Paul, I've got pizzas to make." This time Paul wanted to introduce me to some cool people. When I came out from behind the counter I saw two of my friends. I played dumb and so did they, just for a laugh.

"See these dudes, they are cool. These are the kind of people I want in my restaurant. Give these guys whatever they want tonight, on the house," Paul said. We were all smiling and giving in to the will of this wild man. Something caught Paul's eye out front and he excused himself and sped away with his black apron like a cloak, waving in his wake. Paul was the only one allowed to wear a black apron—we all had red or white ones. I took my friend's order and by the command of Paul, the king of Rockit's, I made them a perfect vegan pizza for free. I sat with them while they ate and I drank my 15th Dr. Pepper of the night. I asked them how they knew Paul. They said that they didn't. They had just walked in and Paul got excited because one of them had blue hair and they both had tattoos. They had barely spoke before Paul left to fetch me.

Rockit's had this one policy, it was an old tradition: If a band brought in a CD or record and a press photo, they got free pizza. Since I was starting to get a feel for Paul and I knew that, more than anything, he wanted Rockit's to be cool, I asked him about extending this tradition to the small time D.I.Y. bands who don't play the bars on the block. He loved the idea, so from then on it was a known fact that if you booked a show for a touring band, you could take them to Rockit's for free pizza. This worked out great for me since working there meant that I had to miss a lot of shows. I'd miss the show, but then the bands would come in and I'd make them free pizza and still get a chance to hang out. I like hanging out with bands more than seeing them play sometimes.

One slow night, Paul came into the kitchen and told me to go up front and take an order. I was getting comfortable with telling Paul no, so I protested. He pushed, and I gave in and took the order pad from him and dusted my doughy hands off. Waiting at the counter were two extremely average looking college girls. I guess they were pretty by the standards of fashion magazines. One was blond, the other one was brunette. I had no clue why I was called up there to take this order. I awkwardly asked them what they wanted. It wasn't awkward because they were girls, it was awkward because it's always awkward when I talk to people whom I don't know. I hate ordering food for myself, and I really hated taking someone else's order. The girls seemed just as perplexed by Paul's behavior as I was. All the while, Paul was out on the floor wiping down tables and trying to act like he wasn't listening. I thought that maybe he was testing me. Maybe he wanted to make me a manager or get me to start doing the counter position. I didn't want either job. I wanted to stay right where I was. I liked being the heart of this dancing drunk. The kitchen was the heart for sure, pizza was the blood, the counter was the face, the manger was the brain, the drivers were the flailing arms and legs, the person sitting outside working the slice box was the... I don't know.

I jotted down their chicken and spinach pizza and said, "it'll be around 10 minutes, Paul will have to ring you up because I don't know how to work the register." I yelled for Paul, and I went back into my furnace to make this puzzling pizza. Paul took their money and chatted with them for a few minutes, then came back to stand beside me at the make table, with his back to the counter.

"Did you see those girls?" he asked.

"Yes," I replied, and kept stretching dough.

"Beautiful, right?"

"They are not my type, but sure," I mumbled. Then he got this far away look in his eyes. His cowboy eyes were looking out over the plains.

"I fucked those girls," he whispered.

I didn't say anything. I kept spreading the sauce. Still in this altered state, he continued. "It was a different time and a different place, but I fucked those girls." I sprinkled on the cheese, making sure it covered the sauce completely and that a little bit got on the crust. "It could have been their mothers." He went on. "Back in the 60's, I used to be with girls like that all the time." He didn't seem to notice or care that I was not really responding. I evenly distributed small chunks of frozen chicken. He started to leave, still talking as I hear his trailing words. "It was a different time..."

Sam came in that night, just like he did every night, for free pizza. While we ate, I told him what happened, and a new catch phrase joined the swelling ranks: "it was a different time and a different place." Every now and then, "I fucked those girls" would come up too. It was always very inappropriate, as was a lot of Sam's behavior. We'd be sitting on the wall in front of People's Park and some random girls would walk by and Sam would pull his version of Paul's mystic gaze and whisper to me, "I fucked those girls."

Christmas was coming again, and Sam was determined not to let it get the best of him this time. He bought a Greyhound ticket to Key West, to get away from winter and family affairs. I asked him why he picked Key West and he said, "because it's the southernmost point I go to." During finals week he decided to make a political statement about Christmas. He put on a red bikini, a Santa hat and a fake beard, and went downtown to pass out coal. He walked into every bank and corporate business on Kirkwood and gave them a huge lump and a note. The note said something about Santa Claus being an evil fat murderer who was going to break into their homes on Christmas Eve and murder them and their spoiled children. It really didn't make sense, but it was funny and confusing. He made it half-way down the street before the cops came. They yelled at him and made him explain what he was doing. He told them that he was just passing out lumps of coal to the naughty people. He asked them if he could go, and finish his work. He told them that he had a final exam to take and needed to hurry. They said no. He insisted that he wasn't breaking the law and tried to leave. They didn't let him. They made him sit on the curb in his bikini in the freezing cold.

A few more cops came and people stopped to see what was going on. He was surrounded by rubberneckers. The cops told him that he couldn't walk into a bank wearing a disguise and hand them a threatening letter. Sam laughed. They didn't like that. They also said that he was dropping chunks of coal and coal dust all over the carpets of the places he went into and he would be lucky if they didn't press charges and make him pay for them to be cleaned. Sam laughed again, and they got really mad at him. They made him wait outside on the curb while they did paperwork in their warm cars and people stared at him, shivering in his bikini with his hands stained black from handling the coal. Eventually, and only minutes before he had to be at his final exam, they got out of their cars and told him what kind of trouble he was in. They said that no one was going to press charges against him, and that he should consider himself lucky. Then, they gave him a trespassing notice that said he was never allowed on Kirkwood Avenue again. He signed some papers, and ran off to take his final. He didn't have time to come home and change, so he went in his red bikini with black hands. He aced the test. He aced all of his finals. School was ridiculously easy for him. Before he left on the bus for sunny Key West, he made a 'zine called Strap Yerself In, and he included his Santa story.

It took him around 48 hours to get there on the bus. He made it there on Christmas Day. He called me and said it was the worst place he had ever been. He hated it. He sounded so sad. A few days later, he called me and left a message on the answering machine.

"Hey, This is Sam Dorsett calling to tell you guys that I met some nice people who are on a bike trip and they asked me to come with them, so I bought a bike and I'm going to ride back to Gainesville with them. One of them is this guy named Rymodee and he's in a band called This Bike is a Pipe Bomb. He's really great and so is his band. I told him that we would release their album on Plan-It-X. It's gonna take me a while to get home, but I'll be home before school starts again. I love you all." Click.

When he finally got back he told me how he had met his new friends. He was sitting on the steps of a health food store eating a bagel that he dumpstered and his fake tooth fell out, the one that he had lost on the slippery rock slide at Cascades Park. He was miserable and toothless, and all alone. Then these punks on bikes rode up and went inside. He wanted to talk to them, but he was too shy, so instead he just gave them his 'zine when they came out. They thanked him and left. A few minutes later, they came back. They asked him what he was doing. He told them. They asked him where he was from, and he told them. Then they asked him if he knew Operation: Cliff Clavin and he told them that he lived with us. They talked for a while and they asked him to come with them. He bought a mountain bike and strapped his stuff to it and then left. Without any training, he was able to keep up with them by the second day of riding. They made it to Gainesville in 10 days, and from there, they got a ride back to Pensacola, where Rymodee lived, and Sam took the bus home from there.

Rymodee told me more of the story a year or so later. He said that they hated Key West too, and they were surprised to see a toothless punk kid with a Discount shirt there. They started reading his 'zine as soon as they were out of his sight. When they read the story about him dressing up as a sexy Santa and handing out coal, they all agreed that they should go back and talk to him. They knew that he was great.

I seldom answered the phone at Rockit's, but sometimes I had to. I'd be the only one in the place. My co-workers would either be gathered around the slice box outside, next door at the bar, smoking weed in the walk-in, or just missing in action. I'd be making pizzas and listening to the same old tapes and the repeated ringing from the counter occasionally interrupted their soft distortion. I knew I had pick it up. I'd stop the tape, getting a little more flour on the dusty buttons of the stereo, and I'd pick up the phone, getting flour on that too.

The tinny voice on the other end would ask, "do you really deliver cold beer?"

"No, sorry we don't. No one does, I think it's illegal," I would repeat the same line over and over like an actor, and I would await the other actor's line, which always came as if it were well rehearsed.

"If you don't deliver cold beer, why does it say that you do in your yellow pages ad?"

It was always the same question, and I always gave the same answer, "my boss is insane, sorry, do you want a pizza?" They usually hung up. I was glad when they hung up. I had pizzas in the oven. I had more pizzas to make. I didn't care about the phone or the people on the other end. Everyone who worked the counter or answered the phone had at least one year of those calls to look forward to, until the new phone book came out. Paul did, in fact, advertise that we would deliver cold beer. He designed and published the ad before looking into the legality of it. We didn't even have a license to sell beer, but that didn't stop Paul from placing that ad or from hanging various neon beer lights in the front window. That was another annoyance that that the counter people dealt with regularly. The frat boys would come in and order their standard, extra-large double pepperoni pizza and breadsticks, then say, "and two pitchers of Miller High Life." When they heard the bad news, that we didn't really sell beer, only O'Doul's (non-alcoholic beer), they always asked, "why do you have beer signs in the window, if you don't sell beer?"

The only answer they would get was, "our boss is an insane person."

Sometimes they'd walk out, pissed off, which was fine by most of us, because despite our differences, we were all united in our hatred of frat boys and sorority girls. We were all musicians for the most part—musicians and misfits—and that was cool. I'd rather hang out with bongo players and potheads than Old-Spice-thugs and ponytail-pulled-through-the-back-of-the-baseball-hat girls.

We all did our part to make Rockit's seem unwelcoming to the mainstream. It wasn't that hard, but when the bars closed and kicked those zombies out into the street, there wasn't anything we could do to keep them away. The drunken brain is helpless to resist the lure of a bright glass box filled with pizza. They stumbled and staggered over to us by the dozens. They were happy to give their two dollars to anyone working the slice box. They didn't care if you were a freak or a punk, you had what they needed. Eventually, we talked Paul into getting rid of the beer signs. I think he sold them. We were all pretty happy the day they disappeared. The cases of O'Doul's didn't disappear though. They stayed in the walk-in for a long, long time. They might still be there.

Sam came to Rockit's every night that I worked and always got free pizza. When I had the chance, I'd make myself something and sit down with him for a while and talk. We both drank inhumane amounts of Dr. Pepper. We had decided for no real reason that Dr. Pepper was the most punk thing in the soda machine. After a few pints of the Pepper, our minds were racing. We talked about everything. Sam would summarize one of the many books that he had read that week. I'd ask questions about science and history, and he always had the answers. One night, Sam said, "I think I'm gonna open an anarchist info shop and used bookstore."

He told me that Ted's Army/Navy was still for rent and he was gonna call about it. If the rent was reasonable, he was gonna go for it. He thought it would be really funny to use his SSI (disability) check, which was a little over $500 a month, to pay the rent on an anarchist bookstore. It would be a government funded anarchist bookstore. He always felt guilty about getting so much money for free, and often donated it to local causes he believed in, and thought that this would be a good way to put the money to use. I was really excited and fully encouraged him to try it. I suggested he call it "Burning Books." I could tell by his expression that he wasn't gonna do that. We drank more Dr. Pepper and we ate more pizza. He went home and I got ready for the rush. A few days later, he signed the lease, and Secret Sailor Books was born. It was a golden age. Free pizza was flowing, and a few doors down, Sam was opening an anarchist bookstore.

My housemate, Dave (aka Dooms Dave, aka The Doctor) lost his job at Kroger and started working at Papa John's for some reason. Sam and I thought it was a pretty good idea, even though neither of us would ever encourage anyone to work at a corporate place. We thought it would increase the frequency and the diversity of our free pizza. It didn't really, the management at Papa John's had really cracked down since the Frankie era, or maybe Dave just wasn't as reckless as Frankie. Regardless, we didn't see much free Papa John's. Dave got off work two or three hours before Rockit's closed, and Papa John's was really close, just few blocks north on the same street, so he would come in after work. Pretty often, he would end up hanging out in the kitchen with me. He was really jealous of our operation.

At Papa John's, the dough came pre-made and slightly stretched, the sauce came out of a can, and the toppings were all frozen in big plastic bags. Now, I'm not saying that Rockit's had the greatest ingredients, but compared to the big pizza chains, we were gourmet. We made our own sauce, starting with cheap cans of tomato paste, but we added our own blend of spices and cooked the sauce in the oven. Our sausage came from the local meat shop a few doors down. We bought plain, unseasoned pork, fried it up and crumbled it, and seasoned it with our own secret spice blend. It was pretty gross to me, but I'm sure it tasted better than the stuff at Papa John's.

Working at Rockit's wasn't always that easy for a vegetarian. I made the sausage a few times, then I just told Paul that I wouldn't do it anymore, and he was really nice about it. Our dough was made in the kitchen too. The day crew made it—well, they were supposed to make it. It was pretty normal to come in at 10 o'clock and find out there was none. That meant that we had around three or four hours before the rush to make dough, weigh it, cut it, and roll it into balls and wait for it to proof. It took around five hours to properly proof, give or take a few hours, depending on the temperature of the walk-in. That meant there was no way the dough would be ready in time, so we would make the dough balls and leave the trays in a stack by the oven for an hour or so, to speed proof it. It kinda worked, but it usually yielded an inferior crust. I was ashamed of some of the pizzas we served. I wasn't proud of my pies on those nights. I'm certain that we were always better than Papa John's though.

The night shift and the day shift were mortal enemies. We hated them. The day shift had it too easy. There wasn't a lunch or dinner rush at Rockit's, no one came in with their families, and it was slow and dead. All the day shift had to do was make dough, make sauce and fold boxes, but instead they smoked weed, made themselves food and sat around drinking soda. The day shift came in at 4 o'clock and we came in at 10. For them, the peak of activity didn't start until around 8 o'clock, when the majority of pizza business starts. They had four lazy hours to do their simple tasks, and, so often, they failed. That's why we hated them. They had no idea what we faced at night. They didn't know what happened after last call.

Anyway, one night Dave asked me if he could make a few pizzas. I let him try it out. He loved it. He loved tossing the dough and putting his hands into our quality cheese. He said that the Papa John's cheese had a powdery coating. He ended up making pizza at Rockit's a lot. He'd come in still wearing his Papa John's uniform, straight from his paying pizza job, and work for free for a few hours with me. We were making slice pies together one night when Paul came in, late as usual. He raised his sunglasses and asked me, "who's the new guy?" He did a double take when he noticed the uniform. I told him that he was my housemate and was just working for fun. Paul's face froze for a minute as he processed the information and thought about what he was seeing, and what I just told him. "Cool," is all he said. Then he went back up front to light candles and turn down the lights.

The Dave era of Papa John's was not nearly as legendary as the Frankie era, but it had its moments. The greatest achievement of Dave's era happened on New Year's Eve, 1999. The world was waiting for Y2K. Everyone was waiting to see if the lights were gonna go out. A lot of punks were hoping for a shutdown, there was talk of revolution, there were kids making plans. I was sure that nothing was gonna happen, and we were taking it pretty easy. We had a show in our basement. I don't remember which local bands were there, but The Insurgent, from Long Island, played. There were 30 or 40 people at the show, which was a pretty good turn out, especially for New Year's Eve, especially on this particular New Year's Eve. There was a big party going on somewhere else, but since I didn't drink and none of us really did, we didn't care. We had a pop punk show instead, in our tiny basement. They played great. It was fun. Shows at The Madison house had to end pretty early, to keep the neighbors happy, so we were all upstairs around 11 o'clock when Dave came in with 12 large pizza boxes. Everyone looked like kids on Christmas morning. Everyone waited to hear what Dave had to say.

"I brought pizza for everyone!" he exclaimed. There was a cheer, and then the boxes were spread out and opened and everyone was eating and happy! Dave told Sam and I that he figured since the world might end in an hour, he should take a risk. He just made twelve pizzas without any explanation, put them in his van and left. It was great.

We ate pizza and watched the clock. Around 20 minutes before midnight I decided that we should get ready for the coming revolution, even though I didn't think that anything was going to happen. The pizza, and Dave's act of defiance, had inspired me. I stood amongst the boxes and the bodies stuffing pizza into their mouths and announced, "Okay, everyone, put on your winter gear and find something to hide your face with. We're going downtown and if the lights go out, we're gonna fuck shit up!"

I got a much better response than I expected. People jumped to their feet and started getting ready. We all knew it was a joke, but we were all playing along and I'm pretty sure we would have played along all the way if the lights had gone out. We put on masks and found makeshift weapons in the garage and started marching downtown.

After a few blocks we started chanting, "time to fear, the end is near." We chanted louder and louder, and used our weapons to keep a beat on the lamp-posts and street signs. As we walked past the community radio station, we pressed our faces to the glass and screamed our mantra and banged on the window. Cops drove by and scanned us. They saw our masks and our baseball bats, but they didn't stop. I think they were afraid. There were a lot of us and our numbers grew as we marched. We passed friends and recruited them for our end of the world party. We decided we should rally at town square, on the courthouse lawn. It's the heart of Bloomington, and in the winter it's shrouded in white Christmas lights. It would be so majestic when they flickered out.

When we arrived we found a party in progress inside the courthouse. It was a formal affair. I guess they didn't believe in the end of the world either. They were dressed up and drinking wine. A few of our mob members rushed in without concern for the doorman or the snobby guests, and they grabbed bottles of wine and handfuls of cheese cubes and ran back outside to join us. A man in a suit chased them out, but froze in his tracks when he saw our ranks. He walked back inside, probably to call the police, but the police were already there. They were pooling up around us. They stayed in their cars, just watching. We drummed and chanted as loud as we could and our numbers were still swelling. Friends and strangers fell under our spell and joined us. One group of friends came because they heard us on the radio. Apparently, the DJ at the radio station thought we were really funny and reported our attack on the station as if it was a true concern, a-la War Of The Worlds, and turned up the mics in the studio so the listeners could hear our warning.

At this point, there were at least 50 of us, and we were getting really wild and anxious. Then the alarm went off at the sporting goods store on the other side of the square. I started to panic. Was it one of our people? Did someone go too far? Red and blue lights exploded, and half of our cop audience quickly circled the square in response to the alarm. We watched as they dragged a middle aged man out of the building and into the back of one of their cars. It wasn't anyone we knew. The clock only had a few minutes left. It was getting really close to the end of the world. We coordinated a prank to pull on the police. We counted to three, and then all of us ran as fast as we could around the courthouse. Again, the lights started flashing and the cars buzzed into action. But, before they could figure out what we were doing or how to stop us, we were back at our rally point, under the statue of some generic World War Two soldier who looks out forever over Kirkwood Avenue. They didn't get out of their cars.

A few minutes later, the clock struck midnight. There was a hush. Nothing happened. Some fireworks went off somewhere, and we were so disappointed. None of us really thought anything would happen, but the last 20 minutes had whipped us into a fury. It was such a let down. Sam started a new chant, "the end of the world sucked!" We walked home, chanting and knocking trash cans into the street. There wasn't a single slice of pizza waiting for us. The world didn't change. All we had to show for Y2K was twelve empty, greasy pizza boxes.

After a few months of long nights and staying up until the sun chased me to bed, I asked Paul if I could try out the day shift. I was sick of the drunks (the customers and my co-workers). I needed a break. I felt like I was burning out. He agreed, and the next Monday I went in bright and early at 4 o'clock. I joined the enemy team. I was a traitor, but I didn't care. I met my new co-workers, this guy named Scott-Rod-Girl, and a girl named Casey. I knew them both already.

Scott was in a band called Hot Rod Girl, so we called him Scott-Rod-Girl. His band used the sexy silver silhouette lady that's most commonly found on semi-truck mud flaps for their logo. They sounded like Fat Wreck Chords style punk, not bad, but not really something I'm ever interested in listening to. He was a nice enough guy. This one time, months later, he was having a party at his house, and he printed fancy invitations and passed them out. I got one, and was told it was for my whole house. The invitations said something like, "this is a formal affair, guys, wear something nice... girls, just show up in your usual hot-ass looking outfits." It also said, "there will be live entertainment, in the form of a lesbian sex show and Jell-O shots." He was really surprised that none of us came. He confronted me about it, and I had to explain that people were offended by the idea of a hired lesbian sex show and that most of the Bloomington punk scene was vegetarian and Jell-O shots were not. He was so confused. I tried to explain that it wasn't personal, but the damage was done—there was no mending the wounds caused by the P.C. punk scene, but this wouldn't happen for months, like I said.

Instead of awkward distance and uncomfortable disagreements, we just hung out. He told me about his band, and asked me about releasing their next album, despite the fact that they were probably breaking up soon. I told him I'd think about it, and I kept rolling dough balls, determined to be the best day shifter ever. No matter how messed up the night shifters were, I would not let them down. When 10 o'clock happened, the weary workers would come in to find trays full of dough balls and buckets full of sauce. They would have the weapons they needed for the battle they faced.

I helped Casey get hired, and I was glad to be working with her and getting a chance to hang out. I met her at one of the open mics that we hosted in our basement. No one knew her before then. She signed up and sat quietly watching the other acts until it was her turn. Then, she took the "stage" and played some really catchy and cute pop songs including a Beach Boys cover of "Vegetables." As soon as she was finished, we swarmed her. We all wanted to know who she was and if she was in band. That turned into, "do you want to start a band?"

A few weeks later, we started a band. It was called "I Like Japanese Hardcore." I played drums, even though I had recently given up on becoming a drummer, and I quit The Sissies because I couldn't play them. I decided to give it a try again, and keep it simple. I just played easy, poppy beats. I think I did okay. We didn't last very long, but it was fun. Paul obviously liked her right away and agreed to hire her. She always worked the day shift.

It was so boring. We made all the dough and sauce and did all the other prep work we could do in a few hours. Then we made ourselves pizzas and sat around until it was time to go. It was too easy. It wasn't fun. After a week of peace and easy days, I was ready to go back to the front line. I missed the excitement. I put myself back on the night shift without asking anyone.

It was good to be back. I liked coming in a 10 o'clock, I liked giving my friends free pizza, and I liked hanging out with Sam and drinking Dr. Pepper. I even kind of liked the late night rush. My first night back was a Thursday, and something was going on at the bar next door, so it was really busy. I was making slice pies as fast as I could. They were sold before they got put into the heat box. It became a habit of mine, to stare up at the counter when I worked. Everyone did it—you had to—and the kitchen was so small and so narrow that you didn't have anywhere else to look. Before I worked at Rockit's, I was always annoyed when I walked up to the empty counter and waited while the cook stared at me. I always thought, "what an asshole, why won't he come up here and take my order?" Now I was one of those assholes. It was hypnotic. I would make pizzas and stare out of the kitchen, over the counter, into the dining room and out the window into the street. If someone stood at the counter, they just became something new to stare at. I rarely considered helping them. I just kept making pizzas and assumed that someone would show up to take their order, and I assumed that they understood why I couldn't help them—I was busy, and my hands were covered in flour.

So it was business as usual for me, back on the night shift, kicking out slice pies and staring at the counter. A guy was standing there. He wasn't the usual looking guy for 11 o' clock. He was older and he was wearing a tie. I stared at him. He smiled at me. I stared at him. Paul showed up at last and started talking to him. I couldn't hear what they were saying because Bright Eyes was blasting, but I saw the guy show Paul some kind of ID and I figured out what was happening. It was the health inspector! I started thinking about how good it would be to get to go home. I figured that we would be shut down for a few days at least, a break would be nice. Then I got overwhelmed with honor for some reason. I didn't want to get shut down, and I didn't want Rockit's to get fined for violations, so I started scrambling to fix whatever I could. There were tons of problems. The first thing I did was take all the meat off the make-table. Our make table was broken and didn't keep the ingredients cool enough— we were supposed to keep all the meats in the fridge until we fixed the table, but of course we didn't do that. I cleaned up a few more things as fast as I could, then I remembered a little thing about the ice machine. I remembered that it was against the rules to allow the handle of the ice scooper to touch the ice. It was supposed to be stuck in the ice, upright. I knew I couldn't save us, but I thought I should at least try to do what I could, so that we wouldn't get too many strikes. I casually opened the ice machine, trying to block the health inspector's view, who was still at the counter talking to Paul. Not only was the handle of the ice scooper touching the ice, but there was also a 6-pack of beer nestled in the cubes.

I gave up. I knew I was on a sinking ship. I washed my hands and started to clean up in preparation for going home. Then I saw Paul and the guy walk away. They went into the dining room. I walked up to the counter pretending to do something so that I could see what they were doing, or maybe hear them. They walked outside. A few minutes later, Paul came back in. He looked slightly alarmed, but didn't say anything about what happened, so I asked.

"Was that the health inspector?"

"Yeah," he said. I waited for more...

"What did he say?" I asked.

"Nothing, it's cool, I took care of it." That's all he said, then he left. I assumed that he paid him off, or made some other kind of deal. He never told me.

Speaking of bribes, whenever Paul was there at closing, and whenever he remembered and if there were left over pizzas, he would tell someone to call the police dispatch and tell them that we had free pizza for them. The first time he told me to do it I was shocked. He just said, "hey Chris, call the police station and tell them we have some pizza for them, for free." I thought he was joking. I had to ask him if he was serious. I didn't take Paul for the kind of person who liked cops. "Yeah, it keeps them on our good side. Everyone loves free pizza."

A few nights later, I noticed that someone had taken the Pepsi logo out of the drink machine and replaced it with a piece of cardboard that said: "1000% PURE", in black marker. We were all joking about it when Paul came in and asked us what we were laughing at. I pointed to the sign and asked him if he knew who had made it.

"I did," he said proudly. We all laughed. "Why are you laughing?" he asked, looking hurt.

"Because there is nothing pure about Pepsi Cola," someone said.

Paul puffed his chest and stood tall. "It's not just the drink machine, it's us, it's this place..."

Chris Resnick was there and with a furled brow and no fear of Paul, and he said "that's bullshit, we're not close to 1,000% pure." Paul was angry.

"Yes we are!" he demanded. Chris didn't back down.

"No we're not, we don't recycle anything, we use shitty ingredients, and we sell Pepsi products. We are not pure!" Paul was really getting angry.

"Okay, Okay, so we're not pure, at least not 1,000%, but we are trying to be," he said, then he went behind the counter and found a marker. He came back and changed the sign to say: "STRIVING TO BE 1000% PURE". We all laughed again and agreed that it made more sense.

Paul told us that we were going to be better and we were going to start ordering better ingredients and get rid of the drink machine. We all shared our support and encouragement, but we knew it was just Paul, being excited. He would soon forget about trying to be pure. A few days later, the Pepsi guy came in to drop of boxes of corn syrup and he noticed the sign. He asked about it. We tried to explain. He told us that we had to put the Pepsi logo back into the machine, it was part of the deal. He told us that Pepsi gave us the machine for free and that we couldn't deface it or remove the Pepsi logo. Paul came out and tried to argue, but eventually gave in and promised to change it back. Before he left, the Pepsi guy also noticed that Paul had replaced the logo on the light up menu board with a poster of Jimmy Hendrix. The menu board came from Pepsi too. He told us that we had to fix it as well. Paul said okay and the guy left. When he was out the door, Paul said, "Fuck that guy, I'll change the drink machine, but I'm not taking Jimmy down."

Paul loved Jimmy Hendrix. One night, Chris and I were busy in the kitchen, and Paul came in. "Come up here you guys." We complained for a second, then followed him to the counter and found everyone else was there too, the slice slinger and the counter girl and a few drivers, all gathered around the counter. Paul looked reverent, like he did in his Polaroid with Steven Segal. "Okay, everyone close your eyes and listen to this," he said. It was Jimmy Hendrix. Chris was the first to snap.

"Fuck this, I've got pizzas in the oven, I'm not gonna stand up here and listen to Jimmy fucking Hendrix." Paul turned from reverent to raging.

"I don't give a shit about those pizzas, this is my pizza place, those are my pizzas, let them burn or fall on the floor, I don't care. I want all of you to close your eyes and listen to this!" Chris stopped in his tracks and muttered something under his breath, and came back to join the circle of Paul's prisoners. I closed my eyes.

"Do you hear that? Do you hear those notes? I was there. I was at this concert. This is a live album." I peeked to see what everyone else was doing. Most of my co-workers had their eyes closed, patiently waiting for this to be over. Chris was drumming his fingers on the counter, and shook his head when I looked at him. I smiled back. Paul's eyes were shut, and his head was leaned back so that he was facing heaven, as if Jimmy might be looking down on him. I closed my eyes again. He went on. "Every note you hear, I saw his fingers make. It was beautiful and magical and I can listen to this whenever I want to. It takes me back to a different time and place."

I giggled, and thought about Sam and how much he loved saying, "a different time and place," in reference to Paul's story of his sexual exploits, whenever he could work it into a conversation.

After what felt like forever, the song was over, and we were free to go back to work. Chris and I raced back to the oven, hoping to save our neglected pizzas. We were too late—they were smashed into each other and ruined, or burnt because they couldn't escape the oven due to the jam up. We started re-making the orders.

There was a homeless guy in town who sold poetry on the street corner near the coffee shop. We all called him Pops. His poetry was terrible, and usually religious. I don't think he was religious, I think that he just thought it would help him sell some of his poems if he mentioned god a lot. He was usually friendly and pretty funny, sometimes a little perverted. He started hanging out on the block. He was either at Sam's bookstore, even though it wasn't open yet, or he was a Rockit's for hours and hours. When he came to Rockit's, he would walk up to the counter and say, "give me a few slices of pizza."

He never had any money, or if he did, he never wanted to pay. That was fine with me, I always gave him a few slices, and most of the people did too. Then he started asking for coffee. We didn't even sell coffee, but we had a coffee machine and he saw it once.

"Give me some coffee," he said. I found grounds and made a pot. From then on we had hot coffee all the time. It wasn't for sale, it was just for Pops and the workers to drink. Sometimes when it started getting crowded, he would want to leave. He would just wait until a driver was going out on a delivery and get up and say, "I'm going with you, I need to get out of here." We all got used to him pretty quickly. It was like we had a crotchety old grandpa. We just gave him whatever he wanted, and it usually worked out fine. We had to kick him out sometimes, when he was really drunk or when he smelled too bad, but most of the time it was fine.

A year or so later, a driver named Mike, a friend of Chris', came back and said, "You'll never believe who I just delivered a pizza to, it was Pops. He was all cleaned up and he had an apartment all to himself. He looked great. He gave me a $20 tip and told me to thank everyone here for helping him when he was down on his luck." We were all shocked and happy.

A few weeks after that, I saw him walking down Kirkwood wearing an open vest, with no shirt underneath and a horrible sunburn. His bald head was bright red and peeling and he was staggering, obviously drunk. He came into to Rockit's that night and said, "give me some pizza and coffee." He never mentioned his apartment or ordering the pizza and giving the huge tip. It was like it never happened.

After months of bookshelf building, painting and planning, Sam's bookstore opened. He decided to call it Secret Sailor Books because he didn't plan on telling anyone the secret source he was using to fund the store. Things started happening right away. Shows were booked, people had meetings there, and everyone hung out there, on the shabby couches. It was great to finally have a place like that, of our own. Sam took full advantage of his proximity to Rockit's too. When the day shift showed up to open the doors, Sam was there, holding his cup, waiting for his free refill. Occasionally, one of the less laid back workers would try to make him pay for his refill or surrender his cup, and he would laugh and tell them to talk to Paul. Paul loved Sam, there was no way he would deny him Dr. Pepper. Everyone who hung out or volunteered at the bookstore ate at Rockit's, it was the closest thing and it was usually free, as long as someone cool was working. After a while, Secret Sailor had their own Rockit's dish bin and a shelf for it by the door, for dirty Rockit's dishes. Sometimes we would run out of bread stick baskets or pizza trays, and I'd have to walk down to Secret Sailor and collect them.

One night I was hanging out with Sam, eating my favorite Rockit's meal, cheese sticks dipped into nacho cheese sauce, when Paul came in with a big can of cheap coffee. He stopped and talked to us for a while. He asked Sam about the bookstore and told him how great he thought it was. He sat down with us and told us that he was an anarchist for a while and might still be one. He said that he was involved in the student riots in the 60's in California, in some famous riot in which the students burned down the student loan offices. We smiled and assumed it was just another one of Paul's tall tales. Then Sam's gaze fixed on the can of coffee. Paul noticed and gave Sam a questioning look.

"You should really buy fair trade coffee," Sam suggested. Paul looked guilty and ashamed. Sam went on to explain why non-fair trade coffee was evil and mentioned Paul's campaign to become 1000% pure. Paul listened, respectfully, nodding in agreement.

"You're right Sam. You're totally right. I'm gonna take this back and return it and I want you to go down to Bloomingfoods and get some good coffee." He reached into his pocket and pulled out his wallet. He got out forty bucks and handed it to Sam. "Go and get however much coffee you can get with this," he said. He stood up, enlivened and excited, and looked to me and said, "I love this guy, he's a genius. From now on, Sam gets free pizza for life."

The words echoed through the empty dining room. Did we hear him right? *"From now on, Sam gets free pizza for life."*

Sam's eyes lit up and a huge smile spread across his face. He looked so happy. He jumped up and I thought he was going to hug Paul, but he stopped himself. We loved Paul and Paul loved us, but he never hugged us. That line had not been crossed yet. Sam was wide-eyed and slightly oscillating. He looked like he was about to explode or boil over with joy.

"Are you serious? Those are pretty strong words," he asked. Paul smiled and grabbed Sam and pulled him in for a hug.

"Of course I am, Sam. I'm serious. It's my place, I can do whatever I want." It was such a great moment to witness. Sam ran off to buy coffee, and Paul left to return the slave labor coffee. I finished my overly cheesy meal and went back to work. Things were good. Sam came back with five pounds of really nice coffee and made a pot for him and Pops to split. He told me that he was considering getting a tattoo of a pizza slice with a banner that said: FREE PIZZA FOR LIFE. He asked me if I would draw it for him. He thought that if he had the tattoo, Paul would have to honor his promise. I assured him that Paul would honor his promise with or without the tattoo.

Sam never got the tattoo, but I've seen a few other people with it. He did get two tattoos that I designed, though. One of them was this random doodle of tribal shapes that roughly formed a person holding a spear. I doodled it on tour once, on a scrap of paper while I was waiting for Joel Biel (from Microcosm Publishing) to answer the phone and give me the address of our show in Mentor, Ohio, that he had booked. He never answered, and we didn't seem to have a show. It was the last day of tour, so we gave up and went home. Later, Sam saw the drawing in my tour notebook and asked, "what is the Mentor?" I didn't know what he was talking about. He showed me the page that I had written Mentor under the sketch.

I explained it to him. "Can I buy it off of you?" he asked. I said no. For months he tried to get me to sell it to him, offering me more money each time, and getting more and more frustrated that I wouldn't sell it to him. Eventually I gave in, and sold it to him for $10. The next day, I found it torn to pieces in the trashcan. I was so mad. I assumed it was some kind of point he was trying to make. I busted into his room to confront him about it. I was just getting started on my rant when I noticed that his arm was bandaged.

"What happened?" I asked, fearing that he had cut himself again.

"Nothing," he said, smiling. I was really worried and I wanted to know why he was wearing a bandage. I didn't give up. Eventually he pulled back the bandage to show me his fresh tattoo of "the Mentor." I couldn't believe it.

A few years later, he was living in Pensacola, and he got a tattoo of a skull in front of a red star that I drew on the back of an envelope that I had sent him. It was evil looking and so random of him to get it tattooed. Those are the two tattoos I designed for Sam, both unintentional.

Paul really wanted Rockit's to become famous, even though, according to the sign, "Rockit's Famous Pizza," it already was. He wanted it to be known as the place for musicians to hang out and eat pizza, and he wanted to have live music, despite the tiny size of the place. He told us that we could only have music on Sunday nights because of some clause in the lease that said that we couldn't compete with the bar next door which was owned by the same landlord. He asked me to book a show, and I was happy to do it. I asked a few bands to play, made some fliers ,and it was done. The first Sunday night show was booked. Paul was ecstatic.

Sam stopped taking his medicine and it had a really strong effect on him. I first noticed when he was in the shower. I heard him arguing with someone and I was really freaked out. I couldn't figure out who would be in the shower with him and why they would be fighting. I stood outside the door and listened for a second and I realized that it was just Sam, no one else was in there.

I heard him say, "fuck you dad, I don't give a shit what you think I should or shouldn't do." Then I knocked on the door. I heard him drop a shampoo bottle. "What do you want? I'm trying to take a shower."

I asked him to let me in. He said no. I asked him if he was okay, and he said yes. I left him alone. A few nights later, I came home from work and noticed his light was still on. I went to talk to him. He wasn't in his room, which wasn't uncommon—he rarely stayed on a normal schedule and he often forgot to turn off his light. I was going back to my room to pretend that I was going to go to sleep, when I heard a howling coming from his closet. I thought he was being funny, then I figured out that he was crying. I knocked on the door, and again, he told me that he was okay and he didn't want to open up. He apologized for crying and asked me to leave him alone. I left him alone. The next day Ali and Sam decided to go hitch hiking. Ali wasn't having a good time in Bloomington and was kind of freaking out. I tried to convince them not to go. I asked Sam what he was going to do about school. He said that he didn't care. They left. A few days later, they were back, and Ali had a broken foot. Sam dropped out of college and refused to take his medication. He became unstable again, but at least he had a lot of projects to keep him busy. I hoped that they would be enough.

Sunday came, and it was time for our first show. I had to work, which wasn't bad. Working on Sunday was nice, because we closed early, and I was looking forward to the show. An hour or so before the show, the phone rang and rang and no one was in the restaurant, so I had to answer it.

"Rockit's pizza, how can I help you?"

"You can help me by explaining why your stupid delivery driver put a stack of encyclopedias on my pizza?" I laughed. "What's so funny? Do you think it's funny?" he asked.

"No, I'm sure that no one stacked anything on your pizza. I'm sorry if it got smashed. Here's what I can do, I'll have him bring you another pizza free of charge and return your money, does that sound good?" I offered.

"No, I want my check back, I gave him a check!" He spat, then said, "can I talk to your manager?" I told him the truth.

"There are no real managers, I'm the closest thing to a manager here," I said, laughing. He was so angry. I tried to calm him down. "Listen, I'm willing to do whatever it takes to make you happy. I'll get you a new pizza and I'll get your check back."

He hung up on me. I didn't care. I started moving tables and chairs out to the sidewalk to make room for the show. Thirty minutes later, he called back and asked to speak to the manager. I told him that it was still just me. He said that he would take my offer, but he wanted to pick the pizza up in person, because he didn't trust the driver. I agreed, and I told him to come in 30 minutes. I made him a perfect pie. I was proud of it. I was sure that it would make him happy, although I didn't really care.

The bands showed up and started setting up their gear. People showed up too and I gave everyone cups for soda. All the seats were filled with punks, waiting for the show, then Paul came in and turned down the lights. He was so happy. He was so pleased with me. I told him about the asshole and the smashed pizza. He told me that I did the right thing. I even showed him the pizza, I was so proud of it. Everything was ready and everyone was waiting, then the guy came in. I handed him his pizza and his check and I apologized. He was still angry. Paul was mingling and noticed what I was doing and came over.

"Hello, my name is Paul, this is my place. I just want to apologize for what happened and assure you..." He was holding out his hand, waiting for the other guy to shake it, then other guy interrupted him.

"I'm not gonna shake your hand or accept your apology, and the next time I order a pizza, I'm gonna order it from Papa John's."

The whole room—filled with punks—was listening. Paul knew we were all listening, and he knew that he couldn't let this jerk talk to him like that. Everything froze for a second, and we waited to see what he would do. No one expected what happened. He grabbed the pizza out of the guy's hands and tried to hit him with it.

"Fuck you, you asshole! Get the fuck out of my restaurant and never come back!" he yelled. The guy took off running and Paul chased him out the door. We all cheered. The cheers turned into laughter. A few people, including me, ran outside to watch. Paul chased him to his car and threw the pizza on his windshield. That beautiful pizza flew out of the box and splattered all over the asshole's car. It was fitting, a perfect weapon. I went back inside before Paul caught me watching. He was so furious and I assumed that he would be embarrassed by his outburst. I rushed back inside and told everyone to act normal. Paul came in, smiling and happy, as if nothing had happened.

"That guy was an asshole, but he's not going to ruin our night." Everyone starting clapping. A few minutes later, he took the mic and gave a speech:

"Hello everyone. My name is Paul and this is my place. We're making history here tonight... we're gonna do this every Sunday night after 10. Punk after

10. Every Sunday and I want all of you here. Everything is free tonight, anything you want and if you have booze, that's fine, just keep it on the down low. We're closed for business, this is a private party with my friends. That's what you guys are, my friends. I want to thank Chris, the governor of punk rock, for putting this together, and I'd like to thank Sam... for being Sam. Okay, let's eat some pizza and listen to some music."

I was so embarrassed about him calling me the "governor of punk rock" in front of all my friends. Everyone was cheering again and Paul was glowing. I didn't have much time to think about my embarrassment, because everyone rushed the counter to get free pizza. I handed out slices and assured everyone that we would make more. I went back to start, then orders started showing up. People were ordering the special pizzas, like the "Johnny Cash" (triple black olives). I had to put my foot down. I went into the dining room and announced that, although all the pizza was free, we wouldn't be making special orders. I said that we would make a variety of vegan and veggie pizzas. Some people hated me. Brad Baute, who was once one of the Ted Dancin' Machine dancers, offered to help in the kitchen, and Paul told him to get back there. It was total chaos. The kitchen was full of people that didn't work there, making themselves pizzas. I gave up and decided to just watch the bands and have fun. It was a magical night. It felt like we really were making history.

Morale was high for weeks after the show. Paul was glowing, and the rest us felt pretty good too. Paul sat down with Sam and I one day and told us more about his involvement in these student riots in California. He talked about breaking windows and throwing Molotov cocktails and watching the buildings burn. I listened and nodded, not really believing a word of it, knowing that he was full of shit. Sam, however had an honest look of interest on his face.

The phone rang and rang and rang, then Paul realized that there was no one working the counter and he knew that I wasn't going to answer it, so he got up, muttering some curses, and went to get it. Sam leaned in close to me. He had a split lip and dried blood on his teeth. I pulled back. He looked annoyed with me, and beckoned me to come close, keeping his eyes on Paul. He whispered, "I think he's for real. He's either for real or he's read a lot about the riots. I've been reading about them myself and he's got all of his facts straight." We only had a few seconds to ponder the possibility before he came back.

Paul changed the subject. "When is the next show?" I talked about some bands and told him I would get working on it right away. Sam's gears were turning. He got up and refilled his Dr. Pepper. He sat back down and humbly suggested that we do an open mic. It was a great idea. The Madison open mics were super fun and it would be really cool to have one in a pizza place. Paul loved it. We decided to do it three weeks from then, and I said that I'd make the flier right away. Paul left to go do something, and Sam and I picked up our conversation.

"I doubt that he's read about the riots, it doesn't seem like something he would do," he said. "He's the right age too."

I shrugged. "I guess it's possible, maybe..."

"I think this is a case for the Thor Detective Agency," Sam said, with a smirk on his face. The Thor Detective Agency was Sam's detective agency. So far, he had solved two cases out of three. One of them was the case of "How does all that snot get in my nose?" He was feeling pretty cheeky about it because he was in the local paper. A reporter came over and did an interview with him about Thor, and took a picture of him wearing a brown blazer with his finger pointed toward the camera and a wild look in his eyes. We didn't think the story would make the cut, but it did. His business didn't really pick up though.

He said that he was going to do some research on Paul. He was going to take the case: "Is Paul full of shit?" He was going to read more about the student riots and ask Paul some questions. He said that he was also going to poke around Bloomingfoods (the local food co-op – that isn't really a co-op at all anymore) to try to figure out if there was any truth to Paul's claim of being one of the founders. I thought of another questionable tale that Paul had told me, and how we could figure out if there was any truth to it.

One day, he told a few of us that he used to be a session musician for a huge major label. A session musician is someone who is really good at some instrument and works in the recording studio, recording tracks for the bands on the label (who often can't do it themselves). Session musicians don't earn royalties, they just get paid by the hour to record. Sometimes they don't even get credit on the album. Paul told us that he played guitar solos on dozens of really famous records and that he had met The Clash and Blondie and a few other huge bands. Of course we didn't believe him. My idea to test him was simple; I would ask him to play at the open mic. Sam looked like a wicked goblin when I told him. He left to go back to Secret Sailor, and I went back to the kitchen to start preparing for the drunken onslaught that was inevitably on its way. Paul showed up again, hours later.

"Hey Paul, Sam and I had an idea. We think you should play something at the open mic," I said. His stoned eyes twinkled.

"Yeah! I will, I'll bring in my telecaster and my harmonica!"

Secret Sailor wasn't becoming much of a bookstore, but it was becoming a meeting place for activist, anarchist, wingnuts, punks and hippies. There were always people in there reading, or shouting about disturbing things they were looking at on the internet. Having a place to express disdain for our culture and meet other people who were equally pissed off really brought people out of the woodwork. We met lots of new folks whom we didn't know existed that had been living in Bloomington for years. It was great.

Things started happening; There were regular critical mass bike rides (where cyclists gather and ride around town, taking up the road to protest driving and to simply celebrate cycling), there were tree sits (that's when someone camps out in a treetop to prevent construction), and people locked themselves to the doors of the Old Navy on their grand opening day and delayed the consumer ceremony for hours. They managed not to get in any trouble (that time) either. It was great. I was so proud of Bloomington and I was so proud of Sam. He knew that simply creating a radical space would create a radical community. That's what happened.

Secret Sailor was great. People hung out all day, various community groups had weekly meetings and there were punk shows at night. We didn't know how well it would work, having punk shows so late at night, so close to the town square. They had to be late, because we had to wait for the other businesses around the store to close, but no one seemed to mind. Our block was great—free pizza at Rockit's and a radical hang out spot just a few doors down.

The open mic night was pretty tame in comparison to the first show at Rockit's, and not very many people performed. It didn't have the same feel as the ones that we had hosted in The Madison basement. Paul didn't give any speeches this time, and he didn't declare free pizza for all, but he did show up, and he brought his guitar. We were so prepared to be embarrassed for him when he got up to play. He sat down awkwardly and muttered something that no one could understand, then he started playing. He was good. It was, by no means, anything that I would ever want to listen to, but he could play. He had his harmonica too. He wailed out solos and played chords smothered in harmonica jams. We were all impressed. Maybe he was a session musician in his day. Sam's investigation had turned up more evidence in Paul's favor too. He was, in fact, one of the co-founders of Bloomingfoods. I was starting to think that everything Paul said was true.

Ten o'clock became the gathering time. Sometimes when I showed up for work, there were already a handful of punks loitering around and waiting for the late shift to come in, the pizza wasn't free until then. Manuel and Marion usually worked the first night shift, then passed the torch to the punks at 10, or 10:30 usually, since people were always late. They were a married couple from Venezuela. They were really nice people, but they didn't like Paul's free pizza for punks policy. Of course Paul was their boss and it was his idea, but they knew, just like we knew, that the business couldn't survive if the pizza was free. I agreed with them totally, but it wasn't my business, and I didn't really see myself working there forever, so I was prepared to go down with the ship. I would sink with my captain Paul. I would sink, eating pizza and giving pizza to my friends. Manuel and Marion couldn't really stop us from our sabotage-like behavior under the orders of our mad captain, but we didn't feel right doing it until they left. They were obviously upset by it, and they obviously had a right to be upset, so we behaved until they left. The pizza punks waited in the booths like hungry hounds. They waited for the wheel to be handed over to us.

As soon as the 'M's walked out, they swarmed the counter. I was fine with giving them pizza, but it was more work for me, so I worked out a deal. I offered pizza in exchange for labor. It was great. I never had to wash the dishes or fold pizza boxes again, none of us did. No one who worked there ever had to do that kind of stuff. There was a constant tower of folded boxes stacked on top of the jukebox, going all the way up to the ceiling, and the dishes were always "clean." Everyone was happy with the deal.

When the ship finally did sink, a year later, Manuel and Marion bought Rockit's. Slowly, they replaced the punk staff with their friends and family for some reason. Who could blame them? Chris Resnick managed to stay. He worked there for eight more years.

Sometime around the open mic (or maybe it was before the open mic), it was Thanksgiving, and Sam made it into the local paper again. This time it was because of a flier that he had made. It said: THANKSGIVING DAY RIOT! It was a call to action. It suggested that people should meet up in the park and "bring baseball bats and gasoline" to protest the holiday that celebrates genocide. It went on to say some pretty specific and crazy stuff, like "let's burn down corporate businesses on Kirkwood, like Streetside Records and Taco Bell," and "let's lynch the racist sheriff, Steve Sharp." I was kind of worried. I asked Sam if he was worried about calling the sheriff a racist and threatening him.

"No, he is a racist and we should hang him." I laughed.

"But aren't you worried about getting in trouble? I think it's illegal to make death threats."

Sam looked at me like I was stupid. "No one is gonna know it's me. I didn't put my name on it or anything." A few days later, someone knocked on our door. It was alarming, since people usually just walked in. I said "come in" as I walked to the living room. It was someone I didn't know. They said they were looking for Sam. I told the stranger where Sam's room was. The guy looked harmless, and I assumed that he was one of Sam's friends, so I wasn't worried. He turned out to be a reporter, and he came to interview Sam about the upcoming riot. Sam was shocked.

"How do you know I made those fliers?" he asked.

"Some kid downtown told me," the guy answered.

"Fuck," sighed Sam. The guy told him not to worry, and assured him that he wasn't going to compromise his identity, and promised to refer to Sam using an alias. He said he was just really interested in the flier and the riot and wanted to do a story on it. Sam agreed, and they talked for a while. The article came out a few days later, using the name Sam as Sam's alias (it was Sam's idea).

It was really funny. The guy interviewed other people about the flier too, including the chief of police. He asked him if the police were preparing themselves for the riot. The chief replied with "there's not going to be a riot in Bloomington unless I.U. wins the final four again." The reporter also interviewed a few business owners on Kirkwood. The best response came from the manager of Bloomingfoods. She said something about how the cops should be there to prevent the riot. She was really concerned about Streetside records getting torched.

She said, "Bloomingfoods is really close to Streetside, if they burn it down, the fire is likely to spread to us." We thought that was really funny that she was only concerned for her business. We hated her because she killed the free box.

There used to be a great free box in the alley by the downtown Bloomingfoods. It was a small shed with shelves inside. It was always full of cool stuff and it was a real community resource. She ordered it to be removed because she said people were using it as a bathroom. Sam argued with her about it and tried to get it back, but she said no. We didn't like her at all, and we were glad to see her looking like a selfish jerk in print. No one showed up for the riot, not even Sam. He sat across from the park and waited for an hour before coming home.

One night when I showed up at work I found little notes taped all over things. They were from Bob, Paul's brother and co-owner of Rockit's. They said things like: "EMPLOYEES GET ONE MEAL PER SHIFT" and "NO VISITORS ARE ALLOWED IN THE KITCHEN." This was very alarming. I was pretty happy with the way things were at Rockit's, and I didn't want them to change. I couldn't handle a normal job with normal rules. Chris Resnick told me that Bob had came in during the earlier shift and was pissed. He knew that we were giving away pizza. He said that the business was in the hole, and that he was paying the bills with the profit that he made from his other business, the snack bar in the new sportsplex, where he sold crappy frozen pizza and other gross shit. I hate frozen pizza. He informed everyone that things were going to change and that new policies were being put in place. Later that night, Paul showed up and tore down all the notes and assured us that we had nothing to worry about.

There was some show at Secret Sailor that needed another band, so Ali (from The Sissies —who had also started working at Rockit's) asked me if I wanted to start a one-night only band with Paul playing guitar. I thought it was a great idea. We asked Paul, and he said yes right away. He asked us about practice and Ali said, "we don't need to practice. Just show up and follow my lead." He smiled and agreed.

She made fliers, and we both kind of forgot about it until the night of the show. I got to the show early and asked her what we were going to do, if Paul actually remembered and showed up. Neither of us thought that he would, but just in case, we sat outside and wrote some simple songs really quickly. We wrote five.

Paul showed up! He had his guitar. "What time to do we go on?" he asked. We decided to get it over with and play first, right away. I played the drums and Ali played bass. Before each song Ali would tell Paul the key of the song and the chord structure and he would basically solo the whole time. We sounded like a real band, for the most part. It was fun.

When we were done, Paul said, "that was great, we should play again sometime." We never played again. We were called The Dog That Ate My Leg.

Paul was right about Bob's new policies, we had nothing to worry about. We didn't see Bob ever again—or at least I didn't—and it was back to business as usual. The workers ate whenever they wanted and as much as they wanted. We all took pizzas home for our housemates. We all came in on nights that we weren't working and made ourselves food, and we all gave free pizza to our friends and to touring bands. We did whatever we wanted. I went beyond the boundaries of pizza-for-punks a few times too.

It started one night when I was left alone in the restaurant, which happened a lot. A guy came in and ordered a pizza to-go. I made it while he waited, hoping that someone would come back before it was done, since I didn't know how to use the register or take credit cards. No one came back, so I just gave him the pizza and said it was on the house. He was freaked out. I assured him that it was okay and that he didn't have to pay. He seemed to think it was a trap. Eventually he accepted my gift and left, but not before putting a $10 tip in the jar. After that night, anytime I was left alone, it was free pizza for all.

I started a new band. I wasn't really trying to start a band, but this guy Grant, who had played in a band called Slingshot Episode, asked Hannah and me to start a band with him. I was really surprised, because Grant is a really good drummer. He was a real musician. I couldn't believe that he wanted to start a band with us—we were sloppy pop punks. He had to tell me multiple times that he was serious before I agreed to do it. We only had around a month to practice before Hannah and I went to Europe for three months, but we decided that it would be cool to at least get a feel for each other and try and write a few songs. We decided to call our band The Devil Is Electric.

It was springtime and everything was exciting. I was in a new band with a really good drummer, and I was about to go on an epic adventure across Europe. Grant asked me if I could get him a job at Rockit's. I told him I would look into it. I asked Paul, and he mumbled something about an interview and told me to tell Grant to call him. I didn't have much faith of this method ever working out, so I decided to hire Grant myself.

Bob's wife, or maybe it was their sister, did all the paperwork for the business and wrote the paychecks. Bob never came in and had no idea who worked there, other than the names on the checks. Paul was in charge of hiring people. When someone was hired, the only thing that happened on his end was the creation of a new time card. The new employee wrote their full name and social security number on the card. At the end of the week, someone took all the cards to the unknown woman to be processed. If there was a new employee, she did all the paperwork and wrote a check, no questions asked, so my idea was to just have Grant come in and fill out a time card and start working. He was a little hesitant, but he did it. He had been working for a few days before Paul noticed him. "Are you new?" he asked.

"Yeah..." Grant answered, and that was that. That's how I started hiring people.

In late April of 2000, Hannah and I went to Europe. We found out quickly that we didn't save up nearly enough money for a three month trip. It was really hard, but it was an epic adventure and that's what we wanted. I had gotten pretty fat working at Rockit's, eating as much pizza as I wanted, but when I came home I was thin again. We walked and hiked a lot, and we didn't have enough money to eat very much. We lived on canned beans, peanut butter and raisins and the occasional order of French fries. Of course we ate pizza in Roma, how could we not? But for the most part, we ate very meager meals and burned the calories off right away, walking with packs on our backs. I had to tighten my waist strap regularly. By the end, it was as small as it could go.

We assumed that traveling in Europe would be like our experiences traveling in the US, but something we didn't consider was that we were not touring, we were just traveling. Touring is way better than traveling. It's very hard to meet people when you're a tourist. We tried a few times; In Amsterdam, Hannah walked up to some punks and asked them about shows. They laughed and answered in a language we couldn't understand. I think they were tourists too. The only people we really met were the people who gave us rides. We met a lot of nice people on the side of the road. We talked with them for a while, then they let us out of their car somewhere and drove away. We decided that we wanted to come back, but that we wanted to tour the next time. On tour you meet cool people almost every day and you get places to stay and sometimes, even food. Traveling is horrible. Touring is great. three years later, we did it with our band Ghost Mice, which we started for just that purpose. I tried to book a tour in 2002 for the Devil Is Electric and This Bike Is A Pipe Bomb, but it was too hard to figure out how to get a van and equipment, so we decided to start the acoustic band that we had always talked about, and tour Europe. We figured that if the Euro-punks hated us, we'd just stop going to our shows (if we managed to book any) and reluctantly become tourist again.

The idea was that we could play anywhere without electricity or without any equipment that we couldn't carry on our backs, and we could travel by hitchhiking or by train. The tour was great, only a few people hated us. We made a lot of new friends and got to experience Europe in a much better way, through its punks and inside its squats.

A few years later, I busted out my Slingshot organizer that I used as a travel diary during our first trip, in 2000, and we wrote a concept album about it, with one song for each country we visited and each body of water that we crossed, so if you want to know more about that first trip, the trip that happened in the middle of my time at Rockit's, listen to Ghost Mice's "Europe." If you get the CD version, you can put it in your computer and look at almost a hundred pictures from the trip.

It seemed like we were gone forever. It was hard to imagine that Bloomington was still there, waiting for us. I felt like a different person. I looked like a different person too. I didn't shave the whole time I was gone, and I came home with a huge beard. Sam laughed loudly when he saw me.

"You're so skinny, and you have fucking beard!" I was happy to see him and to be home. Europe was nice, but Bloomington is way better. He asked me a few questions about my trip and offered me some Dr. Pepper.

"I quit," I told him. He looked betrayed. I had to quit, I knew that soda was more expensive in Europe, and I knew that we weren't going to have much money, so before I left, I quit, so that I wouldn't be addicted to caffeine and have to go through withdrawals on the road. It was hard. I felt horrible for around two weeks, but when I kicked it, I felt so good. It was great being in Europe and only drinking water. I felt better than I had ever felt. I was raised on soda. When I was a little kid, I drank two cans of Pepsi with every meal, even breakfast. It was hard to quit, and I missed it, but I wasn't eager to get hooked again.

Sam was very disappointed. "You're home now and the soda is free. You don't have to worry about those Euro-fascists and their over-priced soda anymore." I managed to resist him for a few weeks before giving in.

When Sam was done pleading his case for soda and I was done telling him about the various sheep fields that we had slept in, he said, "I have some bad news." I asked him to tell me. "What do you want to hear about first? The Madison trouble, or the trouble with the new house that we are moving into?" he asked.

"There is a problem with both houses?" I asked. Sam seemed really worried, and I was pissed that we had just spent hours talking about nothing when he knew there was something important to tell me. I'm sure he just didn't want to bombard me with bullshit as soon as I got off the plane. Eventually, I got both scoops.

When we went to Europe, we moved out of The Madison and Casey and her kid moved in with Sam and Dave. Dave's girlfriend (yes, Dave had a girlfriend) moved in a month later, and Sam gave her his room. He couch surfed for the rest of the summer, or stayed at the bookstore. He left them in charge of the house. They didn't pay the rent. Dave and his girlfriend split up, she moved away, and his appendix burst. He moved out a month early, without paying the rent or cleaning up. He went back to Rockford, and his curse continued.

When the lease was up, the house was filled with left over junk and trash and two months of unpaid rent. The landlord was pissed, and said he was going to sue Hannah. For some reason, he blamed Hannah for everything. I wasn't too worried about the trouble at The Madison, but I was really worried about the trouble at our new house. I was so excited to move in.

We signed the lease on it before we left, and I thought about coming home to it all summer. It was a huge house with four bedrooms, a gigantic living room, a full basement, and a two-car garage. Sam told me that three of the people who were supposed to move in decided not to. We had three days to fill two empty bedrooms. I was starting to miss my simple life, my can of beans, my tent and my backpack. I had to start dealing with people again.

We used the first, primitive version, of the Plan-It-X message board to find roommates. Surprisingly, it worked, and Evan (from Kentucky) and Bernie (from DC) moved in right away. The huge living room had a fireplace in one corner and wood paneling which made it look like a ski-lodge or something, so we called the house "The Limbo Lodge." Yes, we did do limbo, with a bamboo stick and everything, but the name meant more than that. We called it The Limbo Lodge because so many of the people that lived there were temporary.

The best part about the house was my office. Years before we moved in, someone had converted the front porch into a room, and that room was connected to my bedroom. The porch room became the first Plan-It-X office. My dad got a huge desk from the office at the cemetery where he worked, and brought it up. Plan-It-X was becoming a real record label. It was exciting. Of course we still only had around 10 releases and we barely ever sold anything. But, I had an office and a desk!

I was dead broke, so I went back to Rockit's to see if I could get my job back. Paul told me before I left that I could always come back, but I had hoped that I wouldn't have to. I loved Paul and I loved Rockit's, but I don't like working for anyone and I don't like having a schedule. When I walked in, I knew something was wrong but I couldn't figure it out. Paul wasn't there. Someone told me that he was in Hawaii. I decided not to ask anyone about my job, I just grabbed a time card and put my name on it. I found an apron and started making pizzas. It felt great to have the dough in my hands again. It felt comforting to have the warm oven at my back. I was glad to be home. A few hours later, I made one of my old favorites: a no sauce, green olive pizza. I went to the front to take a break and eat it. That's when I noticed what was wrong. The jukebox was gone. I found out that Paul had sold it to pay the power bill. It was so sad. I also found out the power got shut off twice while I was gone. The ship was really sinking now.

My vegan friends were glad to see me in the kitchen again, though not because I gave them free pizza, because they didn't really mind paying for it. They were excited for me to make their pizzas for them again. They had gotten used to my overloaded vegan pizzas with garlic/sesame crust and said that a lot of the other cooks skimped on the toppings. A few of my friends even started calling the pizzas I made for them "The Chris Clavin." They didn't even specify the toppings, they left it up to me. It was really fun. I would alternate between what I called the "meaty vegan" and the "spicy vegan." The Meaty Vegan always had mushrooms, olives, artichoke hearts and a few other random things on it. The Spicy Vegan always had all of the peppers, onions, and garlic. On both variations I would brush the crust with garlic butter and sprinkle on sesame seeds and other spices. Paul got a big kick out of it. He came in the kitchen the first time and said, "This guy out here wants a Chris Clavin. Do you know what he's talking about?"

While I was away, Sam had been writing. He chose the pen name Sterling Grey, and he wrote gay science fiction. He created a fake persona for Sterling and claimed to have discovered him. He swore he wasn't him. Of course, we all knew he was. He reserved the auditorium at the library for a special visit from the author who would be reading some of his work. He made fliers with a sample of his writing, and hung them up all over town. When the day of the reading came, Sam went and waited in the auditorium with the handful of other people that showed up to see the gay science fiction writer speak.

Sterling never showed up.

By the way, the writing was ridiculous and perverse. It was all based on the idea that homosexual men had discovered deep space travel through the use of something called "the ass-cock drive." Only men could pilot space ships, and they had to have anal sex while hooked up to the A.C.D. to make the jump to light speed. It was silly and sexual and kind of offensive, but really funny and well written.

Sometime around then Hannah went on tour with The Sissies again, and I fell in love with someone else when she was gone. Our relationship was dying. We were great friends, but not great lovers. We broke up. It was hard. We got back together. The person I fell in love with hated me and I felt horrible about it all. Hannah and I broke up again, and it stuck for a while. I moved into Sam's old room and Sam moved into the closet in the living room to save money. Hannah started hanging out with someone else and it made me crazy. I hadn't been crazy in a long time. It was an unwelcome feeling.

Paul came back from Hawaii and said that he had met a girl there and fell in love. He told us that she was from Bloomington and that they just bumped into each other over there and hit it off. He said that they were probably going to get married. He told us she was beautiful and only 23 years old. Most of the crew didn't believe him. He kept saying that he was going to bring her in sometime, but he didn't. I believed him though.

I had learned a lot about Paul, and I knew that no matter what else you could say about him, you couldn't say that he was full of shit. Sure enough, he brought in his lover, a few days later. She was young and pretty and seemed to really be in love with him, just like he said. He was happy and that was good, but Rockit's suffered. Paul sold the tuba, to some random guy who came in and asked him about it one day, for a hundred bucks. It was so bleak in the dining room, first the jukebox and now the tuba. Rockit's was losing its style. Then he started selling the more famous bands' autographed photos off of the walls, and it was too much to take. I started working less. Other punks took my shifts, and some of them stole money from the register (something I would never do). It was dark times for me and for Rockit's. I was confused and heartbroken and sick of Rockit's. I was over it. I quit.

I still got hooked up with free pizza for a while, then I went on some tour and when I came back, Paul was gone. Rockit's belonged to Manuel and Marion and I couldn't walk into the kitchen and make myself any kind of pizza I wanted anymore. The era was over. Paul was gone.

After that, I lost interest in free pizza. It just wasn't the same. Eating dumpster pizza isn't as good after you've had a pizza kitchen under your control for two years. I also had more money and didn't need to scavenge food anymore; My band and my record label were growing, and I usually had enough money to buy food and even pay my rent. My life was different. It had been years since I had lived in my van and shoplifted my every need. I also knew that I could never get a job again. After working for Paul and being a part of the golden age of Rockit's, how could I ever settle for less. I decided that I would never work for someone else again, even if that meant living in my van again. I liked living in the van. I'll be happy on the day when I have to get back in it.

Let's say this was 2002.

CHAPTER 21
THE ENDING

One day, I was feeling sad, and I called in an order for a pizza from this place called Aver's. They had this great deal back then, called the "crazy deal" or something. It was a pizza, breadsticks, and two drinks for $8.88. I ordered a green olive and mushroom pizza with pesto sauce, and I got two dipping sauces for the breadsticks: nacho cheese and hummus. I got two cokes to wash it all down with. Twenty minutes later, the driver showed up. I gave him $13. There was no scam. There was no freeganism. I bought a pizza.

The drama of my personal life was killing me. I was in love with someone who was pissed off at me, and I didn't want to let go of someone else. I freaked out. I packed my things and I moved to Pensacola. I lived in a tent, in Rymodee and his girlfriend Jen's backyard for around a month. I wrote songs and played with their cats. It was nice and peaceful. Then Sam came to visit. Then Matte Cathcart (a young Franklin punk, who played drums in my short-lived band, Disarm) came to visit too.

I couldn't get away from Bloomington. Hannah came a few weeks later, and we got back together again. I moved back to Bloomington, and we moved in with our friend Marty. It was great living with Marty and being close friends again. He is my oldest Bloomington friend, and I hope I always know him. It was sometime around then when we started Ghost Mice. The songs I wrote in Florida, living in that tent, became our first few songs. Sometime shortly after that, we were on The Devil Is Electric tour out west with This Bike Is A Pipe Bomb, and my new friend Spoonboy as our roadie. We were standing on a beach somewhere, and I asked Hannah if she would rather just be friends and band mates and not be partners. I expected her to say no. I thought we were getting close again. I only asked to make sure that she felt the same way, but she said yes, and we broke up again, for good.

My muscles started hurting and still haven't quit. They still hurt today, all of them. Abe Froman joined us on the east coast leg of that same tour. There were tons of us, it was crazy. Sam came too, and he was in bad shape mentally. I was in bad shape myself. I was heartbroken and every muscle in my body ached all day long, and I'd have horrible dizzy spells. Sam started drinking a lot and kept talking about wanting to kill Ronald Reagan. I got really upset. I was so mad that he was drinking and I was really pissed at the people who gave him beers. I was pissed at everyone, worried about Sam, and worried about what was going on with my body.

One night in Providence, Sam was drunk. He was helping us load the gear and threw my amp into the van really hard. I snapped. I yelled at him and threw him up against a chain-link fence. Grant (the drummer of The Devil Is Electric) got really mad, shoved me, and yelled at me. I got in the van and passed out. The next day, I told everyone that I was sick and that I was leaving. I assumed Hannah and Grant would come with me, but they stayed. I drove home, alone.

I nearly passed out a few times, and I tried and failed to find the hospital in Akron, Ohio. Instead, I ended up passing out again in the parking lot of a gas station that I had stopped at to ask for directions. I woke up a few hours later and bought some Pepto Bismol for some reason and drank the whole bottle. It made me feel better. I drove the rest of the way home, and went to the emergency room. They didn't tell me anything and charged me $1,000. Then, Hannah called me and asked me if I had seen Sam. She told me that he left the tour and they didn't know where he was. She called me back two days later, and told me that they found him in Albany, New York. He was going to try and kill Reagan.

I met up with the tour for the last show, and The Devil Is Electric played. We patched things up a little. I think they understood that something was wrong with me. Sam seemed to be doing better too. It was good to see him again, as well as the rest of my awesome friends. I regretted leaving and getting so mad at Sam.

When we got home for good, Sam had problems at Secret Sailor. The volunteers, who had been doing all the work at the store, wanted to change things. They wanted to become a real bookstore and a non-profit. They wanted to change the name to help create a new image for the store. They invited Sam to join them or to quit. They were going to leave Secret Sailor either way. Sam was pissed. He decided to quit and to close the store. He made a deal with them. He agreed to walk away and give them the remaining stock and the bookshelves, if they agreed to take over the debts of the store and handle all the final tax work that needed to be done. They agreed, and that was the end of Secret Sailor Books. Sam moved to Pensacola sometime after that.

Time passed. Sam moved to Asheville for a while, then back to Pensacola, and Hannah moved into her own place. A lot of other stuff happened, but that stuff doesn't matter in this story. Sometime in 2004, Sam called me and we talked for a while. Then he said, "I'm a woman now."

"What?" I asked.

"I'm a woman now," she said. There was a pause... and she went on. "I figured it out and I'm much happier." I wasn't surprised. I never really thought of Sam as a man. Sam was just Sam. She told me that she was legally changing her name to Samantha Jane Dorsett. I told her that it was great. I told her I was happy for her. She sounded really happy. She sounded like she did when we first met, and she was young and excited about everything. It was nice. I was so excited for her and hopeful that this metamorphosis was what she needed to feel better. We made plans to hang out. Most of them fell through, and time passed. We lived our separate lives.

I didn't see her again until Plan-It-X fest in the summer of 2004. It was the 10-year anniversary of the label, and Samantha came to celebrate and give a short speech about starting the label. When she got to town, she checked her P.O. box and found final warnings and over due bills from the IRS and book distributors. It was all Secret Sailor stuff. It was all stuff that was supposed to be taken care of. She was really upset about it.

Before her speech, she was nervously pacing around in the alley behind the venue. Some cops drove by and saw her. They yelled at her. They demanded that she come over to their car. She said no, and started running away. They chased her down and grabbed her. We didn't find out until they had hauled her off. They took her to the hospital instead of the jail. Terry (from This Bike is a Pipe Bomb) went over there and pleaded with them to let her go. She told them that Samantha had some mental problems and that the cops were unjust in their assault on her. She told them about the fest and Sam's involvement and promised to take care of her, personally. They let her go and she came back and gave her speech, still shaking from the ordeal. It was a cold homecoming. She almost never came back again.

A year later, she moved to Oakland. I didn't see her much, only when my bands were on tour out west. She was doing good, making 'zines and writing books, getting involved in local activist groups and stuff like that. In the summer 2006 I freaked out again and moved away. I moved to Olympia and lived in my bus. Samantha came up to visit me on my birthday. It was nice. She made me a birthday cake and got a tub of vegan ice cream. It was like old times. We were both scarred and broken, but we were both the same geeky friends that we used to be. We talked about role-playing games and the old days. I bought her a pizza at Old School Pizza. It was their "Princess" pizza, with sun-dried tomatoes and some other stuff. I tried to convince her to move to Olympia. She said that she would consider it. I really hoped that she would. I missed her in my life.

In the winter of 2007, I moved to Gainesville and stayed there for two years. I barely saw Sam at all then, only on tour, and that was only once for a few days. Sometime around then Sam was pushed off of a bridge and broke a lot of bones. The words "hate crime" were used. I had no clue what had happened, no one really did. A few months later, I got a letter from Sam. She told me that she had jumped—she wasn't pushed. She told me that she wanted to die again, and that she was sorry, but then she said that one of our mutual friends, Emmalee, from the band Rosa, came over and brought her coffee and flowers and that the taste of the coffee made her want to live. She said that it was the little things in life that are worth living for. I wrote her back and told her about my life and I asked her, "how could you want to die when there are free refills on soda?"

Then, in 2009, I bought a huge building in the ruined city of Cairo (care-row), Illinois with the dream of creating a punk-rock utopia. I also had the dream of convincing Sam to move there and help me do it. It was an idea we had talked about a lot in the past, and I really wanted her to be a part of it. I called her and told her about it, and begged her to move in. I told her that I was more grown up, and that I could take care of her. She was going to be stuck in a wheelchair for a long time because of her fall from the bridge, and would need some help. I wanted to help her. I owed her everything and I missed her so much. I told her that she could have her own room and as many pet rabbits as she wanted. She said that she would think it over, but that she was a little worried about living in a small town. She was worried about being transgender in a place like Cairo.

Right after I bought the place, I went on an East Coast tour with Ghost Mice and Heathers (twin sisters from Dublin, Ireland). We played a fest in Brattleboro, Vermont, then decided to drive to Albany after the show, since we knew the houses in Brattleboro would be crowded, and we had two shows the next day in New York (a day show and a night show). We drove through thick fog for hours. We got pulled over and the cop didn't seem to mind that we had expired plates and that none of us were wearing seat belts. He just told us to slow down and be careful in the fog.

When we finally made it Albany, we were greeted by a really cute, but really energetic pit bull that kept us up all night. The next morning, we woke up early and our host made us waffles. Mine had a chunk of unmixed baking power, and left a metallic taste in my mouth. Then I noticed that I had seven missed calls, all from Terry (from This Bike Is A Pipe Bomb). I knew that it was bad news, so I went to the van to listen to the messages. There were a lot of people hanging around on the streets who stared at me as I sat in the back seat, too afraid to call Terry back. Eventually I made the call and she told me what I had already guessed. Samantha was gone. I didn't ask her how it happened. I didn't care. It didn't matter.

THE GULF OF MEXICO

Samantha's ashes were spread into the Gulf Of Mexico, in Pensacola. There was a memorial ceremony, but I didn't go. I couldn't bring myself to admit that it was true. I didn't want to see Sam's friends. I didn't want to be with the other people who understood what the world had lost. It was too much to take. I stayed in Cairo, in my big, dirty building, with my new friends that had never even met Sam. I stayed there, working on a hopeless dream, keeping busy.

A few days later, I got a package from Sam's closest friend, Ada. Ada and Sam had lived together in Asheville, Pensacola, and California. They had a falling out near the end, and Samantha moved to San Jose alone. When she got out of the hospital, after jumping off the bridge, she moved back in with Ada. Ada took care of her. I never really got to know her, despite having Sam in common as our best friend. I know it must have been hard for her, and I'm grateful of her love for Sam. I know firsthand that being Sam's best friend is hard job. It's hard to understand why someone so smart and so amazing and so funny would want to die. It was hard for me, anyway, so I had this package in my hands, afraid to open it. I knew it would be some kind of final proof of Sam's death. I knew it would be some kind of artifact that I would treasure forever. It stayed sealed on my desk for days before I finally looked inside.

When I worked up the guts to open it, I found a little blue stuffed rabbit with its eyes closed. It was Sleepy Bunny. It used to be mine when I was a baby. It was on a shelf in my parents' basement for years after I moved out, and every time that Samantha came with me to spend the night there, she would ask me if she could sleep with Sleepy Bunny. I always said no. I was cruel. I would tell her that it was too special to me and I didn't want her to get it dirty or make it smell. It was a game we would play. I would be mean and stern, and she would pretend to be really hurt. Maybe she was really hurt. It went on for years. Eventually, sometime when she was feeling bad, I mailed her Sleepy Bunny. I gave it to her. She was so happy to finally have the bunny of her desires.

I was crushed to see that bunny again. I cried for hours. I finally got it,

Sam was gone for good. I would never see her again.

I wrote this book for her. It was her idea to write about our pizza crimes. Every good story I tell is about her. Of course, the stories in this book are only some of the stories of Sam's life, and I could write so much more about our adventures together. There were also years and years of stuff that I wasn't a part of, stuff that I regret having missed. I regret growing apart and focusing on my own life without Sam. She was the best friend I could have ever wished for, and I owe her everything.

The next time you're you at the Gulf Of Mexico, say hello to her. Tell her that I miss her and that I love her. Tell her your stories. Promise her that you'll keep fighting for our fucked up world.

If you know someone like Sam, suffering from mental problems, please, please, please give them your love and your patience. Don't give up on them.

Drawing, by Samantha.

THE FOLLOWING PAGES ARE
SELECTIONS FROM SAMANTHA'S 'ZINE
"STRAP YOURSELF IN"

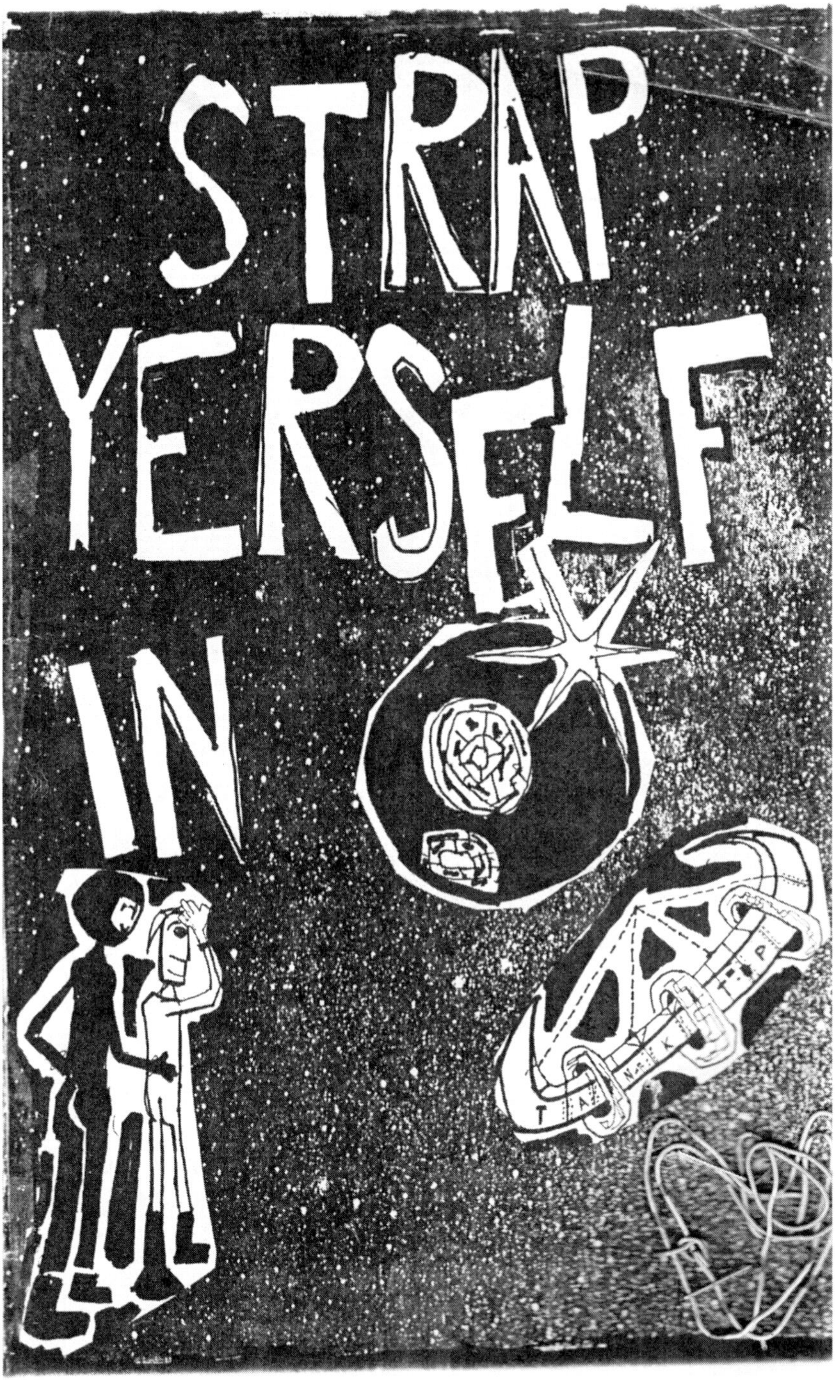
STRAP
YERSELF
IN

good LUCK SAMmy.

I'll miss you.

MY DESK ← masking tape.

♡ -chris

MY ROOM MATES CHRIS + JRD + HANNAH AND MY FRIEND MATT WENT ON TOUR LAST FRIDAY. CHRIS LEFT SOME NOTES ALL OVER THE HOUSE, LIKE THAT ONE ↑ ONLY THE REST WERE ABOUT NOT LEAVING THE BURNER ON + FEEDING THE CAT AND SO ON. ANYWAY I'M A LITTLE BORED AND I MISS THEM TOO SO I'M MAKING THIS. IT ALSO HAD A LOT TO DO WITH STERLING GRAY — HE WAS REALLY UPSET ABOUT NOT BEING ABLE TO MAKE IT TO HIS LECTURE AT THE LIBRARY DEC. 10 (HIS WHOLE BOOK TOUR GOT CANCELED) THAT HE GAVE ME A STORY HE HASN'T GOT PUBLISHED YET AND LET ME DRAW THE COVER. ♡ SAM.

WHAT'S INSIDE

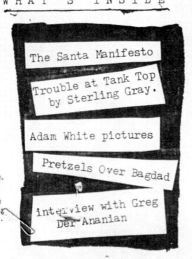

The Santa Manifesto

Trouble at Tank Top by Sterling Gray.

Adam White pictures

Pretzels Over Bagdad

interview with Greg Der Ananian

P.S. CHRIS—I'M REALLY SORRY I LOST YOUR BIKE.

THIS GUY GAVE ME THESE TODAY AND
SAID "THEY SHOULD BE DROPPING THESE
ON IRAQ INSTEAD OF BOMBS... GIVING
SOMEONE FOOD IS HOW YOU GET THEM TO
SEE YOUR POINT, NOT DROPPING BOMBS
ON THEM..." HE TALKED SOME MORE
IT WAS AWESOME. I DON'T THINK MANY
IRAQI'S WOULD EAT FOOD AMERICAN'S
DROPPED ON THEM NO MATTER HOW
HUNGRY THEY WERE, BUT IT IS A GOOD
IDEA I'M SURE.

THE SANTA MANIFESTO

We, Santa Claus, Father Christmas, St. Ni
Kris fucking Kringle have decided that
are very very naughty and don't deserve
have **EVERYMAN** run up his credit card
satisfy your **GREED**.

SANTA CLAUS IS NOT A BIG FAT WHITE M
ANYMORE HE HE IS **UNEMPLOYED** HE IS A PC
STAR HE IS A MIRACLE ON **SKID ROW** HE IS
STRIPPER HE IS SLEEPING IN A **HOMELE**
SHELTER HE IS A **DRUNK** HE IS A **WHORE** HE
FUCKING **PISSED OFF**.

TIM ALLEN IS NOT SANTA!!!!!!!!!!!!!!

Santa's secret army of bastard children l
has fathered will Sneek into your departmen
stores and **SHOPLIFT** all your stupid as
Shitty toys to give away to kids. You wil
be **CLEANED OUT**. Merry fucking christmas t
you and to all a good nite!

SANTA is on strike
Santa is on strike'
Sant a is on strike

THE SANTA STRIKE

december 16, 1998 – bloomington, IN. I had gotten my santa outfit together: a red and white checkered bikini, maroon stockings, a $3 beard from Costume Delights, a feather boa from Vintage Used Clothing, and a Santa hat I'd had for a while and didn't know what to do with it. I needed some better shoes, knee high boots or something but I was running out of time anyway. The manifestos were all printed and my shopping bags of coal were loaded up and I was ready for my first stop: the recruiters office. I was a little disappointed by the reaction I got but when I pulled out the coal they said "You're giving us coal? Why." I didn't say Baby killer or anything like that I just said cause you work for the military and went about my business. "They said for protecting you so you can wear crazy outfits." Oh my they were sure outwitting me but I wasn't there to argue Santa had a lot of stops to make still before Christmas. Some young men were hanging out outside rhino's that night and they had a good laugh I said "Ho ho ho!" and they laughed and said "You're a faggot, man" and "Deck the Halls, motherfucker."

I proceeded to citizens bank where I got an overall good reaction I wasn't being too obnoxious though. Then I went into another bank ONB and shouted Merry Fucking Christmas I could tell they were a lot more scared I deposited some coal and leaflets and got out of there. In Bank One a security guard eyed me as soon as I stepped in the door I stayed low key until I got past him then started yelling. I headed for the alcoves, I was trying to get to the back where the business men were, I didn't want to pick on tellers but I couldn't find any and the security guard started following me. I walked faster and ran into a dead end, turned around and the guard said come here. He told me to take it out on the street, I told him merry christmas and left. A man stepped out of Ladyman's and said "You look nice, Santa." I laughed and said "Ho ho ho."

I walked down college spreading cheer and passing out coal and flyers to the occasional man dressed in a suit. Someone asked me if I was Bart I said No I'm Santa Claus and moved on. On a long shot I went to the justice building I was thinking of delivering some presents to Judge Todd but I doubted they would let me in the building. To my surprise after going through the metal detector, x-raying my shopping bag of coal, and looking under my hat, beard, and bra, they let me in. They asked me where I was going. I said the clerks office, the first thing that popped into my head. I wish I'd picked someplace better but then again I was glad I didn't get arrested. I went into the clerks office and they laughed, one person asked to take a picture. I managed to get a lot of coal and pamphlets passed out to the poor clerks and started to walk out when the lady said Hold on a second let me get a picture. Then someone read the flyers and they said oh my god look at this and someone said "Get Pat get Pat" and the lady that wanted to take my picture said you'd better get out of here. I took her advice. Out on seventh street some naughty construction workers whistled at me and I yelled some cheery Christmas slogans at them.

Next I went into "One City Center" the building with congressman john hostletters office I am really confused about what is the showers building and what is city hall I've never been able to understand that. But anyway it was pretty empty so I went looking for his office. The door was locked with a sign that said knock for entry. I was too chicken to go in so I started heading downstairs. A businessman laughed a bunch and said "Did you come from Andy's? office?" I said know who's Andy. He asked what I was giving out I said coal and he laughed and laughed. " So what are you doing this for? Donations?" I said no. I should have said yes it would have been awesome. He started walking up the stairs saying "Boy, I would love it if someone did that at my office." I called after him "Hey I can go up there if you want me to." He said "Wow that'd be great!" and went up to check on his office. unfortunately no one else was there. I gave him and one of his friends a piece of coal and left.

As I was walking down Lincoln towards Kirkwood a car stopped and rewound. One of the young men inside wanted to have his picture taken with Santa. I asked if he wanted to sit on Santa's lap and he said No. Well his friend took his picture and I continued on my way. I looked at a thermometer it was 42 degrees cold but not unbearable

At McDonalds I passed out coal to all the customers for being so naughty, then the manager asked me to leave. I walked past peoples park where some white people called me a fag, a flamer and told me to get out of here. I ignored them and stopped and talked to a couple of people I knew. one of whom suggested I go in Nick's bar and grill I did, and passed out some coal and flyers to the unsuspecting customers. I decided to try and go to city hall I really wanted to give coal to urban forester lee huss who had caused a tree outside our house to get chopped down. I stopped by this ad agency, and this kid that used to live in collins was working there. They let me come inside and gave me a cup of coffee which I accepted even though I usually don't drink coffee. it seemed a lot colder and I was losing adreniline. I went up to 7th street to try and find city hall but no luck I felt dumb as rocks. I was waiting to cross college when I noticed a police car wasn't moving even though the light was green. I waited until the walk sign lit up then

I start ed across the street only to be motioned over to the police car.
The officer. a chunky male with brown hair asked me a few silly
questions and asked for I.D., I didn't have any. He told me to stand
against the wall. another officer was coming to talk to me about what
I'd been doing on kirkwood. I said I didn't think I'd done anything
wrong and just sat on the curb. I was really freezing now. I asked if I
could wait in the police car because I was cold. he said I wouldn't be
cold if I didn't wear sleeveless tops in winter. I ignored him and got in
the car. When the other officer got there he said "Get out of the car
sweethart" and interrogated me. He had a blond crew cut. He asked
why I was doing this I said "A joke" He said "You think this is funny
huh no one else thinks its funny" I said "What do you mean everyone's
cracking up." He said "Well maybe the outfit is funny but that
literature's not funny. The people at the bank considered it a threat,
that you were going to go in there and take all their money on
Christmas Day," I said "I didn't intend it to be a direct threat, I'm sorry
if you interpreted it that way." The dark-haired officer said "That
coal's not funny" and this gave a new argument to the crew cut cop.
"You were spilling coal all over the county clerk's office. someone's
going to have to clean that up." He asked me if I had a job I said no.
"Well some people have jobs they have to clean stuff like this up." I
felt really really bad then. I told them I had to go at a final at 5 oclock
in Ballantine. the dark-haired office said "What room?" I said 013 he
said "That's a computer lab I believe. is that a computer test." I said no
it is a lecture hall I think I've never been there before. Meanwhile the
crew cut officer said "You were going dressed like that?" I said "no I
was going to go home and change before you gentlemen stopped me,"
and the other one said "Your house is that way. it doesn't look like you
were going home," I said, "I was going to stop by the Shower's
building first" The dark hair officer said "Something's not right." real
sarcastic. I said what, he said "I was talking to him. Something's not
right up there," and pointed to his head. The other officer laughed.
They told me I was officially given trespass notice for all the
businesses I'd went in and that I was free to go. I asked them to give
me a ride to my final they said no. So I walked to my final and
everyone laughed at me a bunch, I was late, took it. It was hard writing
my hands were numb. I hung out at ballantine until the A R A meeting.
Jesse gave me a ride home.

TROUBLE ON TANK TOP
by Sterling Gray

J. R. Tisk could definitely be a lady's man, but the fact is he wasn't. J. R. Tisk was a man's man. He was a troublemaker, a risk taker, a heartbreaker. As far as it went in the rich world, he wasn't amazingly wealthy. Considering the fact that he was a billionaire and he'd never owned stock or had a single employee, J. R. Tisk was doing pretty good. His business card read:

> ## J. R. TISK.
> ## No Masters No Slaves,
> ## Only Predators and Prey.

He was dashingly handsome, *Sexy* was a word no one was embarrassed to use when describing J. R. Tisk, or Mr. Tisk as he was often called. While in space he usually wore his skin tight silver and black flight suit. Rumor had it he was missing one testicle, but if so he never let it slow him down. He was always on the prowl, looking for intercourse.

It was well known that a single night's sexcapade with Mr. Tisk could make or break your career as a homonaut. Many a hot young pilot has been simply because he'd had a little too much to drink and was a little too nervous to satisfy J. R. Of course J. R. didn't mean it to be this way, but people in his business could be just as sheep-like and close minded as the poor heterosexuals. No, take that back. Not that ignorant, but that's not saying much. Let's just say if you reached the point in your career where you had an opportunity to work with J. R., and you blew it, zippers wouldn't unzip when you were around anymore.

The youth he was with right now didn't have anything to worry about. J. R. felt the throb of the ships Ass-Cock Drive synchronize with the rocking motions of the blond haired, well-toned fellow who was riding J. R.'s prone body. He could feel J.R.'s cock deep within his bowels. J. R. absent mindedly fondled the young man's cock and he new that soon he would be in a place beyond space and time, where his primitive, natural ecstasy would be tapped by the ship's drive. Soon there was no more room for thoughts in his head as the rocking reached a fevered pitch and his partner began to moan. All too soon it was over, and the ship's computer turned on some soothing classical music and prepared drinks for the two satisfied space travelers.

J. R. looked at the computer report with satisfaction, unstrapping the young man from the safety restraints and kissing his nipple. "You did it, baby. Simultaneous orgasm. We covered over 600 light years. Three hours of cruising on the hydrogen thrusters and we'll be relaxing in the space port."

When Ian Holmes invented Queer Physics in 2004, he unleashed a vast social change he could never have expected. The act of intercourse between homosexual men and women created enormous *[handwritten: not between men + womyn but men+men and women+women. —ed.]* potential energies of a form incomprehensible until then. These forces, kept leashed inside the minds of most humans, allow the barriers of time and space to be transcended. These amazing theoretical devices led to the Ass-Cock Drive, and, later, the Labial Transmogrifier, allowing queers to dominate space. Indeed, heterosexuals couldn't even be passengers on a ship without destroying the delicate psychic balances that allowed the boundaries to be transcended. Only through months of intense sensuality training could a heterosexual become possibly become aware of his own feelings to the extent that he or she could participate in a space voyage.

He looked down at the exhausted boy, who had fallen asleep. J. R. covered him up with the black satin sheets and tiger striped blanket and laughed.

*

In the cramped corner which served as the ships kitchen, J. R. prepared pasta. He let the task absorb his totally relaxed mind. There was always a lot of worry before an Orgasm, if things got out of control at all you could end up 40 or 50 light years away from where you planned. And if things really messed up, there could be a new black hole where your anus used to be, slurping up planets and stars and people until the end of time. People had always known, intuitively, that the energies behind sexuality were unlimited. Finally science had finally been forced to acknowledge the fact.

J. R. stepped into the drive room to get some garlic out of a cabinet next to his bed, where Peter was awake and thumbing through a book "Why do you have this? You can't tell me you read stuff like this." Peter said. J. R. replied curtly "What I reads my own business, unless you want to borrow it. I take it you don't."

"I understand believing in freedom of the press, but this?! This is homophobic trash!"

J. R. tensed at the harsh accusation. He took a deep breath, and tried to relax. "I don't owe an explanation to you, and your rudeness has lowered my opinion of you a notch. But I'll give you one. That's an interesting word you chose to use. It's meaning has changed a lot over the years, especially its connotations. Consider how the context behind it has changed since when it was first used. Many doctors still considered homosexuality to be a disease that must be cured. Now we are part of a culture, a real, very powerful culture, where queer ideas, emotions, beliefs and thoughts are prevalent and highly valued."

Peter snorted. "You can't tell me you thing homophobia doesn't exist! There's got to be a billion margies on earth, and as far as I can tell they're a lot worse off then ever before. And we brought shit with us from Earth, ideas and conditioning that isn't going away easily – and there's still going to be tact-conditioned hets up here, spying and exploiting as always."

"I didn't say that. This universe is far from perfect, especially Earth. All I am saying is that here and now, the word homophobic has more in common with 'traitorous' than with 'racist,' it implies an admissibly negative bias against a culture."

Peter frowned, uncomfortably. "You're worming around with words. Almost any clever person can do that, anyone can say 'I'm not really speciesist, but those goddamn aliens give me the creeps!' What your saying doesn't have anything to do with that book you have there. I'm not trying to censor you, I'm calling you on your shit."

J. R. took a long look at the book, *Things Never Change*. "This book doesn't say one negative thing about homosexuality, queer lifestyles, or in fact any personal lifestyle choices at all. In my eyes that is what constitutes homophobia, fear of another person's intimate thoughts, actions, and feelings. What it does criticize is the culture and society we live in – a society that is often passed off as utopian, anarchistic, communal, and free. In reality it is a privileged elite culture, created by the exclusion of the minority. Of course this culture is more progressive, more open, and more egalitarian than any other technological society, but we have also inherited an enormous wealth, all the knowledge, experience, and materials that the stars hold. How could we trifle over the small things any decent human being hates to struggle over, food, air, personal space? The margies on earth, the various queers, transvestites, and feminists who can't stand earth and for one reason or another, but are stuck there, they are the ones who pay for our affluence."

Peter gave J. R. a harsh look. "There was a word you were very careful not to use, 'exploitation.' It's implied, though. And I don't see how you can relate what goes on here to exploitation. All the things you say we have inherited have been earned, I don't think we can ever imagine how much work went into turning the cutthroat cowgirl queer outposts into this civilized universe we live in. You know about the Y2K station, right? The hets started killing each other for air and end up wasting it all, ten minutes before Bacti Soor arrived with an emergency tank of oxygen big enough to keep them breathing for three months. Even after that, they still charge for air, and if you can't pay, whoosh, out the door."

"Even after that!" J. R. laughed. "There aren't many places you can go that still charge for air. Tank Top Station's one of them. That's where we'll be in about thirty minutes."

Peter was stunned. Their mission was secret, and J. R. hadn't let him in on the itinerary, mainly because Mr. Tisk didn't know himself. Their destination had been transmitted to the computer by sub-libido transmissions. He let himself be distracted from a discussion he wasn't much enjoying, only asking one more question. "You quoted from that book almost word for word. I guess you must have studied it pretty carefully."

J. R. sat a plate of pasta on Peter's lap and switched the observation windows to transparent. "I guess that might have something to do with the fact I wrote it."

*

Peter walked the corridors of Tank Top Station, full of food and ideas from his voyage. The air had a stale taste, slightly ozony, always reminding you the air had been breathed a thousand times. Based on a physical evaluation, the amount of air Peter inhaled had been estimated at _a lot_ . The Commerce Authorities would charge his account each day for that much air. Yes the Commerce Authorities. There were breeders on Tank Top and they'd brought capitalism and bureaucracy with them.

Tank Top had started out as a little Queer Cowgirl style outpost but a generation ship swarming with about half a million breeders had picked Tank Top Station as its only hope survival, about twenty five years ago. They'd already been told to move on three times, tried to take over one world and been repelled, and been through a civil war by the time they got to tank top.

The rulers of the ship had been in firm control and the sentiments on the breeder ship were peaceful, so the Tank Toppers were pretty impressed. They also were also having a big problem dealing with a non human life form on Tank Top that came close to wiping out the whole human population, and needed the expertise of breeder scientists who'd been in deep space for over a thousand years.

The good will of the breeders couldn't change the fact that they were from a primitive, sadistic, homophobic society, Mexico Earth, and this was internalized in their languages, customs, and social institutions. However these people were desperate and willing to try anything, they were a lot more able to adapt to new conditions than most of the Generation Ships. Most situations like this in history ended in tragedy, for one side or the other.

Peter stepped into the a restroom and used a urinal. When he stepped outside, he noticed a woman carefully scrutinizing him. He nodded at her and began to move briskly forward. She smiled and extended her hand. "I'm Esperanza. Welcome to Tank Top, homonaut."

Peter reached out his hand to shake, but her hand deftly avoided his and she rubbed it across top of her head. "Oh no you don't," she chided "I heard the sink running in there, but your hands are still dry. Who do you think you're fooling, fly!"

Peter was flustered. He didn't really understand what she had just said but he assumed it was some sadistic childish dominance gesture. Now he was trapped in a situation that made him feel very uncomfortable, but he wasn't about to give up. Just retreat a little, to more comfortable grounds. "Do you know where there's a cafeteria around here? I'm a little tired from my trip and I could really use a cup of coffee."

"I'll bet you could." she smiled, showing teeth like a wolf. "The main cafeteria is on Tank Top Central Corridor, go a hundred meters down this corridor, take the lift on your left two levels down, and follow the signs. I'll race you there. Good Wood!"

With that she was off running down the corridor, and Peter had no choice but to take off after her. Her long hair was flowing down the hall but she ducked down a side corridor and disappeared. A shortcut, he guessed, and decided to follow. He came to a dead end, a primitive looking wall of sheet metal with no visible means of getting through. He shouted "Open!" in Mexican, Swahili, Tetum, and three or four less common languages, but no friendly automatic doors would perform their function for him. Defeated, he turned around and began to work his way back to the corridor he started in.

He was slightly sweaty from the short run and a little out of breath. He thought about the tiny oxygen intake monitors some Tank Toppers had attached to their necks, so they could get a little better rates on air, and shuddered. He walked slowly down to the lift, and in about fifteen minutes he was strolling down the Central Corridor.

The Central Corridor was a very different experience from any other he had ever walked down. The art seemed to have no underlying theme or style unless it was, consume, consume, consume. There was very little self expression, and for the most part he found it unnerving and incomprehensible. Glaring, huge clashing letters urged him to Tank Up at Tank Top, Ride the Wild Horse, and Breath Deep To Feed Your Mind. He almost missed the universal cafeteria logo behind a newer commercial display for herbal extracts.

Once inside, he looked around for Esperanza but didn't see her. He walked up to the espresso dispenser and pulled his titanium mug from his satchel. He ordered the machine to fill it but a red light flashed on the console and a unisex voice demanded that he insert five pesos. His account card had only dollars so he was left. An attendant behind him noticed his distress and directed him to a squat, ugly machine called Exchange. He inserted his card and was rewarded with a new card, marked in Mexican. His 20,000 dollar account had been converted into ninety seven pesos. He shook his head. That was about half of what he had, until he and Mr. Tisk got back to Garvey and received their payment. Peter had only been at Tank Top for two hours, not even setting foot on the actual planet, and his nerves were already racked from culture shock. He needed to sit down and relax in a booth, before anyone noticed he was losing his cool.

Peter took a sip of his coffee and leaned back. As he did he felt something moist touch his ear. He stood up quickly and spun around. Esperanza was laughing. "That was fast, homonaut, fast. Is that how they're training you at Stonewall these days! I'm definitely not impressed."

Peter laughed too, and sat down again, still a little on guard. "Why the fuck did you do that, it scared the hell out of me!"

"Maybe I'm in love," she said with an evil grin on her face. "Or maybe I just wanted to see if I could get a whiff of J. R. Tisk's scent on you."

Once again she had left him with nothing to say. J. R. Tisk was infamous, but it was strange for some clueless het on a backwards space station to know where he was and who he was traveling with, especially when everything else was kept as quiet as it was.

"So what are you doing here, exactly? It seems like you'd be kept fairly busy, not just chasing girls around the corridors and wasting all your pesos on coffee."

This was a question easy to answer. "Absolutely nothing. J. R. has some business on the planet, I'm free until I meet him, three days from now. Just as long as I don't waste all my pesos and get thrown out the airlock, whoosh, I'll be fine."

The rest of their conversation was small talk, the obligatory automatic pilot that made up most conversation. She left, without explaining where she was going, and Peter realized he hadn't really learned anything about her, just useless trivia about this shithole planet. He hadn't really much thought about what the planet was like, he hadn't had time to until now. It was a gas giant, one thing he could say was that it was breathtakingly spectacular, a swirling mix of deep reds and purples. He'd watched it in awe as he ate his pasta on the flight in. By the bulky, phosphorescent metal donuts that circled most parts of the station, he could tell that there were also vast electromagnetic fields and violent plasma jets that came with the beauty.

*

As Peter walked, the lighting system activated and dimmed in the areas he was in. He was in a section of Tank Top Station called the Corroded Corridors that had long since stopped functioning. He saw a lot of really fascinating ranch brands, and the image of a barbed wire fence cut in two and rusting that symbolized the Cow Girl movement in space. The old tofu ranches probably were depressurized now, to keep people from messing around in them. A lot of the more paranoid tofu ranchers had tons of booby traps to keep patriarchal authorities away. It wasn't very common but, like the razor blade in the apple, a lot of rumors spread around about children getting castrated fucking around on some old tofu ranch. Peter had grown up on a tofu ranch, when he was six he'd gotten a branded. He'd had it lasered off of him when he turned thirteen, allowing the tissue to heal. No grown man, no matter how queer, had a ranch brand. A lot of people thought it was cruel branding children, but the way it was done wasn't any more painful than getting a tattoo. What little pain there was just made you all the prouder to bear it, to be allowed to be a part of something meaningful, even if it was for just two or three years.

Today was the day Peter was supposed to have left Tank Top Station. J. R. had left a message this morning. "Keep busy. We're going to be here a little longer. Can you feel it?" That's all it said. Peter was getting really tired of Tank Top, and he was sick of J. R. not telling him anything. He knew J. R. dealt mainly in extremely precious substances, and in non-human knowledge. Because he had the enginuity and the balls to do it, J. R. could come up with a lot more stuff that kept the human race on the move than a lot of corporate entities. But it was no fun being treated like a child, left behind on this crappy space station with nothing to do but drink tea all day. He was thinking of taking a trip down to the planet himself, seeing what he could find, and making Mr. Tisk wait.

22

A stunning view of the planet caused Peter to stop his bitter ruminations. The viewports in this corridor had had their radiation protective coating stripped off by vandals. Vandals with a sense of raw natural beauty. The sight before J. R. was like none the somewhat jaded space traveler had seen before. The brilliant swirling purple and red gases of the planet were upstaged by a weblike network of brilliant, retina-searing lights.

A brilliant flash suddenly blinded Peter. He staggered back and covered his eyes. For a moment he was afraid he had been blinded, and would be forced to spend a week in a hostel recovering. After about two agonizing minutes, his vision recovered in a swift rush. Whatever had happened in the planet, it had released an enormous amount of radiation. The viewport's pseudo-glass had a tinted look to it now. The chamber was a lot warmer, and Peter was going to need to try to get out of there as fast as he could and find out what happened. He took one last look at the brilliant planet, when he felt a hand touch the small of his back.

Mr. Tisk's unmistakeable, insistent voice came from a deep black radiation suit with a black, mirrored helmet. "Don't worry. You'll be all right. I've got a shanty built in one of these ranches, and another rad suit for you. There's some medical supplies back there we can make sure that blast of radiation doesn't kill you. There won't be any lasting side effects, except impotence."

Peter followed J. R. back to where he had an emergency pressure suit stashed and a first aid kit. J. R. gave Peter an injection to help him deal with the symptoms of shock he was experiencing. He pretty much had to carry the lithe young man back to his shanty, which turned out to be one of several shanty's sparsely spreading this old ranch. Peter passed out while Mr. Tisk was preparing an infusion of herbs to neutralize the radiation and the tumors that were already boiling up on Peter's flesh.

In the morning Peter was awakened by a loud clanging and J. R. shouting "Soup's On." He got up, feeling as if he had been soaked to the bone in acid. He could feel the bandages on his head, and he guessed that J. R. had been a little more optimistic than candid in reporting his condition. He had probably been scarred for life.

J. R. stepped inside the shanty, and gave me a disapproving look. I've fixed up some tofu scrambler for these womyn about to go out rounding up soybeans all day, and there just happens to be a little left for you and me. But you shouldn't be up and walking around until tomorrow at least. You saw something that no body around here has seen or is meant to see for a long time."

Peter dug into the tofu scrambler with gusto, he found his throat was a little sore but not too bad. J. R. attentively noticed that he had difficulty swallowing and fixed him a cup of tea. After about ten minutes Peter was feeling a lot better and a little more curious.

"What are you doing up here anyway? You're supposed to be down on the planet doing who knows what."

"I am, as far as this world's concerned." J. R. pointed towards a corner of the shanty, Peter assumed he was trying to point at the planet Tank Top. "There's a strange phenomena that happens down there, Storm is a word that I wouldn't care to use for something that displayed such intricate complexity, obvious organization, and a changing period related to the mathematics of prime numbers. But it's a word a lot of people use?"

"Are you implying that this is a sign of life, in these hostile conditions?"

"That's exactly what he's saying," Esperanza stood in the doorway. "Now you two had better get moving before noon, there is a ship taking off to get you two bastards off this goddamn planet before you get killed."

"You're a cowgirl, Esperanza?" Peter asked idiotically.

"Do you see any cows around here? We make our tofu like they did back in the '60s. This is a queer luddite ranch." A cow is a robotic device used for farming, it could make a number of tofu products and assist in the harvesting and planting. Cows were what made the Cowgirl lands communal, they wandered around and ate what they pleased of the crops and shared with whoever was around. As long as everybody did their best to keep the cows fed, there was plenty for everybody, and a lot of extra to trade.

On the way to the ship Mr. Tisk explained what the queer luddites were to Peter, who was leaning on him pretty hard. "It's not something you're expected to learn about. The original group back on

23

Earth believed in a return to man's nature as a socially sophisticated non-tool using life form. The dominant culture at that time took it for granted that that homosexuality was unnatural, and not a part of normal primate life. Even when scientists discovered that homosexual relations were common and useful in primate social patterns this misconception continued. It wasn't until Ian Holmes developed Queer Physics was it shown that homosexuality was not only natural but functional, and could be tapped to produce a non-sadistic, stable culture that could span all time and space. But anyway, these people were proving that you could live naked, free, and queer, but they got massacred by rednecks. It was a lot bigger than some of the other killings that happened about the same time, but nobody really talks about it."

"So what about that explosion? What was it?" Peter said.

Esperanza said, "The web-storm's periodicity has been known for about three months. That gave someone time to get a project ready to go off during the time when all the station's sensors were shut down to protect them from the web-storm. I had disabled one of the pilons that block all contact with the outside, and J. R. set up a sensor array to collect some data on the web storm. The first day went fine then we were hit with a surprise, that shouldn't have been a surprise. Someone tested a weapon of mass destruction on that planet, at least two times in the last few days. Someone's planning on being capable of blowing up whatever they want. After I get back from taking you boys back to Garvey, I'm going to have to find out exactly what's going on."

The ship wasn't equipped with an Ass-Cock Drive. J. R. and Peter relaxed in the kitchen and drank tea all day while the women powered the ship with their lust. "So how'd you like Tank Top? A little too rough for you?" J. R. said,. Poor Peter had fallen asleep on the floor.

SORRY I LOST THE ADAM WHITE page YOU WILL Have to read this one instead. Adam is in a band called pinewood derby they sound like fifteen or the broadways. Here are some other bands I've seen recently.

ambition mission, from chicago, one of their members had a cold when I saw them play but she (annie, the bass player) kept screaming her throat to death. They had a screechy sloppy punk style, if you like the grumpies You'll like ambition mission maybe.

MUSIC

. Also I saw the band, nymb from Chicago, they were good, pretty indie rock, they had lots of energy. The singer broke guitar strings on two guitars, luckily they brought lots of extras. Also I got another chance to see what the new panoply academy line up sounded like - it's pretty good.

7": Spit where the liars live DISGRUNTLED recs 827 Somonauk St. Sycamore, IL 60178

Ali is in a band called the sissies they are having a CD release party at Rhino's Feb. 14. (maybe it's the 15th) I think the c.d. is called "geography." when is that guy at a treyu going to get the new Op.ll. out?

Flying Lesson #two box

pass la secret from me to you ☆

$1

Ali 338 S. Madison Bloomington, IN 47403

24.

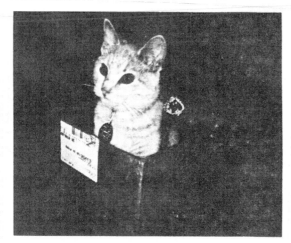

mr. tisk.

if youre nasty

AUBOUT THE AUTHOR

Sterling Gray lives in Ogden,
Utah with his two parents.
He is fourty-two years old.
He keeps busy working on his
new novel and working in an
adult bookstore. In his spare
time, Sterling enjoys watching
the trains go by.

Strap Yerself In

ISSUE #2 $1 PPd

on the ROAD

STRAP YERSELF IN

Strap yerself in is going on the road, with stories about my trip to the west coast a couple of years ago and a trip to Florida a couple of months ago. I couldn't get Sterling Gray to write a story for me I think he was dissatisfied with how the last one came out. the last Strap Yerself In, not his story.

I ♥ Topper

I ♥ Duncan

My name is sam, i live in bloomington, in at a house called the Madison with my friends. We do shows there, if you have a band that wants to play, call (812) 335-8439.

In december I took the greyhound to key west fla, the southernmost tourist town in the continental u.s. please don't ask me why I went to such a silly place it's hard to answer, I knew the town was really pro gay, it used to be a pirate hang out, it was an island and I'd never really spent much time on one. I imagined beautiful beaches but I was really let down by the beaches, and the anti-homeless policies of the locals kind of disappointed me. And meeting anyone I wanted to be around seemed like it was going to be tough. A couple of guys I rode in on the greyhound with, Bob and John, said they would show me the ropes of key west. I didn't really want to hang out with them but we got to town at 5:30 am and it was raining so I kind of went along. We saw a toothless guy sleeping under an awning by the waterfront, and John said "Look at that! How could you lose your spirit in Paradise?" His plan to keep his spirits high involved trying to rent a trailer by the week, getting a job on a fishing boat, getting drunk and stoned every night, and letting me sleep on the couch, they were fucked up rednecks but nice enough, I just couldn't stand hanging out with them. Instead of looking at the classified section, John first looked in the police reports to see if there was anyone he knew in jail that he could stay at their house while they were locked up. I told them I was going to get a room at the youth hostile until I could figure something smarter out, like a good place to sleep on the beaches, they told me that was stupid but once they realized there weren't any cheap trailers rented by the week that close to christmas in the holiday season they had me ask the hostile, the Sea Shell Motel, if they could stay there. I felt like saying, "Are annoying fucked up rednecks in their thirty's allowed to stay at your youth hostile," but I just asked if there was an age requirement and they said no. So my new friends came to the hostile with me. I sat my stuff down and walked around town. I loved seeing palm trees and roosters and if you got away from duvall street there were some pretty houses and really cool gardens but by about 2:00 I was going a little crazy by the trash cans stinking of beer, people's breath stinking of beer, the stupid trolleys. Also I didn't really believe that so many rainbow flags on businesses could be about pride, I was afraid that down in the islands they meant something different, maybe Reggae or Rastifari or something similar. It wouldn't have been bad, but since I was by myself and I was looking forward to three weeks of trying to survive here it sucked. I was losing my spirits in paradise.

I went to the waterfront to look at the boats and that cheered me up a bit. I saw a big sailing ship with a rainbow flag I hoped they weren't just into Bob Marley. I kept gettting lost but since I wasn't really going anywhere I tried not to care. I talked to a homeless guy he was pretty cool I probably would see him a lot.

THEN DOWN TRUMAN AVENUE CAME FOUR BIKES, LOADED WITH BEAUTIFUL, SLIGHTLY DIRTY CAMOFLAUGE PANTS WEARING PEOPLE, AND ALL THEIR CAMPING EQUIPMENT. I STARED IN AWE AS THEY DEFIANTLY RODE DOWN THE STREET, AND WENT RIGHT PAST ME. I STOOD THERE IN SHOCK, KICKING MYSELF FOR NOT SAYING ANYTHING, NOT EVEN WAVING. THEN THEY CAME BACK!

It was love at first sight I was so happy they rescued me. They told me they had came from gainesville, I didn't really know how far that was but I knew it had been at least 100 miles. I told them I hated key west and had been thinking about getting a junk bike and riding to miami. They hated key west to. The one with big soulful eyes and a big mountain beard that I later learned was sideburns said "We can help you get a bike and you can come with us if you want." It was pretty weird for me to have my wish come true and a beautiful vegan come rescue me and take me away on a bicycle adventure I was really scared. They said they were going to split up and meet me back Mallory Square at four. I went to the hostel, got some of my stuff, and wandered around looking for mallory square, I got really nervous, it was driving me nuts to hang out there. I saw a kid with crusty patches drinking beer in a bar.

Well I met them, and we hung out and went on the bike trip. Ryan Modee, the one with giant sideburns, helped me pick out a bike, helped me fix the bike up, helped me strap myself in, and said "Are you sure you're comfortable in that gear?" so many times. I tried to warn them I didn't know shit about bikes, that ten miles was the most I'd ever ridden before, and that I would probably slow them down terribly. Ryan Modee was like a vegan angel straight from heaven with one mission to rescue me from key west, he knew I probably wouldn't be able to make it since I didn't even know how to shift gears right, but him and Sam, the other Sam, a Canadian, really wanted to rescue me, get me out of there before I got arrested for biting a tourist or something. In a couple of hours I had ridden further than I'd ever ridden my bike before. You can read about the whole bike trip in a book Ryan Modee is writing right now. You can read about some of it in this zine PTBH!!!! That Rex writes, he's a person who got sick and had to take the greyhound home right before he made it to key west. **309 N. 6th Avenue / Pensacola, FL 32501.** Write to Ryan Modee and ask how the book is coming or write to PTBH!!! and order #6

My fellow bike pirates, I didn't get a chance to have Rex+Sam draw themselves

my encounter with
a bike god

it was early in the morning the day after christmas

we had been camped out behind a citgo next to some sort of filthy canal. The citgo was closed so we had to drink filthy brown water from the bathroom sinks. I stopped to adjust my basket and everyone else was stopped too. About 40 spandex wearing bikers zoomed passed us. One lagged behind. He said his name was Steve and he was from fort lauderdale but we all recognized his divinity because he had an enormous package his spandex did little to conceal. He was in need of assistance I believe it was a test of our hospitality. He said he had a flat tire and needed a pump. Brian offered him our Blackburn pump warning him it was broken and very difficult to use. In about three pumps re inflated the tires on his fancy road bike to 80 psi. His bulging package distracted us as he tried to give us an alternate scenic route through the clairmont area. He warned us about the dangers of cars and said as long as you have a helmet on, they would leave you alone. He said they would think you were training for the olympics. He said this road had the highest number of fatalities in Fla. we had seen a flyer about a deaf man with a bike with three baskets who had been abducted on this stretch of road so I was scared because I didn't have a helmet. My companions let me ride in the middle. To this day I wish we had taken the alternate route the being who called himself Steve had suggested... I often wonder what we would have found down that county road.

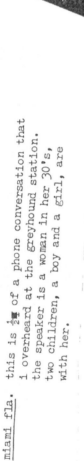

Go Greyhound
and leave the driving to us.

miami fla. this is $\frac{1}{2}$ of a phone conversation that
i overheard at the greyhound station.
the speaker is a woman in her 30's,
two children, a boy and a girl, are
with her.

Hello, I need to talk to Sexy.

I need to talk to Sexy.

She's a dancer there. She said I could call her.

Can you let me talk to Sexy.. She's a dancer there.
It's an emergency.

They aren't allowed to come to the phone?

I can't here you.

I can't HERE you.

i can't here you.

It's an emergency I need to talk to Sexy.

Do you have an address there?

OK.. (... pause ....)

Hello I need to talk to Sexy.

She's my sister, she's a dancer there.

It's an emergency.

Yes, I cando that.

Shit, hold on.

It's 305-871-8954. Tell her it's an emergency.

2

CAMINE CON CUIDADO

At the greyhound station in Lake City Florida I got out to stretch my legs and enjoy the sinful weather. I stepped into the station to check the time when this guy said "How do you do this?" I said what and he said "How do you get food out of this?" He pointed to a vending machine. He had a five dollar bill, so I asked him "How if he had any ones. He produced the doller from his wallet. I told him to put it in his machine, he put it in upside down. I showed him the right way to do it. The dang machine wouldn't take his dollar, it was a little too creased. So I offered to trade him one of my dollars. I put my dollar in the machine. I asked him no money came up on the lcd display. I asked him again what he wanted but my shaky self confidence was getting pretty bad. I pressed A2 and nothing happened. The machine made a tiny noise but no food was released. I pressed more buttons and pulled levers. I couldn't get his dollar back or his food out. It was a moment of great confusion and embarrassment, we were seperated by some great barrier. I bet he was starving. I asked him if he had tried this before he said no. I said we could try to get his dollar back he said, no no that's ok, and he left. I tried anyway but the manager jast said "No, no, I don't know what happened to your dollar. I can't do anything about it." My coach went on and on, I felt like I'd ripped him off instead of the fucking machine, I would have LiKED TO GIVE HIMMY DOLLAR.

WATCH YOUR STEP

especially around people with mullets!

all was swell...

but chaos brewed

An army of naughts took away the heart

they went wit
what they held
DEAR

Who Knows where

FOOLS fled

the wise wild ones stayed

BEFORE the Midwest goes.

2

Sterling gray sent me this letter, it's pretty upsetting I am pretty sad about it.

Dear Sam,

I was really dissatisfied with how your zine turned out. I really expected you to do something a little proffessional, but I guess I should have known. There were numerous editing errors, and I have a sneaking suspision you lost a couple of pages near the end. When I saw you at my lecture about Gays and Lesbians in the Federation at the Star Trek Haters Convention in Miami, FL, I couldn't believe you had the nerve to walk right up to me with a smile on your face like I was an old friend. I admit it was refreshing to talk with you since I'd spent the day with extremely maladjusted anti-trekkies, but it would have given me great pleasure to slap you in the face. If I ever write anything for your little zine again, please have someone else draw the cover. That was the most juveninile attempt at~~xhomageotigxart~~ I have ever seen. I intend to work with
depicting gay men
more   professional writers, like James Brand who writes for the excellent zine Oi-Punk, I think he calls it OxPx. I've never actually seen an issue but I'm sure it's better than strap yerself in.

                              Au Revoir,
                              Sterling Gray

I really hope he'll write for Strap Yerself In again some day.

ACROSS the Missippissi

the rest of this issue of Strap Yourself In is about a trip I took in the summer of 1997 across the Mississippi to the west coast and back. Sometimes I wish I'd never left the three states of Indiana, Ohio, and Kentucky that were the only ones I'd been in until 1996, when I was 21, but I guess I really learned a lot. I definitely met some cool people that really impressed me with what they were doing or how they lived their lives, it made me think why aren't I doing something like that? When I left I was really sick of walking down the same street in Bloomington and seeing the same things every day. I'd decided I wanted to be a male prostitute and had been told I would starve there was too much gay sex to be had for free in Bloomington. On my trip I'd change my mind about being a whore it's an honorable profession but not for me. I'd decided before I left, earlier that summer, that I didn't want to have any more relationships with girls at all, I definitely didn't like it, and that caused huge problems (as you can imagine.) I'd only been in three pretty short ones but that was too much for me. I imagined San Francisco and Berkely were full of cool, polititically conscious vegan boys. Maybe they are but I wasn't there long enough to meet them. ~~Also~~ I left at the end of May, July 1st I had to be back in Bloomington to go to court for Forgery, facing two to eight years in prison. It turned out all right, I just got put on probation (my white privelege saved the day) but I was really worried about it.

THE FIRST FEW DAYS of the trip...

I was traveling with my friends Justin, Ryan, and
Jesse. Jesse, Ryan, and Amanda had hopped trains
from Philadelphia, where they were before. From
Asheville, NC they'd hitchhiked to Bloomington and
stayed there a week or two. I'm not sure about
that. Ryan lived in Oregon in this Anarchist
community called The Land of the Lost or just the
land, that was our destination. Justin was from
Bloomington, he'd just got done with a semester of
college. Amanda, Christie, and Sasha, who was(is)
Justin and Christie's son, and Hannah were going
to meet us inx at the land, and travel by car. We
were going to travel by train. Justin thought it
would be better to leave from Lafayette, IN. so
we split up and hitchhiked there.
Here's a list of what I brought with me on the trip:
A backpack Justin gave me, a sleeping bag, pens and
pencils, $90, "Apocolypse Culture by Adam Palfrey,
a travel journal, a toy dog named Mudpuppy, a grumpies
tape, one spare set of clothes(the ones i was wearing)
a flashlight, an atlas, and maps of berkely, denver,
and San Francisco. Me and Jesse made it to Lafayette
but Justin and Ryan didn't make it until the morning
after next. All the kids in Lafayette were real nice
somebody let us stay at their house I can't remember wh
who. When Justin and Ryan got there, we found the trai
yards and spent the rest of the night there. It
was pretty loud. In the morning a worker asked us
to leave, the rest of the three days we spent there
(maybe two days) we had to hide out. No trains
really stopped there that were going west. We
split up again and headed to Illinois, on the highway
right above the train yard, where we'd try to meet up
again or else just meet back at the land.

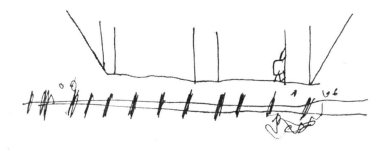

After we got a ride to I-70, a truck driver who was
delivering two u.p.s. trucks to portland oregon
picked us up about nine o'clock at night. He
told me it was dangerous to be hitchhiking at
night, that there were some bad peeple out there.
He said he didn't usually pick people up
but that he was worried about me. Sorry let
me get a few things straight. His name was Bill.
We were on I-74 heading west. And he was going to
Seattle, not portland. I promise to look at my
travel journals before I write any more. But
bill decided that he would let us go all the way
with him. He was kind of quiet and shy. I think
Jesse didn't really feel too comfortable hopping
trains without someone who knew what they were
doing along, and it was a lot easier and faster
to hitch hike, especially if this nice little guy
would take us the rest of the way and let us sleep
in his u.p.s. truck.
As we drove across Nebraska Bill told me that he
had seen all those kh stockyards full of beef
cattle when hey was younger(maxh) and all the
farms full of cows. Now since everyone was
against red meat and there were all those
vegetarians, the cowboy way of life was dying
off. He was real sad. I tolR him I was a
vegetartian. Oh yeah, I crosged the Mississippi.
It was at night. I saw the river Huck Finn went
traveling down none too well. I saw a billboard
for Pair-a-dice, a casino Chris and I have tickets
for. I lost my ticket but he still has his. We're
going to time travel back to '94 some day and
use them. Well the Mississippi's crossed.
Bill decided to stay at a motel, he told us we
could stay in it with him. I'd never slept in
a motel before, I would have rather stayed in
the truck. We spread all our dumster food out
and Jesse sewed a bunch of patches on her stuff,
I guess we made a huge mess. In the morning all
our stuff was in the hotel room and bill was
gone. All this happened in Wyoming.

b THIS GUY JOE gave us a ride to Dnever. He was
pretty cool I guess, he had Beavis and Butthead
toys in his truck that would tell jokes. He
was delivering stuff to Walmart in Utah.
He was from Wk Seattle and interested in
rainbow gatherings, he picked up a lot
of guys hitchhiking and helped them out,
he let a lot of street kids stay at his
house. He was definitely more interesting
to talk to than most of the people we'd
met so far. He told us we could meet him
back at the truck stop if we wanted to and
go on to Utah with him. I think Jess wanted
to, I was kind of sick of hitch hiking and
wanted to try trains again.
DENVER. My feet hurt real bad. We slept under
a bush, in the morning went to the library
and the thrift stores. I got some clean
socks. In my journal for this day it says:
Day 7. A long day in Denver. went to Boulder
too. Rode back from Hell.
A man came up to me outside the thrift shop
and said he couldn't help noticing the
blisters on my feet, and ask if I had new
boots. I said yes. He told me how to oil
up leather boots but my boots weren't really
leather. He told us he dumstered a pair of
jeans and the allen ginsburg book he was
reading. We went across the street to a
coffee shop where Jess' friend was working at
she talked to her and gotcaught up while
the guy who was interested in my feet kept
talking to me. He invited me to jerk him
off in the bathroom, I said no thanks as
politely as I could, and that I was going
to see what Jess was doing. She said it was
my chance to make that $50 I was always talking
about. We went to bouldr, where the college
students had rioted earlier that summer. It
sucked. A crack dealer gave us a ride in a
cab and tried to fondle jess on the way back
to denver and tried to give her $100. He
said she reminded him of New York City.
The moon was five times as big as I'd ever
seen it, Ithink it was because we were up

so high in the mountains. It sucked. we went
back to the train station to plot out strategy
and calm down. Jess drank a beer and told me
stories about people that got injured and
killed hopping trains, she was trying to
scare me out of wanting to do it. She said
she just wanted to get to San Francisco
where she had a place to stay with her ex
boyfriend, as fast as she could. That was
fine with me, it scared the fuck out of me
in boulder, a really rich town with tons of
free food. Also that someone had tolds us
that they used dogs to search the brains for
train hoppers in Utah and that was the next
stop in denver. So that was when we decided
to hitch hike the rest of the trip. A buddhist
gave us a ride to cheyenne, he had skipped
work and he didn't plan on going to cheyenne
he just gave us a ride there. It was nice.
From there we got several small rides, then
it started raining a little and so one of
us would stay under an overpass while the
other one stuck their thumb out, a guy driving
a tree topper to Salem Oregon picked us up.
This is a poem/scribble I wrote about my
friend Vaughan about this time, he told me the
last time I saw him he wanted no further contact
with me, that I disgusted him, and that he
wished he'd never met me before. I hope he's happy.

THINKING OF VAUGHAN, THE GOD OR MAN/PERSON
MY FRIEND. THEY TOOK YOUR FREEDOM, YES
IT DIDN'T MATTER YOU RAGED INSIDE, THEY TOOK
YOUR MIND, IT DIDN'T MATTER WE WERE BY YOUR SIDE.
NOTHING COULD HOLD US AS WE SOUGHT A SAFE SPOT; STEAL
GIVE LOVE FIGHT AND ABOVE ALL PLAY FOOL TRICK
DECEIVE. BUT THEN COMES FALL YOU DECEIVED
YOURSELF, I DECEIVE MYSELF ALONE WE FALL INTO HOLES.
I'M SORRY I LEFT YOU I'M SORRY YOU WISH
NO FURTHER CONTACT THAT YOU REGRET
HAVING EVER BEEN INVOLVED WITH ME
I DISGUST YOU, FUCK YOUR PSYCHOLOGIST.

Class War

we stopped at a truck stop/bar in ꭓꭓꭓꭓꭓꭓ east
oregon where jess and the guy we were riding with was
going to drink. I climbed up some rocks on the
side of a hill that seemed like a mountain
to me. A greyhound stopped and a bunch of kids
got out to take a break. It was beautiful
outside. I xk went inside the bar to see
what was going on. The guy we were riding
with didn't ave a drivers license. Whenever
we passed a weigh station he just had to zip
by. Since the truck wasn't that big we weren't
in too big a risk but no driver's license and
drinking and driving a commercial vehicle was
pretty bad. He read loompanics books, didn't pay
taxes, and was a mercenary so he considered
himself an anarchist. He was racist and didn't
consider the lives of people in africa to be worth
shit. He had gotten paid by corporations to kill
them before so I guess he knows better than
me how much they're worth. Jess just said he'd
been through a lot, he was a vietnam vet. But
anyway when I went in the bar I left my wallet
on the counter after they ID'd me. I went to
the bathroom and wrote class war on the bathroom
wall with a sharpee. Then I went out, the guy
offered me a drink, I declined. Then I noticed
my wallet was gone and started looking for it. I
went back on the hill to see if it fell out when I
fell down the hill. I looked everywhere. They
came outside to help me look. I x eventually found
it in the trash can in the bathroom with all the
money gone. All the people in the bar felt
sorry for me. Now, until chris could mail me my
didability check at the p.o. box at the land, all
the money I'd have would be from what I could
come up with. At least I had some I.D!

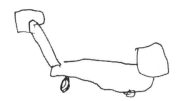

1

Fuck you Portland

we picked up some people, a girl and a nother
girl, named Fred and Manetta, they rode in the
back. I skipped some stuff about me driving
the tree topper and picking up a guy and giving
him a ride to Boise Idaho and sleeping in the
back and getting soaked in rain. Now I was
really stressed out and worried, the guy offered
me a beer I said yes, the first time i ever
got drunk. I'd read that it was easier to
survive wrecks if you were intoxicated and I
was pretty worried we were all going to get
killed. My lips felt real moist and I finally
argued with that ignorant fucking bastard about
racism. He said 'that girl is going to go
to mexico she doesn't know what she's doing
they don't respect human life down there in
a second they'll cut her throat to see
what's inside that backpack.' We stopped
and he said there was room for the ladies up
front, he told me how much he'd like to have
them sitting right next to him. So I sat next
to him when we all got in the car I was smushed
right up against him. I drank another Coors. He
mumbled something under his breath at me but
wasn't too upset. Oh yeah his regualar job was
making copper jewelry with his housemate in S.F.
In another hour or so we were in portland he
dropped us off near Pioneer Square is what it's
called. We crossed the street on a red light
and I yelled Fuck You portland and flipped off the
cars. Pretty soon I was spanging, drinking cheap
beer, and all that really productive stuff.
I got a metal splinter in my finger from a
dumster and had to shoplift some tweezers to
pull it out. We met this homeless guy that took
us to his campsite x that stank of shit. That
night I got to know Fred and Manetta a little better.
Fred was from France, I guess she was going to college
here, she had met Manetta in arizona i think and decided
to go travelling with her. She kind of wanted to
go to the rainbow gathering in oregon, i think
she changed her mind.

Spit on my friend
for a dollar wasㄴㄴ one of the things

Manetta said when she was spare changing, or she
would tell dirty jokes, like "Why does it suck
to be an egg? Eggs only get laid once, and eaten
once." She reminded me of what I think of ℞ Valerie
Solanis being like, the woman who wrote the S.C.U.M.
manifesto and shot Andy Warhol. That's
supposed to be a compliment to beth people, by
the way. Shew as from west virginia and was
wanting to be a herbalist. Me and jess thought
they were good people and we stuck with them while
we were in portland. At a soup kitchen I ate some
bread everyone else ate soup, it had meat in it. I
missed the community kitchen back in bloomington.
We met this kid T, who loved his dog bear more than
anything. He took us to the place he camped at,
under an interstate in the median of a highway, it
was a really good campsite. "The crack heads can't
make it across the highway," he said, and that made
us feel a little safer. I really hate sleeping
around strangers, it was a nice place to sleep. Alex,
the homeless guy we had camped out with last night,
came with us. When manetta was blacked-out drunk he
tried to kiss her and made advances towards her. It
was a pretty fucked up situation, he left. The next
morning he left a fucked up letter, condoms, and stuff
like that at our campsite. He was an artist. We
avoided him the rest of the time we were there.

During the days I would wander off a lot by myself,
looking for food, stealing books from the bookstore,
I went to 22? Burnside, the info shop a lot and tried
to find when food not bombs fed. My favorite park
was waterfront park, i liked the little garden with
all the squares in it xi arranged like a maze.
One said 'Another day another dollar' and had a
business man with a winder like a toy soldier.
Sometimes we'd go up on belmont street and spare
change, there were health food stores there were
I table scored good food like curried tofu. At
a grocerie store we met this guy Jaysen who called
himself a hobo and drank a lot and he became a
part of our little makeshift tribe. Fred hated
carrying herw huge pack, it had a skateboard on it
even, so w she got a grocery cart and jess did to,
We would load all our stuff in them and push them

B

around, taking turns doing that. For a little while everybody was pretty happy it seemed like. One night I hadn't seen anyone for a while and was getting ready to go to sleep behind a buddhist temple when I heard a clatter of grocery carts coming down the street and my friend's loud voices laughing, telling jokes, being themselves. It was so wonderful. I got up and went home with tmen.

The Rose Festival was that week, I'd go down there a lot and pick fries and icecream and so much other food out of the trash. Once I got offered a job as a carny, my best friend from second grade and the first boy i ever kissed had run away from mitchell and became a carny, so i thought about it but i don't think it's the life for me. One time I was digging in this trash can right in front of this family, a mother and her children, and was getting ready to devour my spoils, when the mother screamed "STOP!" and whipped out her wallet. "Don't eat that, Ill give you some money if you just go away! Throw that away and get yourself something to eat!" I was a little offended but took her ten dollars anyway.

I Miss the fire.

I went to this place called the Hangover cafe and ate an awesome Vegan Meal for two dollars. There was a show there that night but instead I went to this J-Church and sicko show someplace else. J-church had already played when I got there, everyone there looked like a jock, and they had little L's written on paper stuck to their heads. I felt out of place a little. Sicko played, they looked like jocks too, they sucked. I went back to the Hangover Cafe and went home with Dan from Bisybackson, to the Dustbin. I got really drunk there, drank two fourty's of malt liquor, and I can't really remember what happened. In the morning I went to reed college with Dan and Damon and made some phone calls, they made some tour calls.

LEAVING PORTLAND. I WAS CONFUSED, LONELY, SCARED.
UNDER THE OVERPASS I'D SEEN FRED AND SHE'D EXPLAINED
THAT THE COPS HAD COME BY THE MORNING BEFORE AND
SHOOED EVERYONE AWAY, AND THAT SHE HADN'T SEEN
JESS, T, OR MANETTA SINCE THEN. I SHOULD HAVE
STAYED WITH HER BUT I REALLY WANTED TO BE
ALONE AND THINK, I NEEDED TO GET AWAY. I LEFT
A NOTE FOR JESS AT THE INFOSHOP 223 W. BURNSIDE
AND WALKED AROUND LOOKING FOR HER, LET HER KNOW
WHAT I WAS DOING. I ATE A MEAL AT SISTERS OF THE
ROAD AND CLEANED UP THE BATHROOM THERE AND
SPARE CHANGED ENOUGH MONEY TO RIDE THE BUS
TO OUTSIDE OF TOWN. FROM THERE I HITCHHIKED
AND MADE IT TO EUGENE, OREGON, BY ABOUT 11 AT NIGHT.
I WENT TO THIS DEAD AREA OF MALLS AND MOVIE THEATRES
AND FOUND A BRAND FUCKING NEW NESTLE CRUNCH
CANDY BAR. I FOUND A BUS STOP AND TALKED TO
THIS LADY ABOUT BOOT-CAMP STYLE SENTENCES
FROM JUDGES SHE WAS STILL ON PROBATION FROM
RUNNING A CRYSTAL METH LAB, TALKED ABOUT
BEING HOMELESS AND STUFF. THEN I RODE THE
BUS INTO DOWNTOWN EUGENE. IT WAS GOING
TO RAIN I WAS SURE SO I STARTED LOOKING
FOR A DUMSTER TO SLEEP IN, OPENED ONE
BEHIND A SALVATION ARMY AND SOMEONE WAS ALREADY
IN IT. SLEPT ON TOP OF A PANCAKE PLACE.

9

THIS QUEER'S NOT BUYING

NO COMMODITY WILL SATISFY ME
NO JOB WILL SHUT ME UP
I DON'T WANT ANY OF THIS HATEFUL PIE
LOVE WILL LIGHT IT ALL UP

I WOKE UP IN EUGENE BY THE RAIN AND HOPPED
DOWN A STUPID EMPLOYEE YELLED AT ME FOR
SLEEPING ON THE ROOF I SAID I WASN'T COMING
BACK. I WANDERED AROUND FOR A WHILE MET
A GUY WITH A CANE AND A THEORY ABOUT STAR
TREK AND GOD FITTING TOGETHER AND THE FIFTH
ELEMENT, HE TOLD ME MOSES WAS A VULCAN.
I WALKED AROUND AND FOUND THE CAMPUS AND FELT
REALLY AT HOME. I FOUND THE UNION AND WENT
THERE AND WENT BACK TO SLEEP ON THE COUCH.
I SPENT THE REST OF THE MORNING LAZING AROUND
DIGGING THRU THE COUCH FOR CHANGE AND STOLE
SOME FOOD FROM THE CAMPUS CONVENIENCE
STORE, READING, AND WRITING BACK TO
CHRIS AND MAILING LETTERS. I FOUND A PSYCHOLOGY
EXPERIMENT THAT PAID $7 AND SOME TACO
TIME EMPLOYEES GAVE ME A BURRITO AND A
COKE. THE PSYCHOLOGY EXPERIMENT WAS
FINDING OUT IF BLIND PEOPLE COULD REMEMBER
VOICES AS GOOD AS SIGHTED PEOPLE COULD
REMEMBER FACES. I RODE THE BUS TO ICKY'S
OR WHAT USED TO BE ICKY'S BUT NOW IS A LIBRARY,
I MET THIS TRADER THERE AND TRADED FOR A BAG,
AND HE GAVE ME SOME WATERPROOF MATCHES, CARDS,
AND A POCKET BOOK ABOUT THE BHAGADA-GITA OR
SOMETHING.

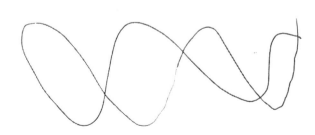

I MADE it to the Land, passing my friend Christie on the way back to the midwest. Justin and Ryan were at Crater Lake camping. So nobody I knew was there at the time. It's a really awesome place, the water comes from a stream and all the electricity is just in this one little area and comes from a few solar panels, that's where the kitchen is. Most people slept under tarps on these really cool tree platforms. I met some really neat people there, Meg, Mandy, Avvram, and Oppio, and Lee, he had a big school bus he lived in. When Justin got back I got made fun of for not being "Straightedge" any more, I was glad to see him though. It was really beautiful there, I got poison ivy from walking around barefoot. I didn't really stay there long, I felt guilty about getting seperated from Jess, and about drinking. I wanted to go to Berkely. The rides I got were short but most people were nice. One guy asked if I was bisexual and dropped me off when I said no. When I entered C.A. and they asked us to declare our fruit, one guy said "You have some fruit to declare! That banana in yer pants!"

JUST OUTSIDE OF REDDING I GOT PICKED UP BY
THIS MINIVAN WITH TWO GUYS IN ROBES IN IT,
ONE IN THE FRONT SEAT AND ONE IN THE BACK SEAT.
THEY HAD ME GET IN THE BACK SEAT. THEY WERE
ON THE WAY TO S.F. TO MEET SOME SORT OF SPIRITUAL
LEADER AND STAY WITH HIM. PALWINDER (the driver)
AND JAGWINDER WERE BROTHERS WHO LIVED IN VANCOUVER,
JAGWINDER WAS NICE HE GAVE ME A COKE AND SHARED
SOME CHIPS WITH ME, BUT HE COULDN'T UNDERSTAND WHY
AN AMERICAN WHO COULD SPEAK ENGLISH WELL
AND DIDN'T HAVE A JOB, CAR, HOUSE, AND EVERYTHING,
I TRIED TO EXPLAIN I WASN'T INTERESTED IN THAT SHIT,
ETHICAL REASONS. PALWINDER ASKED THE TOUGH
QUESTIONS, DID I BELIEVE IN GOD, WHY I DIDN'T HAVE
A WIFE, AND JAGWINDER TRIED TO KEEP ME FROM
HAVING TO ANSWER BUT NOT STOPPING HIS CURIOUS
BROTHER, WHO WAS MAD ABOUT THE ANSWERS.
JAGWINDER SAID IT WAS GREAT I DIDN'T HAVE A WIFE
KIND OF LEERINGLY I WANTED TO BE FREE. HE KEPT
OPENING HIS WINDOW I SMELLED SO BAD. THEY TAUGHT
ME SOME WORDS IN THEIR LANGUAGE TO KEEP
BUSY, AND AVOID AWKWARD TOPICS.

Yes = Han
No = Nahi
Hi = Sat shri-akkal
How are you = kee-hallay
Fine = THEEK
MOTHER = MADA
FATHER = PEDA
Thank you = EHINO

EAGHGURRO
GOD

SIK-
DHARAM

604-853-3361 PALWINDER SINGH

604-572-3618. JAGMINDER SINGH

Around Vancouver

I feel like I've been writing a lot about what happened to me and not much about how I felt. When I say I got a ride to Berkely I leave out how I was really scared by the Indians who had big moon shaped knives and got offended when I touched their chips after buying an underage girl a pack of cigarettes, and they asked me if she was a prostitute. They I stayed up all night, in a gas station then a horrible all night restaurant called pantyhose junction. In the morning I spent five hours by the highway in the hot california sun. I was off I-5 and easy rides were over. I was so close to Berkley but so far away. I had so many ignorant misconceptions about California, now I still do. But out in those beanfields I saw this horrible class division, people in volvos and mercedes ~~cars~~ going towards S.F., and people in beat up old vehicles that would honk and call me a fag. I got a ride to the East Bay ~~and~~ with a roofer who offered me a job. "I'd just have to get a Mexican to do it if I don't hire you."

In Berkely (...) not there yet, in some suburb that could be in a wealthy part of Indianapolis. I bought a walkman at a walmart and rode bus into Berkely. I listened to my Grumpies tape and some thing softened up inside me. I guess hitch hiking was really taking its toll on me. I really don't think I was ready to do all this stuff yet, I really hadn't had time to think. I was afraid I'd never find a place to stay in Berkely but it wasn't that bad. I cried a little on the bart ride it felt pretty good. I'd forgotten I was crazy, and I walked around getting lost and talking to myself again. I went to Smart Alek's and ate a vegetarian burger there, all I'd eaten was trash-picked chips for a couple of days I put my fries on the burger it was good. I called Chris' voice mail and told it I was here. I missed him, I missed Hannah, I even missed Frankie. I was so worried about Jess and stuff, But I figured she was still with Manetta and T, plus she could take care of herself better than I could. I went to the Long Haul, an anarchist info shop in Berkely. I listened to free radio berkely on my walkman. I slept under a bush near the library up at college. I wat people beat on things and get cleared away by cops.

l, in their opinion, becomes 1/3. The first to shout gets l, and the other two divide the rest either by "I cut, you choose" or by moving the knife again and shouting as soon as the perceived value reaches 1/2. (What should they do if two players

I met a juggling midget who was traveling the country by bike. He saw me picking trash and offered to buy me a meal at smart aleck's. I told him I had plenty of money I just liked to eat garbage especially in a clean nice place like berkely. He was a little freaked out I think, I felt bad and stuff because he was a really cool guy. I wasn't joking though, I hate it when the truth sounds like you are being a smartass. A guy with a pentagram tatoo on his forehead told me I looked depressed and offered to buy me an ice coffee (really this is the first thing that happened in Berkely). I told him my story, when I said I was from Mitchell, INdiana he said "I thought so, you talk just like a friend of mine named Marshall." I asked him if Marshall had red hair, it was the same Marshall all right. I used to play chess with him when I was in Junior High. "Yeah, I always had to translate for marshall, no one else could understand his mumbling. He's a cool guy he wants to go to Hell and become a demon. He went back to Indiana though. He likes it there. Hah!"

BARNES WILD ANIMAL CIRCUS

LY MORNING SCENE FOLLOWING THE ARRIVAL OF THE AL.G.BARNES CIRCU

The next morning I slept in the park until about nine a.m. (from about dawn) I met a girl who showed me where a church was that had free food, I ate some muffins and some coffee. She knew about all the places that had shows there. She wanted to go see a Christian band because it had cute boys in it. I'm sorry I can't remember her name, she was really nice to me. She let me stay in the burnt out frat house a lot of people were squatting in at that time. I'd talk a lot more about the people I met then but I can't remember any names. There was a big guy who would say "Hey hippy! Come here hippy, show me some love!" and offered to take me sky diving. He is pretty regular in the park, at least that summer (He was being friendly not hitting on me.) I met a girl named Free, a guy named FroHawk, a guy named Chicago who "owned" the burnt out frat house and had a cool homemade flag that never touched the ground.

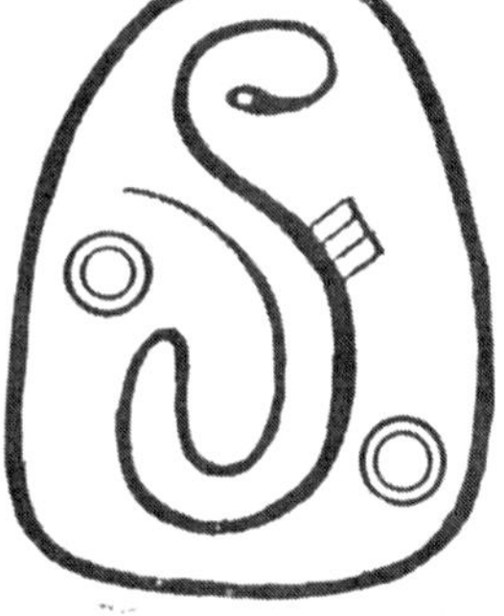

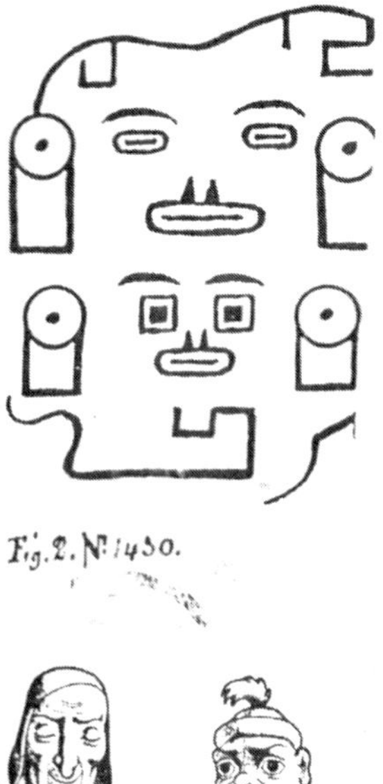

Fig. 2. N° 1450.

TAYCHR

A girl at the long haul told me I could stay
with her friends in a house in South Berkely.
They weren't as excited as her (this was
before I stayed in the burnt out frat
house.) I thought they were really cool
though, they were all freegan. They
had a Bike Library in their garage that
was really awesome: there were tons of
bike frames and parts. You could go there,
pick out a frame and put some wheels on it,
and then it was yours as long as you
didn't sell it. They would ~~put the bike~~
help you out if you needed it. I would have
loved to stay in Berkely longer, see Avail
and the Criminals at the Gilman, get a
bike from the bike library and open
up my own squat. But I wanted to
see Operation: Cliff Clavin, meet up
with them in Texas or New Mexico. I
was kind of worried that they would
be real upset with me (Chris) for fucking
up so bad or ~~free~~ just not able to understand
what was wrong with me. It would have
been hard to just leave them the next
day. I bet they would have put me on a
bus headed home. But I hadn't talked to
my parents for a year and there was no place

LIV:
AILEEN St. House
809 Aileen St.

in Bloomington to go home to.

Well the next night I went to San Francisco.
I had an adress and a phone # this guy
'Lance' lived at, he told me I could
stay at his house, he wasn't there, but his roommates were.
It was on Shotwell Street in S.F. I called them
up, I had lost the scrap of paper he gave me,
but just now found it. I rode the Bart
over there BART costs like $3 to get from
berkely to S.F. His roommates were bike
couriers. The next day I wandered around
the mission, went to epicenter, played
chess and lost money on a street corner.
S.F. is a wonderful place, at least the mission,
so different from anyplace I've ever been.
I would have liked to stay more but I wanted
to go back to Berkely and see this meeting
where gene wolf was going to talk about
her book, Asphalt Nation. One of the
beautiful bike couriers gave me a bunch
of this zines, CHUNK 666, about really
crazy homemade bikes and adventures,
to pass out. That made me a lot of friends
at the lecture, the ger freegans from
the bike library loved CHUNK 666.
Thanks so much Shotwell St. Bike
Couriers!

Library
Shoddy...

*1. Little Planet
bs. Judy's house.
114 Harrison/Kains

'ed. Chateau
2. SF/Hillegass

I couldn't figure out how to hitchhike out of Berkely. When I left I went to Oakland and got a greyhound to Sacramento. I called up Scott, from Secret Center record label, and Mike came and picked me up ~~from the~~ ~~Bananas~~. They were really cool, funny people and I probably had the most fun I'd had on my trip with them. ~~We~~ Also ~~there~~ this guy ~~Scott~~ Tristan was real nice, we hung out and listened to gospel records that were real funny. We played croquet one night. Mike is a musical genius I think, he is in a band called the bananas, In a town of catchy music he stands out, And he's one of the funniest people I've ever met. One day we went to a thrift store ran by two gay priests. It was the only thrift store I've ever been in that sold old food. I had a lot of trouble hitching out of Sacto. got hassled by the cops a lot, and I eventually just took a greyhound to Bakersfield. I hated the road but I felt compelled to keep moving, I'd been in three awesome places where I was welcome and stuff but I would only stay a day or so + move on.

Gilman
19th ...
Oakland

FOOD NOT BOMBS
2:30 PEOPLES PARK

BAKERSFIELD, CA, I RODE THE GREYHOUND ALL
NIGHT AND ENDED UP HERE. A ▓ GUY OFFERS
TO TRADE ME FOR MY BOOTS AND ENDS UP
DUMPSTERING NEAR THE BUS STOP, I WAIT FOR
THE CITY BUS LINE TO GET ME TO THE NEXT
INTERSTATE. I AM IN A HURRY TRYING TO MAKE IT
TO ALBUQURQUE BY JUNE ✶ 21 TO SEE OPERATION
CLIFF CLAVIN AT ALBUQURQUE, THEY WILL WONDER
WHAT THE FUCK HAPPENED TO ME BUT SOMETIMES
YOU GOTTA SWALLOW YOUR PRIDE ADMIT YOU NEED
HELP. I WAS THINKING ABOUT SKIPPING MY COURT
DATE + JUST FINISHING TOUR WITH THEM. ANYWAY
HERE ARE THE RIDES: ✺
AN EX-PROSTITUTE FAT 40-SOMETHING GUY THAT KEEPS
SAYING, YAH YOU KNOW HOW IT IS OUT THERE ON THE ROAD
AND CHUCKLING. BY NOW I AM REALLY USED TO BEING
HIT ON BUT HE OFFERS ME MONEY FOR THE FIRST TIME.
       🚂   NEEDLES, CA. ALL CLEANED
UP A TRUCKER GIVES ME A LOT OF MILES AND STORIES
THAT SCARE THE HELL OUT OF ME INCLUDING FIXING UP
STOLEN CARS VIETNAM STORIES AND THE LAST ONE ABOUT
A WHORE THAT DIDN'T SATISFY HIM SO HE KILLED HER.
THEN HE ASKS ME WHAT I'M PLANNING ON DOING AT THE
NEXT STOP I SAY GETTING ANOTHER RIDE HE SAYS
YOU'RE NOT GONNA DO FOR ME AFTER I TOOK YOU ALL
THIS WAY?

he asked if I wanted out
now. I said yes. I was 40 miles
from nowhere in arizona, no water.
no rattlesnakes crawled in my sleeping
bag.

NEW MEXICO ROLLED BY WITH A 20-something
CONSTRUCTION WORKER HEADED TOWARDS HOME
IN ARKANSAS WHERE HE WAS PLANNING ON GETTING
IN BED NAKED WITH HIS FIANCEE. HE PICKED ME
UP TO KEEP HIM AWAKE. IT WAS REALLY AKWARD
TALKING TO HIM BECAUSE IT SEEMED LIKE WE
WOULD HAVE MORE IN COMMON OR AT LEAST COULD
HOLD A CONVERSATION. BY THAT POINT I DON'T
THINK THERE WERE MANY PEOPLE I COULD
TALK TO ON THE PLANET. HE LIKED HEAVY
ALTERNATIVE LIKE KORN, HE'D SAY HAVE YOU
HEARD OF THIS BAND AND I'D SAY NO. HE TOLD ME
ALL ABOUT WORKING CONSTRUCTION JOBS AND
PHOENIX AND HOW HOT IT WAS, AND WORKING IN THE
BAHAMAS + PAYING $2 FOR A COKE. HE WAS BORING,
HE WAS SAFE. THE CITY LIGHTS OF ALBEQURQUE
STRETCHED OUT BEFORE ME, THEY SCARED THE FLYING
FUCK OUT OF ME, FOR SOME REASON I REALIZED HOW
BIG THE CITIES WERE. MAYBE IT WAS BECAUSE I
NOW HAD A DESTINATION: AN OPERATION CLIFF CLAVIN
SHOW TO SEE MY BEST FRIEND'S BAND. MY DRIVER
ASKED ME WHAT EXIT I NEEDED TO TAKE AND I
SAID THIS ONE WILL DO JUST FINE. HE DROPPED
ME OFF AT A GAS STATION. I SLEPT ON A
ROOFTOP.

Albequrque I woke up feeling the sun so hot on my boots that they were soft. I found the record store Mind over Matter where no one knew about a show. Later I found out it was cancelled. It was about the last thing I could take I was still thousands of miles from home and missed a chance to see someone close to me. Next to the record store was a dunkin' donuts I got a giant garbage bag full of hot, sticky donuts + wished I had someone to share them with. Jess loved ~~hot~~ donuts they were her favorite food back then. When I first met her she had this box of donuts from a grocery store dumster no one else was brave enough to eat. Jess is a really brave, strong person. She's so straightforward about what she's doing, she is always ready to explain honestly to about any stranger anything they would ask. She was a lot better at talking to "normal" people, or grown-ups, and she could pry some really interesting stories out of people. She wasn't ashamed of almost anything she did, she wasn't ashamed of her body, her smell, her parents, what she knew, what she didn't know, her hair, peeing, who she loved, who she didn't love. I learned a lot from her about being honest, standing up for what you do. Maybe I didn't learn a lot, thinking about it again, but she really impressed the fuck out of me, and I was glad to have spent some time on the Road with her. Those donuts sure did bring me a lot of memories and made me want to get back home (less) in one piece and make my court date on July 1st and see the Parade on my birthday and eat at the kitchen and sleep on the rooftops of the only town I knew.

AND I STUCK OUT MY THUMB
FOR FIVE HOURS ON THE
INTERSTATE I-40 AND HAD
TO BITE MY TONGUE SO MANY
TIMES TO KEEP FROM PRAYING.
A SEMI- TRUCK PULLED OVER HE
SAID WHERE YOU GOING I SAID
INDIANA he said
Me too HE NEEDED SOMEONE
TO UNLOAD HIS POTATOES. THRU
Amarillo, TX OKLAHOMA MISSOURI AND ILLINOIS.
HE MADE JOKES ABOUT FAGS ON HIS C.B. AND SAID I REMINDED
HIM OF HIS SON. HE WAS ONE OF THE BLANDEST
PEOPLE I'VE MET. WE DRANK SOME BEER
AND LIE NAKED IN HIS SLEEPER AND HE BEGS
ME TO FUCK be whispers in my ear. HIM IN THE ASS. HE
HATES HIS FAMILY LIFE, HE WANTS TO
BE ON THE ROAD ALL-WAYS. NEAR
INDY THE EVIL TRUCKERS NOTICE ME AND CALL
HIM A FAG ON THE C.B. HE IS SCARED + SAD.

IN INDY I TRY TO CALL SOMEONE I KNOW BUT HAVE NO LUCK ABOUT MIDNIGHT I TAKE OFF MY SHOES + START WALKING HOME. I GET A RIDE! HE DROPS ME OFF AT A BIGFOOT SO I CAN CALL A FRIEND BUT ALL MY FRIENDS ARE GONE SO I JUST wait for him to leave and then I walk away. The pavement is soft under my feet, it is nice to know what is coming next. I see someone I know who didn't know I'd ever left, we don't have much to say to each other. I decide its time to go to sleep. Up on the roof of the Fine Arts Building I find a stash of bagels + empty pans from before I left. I'm starting to realize I haven't been gone for years at all. I didn't run away, I took a vacation from doing nothing. I spread out my sleeping bag and go to sleep, listening to the Janitors take their smoke break and talk about when they were young and out-of-luck, and free. Going to Florida and finishing little kids hamburgers at fast food restaurants. Tomorrow I get back to work, I've got some books I want to steal, go eat down at the kitchen, try + call my Lawyer. If I see Tim I'll probably move in with him like we talked about before I left. Otherwise I'll take a nap in the library. But before I go to bed I'll call the Voice-Mail + tell my friend I made it home, THE END

STRAP
YERSELF
IN #4

(JOHN HINKLEY JR.)   (PEOPLE'S PARK)

(STONEWALL)   (PAPER DOLLS)

STRAP YERSELF IN #4. MAY 1st, 2002

I'M GETTING READY TO LEAVE TOWN ON TOUR AND FINISHING UP THIS ZINE. IT'S MOSTLY TRUE STORIES FROM HISTORY AT THE LIBRARY WITH SOME RANTS ABOUT G.W. BUSH. IT'S BEEN A WHILE SINCE I PUT OUT A ZINE SO THANKS IF YOU ORDERED A COPY AND HAVE BEEN WAITING YEARS. THE FUTURE DOESN'T LOOK SO HOT FOR AMERICANS BUT THAT'S ALLRIGHT I GUESS. I MADE THIS FOR MY FRIENDS IN PENSACOLA they ALWAYS GIVE ME REALLY TOP-NOTCH ZINES WHEN I NEED SOMETHING TO READ. IF ANYONE NOTICES ANY INNACURRACIES IN

THE STORIES in this, please let me know I'd like to learn more.

MY FRIEND BILLY JOE'S IDEA FOR PUNK SOLIDARITY

WHEN RONALD REAGAN DIES YOU HAVE 24 HOURS TO SHOTGUN A BEER

SUPPORT YOUR LOCAL PRISON BOOKS PROGRAM!

CONTACT INFO PO BOX 954 BLOOMINGTON, IN 47402.

TO CELEBRATE INTERNATIONAL Free Comic Day, this zine will be available FREE on May 4th, FREE COMIC DAY while supplies last. They will have some at BOXCAR BOOKS 310A S. WASHINGTON BLOOMINGTON, IN 47402

FREE COMIC DAY!
May 4.

COVER INFORMATION
My friend Paul is on the cover He wrote the stone-gil article. Photo by Riley. Write to him c/o Sam Dorsett PO BOX 954 Bloomington IN 47402. It's taken in People's Park.

WHAT'S IN THE WALKMAN?

Bananas, Cat Stevens, County Z, This Bike is a Pipe Bomb, Iron Maiden, Ramones, Shotwell, Miami, Kill the Hippies, Astrid Oto, Blank Fight, Random Conflict, Johnny Cash, Panty Raid, the Knitters, Devil in Electric

JOHN HINCKLEY JR.

BORN IN 1955 IN OKLAHOMA, JOHN HINCKLEY JR. LIVED THE "UTOPIAN" LIFE OF T.V. SITCOMS AND "DALLAS" AFTER THE FAMILY EVEN MOVED TO DALLAS

HIS MOTHER JOANNE ALWAYS KEPT COOKIES IN THE OVEN AND THE LAUNDRY CLEAN AND IRONED. SHE HAD TROUBLE ADJUSTING TO IMPERSONAL CITY LIFE AND SPENT A LOT OF TIME CRYING.

HIS FATHER KEPT THE FAMILY MOVING CHASING MONEY AND OIL. HE HAD LITTLE TIME TO SPEND ON HIS KIDS

HE WAS A QUIET SHY KID QUITE DIFFERENT FROM HIS BROTHER AND SISTER

HE BECAME **ISOLATED** HE WANTED NOTHING MORE THAN COOKIES, **BEATLES**, AND HANGING OUT WITH MOM

JACK HINKLEY WAS BECOMING **EXASPERATED** WITH HIS YOUNGEST, DIRECTIONLESS CHILD

NO FUTURE

NO FUTURE

IM PUTTING MY FOOT DOWN. HE'S GOING TO **COLLEGE**

I WANT HIM OUT OF OUR HOUSE!!!!!

YOU'RE GOING TO

COLLEGE

TEXAS TECH 1973

AT COLLEGE, JOHN COMPLAINED OF CONSTANT HEALTH PROBLEMS.

I HAVE A ROCKING FEELING IN MY HEAD

PRESSURE IN MY THROAT

I WANT TO COME HOME, MOM

HE GAINED WEIGHT.

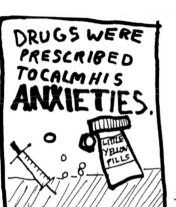

DRUGS WERE PRESCRIBED TO CALM HIS ANXIETIES.

LITTLE YELLOW PILLS

DEAR MOM AND DAD,

BY THE TIME YOU RECEIVE THIS LETTER, I AM NO LONGER IN LUBBOCK. I HAVE DROPPED OUT OF SCHOOL. I KNOW YOU'LL NEVER UNDERSTAND, BUT I'M TOO MISERABLE TO TAKE IT ANY LONGER. I HONESTLY WON'T BLAME YOU IF YOU GET MAD AND CUT ME OFF... I'M SORRY I'M DOING THIS TO YOU... I HOPE SOMEDAY I CAN MAKE YOU PROUD OF ME. LOVE, JOHN.

JOHN WENT TO HOLLYWOOD

LOOKING FOR HIS BIG BREAK AS A SINGER SONGWRITER AND A RECORD DEAL. AND FAME.

JULY

DEAR MOM, I GOT ROBBED. SEND MONEY SOON. LOVE, JOHN

WELCOME TO THE JUNGLE JOHN

MOM I CAN'T MAKE IT PLEASE LET ME COME HOME

WHILE IN L.A., HE SAW THE FILM TAXI DRIVER WITH JODI FOSTER AND HE BECAME OBSESSED WITH HER

JOANNE KEPT HER RECLUSIVE SON

SUPPLIED WITH COOKIES AND CASSEROLES

NO FUTURE

Dear Jodie,

There is a definite possibility that I will be killed
in my attempt to get Reagan. It is for this reason I
am writing you this letter now.

As you well know I love you very much. Over the past
seven months I've left you dozens of poems, letters and
love messages in the faint hope that you could develop
an interest in me. Although we talked on the phone
a couple of times I never had the nerve to simply approach
you and introduce myself. Beside my shyness, I honestly
did not wish to bother you with my constant prescence.
I know the many messages left at your door and in your
mailbox were a nuisance, but I felt that it was the most
painless way for me to express my love for you.

I feel very good aboutthe fact that you at least know
my name and know how I feel about you. And by hanging
around your dormitory, I've come to realize i'm the topic
of more than a little conversation, however full of ridicle
it may be. At leas you'll know I'll always love you.

Jodie, I would abandon this idea of getting Reagan in a
second if I could only win your heart and live the rest
of my life with you, whether it be in total obscurity
or whatever.

I will admit to you that the reason I'm going ahead with
this attempt now is because I just cannot wait any longer
to impress you. I've gotto do something now to make you
understand, in no uncertain terms, that I am doing this
for your sake! By sacrificing my freedom and possibly
my life, I hope to change your mind about me. It is only
an hour before I leave for the Hilton Hotel. Jodie, I'm
asking you to please look into your heart and at least
give me the chance, with this historical deed, to gain
your respect and love.

                              I love you forever,
                              John Hinckley

PAPER DOLLS

Buzz lives in San Fransisco and works in a punk record store and he drew most of the paper dolls.

Amy's in a band called the Mean Agers and she made a sewing zine for the contest

Marc Bolan Lives

50 YARD BUTTERFLY

BASE

BASE

cut here

cut here

cut them out
Glue them on card board WHATever

PAUL WORKS AT BOXCAR BOOKS
AND MAKES PRANK CALLS. HE WROTE
THE STONEWALL ARTICLE. HE'S
ON THE
COVER.

THAT'S
MR
BUZZ MADE
IT

ASK A
LIBRARIAN

CHRIS IS FROM SOUTHERN INDIANA
HE DOES A RECORD LABEL CALLED
PLAN-IT-X. WE'RE IN
A BAND TOGETHER.

UGLY
MEAN
NASTY

the Bulletin of Atomic Scientists MADE this thing CALLED the ~~Atomic~~ Doomsday Clock in the 1940s, when it gets to MIDNight, it's GOOD-NIGHT! for the whole human race. I

7 MINUTES to MIDNIGHT

the hands that COUNT Down Doom

Always thought it was a Real clock At some frightening UNIVERSITY but I think it's just ON the cover of the Bulletin. I'M NOT SURE when it STARTS FROM, RECORDED history OR the DAWN OF MAN. Reading the bulletin MAKES Me a lot less in awe of the DOOMSDAY clock but it doesn't MAKE it easier to sleep. they moved it back after the COLD WAR ~~ENDED~~. they closest its been is 3 MINUTES to midnight DURING ReaganStorm in 1984. IN DeCEMBER + ~~ERROR~~TERRORISTS blew up the INDIAN PARLIAMENT AND KILLED A FEW PEOPLE. AND the whole WORLD WAS ON the VERGE OF NUCLEAR ANNIHILATION BECAUSE INDIA was ~~on the verge of~~ INVADING PAKISTAN. PRACTICING the BRINKMANSHIP LEARNED FROM the UNITED STATES AND THEIR COWBOY MOVIES AND COLD WAR POLITICS. NOW the RUSSIANS lifted A BAN ON IMPORTING NUCLEAR WASTES AND the U.S. is taking MEASURES to SECURE its place AS A to TALITARIAN NUCLEAR POWER READY to REALIZE its apocolyptic MONEY DRIVEN MENTAL ILLNESS BUT I GUESS hat's OLD NEWS. UMM, theyRES a lot of OLD NEWS IN this.

You CAN OFTEN FIND Bulletin of Atomic Scientists AT LIBRARIES.

WHAT I'VE BEEN READING

DESPERATE TIMES #8. This zine by my friend Janelle made me laugh out loud at 8 in the morning when no one else was around. Great comics and writing about poverty bad dates booze gay porn fucking shit up and culture.
Po Box 4047 Berkely CA 94704

TERROR IN the TROPICS: The Army Ants by Tom Lisker. This childrens book is fixated on proving that army and legionary ants aren't superior to humans and won't take over the world and pick the flesh from our bones. The "kiss" of the scout ARMY ANT is a cry for help that can lead to the devouring of animals the size of A HORSE.

I HATE this Part of Texas I read three of these in A ROW one day and they all blurred together but it's a good thoughtful zine about hanging out thinking reading and drinking, folk music, wingnuts, Stonewall Rebellion. Po Box 251766 LR, AR 72225

THE DILINGER DOSSIER This conspiracy theory book claims it made J. Edgar Hoover freak out and fire people, about how the G-men nabbed the wrong guy.

DORIS I just finished READING #19 it's AMAZING from anarchism to cats, nothing else you really NEED TO KNOW, not really BECAUSE it'll MAKE YOU WANT to LEARN everything.
Po BJ734 Asheville NC 28802

FINGER ON the Trigger #3. My friend Ada's zine, about racism AND PUNK Rock with fucked up emails, A story about a bandit named Railroad Bill and other stuff. 1214 N 7th Ave. Pensacola, FL 32503

Singing GARBAGE AND HARDWARE by Ryndee. if you ever thought you couldn't make music because you'd never get any cheap good instruments to play around with get this zine! Us Singing saw, stand up BASS banjo allegedly made from a few parts. 918 E Gozale Pensacola, FL 32501

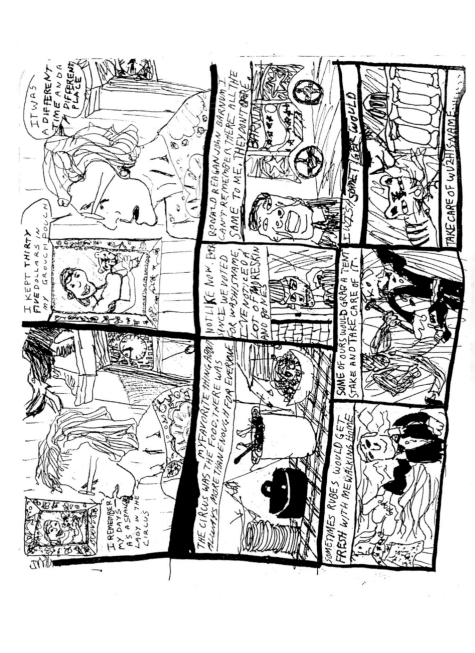

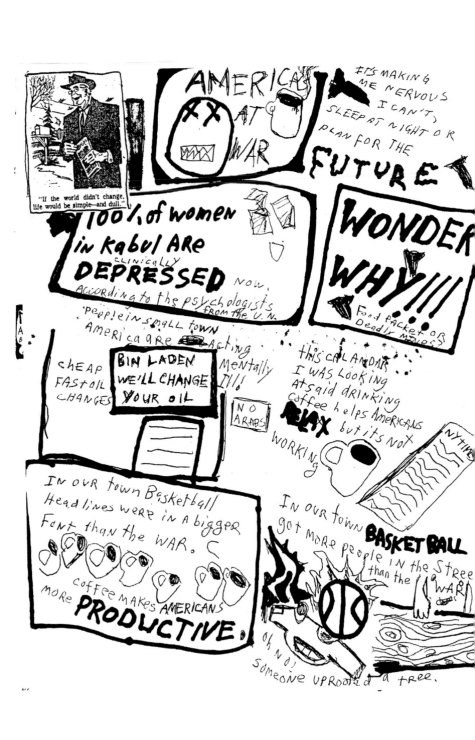

AS THE DEATH TOLLS RISE, I REALIZE A LOT OF INFORMATION IS UNAVAILABLE, THANKS TO CAREFUL MEDIA CONTROL LIKE ARMY PSYOPS AGENTS WORKING FOR CNN

7 MINUTES

THE POLICE HAVE MORE TOOLS THAN EVER AT THEIR DISPOSAL TO ACQUIRE OR CREATE EVIDENCE, AND FEWER RESTRICTIONS ON THEIR ACTION

DNA TESTING

NARC

300 MHz

FABRICATOR

I READ AN ARTICLE ABOUT A MAN IN NOBLESVILLE, INDIANA WHO GOT ARRESTED FOR BURNING ONE OF THE COMMUNITY'S AMERICAN FLAGS IN PUBLIC.

HIS PUNISHMENT INCLUDED A RESTRAINING ORDER TO STAY AWAY FROM ALL UNITED STATES FLAGS. WHERE

AGENTS OF THE POLICE STATE WILL HAVE TOO MANY RESOURCES ON THEIR HANDS.

WHERE DOES HE GO???

IN THE EARLY NINETEENTH CENTURY WHEN THE PINKERTONS BEGAN DEVELOPING THEIR PHOTO FILES (WHICH WERE A PROTOTYPE FOR MODERN LAW ENFORCEMENT) THEY WOULD GO TO GREAT LENGTHS TO GET EVIDENCE ON THE TRAIN ROBBERS AND SAFE CRACKERS AND UNION ORGANIZERS AND INSURANCE SCAMMERS INCLUDING SETTING UP FALSE BARS SIMILAR TO ONES FREQUENTED BY ▓▓▓▓▓ AND SUPPLYING RIVERS OF LIQUOR AND HEAPING PLATES OF HEARTY FOOD TO UNSUSPECTING WORKERS.

IT'S ON THE HOUSE

JACK DANS

XXX

GOMER PYLE IS FUCK

WE'LL ALWAYS HAVE SECRETS.

PLAN-IT-X RELEASES

A somewhat complete history of Plan-It-X Records releases as of April, 2014.

PIX001.1 THE TED DANCIN' MACHINE "SAM" TAPE
PIX001.2 INSTINCT "S/T" TAPE
PIX001.3 THE LATCHKEY KIDS "S/T" TAPE
PIX001.4 THE DIRTYS "S/T" TAPE
PIX001.5 THE TED DANCIN' MACHINE "SON OF SAM" TAPE
PIX001.6 OPERATION: CLIFF CLAVIN "S/T" TAPE
PIX002 OPERATION: CLIFF CLAVIN "TOP SECRET" 7"
PIX003 OPERATION: CLIFF CLAVIN "FREEDOM OF CHOICE"
PIX004 OPERATION: CLIFF CLAVIN / CONNIE DUNGS SPLIT
PIX005 OPERATION: CLIFF CLAVIN "PARADISE LOST"
PIX006 THE SISSIES "GEOGRAPHY"
PIX007 LEFT OUT "25 CENT SERENADE"
PIX008 THE BANANAS "FORBIDDEN FRUIT" SEE 1ST 10 YEARS.
PIX009 PIPE BOMB "DANCE PARTY"
PIX010 ABE FROMAN "S/T"
PIX011 THE BANANAS "SLIPPERY SUBJECT
PIX012 AGAINST ME "CRIME AS FORGIVEN BY"
PIX013 THE BLANK FIGHT "HOUSE BAND FEUD"
PIX014 SHOTWELL "THE DEVIL HAS IT'S DAY"
PIX016 PIPE BOMB "FRONT SEAT SOLIDARITY"
PIX017 CARRIE NATIONS "BE STILL"
PIX020 THE BANANAS "1ST 10 YEARS"
PIX021 THE BANANAS "NAUTICAL ROCK AND ROLL"
PIX022 MADELINE "KISSING AND DANCING" CD
PIX023 ERIN TOBEY "S/T"
PIX024 SOOPHIE NUN SQUADE / ABE FROMAN SPLIT CD
PIX025 THE SISSIES "EVERYTHING IN THE WORLD"
PIX026 SOOPHIE NUNN SQUAD "PASSION SLAYS THE DRAGON"
PIX027 GHOST MICE "DEBT OF THE DEAD"
PIX028 THE DAUNTLESS ELITE "SECURITY"
PIX029 THE DOOR-KEYS "GREEN WOOD PARK MALL"
PIX030 DEFIANCE OHIO/GHOST MICE SPLIT
PIX031 OPERATION CLIFF CLAVIN DISCOGRAPHY 2 CD
PIX031 OPERATION CLIFF CLAVIN DVD

PIX032 THE DEVIL IS ELECTRIC DISCOGRAPHY
PIX033 JAPANTHER "WOLFENSWAN"
PIX034 ROSA "I MISSISSIPPI YOU"
PIX035 SPOON BOY "I LOVE YOU, THIS IS A ROBBERY"
PIX036 MATTY POP CHART "GOOD OLE WATER"
PIX037 LOS GATOS NEGROS "S/T"
PIX038 THE BLANK FIGHT "HOUSE BAND FEUD" CD
PIX039 FOUR EYES "SWEET SOUNDS"
PIX040 PLAN-IT-X FEST 2004 DVD
PIX041 MADELINE REISSUE "KISSING AND DANCING" W/2 MORE SONGS
PIX042 THE DOOR-KEYS "HELL YEAH IT'S THE..."
PIX044 PLAN-IT X COMPILATION VOL 1. "PIX MIX"
PIX045 ANTSY PANTS "S/T"
PIX046 SOOPHIE NUN SQUAD "THE DEVIL, THE METAL..."
PIX047 GHOST MICE "EUROPE"
PIX048 GHOST MICE "FAERIE WAR" LP/CD
PIX050 MICHAEL JORDAN'S TOUCH DOWN PASS "CASH MONEY"
PIX051 YOUR HEART BREAKS "NEW OCEAN WAVES"
PIX052 ONE REASON "ALL RIVERS RUN SOUTH"
PIX053 STRESSFACE "OI YOU'RE WELCOME"
PIX054 FIFTEEN "BUZZ"
PIX055 CAPTAIN CHAOS "BLOOMINGTON VOL. 1" ORIGINALLY BIG
    MAGIC RECORDS
PIX056 MADELINE / DEADBIRD SPLIT
PIX057 DELAY "DON'T LAUGH"
PIX059 THE DAUNTLESS ELITE "GRAFT"
PIX060 ANDREW JACKSON JIHAD / GHOST MICE SPLIT
PIX061 PUNKIN PIE "BROKE TRUCK GOOD LUCK SONG"
PIX062 MATTY POP CHART "EVERYONE DOES EVERYTHING"
PIX064 BEST FRIENDS FOREVER "ROMANCE/CONFLICT/ADVENTURE"
PIX065 THE MAX LEVINE ENSEMBLE "OKAY SMARTY PANTS"
PIX067 HALO FAUNA "DURAK"
PIX071 HEATHERS "HERE NOT THERE"
PIX072 DAVE DEAN'S MUSICAL FORKLIFT DVD
PIX073 BEST FRIENDS FOREVER "SELF TITLED"
PIX074 PIX COMP VOL. 2
PIX075 ERIC AYOTTE "REMNANTS OF STORYTOWN"
PIX076 BEYOND THINGS "OUR CALL OUTS"
PIX077 MADELINE "KISSING AND DANCING" LP VERSION
PIX078 ANDREW JACKSON JIHAD "ONLY GOD CAN JUDGE ME"
PIX079 GHOST MICE / BROOK PRIDEMORE 7" RECORD

PIX080 Delay "don't laugh/jump start my heart"
PIX081 russ substance/james black "split" CD
PIX082 Dead Friends "s/t" CD
PIX083 ghost mice / taco cat. 7" record
PIX084 Delay "plain language"
PIX085 PIX FEST DVD
PIX086 Lycka Till "s/t"
PIX087 Imperial Can "hey fuckers"
PIX088 Eric Ayotte 'wavering"
PIX089 Onsind "dissatisfactions"
PIX090 The Taxpayers "to risk so much for one damn meal"
PIX091 Street eaters "dry eyes and hydrocarbons"
PIX092 The Max Levine Ensemble "Mr. Gikokovich"
PIX093 Small Bones "s/t"
PIX094 Spoonboy "The Papas" TAPE/LP
PIX095 Ramshackle Glory "live the dream" TAPE/LP
PIX096 Fashanu "self titled" TAPE
PIX097 Lion Eater/Will Power "Limestone" TAPE
PIX098.1 Chris Clavin/Kyle Hall "split" TAPE
PIX098.2 Chris Clavin/Sara Cilantro "Secrets" TAPE
PIX098.3 Chris Clavin/Andrew Lips "split" TAPE
PIX098.4 Chris Clavin/Madeline Ava "split" TAPE
PIX098.5 Chris Clavin/Waxahatchee "split" TAPE
PIX099 Wild Assumptions "s/t" 7" record
PIX100 Ghost Mice "all we got is each other" LP/TAPE
PIX101 Onsind "Mildred, Margie, Annie, Clarice" 10"/TAPE
PIX102 Anti-Sociales "LAS MENOS MACABRAS DE LAS VIDAS " LP
PIX103 The Taxpayers "God, Forgive These Bastards" TAPE
PIX104 Los Gatos Negros "self titled" LP version with comic
    zine
PIX105 Ghost Mice "death and hatred to mankind" 10 inch
    collection
PIX106 Emperor X "nineteen live recordings" CD
PIX107 ONSIND "anaesthesiology" LP
PIX108 Kyle Hall "self titled" LP
PIX109 The Taxpayers "cold hearted town" LP
PIX110 Ghost Mice & Ramshackle Glory "shelter" LP/CD
PIX111 Hard Feelings "swell" LP (co-label release)
PIX112 Roman Candles "Riley Versus Jason in the Battle of
    Gracious Living" LP

PIX113 GARRETT WALTERS "I CALL MY YOUNGER SISTER TWICE A DAY" CD

PIX114 BEST FRIENDS FOREVER / THE MIDDLE ONES "SPLIT" LP

PIX115 DOGBRETH "SENTIMENTAL HEALTH" LP

PIX116 WATERCOLOR PAINTINGS "WHEN YOU MOVE" LP

PIX117 MITCH THE CHAMP "LONG WAY HOME" LP